SANDY PYLOS

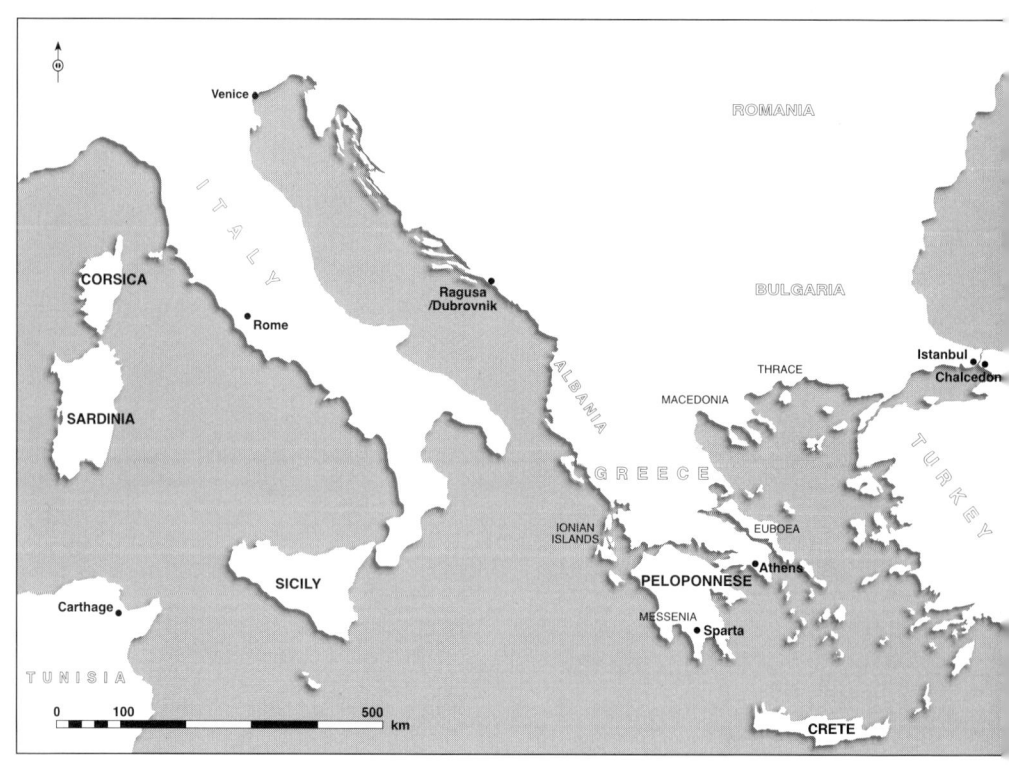

FIGURE 1
Central Mediterranean. Messenia and external centers of power in Italy and the Balkans that have controlled it. PRAP Archive. R. J. Robertson.

SANDY PYLOS
An ARCHAEOLOGICAL HISTORY *from* NESTOR *to* NAVARINO

EDITED BY JACK L. DAVIS

WITH CONTRIBUTIONS BY

Susan E. Alcock
Maria Antoniou
John Bennet
Jack L. Davis
Sharon E.J. Gerstel
Charles G. Griebel
Ann B. Harrison
Sebastian Heath
Kalliope Kaloyerakou
Axel Kampke
Yannos G. Lolos
Michael C. Nelson
Cynthia W. Shelmerdine
Nigel Spencer
David Stone
Charles Watkinson
Sergei Yazvenko
Eberhard Zangger

THE UNIVERSITY OF TEXAS PRESS
Austin

Copyright © 1998 by the University of Texas Press
All rights reserved
Printed in the United States of America
First edition, 1998

Requests for permission to reproduce material from this work should be sent to Permissions, University of Texas Press, P.O. Box 7819, Austin, TX 78713-7819.

∞ The paper used in this publication meets the minimum requirements of American National Standard for Information Sciences—Permanence of Paper for Printed Library Materials, ANSI Z39.48-1984.

LIBRARY OF CONGRESS CATALOGING-IN-PUBLICATION DATA

Sandy Pylos / edited by Jack L. Davis ; with contributions by Susan E. Alcock, et al.
      p.   cm.
Includes bibliographical references and index.
ISBN 0-292-71594-3 (cl.: alk. paper). — ISBN 0-292-71595-1 (pbk.: alk. paper)
1. Messēnia (Greece)—Antiquities. 2. Messēnia (Greece)—History. 3. Excavations (Archaeology)—Greece—Messēnia. 4. Navarino, Battle of, 1827. I. Davis, Jack L. II. Alcock, Susan E.
DF261.M45S26   1998
949.5'22—dc21   97-40652

Dedicated to the memories of
CARL W. BLEGEN *and* ELIZABETH PIERCE BLEGEN

CONTENTS

LIST OF FIGURES   xi

PREFACE   xix
Jack L. Davis

TRANSLITERATION RULES   xxvii

INTRODUCTION
GLIMPSES OF MESSENIA PAST   xxix
Jack L. Davis

CHAPTER 1

THE ENVIRONMENTAL SETTING   1
Eberhard Zangger
THE PHYSICAL SCIENTIST'S ROLE IN
REGIONAL ARCHAEOLOGY   10
Eberhard Zangger
FROM POLLEN TO PLANTS   14
Sergei Yazvenko

CHAPTER 2

THE HISTORY OF ARCHAEOLOGICAL
INVESTIGATIONS IN MESSENIA   23
Nigel Spencer
THE DISCOVERY OF THE PALACE OF NESTOR   42
Jack L. Davis
MARINATOS IN PYLOS   47
Yannos G. Lolos

CHAPTER 3

THE PALACE AND ITS DEPENDENCIES 53
Jack L. Davis
THE PORT OF NESTOR 69
Eberhard Zangger
MYCENAEAN BURIAL AT PYLOS 75
Yannos G. Lolos

CHAPTER 4

THE PALACE AND ITS OPERATIONS 81
Cynthia W. Shelmerdine
THE ANO ENGLIANOS HILLTOP AFTER THE PALACE 97
Charles G. Griebel and Michael C. Nelson
THE PERFUMED-OIL INDUSTRY 101
Cynthia W. Shelmerdine

CHAPTER 5

THE LINEAR B ARCHIVES AND THE KINGDOM OF NESTOR 111
John Bennet
THE PRAP SURVEY'S CONTRIBUTION 134
John Bennet
UMME AND NICHORIA 139
Cynthia W. Shelmerdine

CHAPTER 6

AFTER THE PALACE: THE EARLY "HISTORY" OF MESSENIA 147
Ann B. Harrison and Nigel Spencer
CERAMIC TYPOLOGY FOR BEGINNERS 163
Ann B. Harrison
NICHORIA: AN EARLY IRON AGE VILLAGE IN MESSENIA 167
Nigel Spencer
THE BATTLE OF SPHACTERIA (425 B.C.) 171
Nigel Spencer

CHAPTER 7

LIBERATION AND CONQUEST: HELLENISTIC AND ROMAN MESSENIA 179
Susan E. Alcock

DIALISKARI: A LATE ROMAN VILLA ON THE MESSENIAN COAST 192
David Stone and Axel Kampke

POWER FROM THE DEAD: TOMB CULT IN POSTLIBERATION MESSENIA 199
Susan E. Alcock

BOUKA 205
Ann B. Harrison

CHAPTER 8

MEDIEVAL MESSENIA 211
Sharon E.J. Gerstel

THE ESTATES OF NICCOLÒ ACCIAIUOLI 229
Sharon E.J. Gerstel

VENETIAN METHONI (MODON) 234
Sharon E.J. Gerstel

BYZANTINE SGRAFFITO WARE 239
Sharon E.J. Gerstel

CHAPTER 9

THE SECOND OTTOMAN PERIOD AND THE GREEK REVOLUTION 245
Jack L. Davis

HASANAGA: A GLIMPSE INTO THE OTTOMAN COUNTRYSIDE 262
Susan E. Alcock

THE BATTLE OF NAVARINO 267
Charles Watkinson

CHAPTER 10

FROM PAUSANIAS TO THE PRESENT 273
Jack L. Davis

MESSENIA'S MULTIPLE PASTS 292
Jack L. Davis

COMPUTERS AND MAPS AT PRAP 298
Sebastian Heath
A FIELDWALKER'S PERSPECTIVE ON PRAP 302
Maria Antoniou and Kalliope Kaloyerakou

TIMELINE 307

SOURCES OF QUOTATIONS 311

FURTHER READING 315

INDEX 321

LIST *of* FIGURES

1. Frontispiece: Central Mediterranean.   ii

PREFACE

2. Greece and western Turkey.   xxi

INTRODUCTION

3. Monomitos inscription from the ancient city of Messene.   xxviii
4. The Peloponnese.   xxx
5. Messenia.   xxxii
6. Region examined by the Pylos Regional Archaeological Project.   xxxiii
7. Coast between Navarino and the Langouvardos River (from Profitis Ilias, Lefki).   xxxiv
8. The Englianos Ridge and the Palace of Nestor with Mt. Aigaleon in the background.   xxxv
9. Bulldozed antiquities in the fenced front yard of a modern seaside summer home.   xlii

CHAPTER 1

10. Landslide near the Palace of Nestor, from the northwest.   xlvi
11. The north end of the Bay of Navarino, the castle of Palaionavarino, and the sand bar separating the bay from Osmanaga Lagoon.   2
12. The Englianos Ridge and the uplands around Hora from the top of the Aigaleon Ridge.   3
13. The area of the Mycenaean port basin and the mouth of the Selas River from the town of Tragana.   4

14. Destroyed chamber tombs on the Englianos Ridge.   9
15. Geophysicists measuring subsurface anomalies at the Palace of Nestor.   12
16. Sergei Yazvenko extracting pollen cores from the Osmanaga Lagoon.   17
17. Gulia Ismail-Zade packing sections of a pollen core for storage.   17
18. Pollen diagram showing species of plants represented in cores extracted from the Osmanaga Lagoon.   19

CHAPTER 2

19. Bust of C. W. Blegen by the sculptor Elisavet Valvi erected in front of the Museum of Hora in 1995.   22
20. Bronze figurine of a warrior from the sanctuary of Apollo Korythos.   29
21. Tholos tomb excavated at Malthi by Valmin.   31
22. Site of Malthi with Middle Bronze Age remains.   32
23. Linear B tablet Cn 131 from the Palace of Nestor.   34
24. Plan of the Palace of Nestor, 1953.   36
25. Plan of the Palace of Nestor, 1954.   36
26. Tumulus at Papoulia.   37
27. Headland with the Tomb of Thrasymedes at Voidokoilia Bay from the north, with modern Pylos in the distance.   38
28. Linear B tablets on floor of the Archive Room of the Palace of Nestor at time of discovery in 1939.   43
29. Walter Langsam, president of the University of Cincinnati, Carl W. Blegen, Julia Langsam, and Marian Rawson at the Palace of Nestor excavations.   45
30. Bust of Spyridon Marinatos by Elisavet Valvi erected in the garden of the Museum of Hora in 1994.   49

CHAPTER 3

31. View southwest toward the Bay of Navarino over parts of its Hither Province, from the Archive Room of the Palace of Nestor.   52
32. The citadel of the Palace of Nestor from the northeast.   54
33. The Mycenaean Tholos Tomb IV and the gate to the citadel of the Palace of Nestor, with Mt. Aigaleon behind.   57
34. The Cave of Nestor at Palaionavarino.   61
35. North end of the ridge of Beylerbey.   64

36. Entrance passageway or *dromos* leading into one of the two tholos tombs at Tragana *Viglitsa*. 66
37. Reconstructed prehistoric topography of the area of the Mycenaean port. 70
38. Mechanized drilling equipment at the site of the Mycenaean port. 72
39. Eberhard Zangger examining cores extracted by the mechanized drill. 73

CHAPTER 4

40. Oil-storage magazine at the Palace of Nestor with the Throne Room, hearth, and modern olive trees behind. 80
41. Plan of the Palace of Nestor at the end of excavations by Blegen. 82
42. Artist's reconstruction of Court 3 of the Palace of Nestor, as seen from the southwest. 83
43. Procession fresco with bull, from Room 5 of the Palace of Nestor. 84
44. Broken drinking cups on the floor of Pantry 19 of the Palace of Nestor. 85
45. Bathtub in Room 43 of the Palace of Nestor. 86
46. Nodule Wr 1480 from the Palace of Nestor. 91
47. Curved strip of bronze from Workshop Room 99 of the Palace of Nestor. 95
48. Areas of Dark Age activity within the ruins of the Palace of Nestor. 98
49. Court 88 and Dark Age structures 89 and 90 within the ruins of the Palace of Nestor. 99
50. Storage-sized stirrup jar from the Palace of Nestor. 102
51. Individual-sized stirrup jars from the Palace of Nestor. 103
52. Linear B tablets: Pylos Fr 1184, Knossos K 778, and Knossos K 700. 104, 105
53. Storerooms 23–24 behind the Megaron of the Palace of Nestor. 107
54. Linear B tablets: Pylos Fr 1226 and Pylos Fr 1225. 108

CHAPTER 5

55. Mt. Aigaleon from the southwest, near the Museum of Hora, with Volimidia in the foreground. 110

LIST *of* FIGURES

56. The Aigaleon range from the Cave of Nestor.   115
57. Mts. Maglavas and Lykodimos from the north.   115
58. North end of the Aigaleon chain at modern Cyparissia.   116
59. Explanatory diagram, showing the structure and content of Linear B tablet Jn 829.   118
60. The major Linear B texts relevant to the Hither Province lists of place names: Jn 829, Cn 608, and Vn 20.   119
61. The Mycenaean geography of Messenia.   121
62. From the acropolis of ancient Thouria (possibly Linear B Leuktron) east toward the Taygetus range and Laconia.   124
63. Metaxada Valley from the south.   127
64. View of the prominent hill of Koutsouveri, dominating the modern village of Maryeli.   136
65. Section of a Mycenaean road west of Nichoria, with the built retaining wall that supports it.   137
66. View east from Nichoria into the valley of the Pamisos River.   140
67. Mycenaean street in Nichoria Area III.   141
68. Balloon photograph of Mycenaean House in Nichoria Area IV.   142
69. Finds from tholos tomb at Nichoria: Carnelian sealstone and gold beads.   143

CHAPTER 6

70. Voidokoilia Bay, ancient Coryphasion, Palaionavarino, and the island of Sphacteria, from the north.   146
71. Dark Age tholos tomb at the southwestern end of the Englianos Ridge.   150
72. Pottery vessels from the Dark Age tholos tomb at the southwestern end of the Englianos Ridge.   151
73. Bronze votive statuette of a bull.   152
74. Mt. Ithome as seen from the site of Malthi in the Soulima Valley.   158
75. The house at Kopanaki.   161
76. Tins of pottery awaiting study in museum.   164
77. Table of sherds of pottery being analyzed.   164
78. Reconstruction of Unit IV-1, phase 2, at the site of Nichoria.   168
79. Metal shield boss from Nichoria.   169
80. Fort of Neokastro with the island of Sphacteria and Palaionavarino in the distance.   172

81. Map showing the conjectural positions of Spartan and Athenian military contingents stationed in defense and blockade of Coryphasion.   175

CHAPTER 7

82. The coast at Dialiskari, as seen from the southwest near the church of Ayios Nikolaos, with modern fishing boats in the foreground and new summer villas in the distance.   178
83. Mt. Ithome with the fourth-century wall line of Messene visible on its slopes.   181
84. Arcadian Gate, one of the massive gateways in the fortifications at Messene.   181
85. Reconstruction of the cult group at Lycosura in Arcadia; sculpted by Damophon of Messene (200–150 B.C.).   184
86. Reconstruction and schematic plan of the Asklepieion at Messene.   189
87. Plan of Dialiskari produced by TotalStation.   193
88. "Column House" at Dialiskari in the 1930s and in the 1990s.   194
89. Roman mosaic at Dialiskari.   195
90. Hypocaust from Roman bath at Dialiskari.   196
91. Sherd density at Dialiskari.   196
92. TotalStation in use.   197
93. Location of definite and possible sites of Late Classical and Hellenistic tomb cult in southern Greece.   201
94. View north from the promontory of Coryphasion.   202
95. J. Bennet inspecting Volimidia graves.   203
96. S. E. Alcock at the site of Bouka.   206
97. Magnetometric map showing the plan of an unexcavated building at Bouka.   207
98. Weights for weaving threads on a loom, from Bouka.   208

CHAPTER 8

99. Fortifications of Methoni, as seen from the Venetian marketplace.   210
100. Plan of the basilica of Ayia Kyriaki near Filiatra.   213
101. The church of Zoodohos Piyi, Samarina, Messenia.   217
102. The church of the Transfiguration of the Savior in Hristianou as seen from the southwest.   218

LIST *of* FIGURES

103. Church of the Transfiguration of the Savior in Hristianou, showing Classical blocks used in the construction of its walls. 219
104. Cemetery church at Androusa, from the southeast. 221
105. "Gothicizing" pointed arch in the north wall of the cemetery church at Androusa. 222
106. Pierced handle of a Byzantine double-saucered lamp with traces of burning at the lower edge. 224
107. Aerial photograph of the modern town of Kremydia. 230
108. Relief of the lion of St. Mark in the fort of Methoni. 235
109. Town and harbor of Methoni. Detail from F. de Wit engraving of the Peloponnese. 235
110. Two bases of bowls with sgraffito decoration from Skarminga. 240
111. Fourteenth-century chalice, interior with sgraffito decoration. 241

CHAPTER 9

112. Central square of the modern town of Pylos with a monument to the Battle of Navarino. 244
113. Line of fortifications at Neokastro and the southern end of the island of Sphacteria. 247
114. Two views of the Venetian citadel of Corinth. 248
115. Two sailors at Pylos in the service of the admiral of the Turkish fleet. 253
116. Ali Paşa, vizier of Ioannina, a prominent Albanian potentate of the early nineteenth century. 255
117. The gate of the fort at Neokastro in the early nineteenth century. 256
118. The harbor of Pylos and the island of Sphacteria. 258
119. The church at Navarino after liberation. 259
120. The modern town of Pylos with the Bay of Navarino and Mt. Aigaleon in background. 260
121. S. E. Alcock leaning against enclosure wall with molded top surrounding the yard of a house at Hasanaga. 264
122. The "Hasan Paşa tower" at Troy in Turkey, as it appeared in 1776. 265
123. Painting of the Battle of Navarino with ships of the combined fleet still entering the harbor at the start of the battle. 268
124. Map of the Ottoman formation at Navarino, produced by Codrington on the basis of reports from spies. 270

CHAPTER 10

125. The Gargaliani-Lefki uplands. 276
126. The church of Saints Constantine and Helen. 279
127. Severe erosion of Palaeolithic remains near the mouth of the Veryina River. 282
128. Bulldozed knoll with graves at Tsouka, near Pyrgos. 282
129. PRAP archaeologists surveying in the field. 286
130. Archaic and Classical Greek finds identified by PRAP. 300
131. Roman finds identified by PRAP. 301
132. Leader of a survey team (Charles Watkinson) consulting with the field director of PRAP, John Bennet. 303
133. The makeshift dormitory in the Hora schoolhouse used by PRAP. 304
134. PRAP surveyors washing pottery after the completion of work in the field. 305
135. The PRAP team in 1993. 306

PREFACE

Archaeological projects are both too long and too short. Years flow by swiftly in a predictable stream of frenetic seasons of fieldwork in summer, followed by winters of paperwork and computerized data entry. Away from their academic offices, most archaeologists have no choice but to live in Spartan conditions, in dormitories established in schoolhouses generously donated by villages in which they are guests, or in the least expensive hotels that can be found. Substantial sums of money are required to keep a large team of archaeologists in a foreign country for only a few short weeks, and the need to stretch our dollars as far as possible generally impels us to recreate a summer-camp environment that most of us imagined we had abandoned with puberty.

Fieldwork is not a holiday, nor a paid vacation, nor is the atmosphere always amenable to clear thinking. Back at the university, we find our non-archaeologist colleagues refreshed from a summer of quiet contemplation, while we face both the onset of a new school year and the preparation of technical reports describing and justifying our summer activities. Applications to foundations seem always due, reports always late, and there never appears to be time for reflection—for taking stock of our own research and how it fits into any "big picture."

The conclusion of a project has always left me dazed and exhausted. But then suddenly the hubbub stops, and I experience a real sense of loss. The pressure of preparing for the next campaign evaporates. But so, too, can much of the constant communication with one's collaborators, as a team disperses to the winds—each collaborator returning to his or her respective university. And this dispersal presents very real dangers for our efforts to disseminate the results of our research to other scientists.

Archaeologists are fond of claiming that each field season produces three years of work at home. There is much truth in this, but unless we share an accurate and complete picture of the results of our research quickly,

---

JACK L. DAVIS

there is little point in having done the research in the first place! Yet the road from field to publication is paved with hazards and good intentions. Adequate resources are rarely available to support the preparation of published work, which lacks much of the quick glory of discovery. Colleagues begin work on other projects and are distracted from tasks at hand. The net result is that only a tiny fraction of archaeological fieldwork is ever published, and, of that disseminated, only a small percentage becomes known to the general public.

This small book is a testimony to the determination of a small group of archaeologists to escape from the rat race—to maintain ties among themselves and thus to present the results of their research in a timely fashion, not only to colleagues, but to all interested parties. The many authors of this book are all members of the Pylos Regional Archaeological Project, a program of fieldwork completed in the summer of 1996, at and around the so-called Palace of Nestor, in the western part of the province of Messenia, in southwestern Greece (Fig. 2). PRAP, as we call it, is a multidisciplinary regional-studies project—which is to say that it is a consortium of archaeologists, natural scientists, historians, and art historians who joined forces to study the history not just of one archaeological site, but of an entire landscape, and not just in a single period, but at all times in the past.

The title of our book was chosen intentionally to emphasize the many strands of evidence that it attempts to knit into a single fabric. "Sandy Pylos" is a Homeric term and in the first instance invokes the prehistoric Bronze Age kingdom that occupies center stage in the first half of this volume. At the same time, "Pylos" is a slippery toponym, one that has shifted its meaning and location from earliest times until the present day, and thus provides an inclusive, if elusive, shell for chapters that range over an equally broad timespan.

The continuing migration of the place name "Pylos" itself records significant changes in the evolution of the social landscape of western Messenia. In the Bronze Age, it is clear from archaeological evidence that the name was applied to the area of the Palace of Nestor—but Homer implies that Nestor's home was further north. By the Classical period, the toponym had moved to a coastal area near the Bay of Navarino, where it designated the ancient city-state of Coryphasion—but another Pylos existed in Elea, north of Messenia. Most recently, in the nineteenth century, Pylos was chosen as the official name of the community that now sprawls at the foot of the old fort of Neokastro, at the south side of Navarino Bay, and it is now the only official Pylos in modern Greece.

"Pylos," in this larger sense of the word, was an area, we believed, that offered almost unparalleled opportunities in Greece for exploring the de-

JACK L. DAVIS

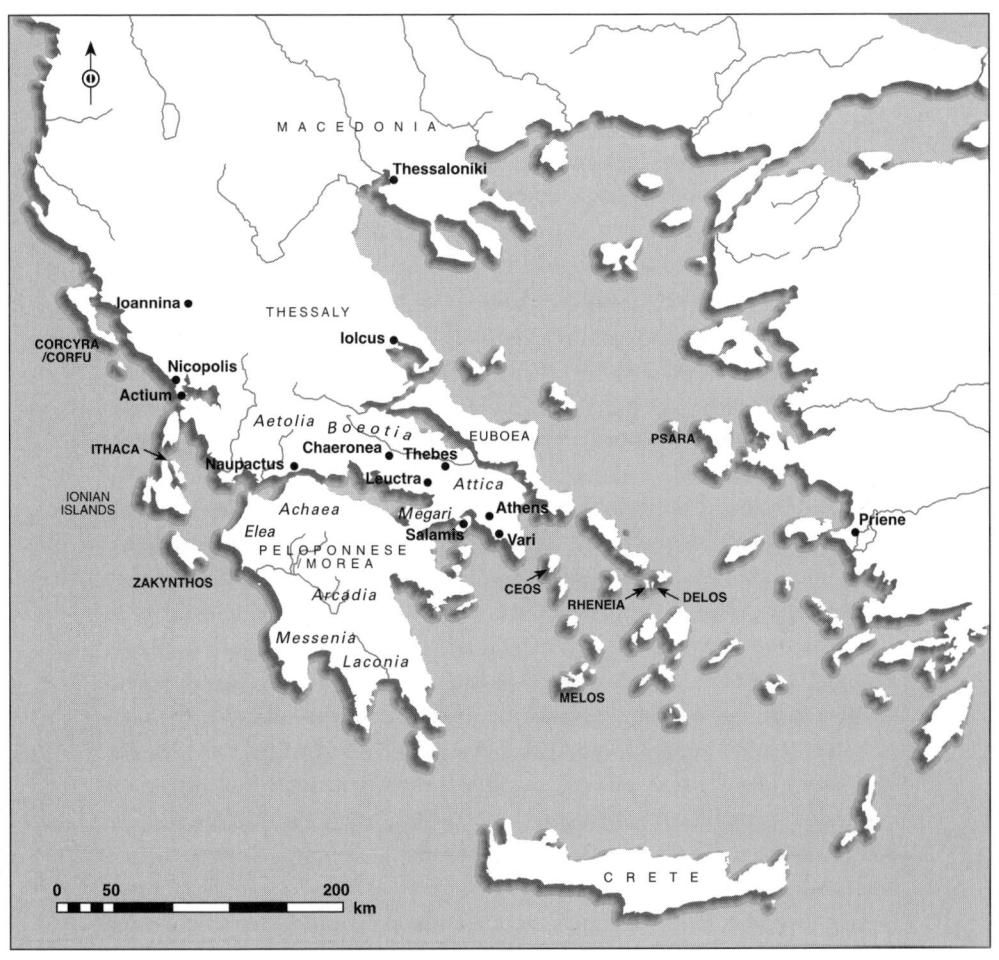

FIGURE 2
Greece and western Turkey. PRAP Archive. R. J. Robertson.

velopment of society in the *longue durée*, to borrow a term from the Annales school of modern French historiography. Our objective was to study the evolution of an entire region over a very long period of time and, we hoped, to learn more about the cultural and environmental forces that have promoted change or stability in the political, economic, and social organization of local populations.

In particular, this area of southwest Messenia offered an extraordinary opportunity to implement a program of research that would fully explore the contribution that archaeology can make to the elucidation of long-term historical processes. What has been the relationship between the environment and human cultures? Can we sort out the immutable from the more ephemeral organizing principles of history? Given the amazing detail provided both by prehistoric archives found in the Palace of Nestor and by rich medieval and early modern written sources, we expected to be able to paint a more complete picture of the Pylos area than we have ever had, or are likely to have, for any other part of Greece. In fact, nowhere else in the Mediterranean region, or in any other part of Europe, can we describe the operations of a Bronze Age civilization with such precision.

Finally, the epithet "Sandy" alludes both to the natural environment that forms the backdrop for the prehistoric and historic dramas that we here sketch and, more literally, to the dunes of sand that line the western coast of Messenia and surround the artificial prehistoric harbor investigated by our natural scientists—necessitating elaborate precautions to keep the port operational.

PRAP included more than a hundred members from a dozen different countries, several dozen universities, and a half-dozen or more academic disciplines. In the direction of the project there has been a partnership among archaeologists from the University of Cincinnati, the University of Ioannina, the University of Michigan, the University of Texas at Austin, and the University of Wisconsin-Madison. For five years (1991–95), with support from our own universities, the National Endowment for the Humanities, the National Geographic Society, and the Institute for Aegean Prehistory, the forty or so archaeologists, earth scientists, and historians associated with PRAP investigated in the field each summer in western Messenia archaeological remains and their natural environment—ancient and modern.

In the winter, both historians and prehistorians on our team collected and read published reports written by archaeologists about earlier campaigns in Messenia. They also synthesized relevant testimonia contained in the writings of ancient Greeks and Romans, including inscriptions carved on stone or inscribed in clay that have been found in Messenia itself. Others collated new information relevant to Messenian history that has hitherto lain unpublished in state archives in Athens, Istanbul, Kalamata, London, and Venice.

We view the archaeology and history of Messenia as a totality. We believe there is significant information to be extracted from study both of its parts and of its whole. The landscape can be broken into its constituents (cemeteries and habitations, farmhouses and cities, or ports and inland communities), but any analysis of one of these components must necessarily include all others. Politics, economics, ideology, and environment are, and always have been, a seamless whole.

JACK L. DAVIS

This volume describes not only how we conducted our inquiry but also how we are proceeding to interpret the data we gathered. And since it is clear to us, at least, that our own research has little meaning outside the context of the investigations of our predecessors, we have devoted as much or more of this book to the work of others as we have to our own. Similarly, our conclusions are only comprehensible within the larger context of Mediterranean prehistory and history. Thus, although the focus of our own pursuits was limited to an area of some 100 square kilometers around the Palace of Nestor, the scope of this book extends to Messenia as a whole and, on occasion, even beyond.

It could hardly be otherwise, inasmuch as the history of Pylos has often been controlled by political and economic vacillations provoked by decisions made far beyond its borders. In addition, for some times in the past, we know so little specifically about the Pylos area that discussion of centers and events outside its borders must justifiably dominate the discourse. No region is an island entirely isolated from external influences, and to understand developments at a local scale almost always requires casting a broad geographical net.

The result is a book that we think is unique. It is the first presentation to a nonspecialist audience of the results of the investigations sponsored by PRAP. At the same time, because we have integrated our own findings with those of other specialists (most of whose research has itself not been extensively discussed outside academic circles until now), we may justifiably claim that this volume constitutes the first complete history of the Pylos area, from before the days of King Nestor until the Battle of Navarino in 1827.

Readers will also learn a great deal about the history and prehistory of Greece from the time of its earliest settlement until the twentieth century. We hope, too, that we have managed to convey at least a flavor of the enormous excitement in interdisciplinary research that brought us all to PRAP and—despite hardships, lack of resources, and academic pressures—continues to renew our dedication to archaeology.

We also regard *Sandy Pylos* as a guidebook for informed travelers in Greece. The general public needs a greater familiarity with the sort of archaeological research that is being conducted in the Mediterranean today. The emphasis is not, as the popular press would have us believe, on achieving success through the "big find" or "discovery of a lifetime," but on the careful description of how people in the past actually lived, of how life changed, often radically, from period to period, and of the causes that have promoted such transformations in society and culture.

It is, however, highly unusual for an archaeological team to present a synthesis of its results to a nonspecialist audience before they have been fully documented in arcane and largely inaccessible scholarly venues. That we have taken such a radical step is a reflection of our commitment to make the history of Pylos and the products of our studies comprehensible to all. In so doing, we gladly fulfill a promise made through the National Endowment for the Humanities specifically to the American people that we would soon present a synthesis of our research in a public forum.

In addition to the NEH and the other foundations and universities already mentioned, many corporate bodies and individuals, private and public, have supported us in the field and out of it. We are especially grateful for financial help from the Society of Antiquaries of London; our home institutions, including the University of Cincinnati, the University of Illinois at Chicago, the Kelsey Museum of Archaeology at the University of Michigan, the University of Michigan, the University of Reading, the University of Texas at Austin, and the University of Wisconsin-Madison; and numerous private donors.

Fieldwork was conducted under the auspices of the American School of Classical Studies at Athens according to terms established in permits issued by the Central Archaeological Council of Greece, on receipt of recommendations from regional offices of the Greek Archaeological Service in Olympia and Sparta. We greatly appreciate the support that we have received from the director of the American School, W.D.E. Coulson; from Katerina Romiopoulou and Yiannis Tzedakis, directors of the Greek Archaeological Service; from Inspectors of Antiquities Mrs. Xeni Arapoyianni (Olympia) and Mrs. Aimilia Bakourou (Sparta); and from their staffs, especially Mrs. Yioryia Hatzi and Ms. Evangelia Malapani. The hospitality extended to our team by the mayor of Hora, Mr. Panayiotis Petropoulos (1991–94), has been nothing short of spectacular, and we are grateful, too, for the assistance of his successor, Mr. Dimitrios Papathomopoulos (1995–96). We are also glad to have the opportunity to thank the University of Athens team of the Voidokoilia Excavations for their collegiality, particularly its director, George Korres; and the Minnesota Archaeological Researches in the Western Peloponnese team, especially Frederick A. Cooper.

The natural and physical scientists, archaeologists, and students of archaeology who have participated in the research of PRAP are far too numerous to be acknowledged here for their individual contributions. It should be obvious, however, that any success that our enterprise has enjoyed rests entirely on the assistance that all have given it. Four PRAP members do, however, deserve special mention. Debi Harlan has managed PRAP's electronic database since its inception, and her behind-the-scenes efforts have allowed the rest of us to begin to think about what the data mean. Sharon Stocker has helped to plan, execute, and publish PRAP. She has been untiring in her devotion to the project and remarkably tolerant of the enormous stress its management has from time to time imposed on our relationship. John Fisher and Kate Bracher fed us, managed our finances in Hora, and made contributions of inestimable value to the progress of scientific research both in the field and in the museum.

The book itself would never have been published so quickly without substantial help from Phoebe Acheson, who assembled illustrations, obtained copyright clearances, constructed the timeline, and in general shepherded the manuscript to press. Others who helped us acquire illustrations include Nancy Wilkie, J. Wilson Myers, and Elizabeth Tucker Blackburn. I am also grateful to Ada Kalogirou, who read much of the manuscript in draft and offered comments, and to the anonymous press referees for especially valuable critiques. The staff of the Burnam Library, particularly Jean Wellington and Michael Braunlin, has, as always, facilitated my research in every way possible. At the University of Texas Press, I am especially thankful for the enthusiasm of Ali Hosseini, who encouraged me to submit this manuscript, and to Jim Burr, who has lent support at every stage of the editorial process. Sherry Wert provided the final copyediting, and her skill has been most appreciated. The production of photographs and line drawings was greatly facilitated by a generous grant from the Classics Fund of the University of Cincinnati, established by Louise Taft Semple in memory of her father, Charles Phelps Taft.

Finally, we gratefully acknowledge the great debt that we owe to the people of Messenia, particularly the residents of the town of Hora. For three years, its young men and women (as students in an educational program sponsored by the European Community) walked with us through the fields of their friends and neighbors (and in some cases even of their own families) and helped us clean and inventory ancient artifacts in the museum. In this way we think that one group of young people has learned, as we have, that the bits of pottery and tile and stone that they routinely find as they execute their daily chores may contribute important chapters to the history of their own past.

TRANSLITERATION RULES

A book like this one, concerned with many periods of the past, can hardly hope to achieve consistency in the transliteration of Greek names into English. In this regard, we have been singularly unambitious, struggling only to ensure that the same word is written in the same way throughout. Ancient Greek names, including those still in use today, are spelled as they appear in S. Hornblower and A. Spawforth, *The Oxford Classical Dictionary*, 3d ed. (New York: Oxford University Press, 1996). Most others are transliterated according to rules suggested by P. Bien and J. Loomis for the Modern Greek Studies Association.

FIGURE 3
Monomitos inscription from the ancient city of Messene. After W. Kolbe, "Die Grenzen Messeniens in der ersten Kaiserzeit," Athenische Mitteilungen *29 (1904): 364.*

INTRODUCTION
GLIMPSES *of* MESSENIA PAST

I, Titus Flavius Monomitos, a land surveyor and freedman of the Roman emperor Vespasian, in the consulship of L. Ceionius Commodus and D. Novius Junius Priscus, on the 14th of December, A.D. 78, in Patras, have checked and certified the aforementioned boundaries [between Laconia and Messenia].

Thus concludes a tedious and superficially commonplace forty-line document carved on two joining fragments of limestone (Fig. 3), discovered more than a century ago at Messene, a metropolis created *de novo* in Messenia on the instructions of Epaminondas, the general from Thebes whose international coalition of city-states brought Sparta to its knees in 369 B.C. (Chapter 7). But this apparently pedestrian document in fact conceals and records in stone a central theme of this volume—a search for Messenian identity. What is Messenia? Why has it been conceived as a distinct region at certain times in the past, but not at others? Why did it matter where the boundaries lay? Indeed, we shall soon see that the borders of Messenia have been fluid, its populations heterogeneous, and its political structures variable. Meaning can thus only be constructed from the archaeological and textual evidence at our disposal by situating it in a specific historical context—itself potentially complex.

ONE MESSENIAN LANDSCAPE

Since the time of Augustus, Messenia had been incorporated into the Roman province of Achaea. Roman colonists were settled in parts of the Peloponnese (Fig. 4), and administrative decrees could be issued, when required or requested, by the governor of the province, by the Senate of Rome, or by a plethora of local administrations that the Romans allowed to continue.

JACK L. DAVIS

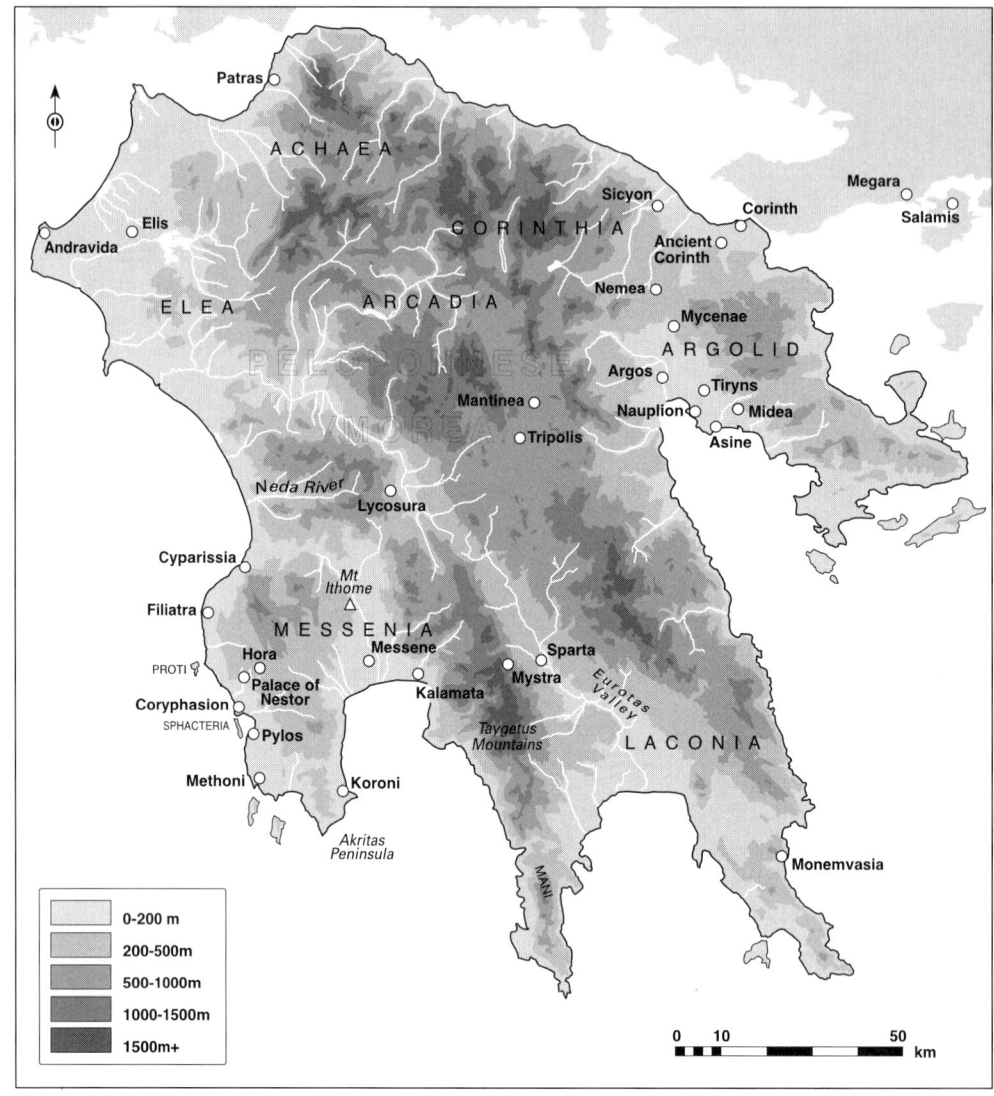

FIGURE 4
The Peloponnese. PRAP Archive. R. J. Robertson.

Messene was one such seat of local government. Before the Roman conquest, it had dominated Messenia, its territorial hinterland, as a sort of federal capital for cities spread from Cyparissia in the north to Methoni in the south, and from Pylos in the west to the slopes of the lofty mountain range of Taygetus in the east, the range that dominates the center of the southern

JACK L. DAVIS

Peloponnese and served as a natural frontier between the lowlands of Messenia and the uplands of Arcadia and western Laconia (Fig. 5).

It is the border on Mt. Taygetus that was a particular bone of contention for all Messenians, and the object of Monomitos's mission. For there the Messenians shared a border with Sparta, the predatory militaristic state that some 700 years earlier had marched its armies into Messenia and, after a protracted series of campaigns, had reduced many Messenians—those, that is, who did not choose or lacked resources to abandon their homes and flee to other parts of Greece—to the serflike status of *helot*, while classifying the remainder as *perioikoi*, literally "dwellers around," who did not enjoy political rights of citizenship (Chapter 6).

In Monomitos's day, the landscape of Messenia was not dissimilar to its appearance today (Chapter 1). Messenia then, as in our own century, enjoyed a reputation for the fertility of its land, particularly the well-watered bottoms of its principal river valleys. These include the Neda, which reaches the sea north of Cyparissia, and the Pamisos, which traverses a broad plain extending north from modern Kalamata, the third largest city in modern Greece. Near the western edge of the plain rises Mt. Ithome, at the foot of which Messene was founded.

It is a steep climb into Taygetus for those traveling northeast to Arcadia, east to Sparta, or south to the Mani, the central "finger" of the Peloponnese that extends southward into the Cretan Sea. West of the Pamisos Valley, passes lead through undulating tableland, then drop rapidly to the coast at modern Pylos. Farther south, in the western "finger" of the Peloponnese, the Akritas Peninsula, the terrain of Methoni and Koroni is rough: flat arable fields are few and far between.

The agricultural resources of western Messenia, the special focus of PRAP's investigations, while paling in comparison to those of the valley of the Pamisos, still offer substantial natural benefits to farmer and sailor alike (Fig. 6). The great Bay of Navarino at modern Pylos is well sheltered behind the island of Sphacteria and provides safe anchorage today, often for very large oil tankers. In earlier times, numerous small inlets between Navarino and modern Cyparissia would have offered safe havens for smaller vessels, as they do now for fishing vessels. A broad coastal plain here is itself well watered and fertile (Fig. 7), particularly in the alluvial flats north of the Bay of Navarino around the modern villages of Yialova and Romanou.

Messenia is both unified and internally divided by its topography. The long northwest-southeast range of Mt. Aigaleon visually dominates Trifylia, the northwestern part of Messenia, and clearly divides coast from interior. A few passes lead east through these hills, across rolling uplands and

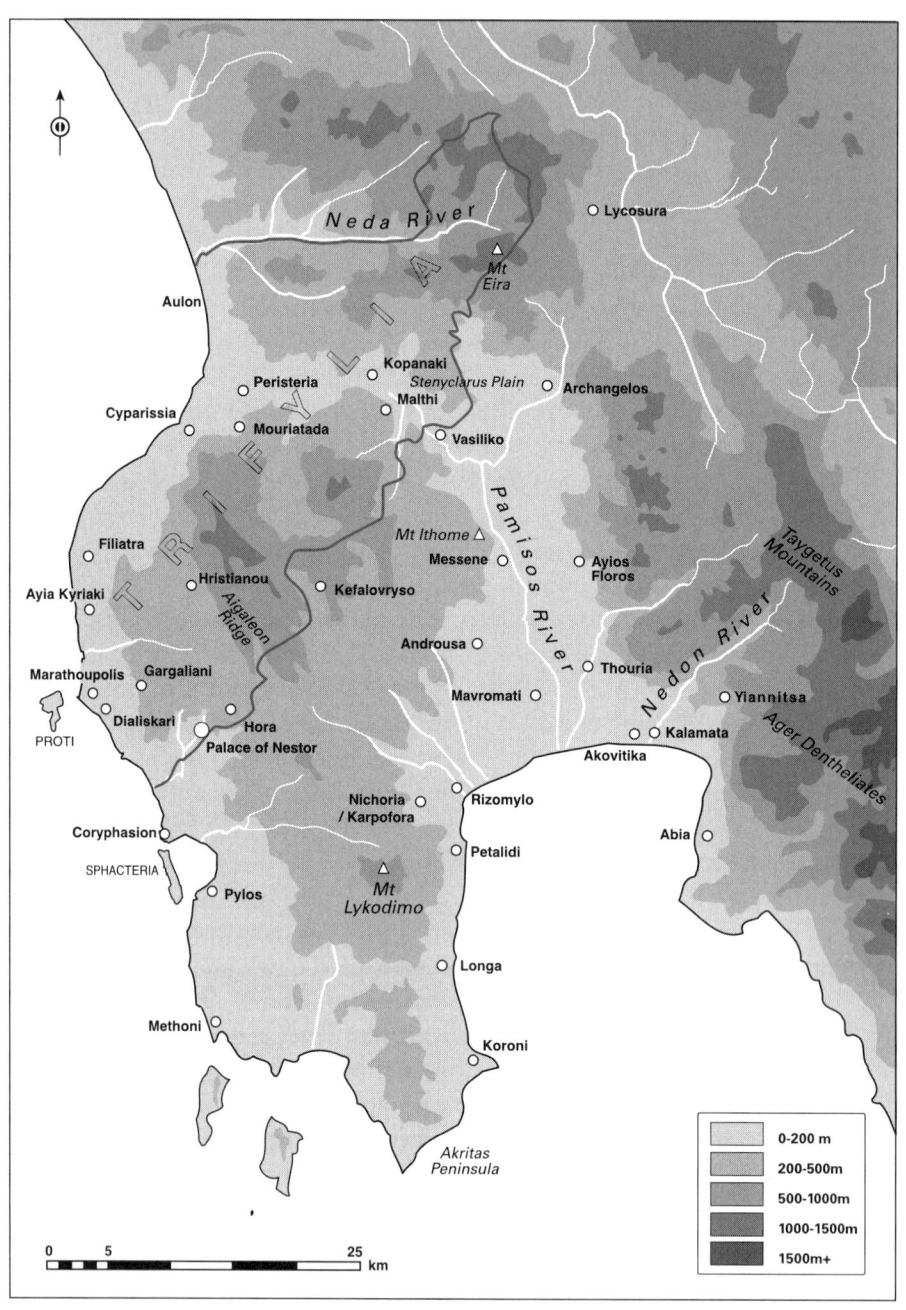

FIGURE 5
Messenia. PRAP Archive. R. J. Robertson.

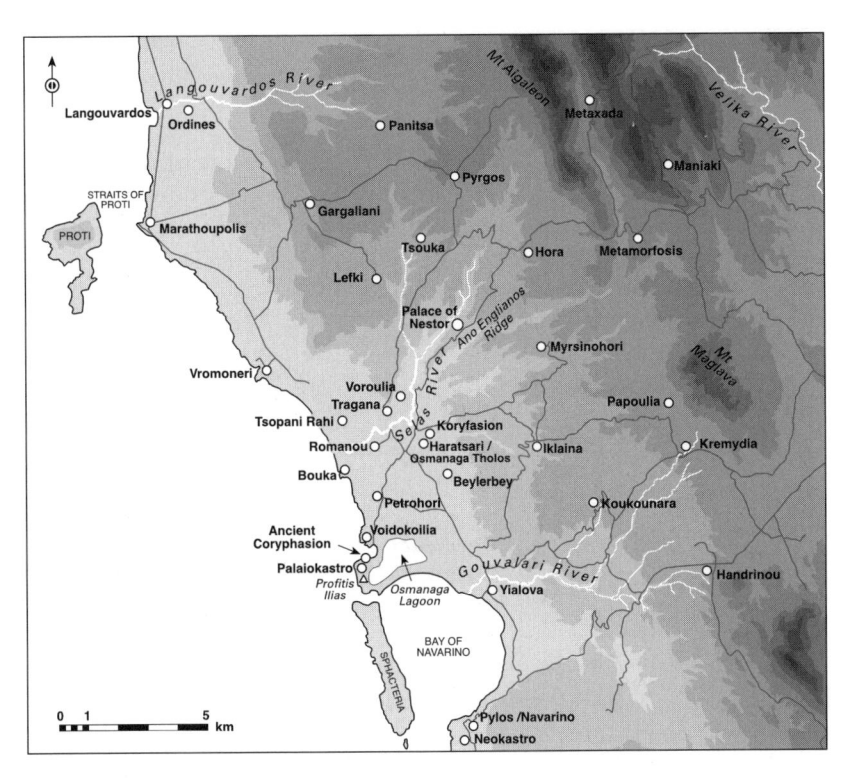

FIGURE 6
Region examined by the Pylos Regional Archaeological Project. 100-meter contour intervals. PRAP Archive. R. J. Robertson.

over the watershed into the valley of the Pamisos. In early times, the Aigaleon range served as a political border between the two provinces of the Bronze Age kingdom administered from the Palace of Nestor (Chapters 3–5), and the palace itself guards what must have been one of the most important routes between eastern and western Messenia. Today its mountains serve to remind travelers of the geographical coherence of the province: for almost nowhere in Messenia does the visitor lose sight either of the peak of Mt. Ithome or of the summit of Mt. Aigaleon (Fig. 8), even from distant Thouria in the foothills of Taygetus.

Flavius Monomitos's view of this Messenian landscape was one of conflict—not only past turmoil, but also strife that had the potential to continue in his own day. Such serious matters required the involvement of the Roman government, whose representative he was. And the motives and strategies of that administration were not consistently munificent.

FIGURE 7
Coast between Navarino and the Langouvardos River (from Profitis Ilias, Lefki). PRAP Archive. Jack L. Davis.

With characteristic capriciousness, the emperor Nero had lately declared Greece free of taxes. However, once the emperor Vespasian had restored order, the central administration sought to clarify boundaries in preparation for the reinstatement of a tax on the Messenians' lands. The resolution of matters like these demanded accuracy if hundreds of years of dispute were to be laid aside once and for all. And indeed, we find precision in this decree: "The 27th marker is set having its inscription turned toward the east and reading 'Boundary of Laconia in the direction of Messenia . . .' and elsewhere . . . on the rock there is cut an 'O' with an 'R' in the middle [for ″ΟΡΟΣ, Greek for 'boundary'] and an 'M' and an 'L'." No chances were being taken this time.

TRAVELERS' VIEWS

Rome and Sparta have not been the only external powers that have shaped the political map of the southwestern Peloponnese. Messenians have often had to fight hard to establish their independence, and indeed, in historical times there has been hardly a period when the affairs of Messenia have not been dictated by centers of power lying far beyond its borders—including (after Rome) Constantinople, Istanbul, Venice, and, since the Greek

JACK L. DAVIS

Revolution, Athens. In no small measure, such external domination has muffled native Messenian historical voices.

Not one work of literature, history, or geography composed about Messenia by a Messenian is preserved before the nineteenth century A.D. Countless foreign travelers have, of course, visited Messenia since the Bronze Age, but their interpretation of Messenian history has unavoidably been filtered through the context of their own preconceptions, dispositions, and expectations, and modern readers, Greek and non-Greek, have in turn construed these accounts in diverse ways, also according to their own presuppositions, beliefs, and convictions. Even a cursory examination of several sources is sufficient to document this point.

The oldest account of a visit to Messenia is the fictional journey related by Homer—that of Telemachos, son of Odysseus, king of Ithaca, to discover the whereabouts of his father, an account that must be at least eight centuries older than the Roman empire. The story is, of course, well known from the *Odyssey*: how Telemachos left his mother, Penelope, besieged by suitors in her palace, to sail to Pylos in the company of Athena, disguised as Mentor, trusted retainer and confidant of the royal house.

On landing, Telemachos found King Nestor of Pylos, his sons, and their subjects sacrificing black bulls on the beach to Poseidon, god of earth-

FIGURE 8
The Englianos Ridge and the Palace of Nestor with Mt. Aigaleon in the background. PRAP Archive. Jack L. Davis.

quakes. With the encouragement of Athena, Telemachos marched right to the heart of the royal party, which he found seated on fleeces of sheep spread on the sand and about to eat sacrificial meat that had been skewered on spits and was roasting over an open fire. Telemachos was welcomed to the feast even before introductions were exchanged and soon found himself fed and bedded in the portico of the nearby palace of King Nestor. The next morning, after sacrificing to Athena, Telemachos, bathed and rubbed down with olive oil by Polycaste, the youngest daughter of the king, departed Pylos by chariot, in the company of Peisistratos, Nestor's youngest son; he arrived by nightfall at Pherae, in the western foothills of Mt. Taygetus, near the border of Messenia and Laconia.

Most scholars today, of course, do not expect that Telemachos's tale should be interpreted in a literal manner. Such direct readings of Homer have been rejected by most historians and archaeologists in the decades since World World II. Still, for many, or even most, contemporary Messenians, and for many visitors, Homer's Messenia is a reality. The seat of power of a historical King Nestor was, without question, situated on the ridge of Englianos near the modern town of Hora, where the archaeologist Carl Blegen, excavating on behalf of the University of Cincinnati, found in 1939 a prehistoric Bronze Age palace. From here it is a short leap of faith to identify other nearby prehistoric installations as the palace of Neleus, Nestor's father, or a tomb, such as the beehive tomb at Voidokoilia, as the burial place of Thrasymedes, another of King Nestor's many sons.

The text of Homer, however, probably reflects the worldview, still imperfectly understood, of this Greek poet of the eighth century B.C., more than it does the historical realities of the later second millennium B.C., the date of Blegen's Palace of Nestor. Indeed, the complex bureaucracy attested in the archives of this palace (Chapters 4–5) finds no accurate reflection in the *Odyssey*, and innocent transformation of a Homeric past into protohistory may divert us from asking many other interesting questions about the Messenian past. When was Messenia first peopled by speakers of the Greek language? To what extent was its prehistoric population really linguistically or culturally unified? What cultural ties does the modern Greek population of Messenia actually have to its prehistoric or historic past?

In the case of the Homeric tales just discussed, it is relatively clear that their interpretation must be approached with great care. But in other instances, it may not be so obvious that a narrative is partial and, colored by the interests and biases of the author, may be only one of many descriptions that could be composed about the same landscape.

It is important, therefore, to re-examine the sources we employ for the

---

JACK L. DAVIS

reconstruction of the Messenian past with an open mind—to identify when possible the agendas of authors and to try to tease out facts from often heavily biased chronicles. Such a goal is difficult to obtain, since all historical texts are highly colored by the perspectives of their creators. A good example is our most extensive ancient account of a visit to Messenia, that of the second-century A.D. traveler Pausanias, who devoted an entire book of his *Guide to Greece* to the southwestern Peloponnese.

What we expect of a guidebook today is lacking in Pausanias's travelogue. As a Greek, Pausanias almost entirely strips the modernity of his own day from the countryside through which he travels. He is instead concerned with establishing the ideological and material blueprint for a Messenian identity, basing his understanding of it on sources that are no longer extant, themselves composed as a charter for an independent Messenian state that only came into existence in the fourth century B.C. (These mythological foundations were indeed given physical form, as we shall see, in the institutions and structure of the pan-Messenian state established at Messene after liberation from Sparta [Chapter 7].) The result is a Messenia that had once been Messenian and was Messenian once again—a goal consonant with Pausanias's overall intention to emphasize Greek identity in the face of Roman imperialism.

We have no other written documents that can directly, by comparison with Pausanias's account, be employed to deconstruct the picture that he offers us. Fortunately, this is not the case for modern Greece, where we have more diverse descriptions of the landscape of Messenia, fabricated by many authors whose interests in constructing their narratives varied greatly. Many of these writers, in following a strategy similar to that of Pausanias, reject the reality of their own day, privileging descriptions of ancient Greek remains.

Fortunately, we may set alongside their histories reports that are less concerned with demonstrating ethnic continuity—for example, the logbooks of Colonel William Leake, a secret agent who traveled extensively in Greece on behalf of the British Crown in the decades that preceded the onset in 1821 of the Greek war for independence from the Ottoman Turkish empire—a period when England and other European powers vied for commercial and martial advantage in the Levant. Although Leake was an astute observer of remains of antiquity, he was also concerned with presenting for military purposes an accurate view of the state of affairs in his own day, one that was cognizant of the present and did not eradicate contemporary elements from the surroundings through which he traveled.

This is not to suggest that Leake admired all that he saw. He, like so many of his northern European coevals, regarded Turkish Greece as only the palest reflection of its ancient glories and its people as pitiful, undeserving heirs to their own antiquity:

> The very limited success of the principal works descriptive of Greece, which have lately been published, shew how difficult it is to render travels in that country agreeable to the general reader, and may serve in part to explain the long delay which has occurred in the publication of the present volumes. The new condition of the Peloponnesus will equally account for their being now submitted to the public. Greece, in fact, abstracted from its ancient history, has, until very recently, been no more than the thinly peopled province of a semi-barbarous empire, presenting the usual results of Ottoman bigotry and despotism, relieved only by the occasional resistance of particular districts to their rapacious governors, or of armed bandits to the established authority.

Leake's Messenia could hardly be more different from the province that the modern traveler will discover. Marauding bands of revolutionaries had destroyed olives, an act of war that finds no parallel in northern Europe in its long-term destructiveness to the productivity of the land. The Peloponnese was under siege from forces that threatened the stability of this Ottoman province, and the Turkish governor had summoned local Messenian leaders to Tripolis to discuss plans for defense.

The population was ethnically diverse. The largely Greek population of Kalamata practiced its religion without molestation from the Turkish minority. An Albanian chief-of-police patrolled the countryside to keep it free of bandits. The Greek city council that he served paid taxes in response to levies exacted by a Turkish tax-farmer. He, in turn, had bid for his contract in Istanbul.

Kalamata was extraordinary in the homogeneity of its population and the freedom it enjoyed. Elsewhere, ethnicities were intermingled to a greater extent, and Greeks were likely to be abused. It was difficult to predict the composition of a village by its appellation. In the Pamisos Valley, many villages with Turkish names were Greek; others with Greek names were largely Turkish. Greeks who resided in mixed communities were not free even to conduct Easter services in the open. Monks in the monastery at Voulkanou on Mt. Ithome were harassed. An industrious merchant at Navarino was constantly being shaken down by the Turkish military that manned the fort at Neokastro. Tax collectors were feared.

As today, Kalamata served as an important regional marketplace and the site of export for goods produced in the interior of the Peloponnese.

JACK L. DAVIS

But the agriculture and industry in its vicinity at that time differed substantially from what exists in the present. Husbandry of silkworms and fabrication of silk cloth were going concerns—the thread employed to produce handkerchiefs as well as mosquito curtains was greatly in demand in the Levant. Much of the Pamisos Valley was dominated by large farms, some owned by members of the imperial Ottoman family, others by Turks who had been granted their lands in return for obligations of military service. In all cases, their fields were worked by Greeks.

DIVERSITY AND MODERN MESSENIA

In the chapters that follow, we further explore these and many other testimonia that also describe the great diversity of traditions that have contributed to the formation of modern Messenia. We, of course, reject any notion that the Messenia discovered by the modern traveler is "timeless." Indeed, the modern homogeneous cultural landscape composed of the highly fragmented landholdings of almost exclusively Orthodox Christian, Greek-speaking, democratic small-scale farmers is a creation largely of the past century.

The great ethnic and cultural homogeneity enjoyed both by modern Messenia and by the rest of Greece is, in fact, a triumph of political and educational institutions established by the modern Greek state, which, since its formation in the early nineteenth century, has often sought to build internal solidarity through emphasizing Greek pasts to the exclusion of alternatives. Purification of the language by excising foreign vocabulary, alteration of toponyms to exclude non-Greek place names, subsumption of medieval and early modern archaeology and history under the rubric of "post-Byzantine"—these are ongoing processes that serve to create an impression of stability in population and cultural traditions, even where none may exist. These courses of action have often been indirectly promoted by forces outside Greece: Western attitudes have encouraged a definition of Greek nationality that emphasizes its Classical past. Continuing threats to the security of its borders have prompted expressions of national unity, as did the dominant philosophy of European nationalism in the nineteenth century.

Seen in this light, it should not occasion surprise that myth has been employed as a charter for the present and that Homeric tales have served contemporary political agendas by emphasizing the ethnic solidarity of Greece—its essential Greekness—since prehistoric times. For Homer describes a Greece populated by Greek speakers, with few traces of barbarous populations—a powerful pedigree with which to forge a modern nation with uniform traditions from the variegated ethnic landscape of Turkish Greece.

Our primary goal is to make our readers aware of the extent to which the histories of the past we have all composed are unavoidably constructed in the context of our presents. We believe that a multicultural history that incorporates the diversity of experiences that have shaped the past is a richer history—and also more enjoyable reading! Thus the preceding discussion is by no means to be construed as a criticism of the policies of modern Greece. Indeed, the success that it has achieved in establishing a sense of ethnic unity is enviable—particularly if one compares the striking failure of similar endeavors by several of its Balkan neighbors.

THE PRAP PERSPECTIVE

As we have already seen, Messenians have themselves left us only the most scanty narratives of their own past. For this reason, we believe that any attempt to write a history of Messenia can only succeed if it integrates a vast array of information, gleaned from the careful analysis of artifacts as well as texts. Unlike historians of more central areas of the ancient Greek world, where written testimonia are relatively abundant, students of Messenia, like ourselves, have no choice but to turn to sources of information that are not available in any library.

A need for additional information spawned the genesis of our own program of investigations, and the results of our own endeavors figure large in the chapters that follow. At the heart of our research has been an archaeological technique called "surface survey," in which teams of archaeologists systematically explore parts of the countryside, carefully chosen to reflect the diversity in types of land, mapping the distribution of artifacts they find on the surface of the earth. Unlike excavation, this technique allows a team of investigators to explore an entire region, rather than merely a single site. Surface remains, at least in a landscape that is intensively cultivated, like that of modern Greece, can provide clear indications of buried archaeological deposits, and thus of the locations where past inhabitants have lived, worked, worshiped, and commemorated their dead.

The path that runs between the basic collection of old pottery or stone tools in the field and the composition of an interpretive synthesis such as this book is, however, a long one. In the first instance, finds need to be described and dated so that we can know not only when archaeological sites were in use but also something about the activities that were conducted at them (Chapter 10). This analysis requires that a project like ours include experts who are knowledgeable about the typologies of artifacts from periods as chronologically disparate as the Palaeolithic (or Old Stone Age) and the early twentieth century.

Geologists on our staff help us appreciate the extent to which human beings have modified the landscape, as well as the degree to which erosion, ancient and modern, hampers our efforts to find archaeological sites. Botanists add another dimension to our construction of the past by providing information about ancient agricultural systems, through the analysis of fossilized pollen. Experts in Linear B, the script employed by the bureaucrats who managed the Palace of Nestor, and historians, skilled in finding and interpreting documents stored unindexed in sometimes chaotic medieval and modern archives, construct their version of the past with both texts and archaeological evidence.

This volume is the result of our individual efforts—a story of Messenia assembled from the contributions of more than a dozen authors who were invited to collaborate in its composition. A dialogue among PRAP members that began around the dinner table in the field in Messenia was developed in weekly seminars held at our temporary quarters in a public schoolhouse in the town of Hora, near the Palace of Nestor, and here continues. We do not, of course, believe that this book contains the only "correct" story that could be written about the Messenian past.

Nor should this book be construed as the official or final interpretation of the results of our research. Indeed, we have not been, are still not, and probably never will be in total agreement as to the best interpretation of the data we have gathered. We consider any such difference of opinion to be a virtue, not a fault. For in our view, the real fun of archaeology lies in dialogue among members of an interdisciplinary project, a dialectic that can sometimes engender striking new perceptions of the past. Each individual has therefore attempted to give an interpretation of Messenian history that in his or her mind provides the best explanation for certain specific aspects of the archaeological and historical information now available to us. The result is, we hope, a collection of perspectives that reflects the multiple voices of our own personnel, differing in gender, nationality, specialization, and position in the archaeological hierarchy.

REGIONAL STUDIES AND THE VISITOR TO GREECE

Although our project is perhaps unusual in its scale and its ambition, similar endeavors to explore many other regions of Greece have been recently completed or are under way. Yet modern visitors to Greece (and most permanent residents) are hardly aware of this work, since it offers little or nothing that is visually comprehensible in an instant. Tour buses stop only at excavated sites and at the museums where the finds are displayed. Guidebooks similarly emphasize individual excavations rather than entire landscapes.

In contrast, it is our hope that informed visitors to Greece will make the effort to comprehend the bigger picture that this volume offers and to understand in greater depth the history and prehistory of a Mediterranean landscape that is typical of much of Greece as a whole, yet fascinating in its own right. Readers should also understand that the approach to archaeology that we here espouse is vital to the preservation of the Greek past.

The countryside of Pylos is today being reshaped in ways more all-encompassing than ever before. The past that we have investigated and here describe will not survive intact, as its physical remains are rapidly being destroyed by the mechanization of agriculture, industrialization, and the expansion of the touristic infrastructure so important to the Greek economy.

Until recently, Messenia lay far from the main tourist paths. But in the past decade, a number of factors have combined to make it easier for foreigners, Greek and non-Greek, to reach Pylos and to reside there. The number of charter flights to the Kalamata airport has increased dramatically. Ferry-boat service between Italy and Patras expanded substantially

FIGURE 9
Bulldozed antiquities in the fenced front yard of a modern seaside summer home, and PRAP archaeologist David Stone. PRAP Archive.

JACK L. DAVIS

following the sundering of Yugoslavia. Membership in the European Community has made it easier for northern Europeans to build summer homes. The construction of a superhighway linking Corinth to Tripolis leads Athenian holiday-makers to Messenia by the thousands each weekend of the summer.

This boom in tourism has led ineluctably to the construction of scores of new coastal tourist facilities and private villas (Fig. 9) and threatens with destruction archaeological resources that have remained untouched for millennia (Chapter 10). It is important for newcomers to Messenia, like many readers of this volume, as well as its long-time residents, to realize the severity of the threat. Only a very few of the many archaeological resources of Messenia are currently protected as official archaeological sites. The remainder may be ravaged at will.

The scale of the problem is almost incomprehensible, since it is the entire archaeological landscape that is at risk, not just a few dozen sites. No number of additional antiquities guards would be great enough to protect it. It is our hope, however, that a program of education, to which this volume may make a small contribution, might succeed. An informed public, more aware of the magnitude of the challenge and the importance of preserving its heritage, may ultimately accomplish what lies beyond the reach of governments.

SANDY PYLOS

FIGURE 10
Landslide near the Palace of Nestor, from the northwest. PRAP Archive.
R. J. Robertson.

CHAPTER 1
The ENVIRONMENTAL SETTING

Messenia is the name both of a region and of an administrative district in the far southwest corner of Greece—an area segregated from the central Greek mainland by several mountain divides, bordered on three sides by the sea and on the fourth by the Taygetus Mountains, which rise to a height of 2,400 meters. Because of its remoteness, much of Messenia is only sparsely inhabited, and the entire province has a single regional center of traffic and commerce, its capital, Kalamata.

Although Kalamata possesses a port with ferry connections to Crete and a small airport with scheduled flights to and from Athens, most who visit Messenia will drive by car over winding roads through the center of the Peloponnese before arriving in one of the most beautiful parts of Greece. A mere 150,000 people in an area of 3,000 square kilometers share the best soil and most favorable climate in the entire Peloponnese. Most live in the city of Kalamata and in the towns of Pylos, Hora, Gargaliani, and Cyparissia; thus the spectacular coastal scenery of western Messenia, including the Bay of Navarino, remains almost unspoiled by modern buildings.

The great Bay of Navarino, the extensive swampy lagoon known as Osmanaga, and the beach barrier dividing these two are among the most prominent geographical features of western Messenia. West of the lagoon is a shallow sea inlet, ringed by tall sand dunes at a place called Voidokoilia ("ox-belly") because of its distinctive shape. Voidokoilia, crowned by the so-called Cave of Nestor on the nearby Navarino Ridge, certainly ranks as one of the most enchanting landscapes in Greece (Fig. 11).

To understand how this landscape evolved, it is necessary for us to widen our perspectives beyond those normally considered by historians and archaeologists, and to consider geological scales of time and space. The main geological and physiographic characteristics of Messenia are the result of a collision between two units of the earth's crust that are called the African and the European plates. These plates have been moving toward each other

EBERHARD ZANGGER

FIGURE 11
The north end of the Bay of Navarino, the castle of Palaionavarino, and the sand bar separating the bay from Osmanaga Lagoon. PRAP Archive. R. Dupuis-Devlin and E. Dallagher.

at a rate of approximately 1 centimeter per year, and during the past two million years, it seems that probably as much as 20 kilometers of the earth's crust has subsided between them.

These horizontal plate movements are accompanied by vertical displacements of the earth: mountain ridges are uplifted along tectonic faults, while coastal plains temporarily sink below sea level, where they accumulate large amounts of sediment. Subsequently, they may rise above sea level again, thus exposing their marine deposits.

Messenia's landscape was shaped by a combination of these processes. Precipitous slopes occur along tectonic faults: the island of Sphacteria and the Aigaleon range of mountains in western Messenia are good examples of such landforms. Extensive terraces of uplifted marine sediments now cover areas between ridges. In places, deposits that formed at the beginning of the Pleistocene, two million years ago, are now located as high as 400 meters above sea level. Streams that drain the mountain basins cut their beds deeply into these young, soft deposits and, in so doing, fashion the soft powdery marl bedrock into spurs (Fig. 12).

Since natural resources such as arable land, abundant fresh water, protected harbors, and mineral resources have all, to a greater or lesser degree, influenced the fate and fortune of both ancient and modern cultures, any attempt to reconstruct Messenia's history requires an understanding of the habitat in which Messenians, past and present, have lived. What is more, the success of royal palaces, trading cities, and even entire states has often reflected their geographic position either in their immediate landscape or in a larger geopolitical world-system.

Interrelations between the natural environment and the history of its human habitation are complex, and require that archaeological field projects like the Pylos Regional Archaeological Project engage physical scientists, including geologists, geomorphologists, geophysicists, botanists, and soil scientists. Their job is to investigate the evolution of the landscape around the archaeological sites that are of interest to the archaeologists. Specifically, the scientists aim to find out how the landscape has changed since it was first settled, how the environment has influenced the choice of places to live or land to farm, and how the natural habitat, in turn, has been affected and changed by people.

These were the goals of the physical scientists who participated in PRAP and who formed a significant percentage of its staff. And after several years of fieldwork and laboratory analysis, we are now in a position to sketch the

FIGURE 12
The Englianos Ridge (distant center) and the uplands around Hora from the top of the Aigaleon Ridge. PRAP Archive.

The ENVIRONMENTAL SETTING

FIGURE 13
The area of the Mycenaean port basin (open area right of the large house in center) and the mouth of the Selas River from the town of Tragana. PRAP Archive. R. Dupuis-Devlin and E. Dallagher.

following history of the landscape of western Messenia, in the areas around the Palace of Nestor that formed the focus of detailed research by PRAP.

Ten thousand years ago, sea level was lower than at present, and the Bay of Navarino would have extended several kilometers farther north than it does today, reaching the foot of the ridge on which the modern village of Tragana is located. Osmanaga Lagoon, the beach barrier that separates it from the Bay of Navarino, and the dune fields at Voidokoilia did not exist at that time, although there *were* extensive stabile dunes north of Romanou. The two biggest rivers in the Pylos region today are those which run immediately north and south of the Englianos Ridge, then unite at its southwestern end to form the Selas River; several thousand years ago, this combined river would have exited into the Bay of Navarino (Fig. 13).

There is no doubt that these streams then flowed perennially. Rain would have been caught and preserved by a thick vegetation cover and by mature soils, which would have released their water slowly but steadily. Botanical investigations by our project allow such a reconstruction since they indicate that warmer and wetter conditions that followed the Ice Age supported open oak forests that, at low elevations, contained beech, holly, hornbeam, pistachio, and almonds with pine forests and evergreen shrubs at high elevations and on poor sandy soil.

At the end of the last Ice Age, it appears that Greece was largely deserted. The first farmers seem to have traveled from the Near East to northern Greece during the seventh millennium B.C., and to have chosen to settle in the most fertile plains facing the Aegean Sea, across which they would have traveled from Turkey. They brought with them the knowledge required for both agriculture and animal husbandry, including the ability to produce all tools needed for woodcutting and farming. Messenia, being far from the Aegean Sea, was settled later in the Neolithic. Pollen remains from this period are not exceptionally well preserved but are adequate to show that the first settlement by farmers was not accompanied by major land clearance. In a natural replacement, the extensive pine forests gradually gave way to deciduous oaks.

Until the third millennium B.C., agriculture was limited to the most fertile floodplains, where the soft soil could be manipulated with primitive tools. With the introduction of the plow around 3000 B.C., even fields of marginal quality became arable on a relatively large scale. As a result, hill slopes surrounding the fertile floodplains were cleared of forests to make space for new fields and pastures. The population expanded rapidly, and more deforestation and land clearance ensued.

These major changes in agricultural practice occurred first in Thessaly, then in the Argive Plain, and finally, after a delay of about a millennium, in remote areas such as the southern Argolid and western Messenia. By the time that the southern Argolid was cleared for large-scale agriculture (around 2000 B.C.), the agricultural potential of Messenia seems to have been exploited, too. Since then, the Messenian landscape has undergone rapid and long-lasting changes on four occasions.

Our pollen cores from Osmanaga Lagoon show that by 2000 B.C., pine forests had been reduced to a fraction of their former size. The sedimentation rate accelerated sharply, and the amount of organic matter in the sediments increased. We also found a 15-centimeter-thick sediment layer containing much charcoal, possibly stemming from forest fires, which may have been set intentionally to clear the pine woods. It appears that this first phase of deforestation brought about landscape instability and triggered a phase of increased fragility that has lasted until the present day.

The second period of significant environmental change coincides with the formative stages of Mycenaean civilization. Although the landscape seems to have regained stability between 1800 and 1600 B.C.—when even the pine forests were able partly to recover—shortly thereafter, between

1600 and 1400 B.C., the pines were suddenly and completely wiped out. Dramatic environmental destruction seems to have accompanied early Mycenaean agriculture. In addition to the total disappearance of pines, the number of oak trees dropped by half, making space for plants that are indicative of steppe and macchia communities. This radical change in the vegetation cover is best explained as the result of human-induced deforestation combined with subsequent overgrazing, which suppressed the recovery of trees.

Around 1400 B.C., however, the environmental situation took another turn. The steppe communities declined, and olive trees replaced them. New species of plants appeared, including rye, walnut, plane tree, and Judas tree. At the same time, sediments from Osmanaga Lagoon record a time of relative landscape stability between 1400 and 1200 B.C. Considering how prone to erosion the Pylos area is, it is more than likely that the steep slopes of Englianos were protected by terrace walls to prevent them from slumping. But whatever system the Mycenaean Greeks used to obtain landscape stability, it could not be maintained after the collapse of the kingdom, when archaeological evidence suggests that population density dropped precipitously.

During such phases of social and political readjustment in Greece, natural resources tend to be abused. In this instance, however, it did not take too long before the landscape became stabile once more, as its surface was protected by vegetation that grew almost without restriction. Indeed, deciduous oaks spread to such an extent that they may have covered over half of the total surface of the Pylos area. Although deciduous oaks are much less resistant to grazing than are evergreen oaks, with a deemphasis on husbandry, deciduous oaks have the competitive advantage of faster growth. At the same time, the number of olive and pistachio trees decreased, presumably because there was nobody resident on the land who would cultivate and maintain them.

The physiography of the Pylos area has not experienced any major changes since the end of the second millennium, except that the sand barrier at the northern end of the Bay of Navarino closed between 800 and 500 B.C., isolating Osmanaga Lagoon from the remainder of the gulf. What *has* changed significantly during the past three millennia is the plant cover.

The third phase of major environmental change coincides with the Classical to early Roman periods and marks one such alteration in plant communities. The study of the vegetation argues for a dense population and a high level of agricultural production between 500 and 100 B.C. After the end of the Spartan control of Messenia in the middle of the fourth century B.C. (see Chapters 6–7), the olive reaches an all-time peak (between 350 and 100 B.C.), when a quarter of the entire surface of the Pylos area may have been covered with olive trees. Many of the plants that are likely to have been cultivated at that time, including cereals and grapes, are hard to discern in fossil assemblages. This intense land use was accompanied by a significant drop in deciduous oaks and above-average erosional rates, as reflected in the physical parameters of sediments from our cores in Osmanaga Lagoon.

Land use diminished during the time of barbarian raids and Slavonic invasions in the later first millennium A.D. Fewer olives were cultivated and deciduous oaks recovered, each trend indicating decreased human activity. The sedimentation rate—an indicator of landscape instability—slowed down to a third of its previous value. During the Middle Byzantine period, the environmental data points to more intensive agriculture, while archaeological evidence suggests settlement was also more widespread (see Chapter 8). But no major changes in the environment occurred before the modern period, the fourth and last phase for which there is abundant evidence of human interference with the landscape.

Core samples from sediments just beneath the floor of the lagoon confirm what can be observed by eye in the present landscape. Agriculture has had such an impact on the vegetation that almost no examples of undisturbed natural plant communities can be found anywhere in the landscape. A mixture of cultivated land and pasture covers southwestern Messenia. Natural forests have completely disappeared, and macchia, a seminatural shrub vegetation, has spread over steep and inaccessible slopes. In many places, where grazing is most intense, the macchia has been degraded even further into another kind of plant community, called phrygana (or garrigue), a light, open, shrub plant community of 0.5–1 meter in height that covers many dry, sunburnt, eroded slopes with thin soil. Phrygana tends to look patchy, because many of its plants are cushionlike, and some parts of the community are dominated by only a single species of plant.

A flight to the cities and economic oscillations have forced most landowners to emphasize low-labor monocultures, mainly olives. The invention of deep plows, bulldozers, rototillers, and herbicides in this century was accompanied by a massive destruction of soils and shrubs. Today, in many areas, no low vegetation exists between the olive trees. Almost everywhere on the soft marl bedrock, soils have already been destroyed to the point that it is hard to find remains of them. Most farmers are simply plowing bedrock! For them, however, this is no cause for alarm, since the silty marl has very good physical properties for agriculture, and what it may lack in terms of minerals and organic compounds can be added with modern chemical fertilizers.

Widespread erosion has far more serious consequences for archaeologists, however, because artifacts contained in the soil are washed away, too. Hence, the loss of soil has, in many instances, destroyed archaeological strata. How much of the surface has been destroyed in recent years can often be measured at the bottoms of olive trees, where it is clear that in some instances the roots have been exposed to a depth of 1 meter.

Although calculating the total amount of natural and human-induced erosion that has occurred since prehistoric times is difficult, there are a number of ways to derive estimates. As a general rule, geologists hold that 1 meter of uplift in one thousand years should be equivalent to 1 meter of erosion in one thousand years—for internal mountain-building and external destructive processes on earth are roughly in balance. For western Messenia, we can be more specific if we examine the state of preservation of rock-cut chamber tombs, one of the most typical forms of burial employed by the Mycenaeans at the time of the Palace of Nestor.

Although the size and shape of these tombs vary considerably, in the Pylos area they tend to consist of a chamber that is 2.5–4.5 meters deep, with a doorway (or *stomion*) and an entrance passageway (*dromos*) that are together 4–9 meters long. Of those examined by PRAP in detail, only the rear wall and less than 1 meter of the chamber of several such tombs located on the Englianos Ridge itself were still preserved. In other words, it is obvious that since the later second millennium B.C., a few vertical meters of soil and bedrock have been removed from the surface of the slopes of the ridge in these locations (Fig. 14).

More evidence for very recent environmental destruction exists in the form of conspicuous, well-defined knolls, consisting of undisturbed marl bedrock, usually 3 to 5 meters high and several meters wide. Their surfaces are level and overgrown by grass and bushes, whereas their sides are usually vertical. Some of the mounds bear trigonometric markers, some ancient graves, some both. Apparently these mounds represent leftover bedrock prominences that have been spared from plowing and bulldozing. Their tops are remnants of the former surface, which used to extend laterally before the surrounding area was lowered by excessive plowing. The date of the destruction most likely falls between the erection of the trigonometric stations and the planting of the olive trees on the lowered surface around them—in most cases, in the last thirty years. In two instances, these "leftovers" suffered even more destruction shortly after we had investigated them (see Chapter 10).

EBERHARD ZANGGER

FIGURE 14
Destroyed chamber tombs on the Englianos Ridge. PRAP Archive. J. Bennet.

At the end of this journey through the last few thousand years of environmental evolution in southwestern Messenia, we return to our starting point: the present landscape around the Palace of Nestor. Those factors which characterize today's landscape—high rates of tectonic movement, erosion compensating for uplift, and intensive human land use—have also determined the landscape in prehistoric and historic times. Messenia was always blessed with fertile soil and relatively abundant fresh water. Geopolitically speaking, however, it has almost always lain far away from the pacemaking centers of culture. We shall explore the effects of this isolation in subsequent chapters.

The ENVIRONMENTAL SETTING

FOCUS

The PHYSICAL SCIENTIST'S ROLE in REGIONAL ARCHAEOLOGY

Reconstructing the history of the Pylos region—or of any other landscape—means determining a sequence of events, like the scenes in a motion picture, showing when and for what reason landscape changes occurred. In environmental reconstructions—much as in screenplays—important moments are emphasized and presented in detail, whereas periods when little or nothing happened are simply omitted. The organization of the physical scientific work on an archaeological field project is also somewhat similar to that needed to shoot a film. In both instances, a team effort, involving experts from many different fields, is required. While some people are dedicated to solving special problems, others concentrate on the ultimate results of the combined efforts.

The movie director, however, has a script that contains the story, scene by scene, leading up to the film's climax, whereas the director of the physical scientific work on an archaeological project only has the last scene of events from which his teams will have to work backward, collecting clues during fieldwork to determine which processes were responsible for environmental changes. This last scene is simply the present landscape—the product of a long evolution, yet a momentary frame in the eternal evolution of the earth. To decide which methods are needed to reconstruct the landscape and who might be the right people to employ these methods, it is important to start with a careful interpretation of the present landscape. Hence, conducting a reconnaissance is as indispensable for an environmental reconstruction as reading the script is for the production of a movie.

In 1991, during a first visit to our study area, we established four main areas in which intensive physical scientific work was required. First, the modern floodplains had to be investigated to determine how much sediment had accumulated in recent times and how deeply some archaeological sites might have been buried under the surface. Second, at places

EBERHARD ZANGGER

where architectural structures were likely to be hidden under the surface, we wanted to conduct a geophysical reconnaissance to trace these constructions without excavation. Third, the vegetation history of the past several thousand years had to be determined to find out about the extent and character of ancient land use. Finally, the soils had to be studied to establish their state of preservation and the past and present agricultural potential of the landscape.

We invited a total of twenty-seven scientists and graduate students for the physical scientific fieldwork on PRAP, and many more experts conducted laboratory analysis on material collected in the field. The idea was to stimulate new ideas for landscape reconstruction in Greece by bringing in scientists who had worked outside the Aegean. Specialists came from many disciplines, including geoarchaeology, geomorphology, geophysics, geochemistry, soil science, palynology, geochronology, micropalaeontology, and hydroengineering. They came from eight different universities and research institutes in the United States, Greece, Germany, Canada, Russia, and Switzerland.

In contrast to many other archaeological projects in the Aegean, the ultimate goal of the physical scientific work on PRAP was not to produce individual contributions from the experts involved, which—again using the comparison with movie production—often appear like disconnected takes and scenes that bear little or no relation to each other. Instead, we were aiming for a complete integration of the many disciplines involved, which would lead to a comprehensive story of the evolution of the landscape, not as a substitute for, but as a complement to, highly specialized articles in scientific journals.

The first expert to join our team was Sergei Yazvenko from the Department of Higher Plants at Lomonosov University in Moscow. Yazvenko had written a dissertation about the Holocene vegetational history of the Black Sea's coastal region and received a grant shortly after the commencement of PRAP that permitted him to move to Canada, where he now lives. Yazvenko's botanical research for PRAP led to one of the most detailed, complete, and accurately dated vegetation histories of southern Greece. The methods he employed are the subject of a separate focus in this chapter.

To locate buried architectural structures, we invited a group of geophysicists from the Polytechnical University of Braunschweig in Germany. Guided by Falko Kuhnke, this team had already mapped an entire Roman settlement in southern France without moving any soil. Geophysical mapping rests on measuring minute variations in the earth's magnetic field, which are often caused by accumulations in the soil of natural building ma-

FIGURE 15
*Geophysicists measuring subsurface anomalies at the Palace of Nestor.
PRAP Archive.*

terials such as stones or mudbrick. A second, equally useful technique measures the electric resistivity of the soil between two probes. Many thousand such measurements, at 1-meter intervals, produce a map that provides important clues about the size and extent of subsurface structures. These geophysicists systematically investigated a substantial area adjacent to the Palace of Nestor (Fig. 15), as well as three other sites (Bouka, Dialiskari, and Ordines; see Chapter 5 for the palace area, Chapter 7 for the other sites).

The next expert to join our team was Michael Timpson, from Northern Arizona University. For several years Timpson had worked as a soil scientist on American archaeological projects in eastern Crete. His role on the Pylos project was to determine how much of the prehistoric surface has been preserved until the present day and how much has been destroyed by erosion. Soils form in the uppermost epidermis of the earth through the movement of water, ions, and clay combined with the activities of plants and microfauna. The maturity of a soil mainly depends on the climate, the duration of exposure at the surface, and the type of vegetation that covers it. In Greece, at least one to two thousand years of landscape stability are necessary to generate a distinct soil with several different horizons. Timpson found that because of high rates of erosion, such undisturbed soils are extremely rare in the center of the study region. He was also able to distinguish between areas that now contain few archaeological sites due to soil erosion and areas that were never densely inhabited.

During the final season, we invited a few well-known authorities to examine specific problems that had arisen in the course of fieldwork. Jost Knauss, from the Polytechnical University in Munich, a specialist in Late Bronze Age water management, investigated the hydrological parameters of a basin near the town of Romanou, west of Pylos, and arrived at the conclusion that it was probably, at least in part, not natural (see Chapter 3). He also examined the Selas stream, which changed its bed not too long ago and now passes through the artificial basin. Günther Wagner, from the Max Planck Institute of Nuclear Physics in Heidelberg, and his colleague Yiannis Bassiakos, from the Demokritos Institute in Athens, were asked to help us date the first two Palaeolithic sites in Messenia—both of which were discovered by PRAP. Using a technique called thermoluminescence dating, they were able to determine when the sediments surrounding the stone tools were last exposed to sunlight, which in turn has provided a date for the deposition of both sediment and tools.

During the final season of the project in 1995, the physical scientists present in the field at times outnumbered the archaeologists—perhaps hinting at the increased significance of the role of physical sciences in archaeological research in Greece.

FOCUS
From POLLEN to PLANTS

Since climatic shifts as well as changes in human land use have a profound effect on plant cover, knowing the history of vegetation is extremely important for the reconstruction of landscape changes. Vegetation, especially forest, is the glue that binds the surface of the earth and keeps erosion low, the soil in place, and the water supply stable. Once the forest is removed, Pandora's box is open: erosion increases, stripping slopes of productive soil; streams and rivers choke; torrential floods during rainy seasons damage fields and villages; and ultimately the very basis of life, productive land, may be exhausted.

Throughout their history, people have had difficulty learning this simple lesson. From the Mediterranean to the Mayan Yucatan to tropical Africa and Amazonia, deforestation is commonly associated with human habitation. People have changed the environment both by clearing the forests and by introducing exotic plants as crops or weeds. The course of such changes has varied greatly in different areas of the world. Left alone, forests can make remarkable comebacks, but may be different from the ancient, undisturbed plant communities that existed before human interference.

Human-vegetation interactions of these sorts could have had profound effects on the development of many early civilizations of the world, and both botanists and archaeologists study them with great interest. However, to reconstruct vegetation of the past is not a simple task. Historical accounts may be used, but they often give only patchy, scattered evidence that can hardly be quantified.

There is an alternative way: the study of plant pollen in the sediments of marshes or lakes. Pollen is not only a nuisance for millions suffering from pollinoses (including myself!). It is also a unique natural chronicler that continuously and tirelessly records changes in vegetation. Pollen is ubiqui-

SERGEI YAZVENKO

tous. Every season, trees, shrubs, and herbs all over the world produce perhaps sextillions (10^{21}) of tiny (10–150 microns in size) pollen grains, amounting to millions of tons. Every square inch of the Earth, even Antarctica, receives annually up to millions of pollen grains.

Pollen is dispersed by wind, water, insects, and other animals. Hummingbirds carry pollen to flowers, some cacti are pollinated by bats, and some desert shrubs can even receive pollen from snakes. Pollen of plants pollinated by wind may travel particularly far. The great majority of pollen grains are, however, deposited within several kilometers of source plants, and consequently the study of these ancient pollen grains can tell us about vegetation that once grew in the area.

Though some plants, such as grasses, sedges, and most ericoids, have morphologically uniform pollen and thus are difficult to identify, many other plants have pollen that is quite specific in its shape and surface sculpture—so much so that an experienced botanist can recognize many plants at the genus level (pine, oak, olive), and can even discern precise species (walnuts, plantains, many knotweeds). The greater the proportion of a certain plant species in an area, the more pollen of its type is deposited in swamps or lakes. It is possible, therefore, to estimate from the quantities and percentages of various pollen types preserved in sediments the abundances of plant species that once grew in a region.

Pollen grains and spores of ferns and related plants are like nuts: a living cell is enclosed in a shell (cell wall) made of a complex polymer called sporopollenin. This polymer is one of the strongest organic substances on earth. It can withstand alkali and acids that eat metals and glass. Under some conditions, pollen and spore "shells" can survive for hundreds of millions of years, although the soft protoplasm of the cell dies within days. Scientists have found spores as old as the first vascular plants, and by the mid-Mesozoic period, there were already hundreds of pollen types.

At the same time, pollen cannot long survive oxidation and microbial attack. For our purposes, pollen must land in a permanently anoxic site, where there are no microbes or fungi. If pollen falls in a wetland that sometimes dries out, it may decay. If sand and gravel are deposited along with the pollen, it may be mechanically damaged.

Ancient pollen is thus best sought in calm, permanently wet, preferably low-oxygen (but not necessarily acidic) beds of seas, lakes, lagoons, and mires, where organic sediments and/or clay have constantly accumulated in thin layers over thousands of years. The continuous deposition of pollen can often provide an annual record. No wonder that after 1916, when the analysis of pollen was developed and publicized by prominent Swedish botanist Lennart von Post, the method rapidly became very popular; now thousands of scientists throughout the world study pollen and call themselves palynologists. Applications of pollen analysis range from dating oil- and coal-bearing deposits, to studying the responses of vegetation to climate changes in the past in order to predict more accurately the future of the biosphere. Among its many archaeological applications, pollen analysis is one of the few methods that can be employed to assess the extent of the pressure exerted by humans on vegetation, and thus allows us indirectly to speculate about the size of past populations.

Both fieldwork and laboratory analysis are extremely labor-intensive. Since palynology begins in the field, let us begin by describing how palynological research was conducted in Messenia under the auspices of PRAP. Pollen was extracted by drilling holes into sediments. The drill pipe is hollow, so that a cylindrical tube, or core, of sediment is contained inside it when it is removed from the lake. The PRAP cores were taken from a coastal lagoon, in water 1 meter deep, several hundred meters offshore. We had to wade into the lake and stay there for hours (Fig. 16). Several cores are usually collected from each site. One core is used for sediment, pollen, and physical and geochemical analyses; another core is for radiocarbon dating; and the remaining cores are stored permanently as archives.

Sediment was described in the field, then the cores were wrapped in plastic film and in aluminum foil (Fig. 17), labeled, and shipped from Greece to our laboratory in Canada. There, small samples (1–5 cubic centimeters) were taken from the cores at intervals of 5–20 centimeters and processed using a series of acids (including strong hydrofluoric and hydrochloric acids) and alkalines to remove mineral and organic debris, leaving only the pollen.

What a thrill I felt when taking samples of the cores in the laboratory! A seed of a plant or a shell of a mollusk might fall out—fresh in appearance, despite being several thousand years old. Dodo Chochieva, a prominent palaeobotanist from Tbilisi, Georgia (the former Soviet Union), told me once that perhaps the most extraordinary experience in her entire life was a day when she was standing on the shore of the Black Sea washing a 30-pound lump of clay. Suddenly, as the clay washed away, she was left holding an entire bunch of redwood twigs, complete with leaves and cones. They were 1.5 million years old—but they looked and *smelled* like fresh redwood. For a minute, she even dreamed that she saw the ancient forest running all along the coast, extending to the horizon, and she could hear it rustling and sighing. Such moments add excitement to days and weeks of hard, often monotonous, work.

SERGEI YAZVENKO

FIGURE 16
*Sergei Yazvenko extracting pollen cores from the Osmanaga Lagoon. PRAP Archive.
J. Bennet.*

FIGURE 17
*Gulia Ismail-Zade packing sections of a pollen core for storage. PRAP Archive.
J. Bennet.*

After the samples were processed, 400–500 pollen grains from each sample were identified and counted under the microscope to produce what is called a "pollen spectrum"—a list of the percentages of various pollen types contained in the sample. Finally, the pollen counts for all levels in the core were compiled in a "pollen diagram," a chart that illustrates changes in pollen percentages (x-axis) through depth/time (y-axis), as is shown in Figure 18. Accelerated Mass Spectrometer (AMS) radiocarbon dates allowed the layers of pollen to be dated.

From pollen to plants in a direct route? Hardly! The path to environmental reconstruction is mined with potential pitfalls. Different plants produce different quantities of pollen; some pollen types are dispersed more widely than others. Wind-pollinated trees can produce enormous amounts of pollen that travel far. Pine is the champion in both quantity (its yellow powder scattered everywhere on a June day in Canada) and distance (pollen in Antarctica is mostly pine). Pine is followed by birch, alder, oak, sagebrush, and grasses in amount of pollen dispersed. Pollen of these plants is present in virtually any pollen sample outside the tropics, often dominating the pollen spectrum. In contrast, many insect-pollinated herbs produce millions of times less pollen; much of what is produced is eaten by the pollinators themselves, whereas much of the remainder simply drops in place from the source plant. Such types are underrepresented or absent in most pollen cores.

Certain pollen types are more resistant to decay than others. Often, pollen samples from archaeological sites are dominated by the sunflower family, the parsley family, and/or ferns. The likely explanation is not that these plants were most common in the past, but that their pollen is armored and has survived where most other pollen has been destroyed. Such is an extreme and obvious case. Often, pollen suffers less-obvious damage that is nonetheless sufficient to alter the proportions of the pollen types that we observe.

Many pollen types can be identified no more closely than a genus or a group of genera. Even in cases where distinct pollen types exist, it can be difficult to discriminate between complexes of vegetation (e.g., an oak forest and intensively grazed knee-high oak maquis) when they are dominated by the same taxa.

The bottom line is this: percentages of pollen in a fossil sample may not accurately reflect the percentages of plants that grew in an area in the past. To "convert" pollen counts into meaningful descriptions of ancient vegetation, it is necessary to examine in great detail the relationship between pollen production and modern vegetation. It is assumed that the relation between modern pollen and modern plant assemblages may be applied

FIGURE 18

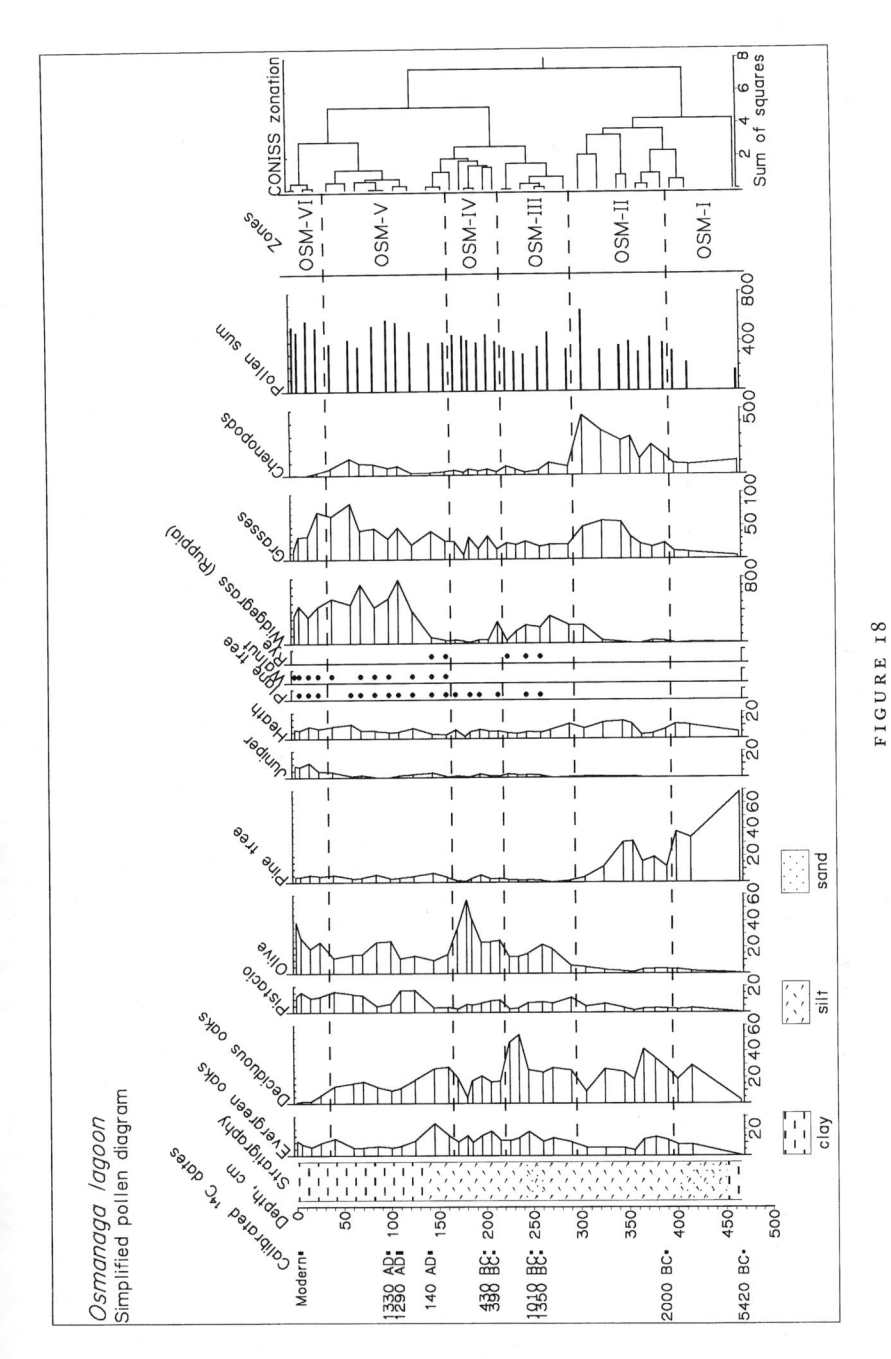

Pollen diagram showing species of plants represented in cores extracted from the Osmanaga Lagoon. PRAP Archive. S. Yazvenko.

to estimate the relation between fossil pollen assemblages and past plant cover, an assumption that has been tested in other regions of the world, mainly in northwest Europe and eastern North America.

There have been in the Mediterranean several excellent studies of present vegetation and its pollen production. However, for this entire region, ours is the first study that quantified the relation between the modern pollen production and its source vegetation. For this purpose, we studied a wide variety of modern vegetation types, including coastal dunes; oak macchia; mixed shrubland with mastic trees, heaths, wild olives, myrtle, strawberry trees, etc.; open low-shrub frigana, with many aromatic plants; olive orchards; and vineyards. Some vegetation types that we know to have once been prominent in Greece, like pine forests or deciduous oak forests, are now virtually gone.

So we had to travel extensively to find them and study their pollen production. In this way, a comprehensive database of vegetation types and their pollen spectra was compiled, which allowed us to construct mathematical equations that literally converted pollen counts into vegetation abundances. The work is still in progress, and there are, of course, many difficulties yet to be confronted; for example, it is hard to quantify the effects of the different air currents that carry the pollen, or the influence of pollen carried into the lagoon by water rather than by air. But the journey of a thousand miles begins with the first step.

FIGURE 19
Bust of C. W. Blegen by the sculptor Elisavet Valvi erected in front of the Museum of Hora in 1995. PRAP Archive. R. J. Robertson.

CHAPTER 2

The HISTORY of ARCHAEOLOGICAL INVESTIGATIONS in MESSENIA

> *It was upon . . . Cape Coryphasium, that stood the town built by Pylos the son of Cleson, where Nestor received the young Telemachus, and gave him a car to transport him to Sparta. Perhaps the cavern might yet be found which served as a stable for the flocks of his grandfather Neleus and his own. The temple of Minerva would, however, be sought in vain; not the slightest vestige of it has been spared by Time.*
>
> FRANÇOIS POUQUEVILLE, *Travels in Greece and Turkey* (1820)

A search for the past of Messenia is a search among many renowned figures of legend (Homer's wise King Nestor; Aristomenes, the ancient Messenian national resistance hero), classical history (Epaminondas, conqueror of the Spartans), and modern archaeology. The focus of this chapter is the latter, the antiquaries and archaeologists who have shaped our vision of Messenia—men like Carl Blegen, excavator of the Palace of Nestor; Spyridon Marinatos; and Natan Valmin. But Messenia is significant not only because it can boast of many famous archaeologists who have investigated its past. It is no exaggeration to say that archaeological projects in Messenia have often established new standards in their innovative approaches to fieldwork, especially interdisciplinary research (an approach on which PRAP itself has focused; see Introduction).

Messenia's importance in Greek Bronze Age archaeology was ensured by Blegen's excavation of the Palace of Nestor at Ano Englianos and his discovery of the largest collection of prehistoric documents yet found in mainland Greece (see Focus in this chapter and in Chapter 5). But the decipherment of the Linear B script in which these documents were written and the realization that the language of the tablets is an early form of Greek also marked a sharp turning point in the history of archaeological investigations in Messenia.

NIGEL SPENCER

The following account is therefore a story, with the central plot revolving around how, after the discovery of the tablets, there resulted an explosion of interest in the Greek Bronze Age in Messenia at the expense of the historic periods, a bias not corrected until PRAP's more balanced view (shown throughout this volume). Ironically, however, the boot was once on the other foot, and it is easy to forget that before work began in earnest at the Palace of Nestor in 1952, it had been the historical periods that were of greater concern, and it was prehistoric Messenia that had been the object of archaeological neglect. Such are the dramatic swings that the central characters in the plot induced, affecting research for decades after their time.

ANCIENT WRITERS, BYZANTINES, AND TURKS

Despite the legendary, heroic past of Messenia and, later, its well-attested struggles with Sparta, early travelers and antiquaries found it virtually impossible to recognize physical evidence of Messenian glory "on the ground." Even by the first century B.C., the ancient Greek geographer Strabo felt obliged to curtail his discussion of Messenia because the area had become a backwater. Two centuries later, the Roman traveler Pausanias was even more frustrated in his search for antiquities, stating that "the catastrophes that the Messenians have suffered and their long exile from the Peloponnese . . . have obscured much of their ancient history, and, since the Messenians themselves don't know the facts, whoever wants to do so can dispute their claims" (3.13.2).

As for much of Greece, knowledge of Messenia in the centuries following the collapse of the Roman empire is scant. The only places regularly visited by travelers were the important ports of Methoni and Koroni, on opposite sides of the southern peninsula of Messenia. The Venetians gained control of these two towns after 1204, and both became safe havens for shipping en route from Italy and the Ionian islands to Crete, itself a colony of Venice for over 300 years. Brief descriptions of medieval Methoni and Koroni survive (see Focus in Chapter 9), but none specifically examines their antiquities.

THE EIGHTEENTH AND NINETEENTH CENTURIES

Following the French Revolution, Greece overtook Rome and Renaissance Italy as the focus of intellectual thought in Europe: a nostalgia prevailed for the loss of the original, "ideal," and largely imaginary Greek culture of ancient times. "Hellas," as the Greeks have always called Greece, had tremendous political and philosophical potential as a model within developing Western European humanism and romanticism. Its reputation precipitated a great influx of travelers to Greece—clerics, Oxford scholars, aristocratic dilettantes, ambassadors, merchants, and adventurers.

And traveling in Greece at this time certainly was an adventure. If one eluded capture at sea by pirates or on land by brigands, at the final destination might await sickness, even plague. Many travelers were far from expert in the history, literature, and archaeology of Greece; nonetheless, many enthusiastically carried information home to scholars who lacked such wanderlust. Countless corrections were conscientiously made by those who walked later in the footsteps of the pioneers, and gradually mistakes in earlier topographical accounts were eliminated, and the record of the material remains of ancient Greece became more completely and correctly known.

In contrast with several other parts of Greece, such as Athens or the Cycladic Islands, in Messenia the search for ancient remains began late; it was not until the beginning of the nineteenth century that systematic investigations ensued. Then, English travelers such as Edward Dodwell and Sir William Gell began to describe ancient remains at Cyparissia and ancient Messene. But the most detailed of the early investigations was published in 1831 by the Expédition scientifique de Morée under the direction of Abel Blouet. This French team is the first in our story to have attempted interdisciplinary fieldwork in Messenia (and arguably in the whole of Greece), a tradition that has persisted in the area to this day (see Introduction and Chapter 1).

In the nineteenth century, the most popular touristic attraction in western Messenia was the old medieval castle northwest of the Bay of Navarino, partly because of remains of the ancient Greek city of Coryphasion, mentioned by Pausanias, but more importantly because the site had come to be associated with the Homeric Pylos of King Nestor (for the wandering nature of this toponym, see the Introduction). This association was not altogether surprising, since the shores around Coryphasion clearly matched the "sandy" epithet given by Homer to Nestor's town, and the possible identification with Nestor did not escape the attention of the next major figure in the story of Messenian archaeology, and probably the greatest Homeric archaeologist of all time, the German archaeological entrepreneur and self-made millionaire, Heinrich Schliemann.

After three seasons' work at Troy, Schliemann returned to mainland Greece in 1874, intent on exploring other famous Homeric sites; in addition to Mycenae "rich in gold" in the Argolid, he fixed his sights on the western coast of the Peloponnese, where the venerable and wise Nestor had ruled his kingdom from the "stately citadel" of Neleus, his father. Perhaps because he came from outside the field of Classics, Schliemann (like the

Expédition scientifique) brought with him innovative ideas about interdisciplinary fieldwork. So, into the field he would bring engineers, artists, architects, and scientists, reporting on everything from stone blocks to botany, from topography to ethnography.

At Coryphasion, specifically in the so-called Cave of Nestor on the northern slope of the ancient city, Schliemann found fragments of broken pottery, some of which he declared to be of "Mycenaean" type, from the time of Homer's Trojan War. Encouraged by these finds, Schliemann's team opened trenches within the ruins of the medieval castle in search of Nestor's palace late in November 1888, but the results proved disappointing, and Schliemann left Messenia, concluding (quite correctly, as it turned out) that the capital of Nestor's kingdom lay elsewhere.

In the last decade of the century, our story takes its first major swing toward the historic periods as the focus for archaeological interest in Messenia. First, in 1894, the German archaeologist Erich Pernice found ancient Greek and Roman inscriptions together with squared marble blocks at a place called Yiannitsa near Kalamata, and wondered whether these finds might be the remains of Homeric Pharae—where Telemachus had lodged overnight at the house of Diokles on his journey from Pylos to Sparta (see Introduction).

Second, however (and more important), was the first serious excavation at Messene, the imposing city on the slopes of Mt. Ithome. In antiquity, this was the largest and politically most important ancient Greek city in Messenia, and the historical periods came to dominate the thoughts of most archaeologists interested in the area until after World War I.

In 1895, Themistoklis Sofoulis undertook a season of excavation for the Greek Archaeological Society amidst the ruins of Messene, claiming to have found both a fountain mentioned by Pausanias and a large part of the ancient marketplace, or agora, of the town (although we now know that the latter was a sanctuary of Asclepius, the Greek god of healing). Unfortunately, Sofoulis was taken seriously ill and later confined to bed, meaning that the results of his excavations were never published and investigation of this highly significant site was suspended.

Interest in the historical periods was not suspended, however, and the great naval battle that had occurred between Athens and Sparta in 425 B.C. at Pylos now attracted considerable attention abroad, particularly in Britain. There, scholars had been arguing about the topographical details of the island of Sphacteria, where Spartan forces had taken refuge following their defeat. In October 1895, one of the principal "combatants" in the debate, G. Beardoe Grundy, came to Pylos to inspect the topography of the battlefield firsthand. It is ironic that while standing on the north shore of the small inlet of Voidokoilia, he made by accident one of the most important discoveries in the history of Messenian archaeology.

Seeing a shallow quarry hollowed out of the side of the hill, Grundy reports that

> [I] made for that, planted my instruments in the middle of it, and took sightings for about half an hour. Stopping for a moment in the course of the work (to light my pipe as a fact), I noticed that I had planted my table in the middle of what had evidently been an enclosure of very large stones. The reason that I had not noticed it before was that the surface of the stones was practically flush with the ground, and they were worn on the surface by weathering and other causes into an irregular shape.... The general characteristics reminded me of the stone circle at Mykenae, which I had but lately seen . . . but there were in this case no upright slabs.... This space is, I am almost sure, artificial. It commands a magnificent view of the lagoon and Navarino Bay. That it deserves further attention I am sure.

Grundy seems to have been standing in the ruins of a Bronze Age beehive or tholos tomb, the "Tomb of Thrasymedes" that Pausanias described just outside the walls of Classical Pylos, but blinded by his interest for the historic battle he did not examine the ruins further! No excavations of this monument were carried out, Grundy left Messenia, and it was to be sixty years before Spyridon Marinatos would systematically explore the tomb and the important Bronze Age village beneath it at Voidokoilia. Thus, the Bronze Age past of Messenia still lay dormant.

THE EARLY TWENTIETH CENTURY

Despite Sofoulis's illness and the lack of work at Messene since 1895, the potential of the site meant that it was soon the focus of further investigations, this time by the Greek archaeologist Yioryios Oikonomos in 1909. In just two months, Oikonomos uncovered part of the stadium of the city and parts of two large public buildings—the Propylon, a monumental gateway, and the Synedrion or Bouleuterion, a meeting hall on the eastern side of what was still perceived to be the "agora."

In the same year, there was one of the first signs of interest in the prehistory of Messenia when the provincial director of antiquities, Andreas Skias, investigated reports of a tomb to the north of ancient Coryphasion near the village of Tragana. There was unearthed a Bronze Age tholos tomb that Skias compared in form and size to the "Royal Tombs" at Mycenae (as

Grundy had done at Voidokoilia). Three years later, the tomb was explored more thoroughly, and although the site had obviously been plundered long before, there were still finds of gold and other jewelery in addition to Mycenaean pottery.

But despite this excavation, which clearly indicated the exciting potential of the Bronze Age culture of Messenia, the overwhelming interest in Messenia continued to be in the historical periods. However, luck also played a large part in the discovery of the next major historical site, the "extremely ancient" shrine of Apollo Korythos, which Pausanias had spoken of as being on the shore of the Messenian Gulf, 80 stadia (approximately 16 kilometers) south of ancient Koroni (the modern town of Petalidi). Pausanias had described how this sanctuary had been especially revered by the Messenians not only for its great antiquity but also for the therapeutic powers of the god there.

In November 1914, a farmer whose land lay around a chapel of Ayios Andreas near the town of Longa was cultivating the plot when his plow struck a column drum inscribed with a second-century B.C. dedication to Apollo Korythos. A find such as this, testifying to a hitherto unlocated sanctuary of ancient Messenia, sparked great local interest, and only a few months later, formal excavations brought to light four temples and several associated buildings. Pausanias's claim that the shrine was of great significance to the Messenians was borne out by the high quality of the offerings that had been presented to the god. In addition to much fine pottery, terracotta figurines, and fragments of marble sculpture, there were exquisite bronze figurines (Fig. 20), remains of bronze vessels, and inscribed spearheads.

BETWEEN THE WORLD WARS: VALMIN AND BLEGEN

World War I brought almost complete cessation of fieldwork in Messenia for ten years, and it is during this break that the plot of our story begins to twist.

First, bureaucratic wranglings meant that the tempo of the work at Messene was still slow by 1926, and Yioryios Oikonomos, now secretary of the Greek Archaeological Society, made his frustrations quite clear in his annual address to the society's members. His impassioned plea called for the government to realize the importance of his beloved Messene and to support systematic work there:

> Messene is a vitally important archaeological place, and the uncovering of the site can be described as possessing great significance, the like of

FIGURE 20
*Bronze figurine of a warrior from the sanctuary of Apollo Korythos.
R. J. Robertson, after Freiderikos Versakis,
"Τὸ ἱερὸν τοῦ Κορύνθου Ἀπόλλωνος," Ἀρχαιολογικὸν Δελτίον 2 (1916): pl. A.*

which few other places in Greece can boast. But the discoveries cannot be completed quickly because of the great hindrance caused by the cultivation of the place by the settlers of the modern hamlets around it. We hope that the Government, which has the matter in hand, wishes shortly to address the issue of compensation for the villagers' loss of cultivation land so that the archaeological work can progress more quickly.

However, little did Oikonomos realize that it would be not the neglect of his government but the arrival of two foreign scholars that would turn attention away from Messene and change the focus of Messenian archaeology to our own day.

The Swedish archaeologist Mattias Natan Valmin arrived in Messenia in 1926, attracted by prospects for rich discoveries in a region where there had previously been relatively little archaeological fieldwork. To Valmin, Messenia "seemed to be a good and untouched field for prehistoric researches in particular," and his place in the history of archaeological work in the region is especially important. During the next ten years, not only did Valmin follow his immediate predecessors by doing extensive reconnaissance of historical sites, but (significantly) he also began to swing the pendulum back toward prehistoric research, excavating a number of Bronze Age tombs and undertaking the first detailed examination of a settlement of similar date.

First, during a brief visit to northern Messenia in Easter week of 1926, he recognized that two earthen mounds (tumuli) in a cornfield at the foot of a hill named Malthi, near the village of Vasiliko, covered Mycenaean tholos tombs, one of which still had its vaulted roof intact (Fig. 21). In the summer of that same year, Valmin spent six weeks excavating the two tombs, finding gold and steatite ornaments and bronze weapon blades in the second (which had suffered less from plundering because of its collapse).

The following year, happenstance led to an even more significant discovery atop the hill of Malthi itself. A dispute with owners of the railway line that ran near one of the tholos tombs briefly halted excavations; during the delay, Valmin made a visit to the ridgetop of Malthi, no doubt curious to see if he could find the ancient settlement where those buried in the tombs had lived. In just four days, parts of several rooms of the prehistoric town were excavated. In subsequent campaigns, Valmin uncovered a large part of this settlement: the entirety of the fortification surrounding the settlement was cleared, and more than 100 rooms within it (Fig. 22). At the same time, he also extended the scope of his researches throughout almost all of Messenia. Traveling widely, he chatted with villagers and investigated their reports of ancient remains. This fieldwork formed the basis for

FIGURE 21
Tholos tomb excavated at Malthi by Valmin. Reproduced from M. N. Valmin,
The Swedish Messenia Expedition *(Lund: C.W.K. Gleerup, 1938), 209, fig. 36.*

the impressively comprehensive *Études topographiques sur la Messenie ancienne*, published promptly in 1930.

In continuing the tradition of exploration of historical Messenia, Valmin was in part guided by the earlier surveys by Pernice and Skias, but he made his own original contributions. At Ayios Floros, near the strong springs of the Pamisos River, north of Kalamata, Valmin noted the remains of a small temple, and even attempted an excavation; but the site flooded in just a few

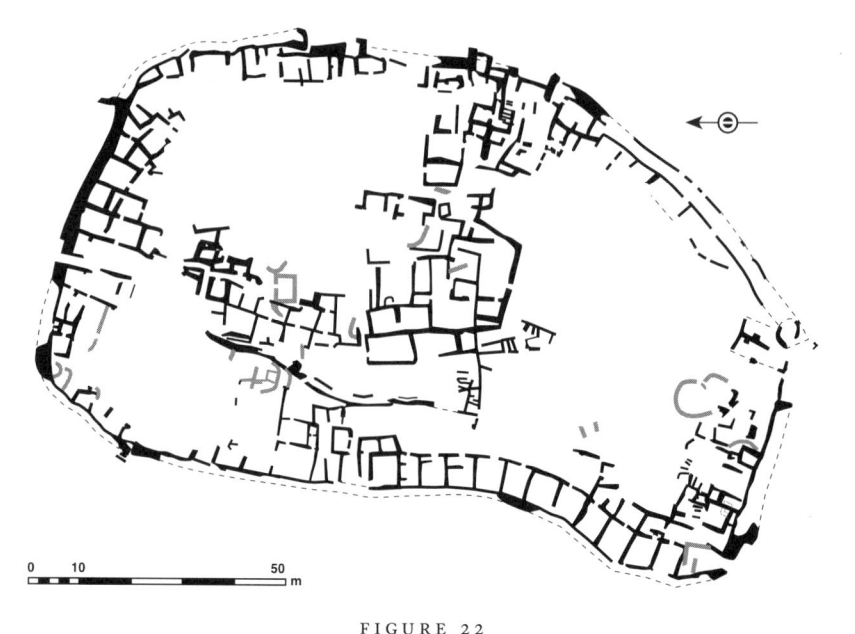

FIGURE 22

Site of Malthi with Middle Bronze Age remains; two phases, the earlier in gray. PRAP Archive. R. J. Robertson, after M. N. Valmin, The Swedish Messenia Expedition *(Lund: C.W.K. Gleerup, 1938), plan I.*

hours, and he was forced to stop. After a four-year break, Valmin returned in early September 1933. He arrived to find that a summer dry spell, abetted by the extensive digging of agricultural drainage ditches, had lowered the water level by a full meter. The temple could now be cleared and a plan made of the remains. Investigations were completed in the following years, and by 1935 artifacts from Malthi and Ayios Floros had been installed in a newly dedicated museum at Vasiliko.

In addition to excavations, Valmin devoted his efforts to the elucidation of outstanding problems in Messenian geography. One question that had vexed early explorers of Messenia was the location of Erana, a town described by the Roman geographer Strabo as lying between Cyparissia and Pylos on the western coast of Messenia. Already in the early nineteenth century, William Leake had placed Erana at Ayia Kyriaki, north of Marathoupolis, but Valmin found there only some unfluted columns and the ruins of a Byzantine church.

Valmin was more taken by the impressive remains that he charted in 1934 along the coast south of Marathoupolis. There at Dialiskari (see Focus in Chapter 7), he found architectural fragments, including columns; parts of what looked like a Roman bath were visible, as well as dense scatters of ancient Greek and Roman pottery. These finds, he concluded, belonged to Erana. His tour of Messenia this same year ended with an unsuccessful search for the temple of Artemis Limnatis, where, according to tradition, the bitter struggle between Messenia and Sparta had begun.

Valmin departed Messenia for the last time in July 1936, leaving an indelible mark on the archaeology of the province, not only because of the range of his research but also because of his conscientious attitude toward publication. In addition to his *Études topographiques sur la Messenie ancienne*, Valmin published preliminary reports describing each of his excavations, and only two years after his final departure, in 1938, there appeared his detailed publication, *The Swedish Messenia Expedition*.

The second foreign scholar to enter Messenian archaeology at this time cast a long shadow over nearly all subsequent work here, and Oikonomos's calls for resources to be directed toward historical research were drowned out for many years simply by the immense scale of this scholar's discoveries relating to Messenia's Bronze Age past. This man was Carl Blegen, and his major discovery was no less than the Palace of Nestor itself.

In 1926, Konstantinos Kourouniotis, director of the National Museum in Athens, invited Blegen to assist him in his exploration for Mycenaean settlements and cemeteries. Kourouniotis had himself excavated a tholos tomb near the village of Koryfasion in 1926. Among newly discovered Mycenaean sites visited by Blegen was one on the ridge of Ano Englianos, 3 kilometers southwest of the village of Hora. This was the largest site explored by Kourouniotis and Blegen, and it occupied a position that dominated the local topography, visible even from the coast at ancient Coryphasion. On the first day of excavation in 1939, when Blegen's team uncovered substantial walls and even fragments of clay tablets (Fig. 23) with writing similar to those previously found by Arthur Evans in the Palace of Minos at Knossos on Crete (see Focus in this chapter), it was obvious that they had found the Palace of Nestor. But after these brief soundings, the outbreak of World War II in September of that same year halted work. It was to be another thirteen years before Blegen could resume his research.

Blegen, however, had learned a great deal, not only from this single season of excavation but also from the experience gained in some twenty-five years of mapping ancient sites and studying their surface remains. In 1940, he addressed a symposium at the University of Pennsylvania on the topic "Preclassical Greece." In this address, he foretold the future direction of archaeology in Greece, speaking almost prophetically.

He made two appeals. First, he called for "a systematic, comprehensive survey of the districts of Greece, province by province, with the recording and mapping of all the ancient sites." After his experience at Ano

FIGURE 23
Linear B tablet Cn 131 from the Palace of Nestor. Archives of the Department of Classics, University of Cincinnati. With permission of E. L. Bennett Jr. and the Department of Classics, University of Cincinnati.

Englianos, he was further convinced that surface scatters of ancient potsherds were representative of the artifacts buried under the ground, and therefore that study of surface remains could help locate "scores, not to say hundreds, of smaller settlements." Second, Blegen recommended that all archaeological projects follow the example set by Schliemann and collaborate with scientists, especially physical anthropologists and palaeozoologists, because, he argued, archaeologists were going to need specialist information to help solve the problems facing them. He argued that only in these ways could we form a coherent picture of the Bronze Age.

It was the implementation of a program of research evoked by Blegen's remarks that changed the face of Messenian archaeology in the decades immediately following World War II, altering the focus from specific sites to a wider, regional picture (ultimately serving, therefore, as the inspiration for our own research, as outlined in the Introduction). Moreover, Blegen's finds at the Palace of Nestor ensured that the Mycenaean period in Messenia was at the forefront of research for decades to come, returning Bronze Age research in the area from its poor-relation status compared to historical studies to its original position of prominence. The wheel had turned full circle.

MARINATOS, MCDONALD, AND THE UNIVERSITY OF MINNESOTA MESSENIA EXPEDITION

Although Blegen's collaborator, Konstantinos Kourouniotis, had died in 1945, the decision was taken after World War II to continue a Greek-American collaboration at the Palace of Nestor (Figs. 24, 25). Blegen offered Spyridon Marinatos, Kourouniotis's successor, a share of the palace excavations, but Marinatos preferred to turn his attention to the hinterland, where he searched for Mycenaean cemeteries and undiscovered settlements. Marinatos's description of the first results of his search as "very encouraging" was extremely modest, since already by 1952 he had discovered a very large group of rich Mycenaean chamber tombs at Volimidia, on the northeastern outskirts of the village of Hora, scarcely 5 kilometers from the Palace of Nestor.

The next few years of exploration proved even more fruitful, and discoveries were not limited to cemeteries. Southeast of the Palace of Nestor, near the village of Iklaina, Marinatos excavated remains of an opulent building with frescoes on its walls. Not far away, at Papoulia, he discovered an impressive burial mound, or tumulus; bodies had been deposited inside large storage jars (*pithoi*) that were then inserted in the mound (Fig. 26).

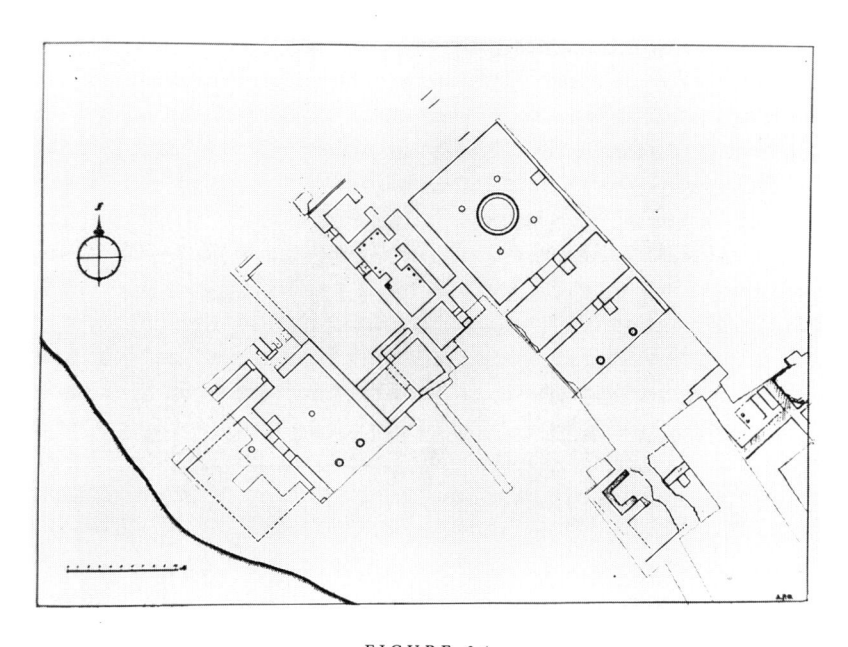

FIGURE 24
Plan of the Palace of Nestor, 1953. Reproduced from C. W. Blegen, "Excavations at Pylos 1953," American Journal of Archaeology *58, 1 (1954): pl. 4, fig. 2. With permission of the* American Journal of Archaeology.

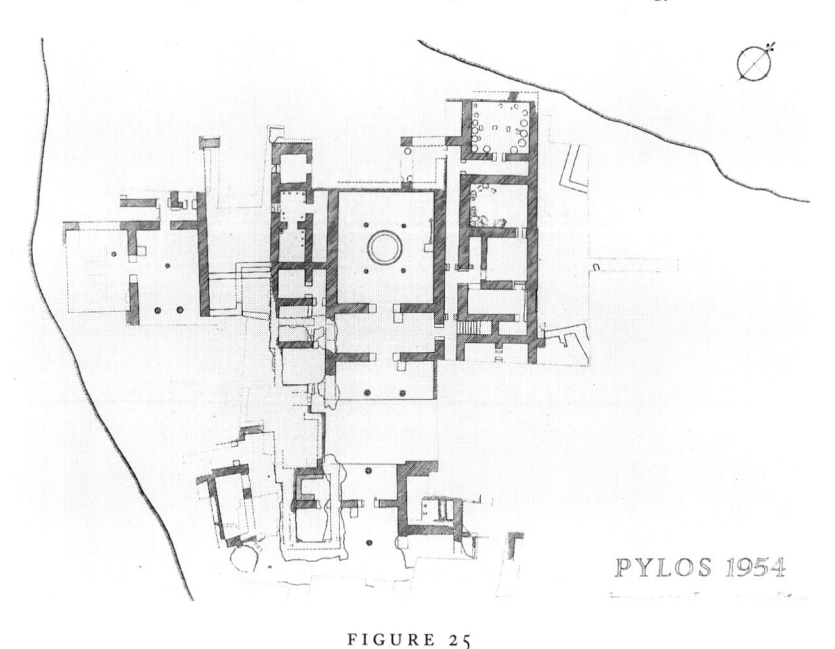

FIGURE 25
Plan of the Palace of Nestor, 1954. Reproduced from C. W. Blegen, "The Palace of Nestor: Excavations of 1954," American Journal of Archaeology *59, 1 (1955): pl. 24. With permission of the* American Journal of Archaeology.

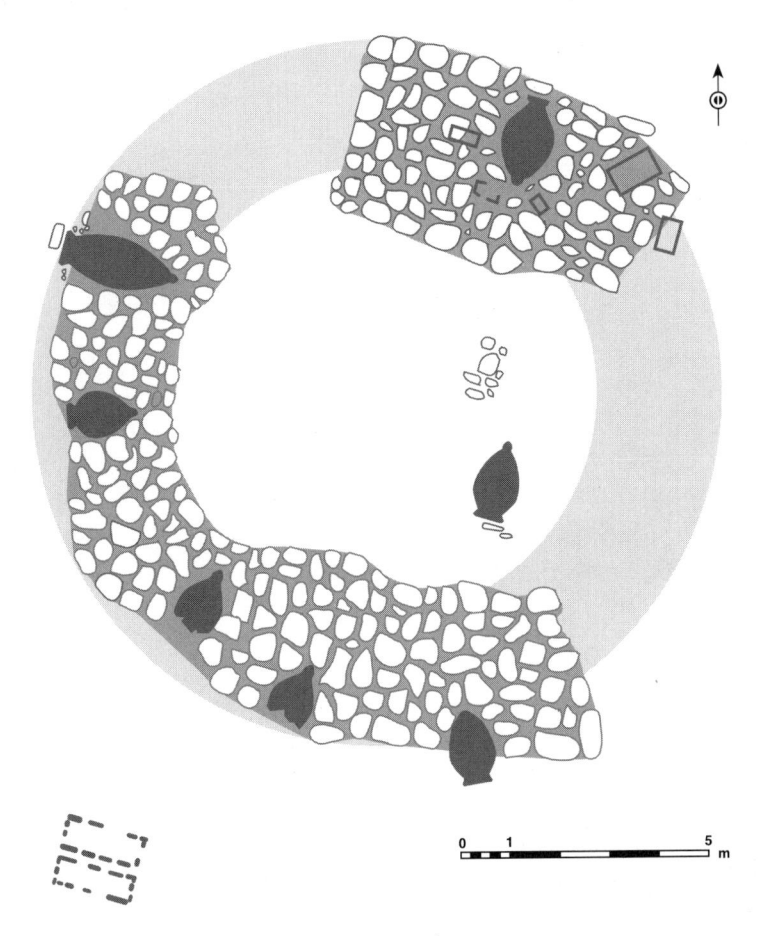

FIGURE 26
*Tumulus at Papoulia. PRAP Archive. R. J. Robertson, after S. N. Marinatos,
"Ἀνασκαφαὶ ἐν Πύλῳ," Πρακτικὰ τῆς ἐν Ἀθῆναις Ἀρχαιολογικῆς Ἑταιρείας
(1954): 315, fig. 12.*

A second tholos tomb was excavated at Tragana near Koryfasion; bronze weapons, gold jewelery, and a steatite seal were recovered.

Other spectacular discoveries followed in rapid succession. At Voidokoilia, the tholos tomb found fifty years earlier by Grundy was excavated at last (Fig. 27). A Mycenaean house northeast of the Tragana tholoi at first seemed to be an ancient storeroom, so great were the numbers of fine pots found in it. Still more impressive were two tholos tombs (one unplundered) at Myrsinohori, which yielded spectacularly rich finds of late Bronze Age date, including two daggers inlaid with gold and silver (very similar to

FIGURE 27
Headland with Tomb of Thrasymedes at Voidokoilia Bay from the north; modern Pylos in the distance. PRAP Archive. J. L. Davis.

the daggers from the Shaft Graves at Mycenae), many other gold and silver objects, sealstones, and fine pottery.

Marinatos was also drawn to the village of Koukounara, some 15 kilometers northeast of Pylos. In the course of 1958, he became convinced that Koukounara was a major Mycenaean center, one of the principal towns of the Pylian kingdom listed on the Linear B tablets. Not only were there seven tholos tombs in its vicinity, but their finds included gold, bronze vessels, bronze weapons, stone arrowheads, and even pieces of boars'-tusk helmets; a contemporary settlement was investigated on a low promontory to the northeast of the village.

The Mycenaean era of the Late Bronze Age came to dominate scholars' thoughts on Messenia. The interest was especially stimulated by a student of Blegen's, Emmett L. Bennett, who had transcribed the tablets from the Palace of Nestor—an assignment he received in one of Blegen's graduate seminars at the University of Cincinnati. With these new data at hand, a young British architect and linguist, Michael Ventris, soon offered a decipherment, with the exciting conclusion that the language of the Mycenaeans living at Pylos had been an archaic form of Greek (see Chapter 4).

Scholars were not slow to realize that the research potential of this new, detailed information from the tablets was immense. No other site in mainland Greece could now boast such detailed documentation about such an early period, and one of the debates that immediately followed from the new data, over the geography of the kingdom of Nestor, continues to this day (see Chapter 5).

The new information from the Linear B archive also profoundly influenced field research, however. William A. McDonald began a series of surface reconnaissances in 1953, not only near the palace but also in its hinterland, prompted by a desire to relate place names mentioned in the tablets to actual archaeological sites. As McDonald would later write, the purpose of his regional-scale research was "to discover whether any of the toponyms in the Pylos tablets might have remained in continuous use in out-of-the-way spots."

McDonald and his co-worker, Richard Hope Simpson, used air photographs and hydrographic and large-scale topographic maps to identify likely locations for ancient sites. They then visited these places to check for surface scatters of ancient pottery and other artifacts. The two scholars also followed Blegen's call of 1939 for a restoration of interdisciplinary research, enlisting linguists, geologists, civil engineers, chemists, metallurgists, palynologists, and anthropologists into their University of Minnesota Messenia Expedition (UMME) to widen the focus of their fieldwork. Thus, the tradition of the French Expédition scientifique of the 1830s was renewed, and Messenia became the first region of Greece in which interdisciplinary research was carried out on a large scale in the twentieth century, laying the foundations for the kind of fieldwork championed by PRAP, which has become the norm all over the Aegean today (see Introduction).

Against the background of these high-profile investigations, focused on the Messenian Bronze Age, the 1950s also marked the long-anticipated resumption of archaeological investigations at Messene. Anastasios Orlandos was placed in charge of the excavations, and after clearing the site of undergrowth that had accumulated since Oikonomos's last season, Orlandos focused his attention upon the three buildings of the "agora" found by Sofoulis and Oikonomos. By the early 1960s, it had become clear from the discovery of inscriptions and sculpture that this architectural complex was, in fact, the city's Asclepiea, and that the agora must lie further to the north.

NICHORIA

An important outgrowth of the Minnesota research program was the excavation of Nichoria, a Mycenaean town, like Koukounara, almost certainly mentioned in the Pylos tablets. Indeed, McDonald and Hope Simpson had always intended that their survey would be the first step toward the excavation of a site that appeared promising from surface inspection.

The site eventually chosen lay on the long ridge of Nichoria near the village of Rizomylo, west of Kalamata. The Greek Archaeological Service had previously excavated Mycenaean, Protogeometric, and Geometric tombs there, and McDonald was keen to supplement the excavation of the cemeteries with an examination of the accompanying settlement. Aside from the basic aim of discovering the main periods of occupation and the extent of the settlement, McDonald was eager to experiment with scientific aids to archaeological research. He employed not only a resistivity meter, but even infrared aerial photography from a balloon, to detect subsurface archaeological features by mapping areas where electric current did not pass through the ground easily (possibly disturbed by buried walls) or where the location of buried buildings might be reflected in differential patterns of vegetation (similar to techniques later employed by PRAP; see Chapter 1).

Even though the stated goal of the project was to examine day-to-day life in the Bronze Age, McDonald confessed that he would welcome "treasure" in the form of a new archive of tablets that might reveal the name of Nichoria. Linear B expert John Chadwick, an early collaborator with Ventris, had suggested that Nichoria was the site named *re-u-ko-to-ro* in the palace archives, the eastern subcapital of the Pylian kingdom's "Further Province." Chadwick later revised his opinion, since the town named *ti-mi-to-a-ke-e* was also a likely candidate (see Focus in Chapter 5). We can now be reasonably certain that this latter identification is correct.

While excavations continued at Nichoria, discoveries of great significance for the earlier prehistory of Messenia were made not far to the east, at Akovitika, near Kalamata. The opening of a drainage channel in 1968 in the delta of the Pamisos River revealed parts of an Archaic temple of Poseidon, the ancient Greek god of the sea and earthquakes, particularly appropriate in an area that has frequently been devastated by violent tremors. The following year, excavations expanded about 200 meters farther northwest to uncover a huge rectangular building of the third millennium B.C., more than a thousand years older than the Palace of Nestor.

By 1970, the first two volumes reporting the results of Blegen's excavation had already been published as *The Palace of Nestor at Pylos in Western Messenia*. In 1972, the results of the University of Minnesota Messenia Expedition were published by McDonald and George Rapp, his geologist colleague and director of scientific studies at Nichoria. The first volume in a series describing the results of the Nichoria excavations, *Excavations at Nichoria in Southwest Greece*, was designed to set the site fully in its environmental context.

THE RECENT DECADES

Major archaeological fieldwork continues each year in Messenia, much of it, like the Pylos Regional Archaeological Project, resting solidly on the foundations laid by the pioneers whose dedicated research has been the focus of this chapter. George Korres succeeded to the direction of excavations at many of Messenia's major Bronze Age sites after Marinatos's death in 1974. Since Orlandos's death in 1975, Petros Themelis has resumed excavations at Messene in the ancient theater northwest of the Asclepieia, in the Asclepiea itself, and in the stadium, agora, and gymnasium.

But here our twisting story of past research, which has fluctuated between the Bronze Age palaces and Classical acropoleis, merges with the present.

FOCUS

The DISCOVERY of the PALACE of NESTOR

Tuesday April 4 [1939]
Dark and threatening weather. Macdonald [*sic*] and I go out to Ano Eglianos [*sic*]. Lv. 7:30 Arr. 8:15.
We find Charalambos [Hristofilopoulos] and many men.
Start work with 20 men at 8:30.
Lay out long trench approx. N-S ca. 50 m. long 2 m. wide . . .
5 sections ca. 10 m long each.
Macdonald takes charge of trench.
Soon find stone walls—several at intervals. all running approx. NW-SE. . . . Looks like walls of large building. Earth black and red. all burned. Sherds few but look LH III.
In section A find ca. 30 [viz. cm] deep a deposit of inscribed tablets. plano-convex in shape. Lined out on flat side and inscribed w. Minoan signs. Workman gets out two. Mac and I three more—all complete. One more at least left. But we leave and cover for a drizzly rain sets in and hard to photo and to cut out.
Stop work ca. 4:15 on acct. of rain.

Thus reads *in toto* the laconic notebook entry made by Carl Blegen the first day of excavation at the Palace of Nestor on the ridge of Ano Englianos. Nothing in his matter-of-fact tone hints that the eight hours spent on the ridge of Ano Englianos that day would soon change the entire course of Aegean prehistory forever, with discoveries that were unquestionably the most important for Mycenaean archaeology since Schliemann's very excavations at Mycenae began almost sixty years before (Fig. 28). For Blegen, the day was the culmination of eight years of planning. The foundations for this work had been laid already in 1929 when, at the invitation of Konstantinos Kourouniotis, he had been invited to cooperate in systematic exploration of the prehistoric antiquities of western Messenia.

JACK L. DAVIS

As the two explorers noted in their triumphant report published expeditiously in the *American Journal of Archaeology* in this same year:

> The Dorian Invasion, whatever its source and however it ran its course, has left a broad gash, like a fire-scar in a mountain forest, cutting through the archaeological panorama of ancient Greek history. Many towns and settlements that flourished in the preceding Heroic Age were henceforth abandoned or declined to a state of insignificance. Even some of the great and noted strongholds sank into virtual oblivion, and the places where they had stood were lost from the view of man . . . exactly the same fate overtook Pylos, Sandy Pylos, the seat of the Neleid King Nestor, where Telemachos was so hospitably entertained on his famous journey described in the *Odyssey*.

The problem of the location of Nestor's palace had been much in dispute, but as Blegen and Kourouniotis note, the matter had never been "put to the practical test of the spade." This was their intention.

Kourouniotis had noted a pattern in the distribution of monumental tholos tombs in western Messenia—in particular, that they appeared to point to the long ridge that ran from the modern town of Osmanaga

FIGURE 28
Linear B tablets on floor of the Archive Room of the Palace of Nestor at time of discovery in 1939. Archives of the Department of Classics, University of Cincinnati, with permission.

(officially rechristened Koryfasion) in the direction of the modern town of Hora. On the ridge itself, several such tombs had been noted, and it was they that led Blegen on April 4 to a field belonging to Periklis Tsakonas and Leonidas Spyropoulos; the humor of the situation (the great Athenian statesman Perikles and the Spartan king and general Leonidas came from cities that were mortal enemies in the fifth century B.C.!) could not have been lost on either Blegen or McDonald.

The location was promising. Several long ridges run toward the sea from the foothills of the lofty Aigaleon Mountains. To the north of the Bay of Navarino, these converge on the broad lowlands that support the modern towns of Romanou, Petrohori, and Yialova. The Englianos Ridge, on which the palace sits, carries on its back the major modern route of communication that links the towns around the Bay of Navarino with settlements near Cyparissia and in the Soulima Valley, areas where the important Mycenaean sites of Mouriatada, Peristeria, and Malthi, among others, are located. From Koryfasion, the ridge is bordered on both sides by steep ravines; about halfway, it rises more abruptly. The palace sat on a knolltop here, dominating both the inland and the coastal approaches. The beehive tombs had led the way to it.

The project had begun in 1939 as a joint expedition of the Greek Archaeological Service and the University of Cincinnati. Kourouniotis, the senior partner in the venture, had become director of the National Museum at Athens, and it was agreed that Blegen (Fig. 29), as junior partner, would organize fieldwork. The team, consisting of Elizabeth Blegen, William McDonald, and the Blegens' lifelong friends, Bert Hodge Hill and Ida Hill, had arrived in the modern town of Pylos on March 25. After arranging for the rental of a house and hiring a chauffeur, the team members spent nearly two weeks visiting archaeological sites in the surrounding countryside, to which they were led by Haralambos Hristofilopoulos, their foreman, who had already brought so many of the tholos tombs investigated previously to the attention of Kourouniotis. But in this instance, their interest was in the discovery not of tombs, but of sites that had likely been the locations of prehistoric settlements. Only after this initial reconnaissance had been completed did the team turn its efforts toward the site on the Englianos Ridge.

Blegen had already visited the palace site in 1929 and had collected samples of pottery on the surface; Kourouniotis had led the way. Of particular interest to them both was what might, they hoped, be the remains of monumental architecture, the limestone blocks of the wall calcined by fire. The Mycenaean pottery present in substantial quantities on the slopes of the hill of this citadel was plain, for the most part undecorated, and of

FIGURE 29
Walter Langsam, president of the University of Cincinnati, Carl W. Blegen, Julia Langsam, and Marian Rawson at the Palace of Nestor excavations. Archives of the Department of Classics, University of Cincinnati, with permission.

types in use at Bronze Age sites of the later prehistoric phases. Blegen was very familiar with it now from the half-dozen or so excavations in Mycenaean sites he had already completed in the Argolid and Corinthia. These had in fact established the first reliable stratigraphically based chronology of ceramic types, outlined with his friend and frequent collaborator, noted British prehistorian Alan Wace.

The groundwork laid by years of preparation paid off on this fateful day in 1939. The "dark and threatening weather" noted by Blegen, counter to expectations, proved an omen of great good luck. More than one more tablet inscribed in the Linear B script would emerge—in all, hundreds were recovered in this first year of excavation alone. The rapid dissemination of the texts inscribed on these in the peculiar system of pictorial signs that we call Linear B led directly to its decipherment as an early form of

Greek, resulted in the foundation of an entire new subdiscipline of Classical scholarship devoted to their study, and has provided us with our most detailed picture of the day-to-day operation of a Bronze Age kingdom on the European mainland. Blegen's very first trench had hit the archive room of the best-preserved palace of the Mycenaean period yet found.

FOCUS

MARINATOS *in* PYLOS

"The oak tree of archaeology has fallen." That headline in bold letters appeared in an Athens daily newspaper shortly after the death of Spyridon Marinatos on October 1, 1974. His sudden passing, the result of a tragic accident at his excavations in the Late Bronze Age town of Akrotiri, on the Cycladic island of Thera (Santorini), marked the end of a brilliant archaeological career. By the time Marinatos arrived at Pylos, he had already brought to a successful conclusion major investigations in Crete (1919–52). His excavations at Akrotiri (1967–74)—an undertaking that would bring him world fame, as he unearthed this unique prehistoric Pompeii of the Mediterranean—were yet a dream.

Marinatos made his first appearance in the Pylian landscape in 1952, as a representative of the Archaeological Society of Athens and successor to Konstantinos Kourouniotis in the joint Hellenic-American Pylos excavations at the Palace of Nestor. His work in Messenia continued until 1966, parallel to Blegen's researches at the Palace of Nestor. Deciding "to leave the Palace to the skills of its discoverer," he chose instead to devote his own efforts to the exploration of other nearby prehistoric settlements and cemeteries. From villagers and hunters he garnered information about the existence of surface archaeological remains in places with names hitherto unknown to the archaeological community. Such reports led ultimately to the study of more than twenty archaeological sites scattered over a wide geographical area—from the imposing early Mycenaean acropolis of Peristeria in the north (where the great Tholos Tomb I was discovered in 1960) to the isolated tholos tomb at Harakopeio, near Koroni, in the south.

Marinatos's presence was commanding: in his pith helmet, he entered the "battlefield" of an archaeological excavation with the boldness and confidence of a helmeted Mycenaean warrior. In his archaeological explorations, he was led by his sharp archaeological instincts, a general vision of the ancient world, and an impressive command of ancient Greek literary

YANNOS G. LOLOS

testimonia. He had the uncanny ability to assess the importance of buried ruins, almost from the first turn of the spade.

He is best known for his excavations of funerary monuments (tumuli, tholos tombs, and chamber tombs), and certainly his finest hours included the excavation of the three early Mycenaean beehive tombs at Peristeria (1960–65) and of the unplundered second tholos tomb at Routsi (1956–57). Nonetheless, we should not lose sight of the fact that he also discovered and excavated, in whole or in part, large Mycenaean buildings and settlements at Peristeria; Mouriatada; Katarrahaki and Palaiohoria in the Koukounara area; at Iklaina; at Volimidia; and at Voroulia.

It is unfortunate that Marinatos did not live to publish the results of his many excavations in a full and definitive form. The significance of his research in Messenia is, however, clear, since it was he who constructed, so to speak, the first map of Mycenaean Messenia. This map—now substantially enlarged and supplemented through the work of the University of Minnesota Messenia Expedition, and through the excavations of George Korres, Marinatos's successor in Messenia, of individual members of the Greek Archaeological Service, and of PRAP—still provides a solid foundation for archaeological research. Moreover, Marinatos's thirty-five publications concerning Late Bronze Age Messenia, including carefully composed annual excavation reports, packed full of useful information, are *in toto* a first and essential commentary to this map, whereas other articles treat in detail the many thorny problems of Mycenaean and Homeric topography of the region.

Marinatos was an archaeologist in the grand tradition, possessing an air of certainty that he was embarked on a special mission—to provide his native land with its past. His wide-ranging interests extended into the fields of medicine, astronomy, biology, and botany—and his knowledge in these disciplines is often evident in his archaeological writing. In person, he presented an austere and imposing figure. But he was a gifted speaker who captured both Greek and foreign audiences with his deep voice, his clear and elegant style, and his ability to combine archaeological and literary evidence to create a convincing theory. Marinatos was always ready to enter into a scientific debate. And despite mistakes and misinterpretations, many of his arguments are still highly relevant to current discourse in the field of Greek prehistory.

He was restless and indefatigable as an excavator, his spade halted only by the turbulent years of World War II. And in all places where he excavated, he left his stamp—his passage preserved in the memory of his assistants, hired workers, and local populations. He was also an everlasting influence and inspiration to those young scholars who were so fortunate as to

FIGURE 30
Bust of Spyridon Marinatos by Elisavet Valvi erected in the garden of the Museum of Hora in 1994. PRAP Archive. R. Dupuis-Devlin and E. Dallagher.

have the opportunity to work with him—including the writer of this Focus, whose very first archaeological excavation was Marinatos's dig at Akrotiri in the summer of 1972.

In recognition of all the preceding accomplishments, his bronze bust (Fig. 30) now stands opposite that of Blegen in the garden in front of the archaeological museum of Hora, a museum brimming with the finds from both men's excavations. The joint role that these two men have played in the exploration of Nestor's Pylos is symbolized not only by this union, but also by the commemoration of their names in the principal streets of Hora, which today, at the corner of Marinatos and Blegen streets, intersect to form the town square.

YANNOS G. LOLOS

FIGURE 31
View southwest toward the Bay of Navarino over parts of the Hither Province, from the Archive Room of the Palace of Nestor. PRAP Archive. R. J. Robertson.

CHAPTER 3

The PALACE and Its DEPENDENCIES

In the thirteenth century B.C., the Palace of Nestor stood atop its bluff, a two-story, lavishly frescoed building visible for miles around as a symbol of power. The Palace of Nestor still stands atop its bluff (Fig. 32), surrounded by iron fencing and decorated by flower beds lovingly maintained by its guards. The megaron (or throne room) itself, the archives room, the state apartments, the storerooms—all have been covered since the completion of excavations with a corrugated steel roof supported by metal pylons, a modern construction that ensures the palace's visibility across much of the region. Such protection, the fence and roof, is, of course, necessary to secure the fragile remains of plaster, mudbrick, and stone both from the elements and from ravages that might be willingly or unwillingly inflicted on them by tourists or vandals.

The average visitor (a quarter-century ago on my first trip to Pylos, I was one myself) arrives by bus. The buses pull into the gravel parking lot beneath the citadel to its east. Passengers enjoy a cool respite provided by water now piped to a cemented springhead, then take the short trudge uphill to the gates of the *official* archaeological site. Most arrive in the dead of summer, and are winded, as was I, even from this minor exertion. For me and for the others in my group, the shelter of the palace roof provided an immediate and welcome refuge from the sun. We rarely strayed far from the shade; after a brief lecture from a guide and moments of frenetic photography (having paid, of course, a proper surcharge at the ticket booth), we filed back down the slope, across the parking lot, to visit the rebuilt Tholos Tomb IV (see Lolos's Focus, Chapter 3). There, too, was relief from the midday heat.

As consumers of packaged holidays hasten from the luxury of their air-conditioned buses to the ancient structures on the Englianos Ridge, few are encouraged to stop to ponder the magnitude of their sacrilege. To tread on the floors, to march past the throne, to wander oblivious to the sacredness of the hearth of the megaron of the lord of all of Messenia; then to en-

---

JACK L. DAVIS

FIGURE 32
The citadel of the Palace of Nestor from the northeast. PRAP Archive. J. L. Davis.

ter the very chamber of the dead of the dynasty that held sway here—all without respect for ritual; all without realizing that in the thirteenth century B.C., few of our ancestors would have been of sufficiently high station in life to warrant admission to these structures. For, as we shall see in Chapters 4 and 5, the kings who ruled from this seat of power had succeeded in establishing a strongly hierarchical rule over the surrounding countryside—indeed, over most of modern Messenia—one that recognized their suzerainty in temporal and leadership in heavenly matters.

But what of the countryside that lay under their control? Only the more adventuresome tourists can acquire an appreciation for the landscape over which the Palace of Nestor once held sway, those who have set out on their own, spending the night in modern Pylos, hiring a car or a motorbike, or even hiking the distance from the coast on foot. Only in this way can the situation of the palace and its relationship to the countryside that surrounds it be fully appreciated.

We who have been raised in the West, particularly in North America, are accustomed to clear divisions between town and country: townsfolk live in our towns and cities, farmers don't. Greece, then, comes as a bit of a shock

JACK L. DAVIS

to those foreigners who stop long enough to think about it. The countryside simply lacks farms in the sense we use the word. Towns, instead of providing markets and services for largely scattered rural populations, integrate agricultural practice and centralized residence to an extent that may be truly unfamiliar. Farmers live in towns. The edges of town and countryside are blurred; farmers farm in towns as well as outside them. In a sense, towns are farms, thus usually making a sham of the response of an archaeologist to the U.S. Department of Agriculture's standard question to a returning vacationer: "Have you been on a farm in the past two months?"

The structure of modern tourism, even of archaeology until late, has discouraged all of us from comprehending the full importance of this interdependence between town and country. The tourist is in a rush to visit the "important sites" of Greece. The archaeologist is keen to comply by packaging sites in easily comprehensible parcels. The whole approach sometimes smacks of mechanization: off the bus, pay the fee, walk along prepared paths, hear a special spiel, and buy postcards. Yet rarely is the most important question posed: "What is an archaeological site?"

At Pylos at least, the "site" that is dished up to tourists is only one small part of a total archaeological landscape, the entire structure of which we must attempt to grasp. The Palace of Nestor did not stop at the fence, and the goal of this chapter is to give the reader some appreciation of the nature and significance of archaeological remains outside the fence, in the vicinity of the official site (the palace itself is described in Chapter 4). To accomplish this, it will be necessary for us to move off the beaten tourist path, first concentrating on the Englianos Ridge itself, then traveling beyond it to a discussion of other Mycenaean sites nearby.

But deviations from the official path can be confusing. A jumble of walls confronts the more adventuresome tourist who strays northeast or northwest from the roofed remains inside the fence. The palace itself stood near the western edge of a flat plateau atop the citadel. There is little depth to the archaeological deposit beneath it; this is not a tell site of Near Eastern type, nor a *magoula* of the sort that litters the landscape of Thessaly and the more northerly parts of the Greek peninsula. Along the slopes of the citadel, however, the deposits are preserved more deeply. There and beyond, we can gain some idea of the extent, character, and duration of the community that dwelt at the feet of the lords of Pylos.

THE CITADEL BEFORE THE PALACE OF NESTOR

Of the principal Bronze Age centers, Pylos is among the oddest in that it does not appear to have been defended by a fortification wall in the later

Mycenaean period (in the thirteenth century B.C.). In this regard, its aspect is strikingly different from that of other centers of the prehistoric Peloponnese and central Greece—Argos, Tiryns, Midea, the Akropolis at Athens, the "Wall of the Dymaians" at Araxos near Patras, and Mycenae itself. The absence of a wall blurs the distinction between those spaces reserved for the elite residences of the kings of Pylos, the supporting facilities for the palace, and the houses of the townspeople.

This apparently had not always been the case. In the earliest phase of the Late Bronze Age, the citadel at Pylos *had* been walled. The traces of the fortifications, however, are hardly obvious today. Blegen was forced to conclude that, if the enceinte was ever completed, it had been largely destroyed by erosion, probably accelerated by the scavenging of its fabric for reusable building materials in the Dark Ages (see Focus in Chapter 4) and in historical times, since in most places where the circuit has been preserved, it has been dismantled down to its foundations. Because it was built of much smaller stones than the Cyclopean marvels of the Argolid, later Messenians would have found such a wall to be an inviting resource. On this ridge of soft marly bedrock, even stones have been precious prizes for those farmers who have subsequently constructed their fieldhouses and threshing floors in the vicinity.

At the northeastern edge of the citadel, however, it is still possible today to gain some idea of the original appearance of these defenses. There, Blegen's team uncovered the remains of a broad (3.5 meters wide) sloping roadway, stepped in places, that ran from the top of the plateau east of the palace down the slope of the citadel, passed through a gateway, and continued to the northeast. Both the road and the gateway appear to be directed rather precisely toward Tholos Tomb IV (Fig. 33), and it is difficult to avoid the conclusion that this orientation was intentional on the part of the builders: that is, that the road, at least occasionally, served as a processional way to the tomb for the elite residents of the citadel who buried their dead in it. There come to mind similar associations in the settlement plan of Mycenae: for example, the strategic placement of beehive tombs just outside the gate to the citadel and along the road leading through the settlement; or the intentional usage of conglomerate stone for both the facade of the Atreus tholos and the facade of the Lion Gate.

The original thickness of the fortification wall at Pylos is unclear: the passage through it was at least 5 meters long, but the preserved width of the wall itself, west of the gate, was as little as 1.4 meters, hardly on the scale of later fortifications at Argolid centers like Mycenae (and even slimmer than the fortifications at Malthi, which range between 1.6 and 3.6 meters).

FIGURE 33
The Mycenaean Tholos Tomb IV and the gate to the citadel of the Palace of Nestor, with Mt. Aigaleon behind. (= C. W. Blegen, M. Rawson, W. Taylour, and W. P. Donovan, The Palace of Nestor at Pylos in Western Messenia, *vol. 3:* Acropolis and Lower Town, Tholoi, Grave Circles and Chamber Tombs, Discoveries Outside the Citadel *[Princeton: Princeton University Press, 1973], fig. 4.) Archives of the Department of Classics, University of Cincinnati, with permission of Princeton University Press and the Department of Classics, University of Cincinnati.*

Blegen suggested that a tower originally stood at each corner of the gate and that the passage through the wall may have been roofed.

THE TOWN AROUND THE CITADEL

Blegen believed, too, that fairly extensive remains of a nonpalatial settlement surrounded the citadel. The extent of this occupation was explored in a series of small excavations, or "test trenches," as they are known to archaeologists. None was far distant from the citadel. To the northwest, beneath the citadel, plentiful surface finds were noted in vineyards, but there was no excavation. Tests here against the steep slope of the citadel, however, uncovered sufficient remains of walls to demonstrate that buildings had been set against its very scarp.

The most distant of Blegen's test excavations in the settlement was west and southwest of the palace, about 100 meters away from buildings on the citadel. Here the ground was more level than in the northwest, and archaeological deposits were deep, substantial, and fairly well-stratified in places; phases in the history of the site were represented that both preceded the palace of the thirteenth century B.C. and were contemporary with it. This was also true of the exiguous space southeast of the palace and west of the modern road. Geophysical investigations sponsored by PRAP have subsequently identified extensive remains of buried walls in areas more distant from the citadel than were Blegen's tests.

East of the road, furthermore, Blegen noted a considerable amount of broken pottery on the slopes leading steeply into the ravine. Finally, to the north of the palace, at a distance of some 50 meters from the citadel, well-stratified remains both of the Middle Helladic period (the earlier second millennium) and of the period of the Palace of Nestor (the thirteenth century) were uncovered. Each of these exploratory soundings suggested that a settlement of some size had surrounded the palace and its associated structures. Our own research in the past five years has contributed greatly to the clarification of Blegen's findings, and we now believe that the town of Pylos was several times larger than earlier scholars envisioned it. Fieldwork organized by PRAP has also provided a clearer regional context for this town (see Focus in Chapter 5).

PREHISTORIC COMMUNITIES NEAR THE PALACE OF NESTOR

Archaeological explorations in the countryside around the Palace of Nestor, particularly since World War II, have shown us that the settlement on the Englianos Ridge was just one of a number of prehistoric communities in the area. One of these lay a mere ten-minute drive to the northeast of the Palace of Nestor, strategically situated at the junction of the Englianos Ridge and the expanse of flatter tableland that sits at the foot of Mt. Aigaleon, within the modern town of Hora. Hora commands virtually the only convenient routes leading from the Palace of Nestor north, south, or east, and it has been a center of some importance since very early prehistoric times. Indeed, Spyridon Marinatos discovered there, in a cave called Katavothra, only a few minutes walk southwest of the town square, one of the very few traces of Late Neolithic (fourth millennium B.C.) occupation in western Messenia.

After a gap of more than a millennium during which we have no evidence whatsoever for occupation, our next signs of human activity at Hora are at the northeastern edges of town in the suburb known as Volimidia. Here at Kefalovryso are ample springs that supply the modern town of several thousand souls and that must also have been of interest in prehistoric times. It has long been known that there are Mycenaean tombs at Volimidia. But the location of the settlement associated with them remained a riddle until Marinatos conducted test excavations in 1953 in what is today the backyard of a villager's house by the main road (see Focus in this chapter). As he wrote in the same year, Volimidia was a beautiful and fertile location, a wonderful place to be buried, and so it is still, despite the expansion of the modern town of Hora around it.

Nothing at all is today visible of the settlement that Marinatos found, and goats graze over what must have been the excavation trenches. Nor were the architectural remains impressive. Only in the uppermost level, associated with pottery contemporary with the final thirteenth-century phase of the Palace of Nestor, was a single wall discovered. Lower down, in a deposit about 1 meter deep, Marinatos found important remains of habitation, dating to the formative stages of Mycenaean civilization—but not the actual houses themselves. Sherds of one-handled cups of the type called "Keftiu," after their appearance in the hands of the Keftiu people (almost certainly Minoans) depicted on the walls of Eighteenth Dynasty tombs at Egyptian Thebes; sherds from large storage jars decorated with bands of clay in imitation of rope; pieces of mud brick, ash, and charcoal—such finds and more were retrieved from Marinatos's soundings.

Indeed, there may have been, as Marinatos suspected, a prosperous Mycenaean town at Volimidia, but it never proved possible for him to resume his work, and the site has not been further investigated since his death. Study of the pottery from the excavation has, however, shown that much of it belongs to the first (or Late Helladic I) phase of the Mycenaean period, and was thus produced in the seventeenth century B.C. This was also, of course, approximately the time when the great Tholos Tomb IV at the Palace of Nestor (and of the "Grave Circle," not far from it) was constructed, and when the monumental fortifications of the citadel itself were built. Occupation seems to have continued at Volimidia in a relatively unbroken sequence through the following centuries until the end of the thirteenth century B.C.

But however long-lived or extensive the Mycenaean settlement at Volimidia may have been, the character of the site differed considerably from that of the settlement at the Palace of Nestor. For, unlike the Palace of Nestor, no true tholos tombs were ever built (although large chamber tombs were constructed). If such monumental graves are the visible manifestations of the power of early Mycenaean elite families (see below), their absence at Volimidia may suggest that this area already belonged to the settlement on the Englianos Ridge in Late Helladic I.

There are, however, several other major sites with important remains of the early Mycenaean period only a few hours' walk from the Englianos Ridge, to either the east, the south, or the west, with monumental tholos tombs at Routsi, Koryfasion, Tragana, and Voidokoilia. These settlements are likely to have presented more of a challenge to political expansion by the elite of Englianos. Marinatos and his successor at the University of Athens, George Korres, have explored the tombs, but Korres's University of Athens team has especially focused on the site of Voidokoilia and its surroundings, at the northwestern side of the Bay of Navarino.

The modern town of Pylos sits near the south end of this bay and is afforded an excellent harbor, protected as it is by the long and narrow island of Sphacteria, which figures so prominently in the post–Bronze Age history of Messenia (see Chapter 6). A substantial number of prehistoric finds have been found in its vicinity: at Palaionavarino, in the Cave of Nestor, and at Voidokoilia. Palaionavarino is the lofty Classical and medieval citadel of Pylos, just to the north of Sphacteria and separated from it by only a few dozen meters of sea. This was the ancient Coryphasion (its name in modern times has been expropriated by the inland village of Osmanaga). Shifting onomastics make the Pylos area a touristic (and archaeological) nightmare.

Two-thirds of the way up the northern ascent to the citadel of Palaionavarino is a cave that has been locally known as the "Cave of Nestor" since time immemorial; it was so called already by the Greek Pausanias, who traveled in the Roman world of the second century A.D. Today the cave is dark and full of bats, its ceiling pierced by a large aperture that permits some natural illumination in its interior. Few remember that it was Heinrich Schliemann himself who first came here in his search for Nestor's Pylos (see Chapter 2). Schliemann reported to the Athenian Division of the German Archaeological Institute on January 23, 1889, that he had inspected the citadel of ancient Coryphasion and had dug trenches amidst the ruins of Venetian and Turkish houses without finding traces of either Classical or pre-Classical occupation.

Still, Schliemann did not waver in his resolve that Nestor's palace lay here, its ruins long since eroded from this steep acropolis by the winter rains, and on the north slope of Palaionavarino in the spacious "Cave of Nestor" he struck pay dirt (Fig. 34). Schliemann found Mycenaean pottery in his soundings at a depth of 3 meters. More recent excavations and surface investigations in this century have made it clear that Mycenaean pottery is to be found elsewhere at Palaionavarino (particularly to the south, near the straits that separate the headland from the island of Sphacteria). We now also know that the "Cave of Nestor" preserves some of the oldest evidence of occupation yet recognized in Messenia: here, in recent excavations by the University of Athens, have been found strata dating to the later phases of the Neolithic.

North of the "Cave of Nestor" lies a rocky headland that clearly formed part of the Classical settlement of Coryphasion, and is today littered with

FIGURE 34
The Cave of Nestor (center) at Palaionavarino. PRAP Archive. J. L. Davis.

The PALACE *and* Its DEPENDENCIES

sherds of ancient pottery and tile. Scanty evidence of Mycenaean occupation has been found in the hollows of the bedrock, beneath houses and graves of the historical periods, and in the shifting sand dunes that cover them. But more impressive than any of the other prehistoric remains is the site of Voidokoilia, which occupies a second headland, at the northern end of a sandy beach and a small and serene cove that is almost entirely cut off from the Ionian Sea.

It was, of course, Marinatos again who first excavated prehistoric remains at Voidokoilia, although it was *not* he who first discovered finds of archaeological interest (see Chapter 2). Marinatos unearthed a small tholos tomb, built in Late Helladic I and used afterward for several centuries; it was constructed on the natural bedrock and does not appear to have been buried in the earth at all. Pausanias had mentioned the monument of Thrasymedes, one of the sons of King Nestor, a little distance outside the Classical town of Coryphasion at Palaionavarino, and Marinatos believed this to be his final resting place. Despite considerable disturbance in historical times, two human skeletons remained *in situ*; the complete carcass of a cow appears to have been set into the tomb as a grave gift. Apart from the cow, the dead had been accompanied by many arrowheads of obsidian and chert, necklaces of amethyst and sardonyx, gold bands with spiral decoration, and Mycenaean pottery.

Korres's recent research has unraveled further the extremely complicated history of the site. Scattered sherds of the Neolithic period attest to a Neolithic presence, also recognized on the hill of Profitis Ilias immediately north. The first substantial remains, a small village of more than a dozen houses, date, however, hundreds of years later, to the latter part of the third millennium B.C., in the Early Bronze Age.

The houses then were rectangular, with walls of the so-called herringbone masonry style so characteristic of third-millennium architecture elsewhere in Greece. Signs of trade and contact with the wider Aegean world are typical of settlements of this period, and Voidokoilia is no exception: obsidian from Melos is found in some quantity, while many pottery shapes and fabrics are of types characteristic of contemporary sites in the eastern Peloponnese (e.g., "sauceboats" and shallow saucers).

At the end of the third millennium B.C., this settlement was deserted and the promontory transformed into a cemetery. After some time, a roughly circular mound of earth and debris (a tumulus) about 1.5 meters high was heaped up over the remains of the settlement, and nine large jars, their mouths radiating out to the periphery, were set into it as containers for human remains. (A second tumulus appears to have been constructed a bit farther north, on the lofty hill of Profitis Ilias.) In early Mycenaean times, much of it was totally obliterated when the tholos tomb excavated by Marinatos cut through the tumulus and foundations of the Early Bronze Age structures.

Voidokoilia, like several other sites in the wider Pylos area, has produced rich Mycenaean burials, but as yet the location of the associated settlement has not been determined with certainty. One cluster of Mycenaean centers nearby, where both settlements and cemeteries have been located, however, lies near the southwestern end of the Englianos Ridge, about halfway between the Palace of Nestor and Palaionavarino. The settlements include Romanou, Portes, and Beylerbey; the graves, the impressive early tholos tomb at Haratsari (see Lolos's Focus in Chapter 3). Each of these sites has been known for many years. Most were, in fact, discovered through the wanderings of Blegen's collaborator, Konstantinos Kourouniotis, and his excavation foreman, Haralambos Hristofilopoulos (see Chapter 2). Our own recent investigations have, however, clarified considerably the extent and duration of Mycenaean occupation.

The low ridge of Beylerbey (Fig. 35) lies not far from the modern village of Koryfasion (formerly Osmanaga). Hristofilopoulos brought this important Mycenaean site to the attention of Blegen, and, before beginning excavations at the Palace of Nestor, Blegen and McDonald visited it on March 31, 1939, after collecting Hristofilopoulos by car in Osmanaga. They proceeded to the site, where Blegen recorded in his field notebook:

> Exploring hill, south of village, in a place called 'Beyler Bey'. Found a good many sherds—probably a site of habitation. We collect some and take back to Pylos for washing. Date not certain. Some look Mycenaean. others earlier. perhaps Neolithic.

Many years later, Marinatos excavated and found that the ridge on the whole has been very badly eroded since antiquity and that soft marl bedrock lies almost immediately beneath the plowzone. We have confirmed this sorry state of affairs. Exploration by PRAP geologists with a hand auger failed to reveal undisturbed cultural deposits, while geophysical researches with a magnetometer did not find a single preserved trace of architecture. Nonetheless, there are significant questions to be asked about the settlement at Beylerbey that can be addressed now that systematic surface exploration has been completed. For example, collection of surface artifacts from the entire site allows us to estimate that the thirteenth-century B.C. settlement contemporary with the Palace of Nestor covered 3.5 hectares, an area a quarter as great as that of the settlement at Englianos.

FIGURE 35
North end of the ridge of Beylerbey. PRAP Archive. J. Bennet.

Several hundred meters north of Beylerbey, on the outskirts of modern Koryfasion, one can locate with some difficulty the tholos tomb at Haratsari, excavated in 1926 by Kourouniotis. The latest pottery found in it dates to the fifteenth century B.C.; recent restudy of finds by Yannos Lolos, one of the contributors to this volume, suggests that this so-called Osmanaga Tholos is quite probably the earliest *real* tholos known on the Greek mainland, and may have been built toward or at the end of the Middle Helladic period. The walls of the tomb appear to have been founded on virtually flat ground, but Kourouniotis noted evidence that a tumulus of earth had once been heaped over it.

The preceding are hardly the only Mycenaean finds north of the Bay of Navarino. These lowlands were, as already noted in Chapter 2, a focus for beehive tombs and settlements. Just a couple hundred meters northwest of Haratsari, there is another Mycenaean site at Portes. PRAP survey teams have even found evidence for Mycenaean occupation within the modern town of Romanou—on the north side of the town overlooking the tiny harbor of Bouka, near the prehistoric harbor of Pylos (see Focus in this chapter). And a bit farther north, near the western end of another of the principal ridges that slope down to the sea from the foothills of Aigaleon, archaeologists have found even more Mycenaean remains.

There, on the outskirts of the modern village of Tragana, Marinatos in 1956 excavated one room of a house that contained finds exclusively of early Mycenaean date (Late Helladic I); the room appears to have belonged to a structure of modest dimensions, exactly contemporary with the earliest settlement at Volimidia (above). Finds included triton shells and more than 100 pottery vessels; most were coarse handmade fabrics. Our own survey of the area failed to produce any evidence that Marinatos's structure belonged to a larger village or town, and it is possible that this site (and perhaps others in Messenia) is a remnant of an isolated mansion. If so, such mansions may have functioned similarly to the nearly contemporary country houses of Crete and would be without parallel elsewhere on the Greek mainland.

The low hill southwest of Tragana called Viglitsa affords a commanding view of the coast, the harbor of Bouka, the town of Romanou, and even the Bay of Navarino several kilometers south. Viglitsa was chosen as the site for two early beehive tombs (Fig. 36; see Lolos's Focus, Chapter 3), although we do not know for certain where those Mycenaeans who built them actually resided. Re-examination of these monuments by Korres's University of Athens team has once again clarified many details about the history of an important site. It now seems, for example, that, as at Voidokoilia, the beehive tombs at Tragana were set into remains of an earlier settlement. Elements of occupation as old as the Early Bronze Age have been recognized, whereas Middle Helladic and early Mycenaean potsherds appear to derive from the debris of houses rather than from funerary contexts. The tombs themselves are of an early type; one appears to have been built in Late Helladic I, the other in Late Helladic II.

Thus far in our tour, we have only visited sites that lay south and west of the Palace of Nestor, near the sea, or at least closer to it than the Englianos Ridge. But to the east there are also important complexes of early tombs and settlements. Those nearest to Englianos lie near the modern village of Myrsinohori, separated by a deep gorge from the uplands around Hora. Northeast of the village, a still-well-traveled track makes its way along the back of a ridge called Routsi through the Aigaleon mountain chain to the modern town of Metamorfosis, where it joins the asphalt highway that climbs the Englianos Ridge and passes through Volimidia.

No settlement has yet been found along the road, and the ridge itself was not the target of intensive surface investigations by PRAP. But the two tholos tombs of Routsi are impressive. (Their contents are described in Lolos's Focus, Chapter 3.) Many of the luxury ornaments that adorned the burials have close parallels in the rich Shaft Graves at Mycenae. One tomb was exceptionally rich in beads made of amber, thus reinforcing a pattern

FIGURE 36
Entrance passageway or dromos *leading into one of the two tholos tombs at Tragana Viglitsa. PRAP Archive. R. Dupuis-Devlin and E. Dallagher.*

long recognized in the Peloponnese in the period of the Shaft Graves. Mycenaean burials in the Argolid and Messenia account, in fact, for the bulk of amber found in Greece at this time; the raw material is indisputably an import from the shores of the Baltic Sea.

Recent study of the pottery found there suggests that both tombs must have first been built in the early Mycenaean period, in Late Helladic I. Details of their construction also point to an early date: stones of the walls are carelessly worked and set; the sides of the *dromos* are not walled in stone. Both tombs fell into disuse after the early Mycenaean period and were not replaced by others—in contrast to the situation at Nichoria, in an area much farther from the Palace of Nestor, where the construction of a tholos tomb in Late Helladic IIIA2 may reflect incorporation of the area around the Gulf of Kalamata into the Pylian kingdom (see Chapter 5).

We now know that the tholos tombs of Myrsinohori were successors to an older tradition of elite burial. About a kilometer or so to the northeast, on the Kaloyeropoulos property, the University of Athens team under the direction of Korres has excavated a tumulus of stone and earth containing a large cist grave constructed of stone slabs; several burials were also deposited in large storage jars (*pithoi*) set along its periphery. The mouths of these *pithoi* were framed by stone slabs so as to form a threshold and lintel with door jambs, thus monumentalizing the entrance to the tomb.

DEPENDENCIES OF THE PALACE OF NESTOR?

With the tombs of Myrsinohori, we complete a brief survey of those antiquities that lay nearest the Palace of Nestor on its north, south, east, and west, but we leave as yet unaddressed one fundamental question begged in the title of this chapter. Were these sites dependencies of the Palace of Nestor?

This question is easy to answer for the thirteenth century B.C., when written documentation is available. At that point, all of the sites had long since been incorporated into the kingdom administered from the Palace of Nestor (see Chapter 5). But how much earlier did this settlement on the Englianos Ridge begin to display exceptional power and to manage politically its nearest neighbors? When did neighbors become subordinates?

For clues, we need to search the archaeological evidence carefully and to apply a modicum of common sense. One analytical strategy is to try to work forward in time from the Early Bronze Age (the third millennium B.C.) toward the final destruction of the Palace of Nestor (ca. 1200 B.C.), and in this way to establish chronological "brackets" around the moments when the settlement on the Englianos Ridge is most likely first to have dominated surrounding areas. (Expansion of its power further afield is discussed in Chapter 5.) The evidence, when considered in this way, seems to point to the seventeenth to fifteenth centuries B.C. (that is, the Early Mycenaean period) as the critical time during which new relations of power were being established in the region.

We can be reasonably confident, for example, that the settlement on the Englianos Ridge did not emerge as a regional power until *after* the Early Bronze Age—that is, until sometime in the second millennium B.C. Habitation in the third millennium appears to have been focused on the coast, with centers such as Voidokoilia and Tragana dominant over inland territories. In contrast, although there is no solid evidence that a palace was built on the Englianos Ridge before the fourteenth century B.C., there is some purely archaeological evidence that several centuries earlier, this settlement had already become powerful enough to exert control over its neighbors.

One of the earliest expressions of that power is the early fortification wall around the Englianos citadel. Confusing stratigraphy made it impossible for Blegen to date the wall with precision, but it appears to have been built around the time of transition between the Middle and Late Bronze Age, that is, around 1700–1600 B.C. It is interesting, moreover, that similar fortifications have not yet been recognized at any of the neighboring sites discussed in this chapter (the closest possible parallels being at Peristeria and Malthi, in the Soulima Valley, and perhaps at Ayios Hristoforos near Filiatra).

On the other hand, the tholos tombs built at Myrsinohori, Voidokoilia, Tragana, and Haratsari suggest that influential individuals capable of commanding the substantial resources required to build and equip such monuments lived in areas near the Englianos Ridge in the seventeenth and sixteenth centuries B.C. (see also Chapter 5). Who were they, and what was the basis of their power? Is the replacement of tumuli by this new form of burial to be interpreted as an expression of shared values by powerful individuals who found more in common with peers in neighboring communities than with the powerless in their own? Should we imagine that the builders of these tombs were competitors with the elite of the Englianos settlement? Did they construct tholoi to boast of their might and independence? Or is it possible that the entire area described in this chapter had already been politically unified in the seventeenth century B.C., and that the tholoi we have discussed were built by functionaries anxious to follow a lead in mortuary fashion set by a central authority now based on the Englianos Ridge?

The evidence we do have is frustratingly murky in places where clarity is required. Considerably more archaeological data from excavation of settlements are needed if the nature of relationships between the Englianos Ridge and other Early Mycenaean centers in the region is to be specified more accurately—if we are to discriminate among the possibilities outlined above. But certain conclusions seem worth stating—at least as hypotheses that can be tested in the future. The early fortifications at Englianos suggest that this center may have dominated its nearest neighbors already by the very beginning of the Mycenaean period. Elaborate tholos tombs, on the other hand, must have served as visual manifestations in the landscape of the presence of an elite; their broad geographical distribution implies, moreover, that already by the Early Mycenaean period, there existed a regional privileged class that lusted for exotic goods from other parts of the Greek mainland and from Minoan Crete. These hints of conflict and avarice are the foundations on which was constructed the kingdom of Nestor—subject of the next two chapters of this volume. The interpretive ground will there be more solid. Now we enter the age of proto-history, where text and artifact complement one another.

JACK L. DAVIS

FOCUS

The PORT of NESTOR

During the course of PRAP's explorations, some of the natural scientific research evolved into a clue-gathering investigation reminiscent of a whodunit detective novel. It all began with an earlier study of the landscape evolution of western Messenia. Almost twenty years ago, our colleagues John Kraft from the University of Delaware and George Rapp and Stanley Aschenbrenner from the University of Minnesota realized that the bed of the Selas River, which passes along the western side of the palace, appears to have been diverted by human interference. A few thousand years ago, the river exited into the Bay of Navarino, but it has since abandoned this old bed and now takes a right-angle turn to the west, thereby avoiding its former floodplain and exiting into the Ionian Sea.

Kraft and his colleagues assumed that this diversion was constructed artificially to prevent the fertile floodplain at the northern end of Osmanaga Lagoon from drowning during annual river floods. They also argued that the most likely period during which this kind of human interference with the hydrological environment might have occurred would have been the Late Bronze Age, because several Mycenaean engineering feats of a comparable character are already known. Among these is a similar river diversion at Tiryns that is still functioning today, over 3,000 years after it was constructed.

These arguments, however, remained on the level of a hypothesis meant to stimulate further research. The close examination of the Selas River consequently became a focal point of the physical scientific work on PRAP—one that kept us busy for five years, until we finally found what appears to be a simple explanation for a complicated system.

During the first season of fieldwork, while trying to collect clues about the peculiar course of the Selas River, I noticed that the stream passes through an alluvial plain of unnatural rectangular shape just a few hundred meters before it exits into the Ionian Sea north of the village of Romanou

EBERHARD ZANGGER

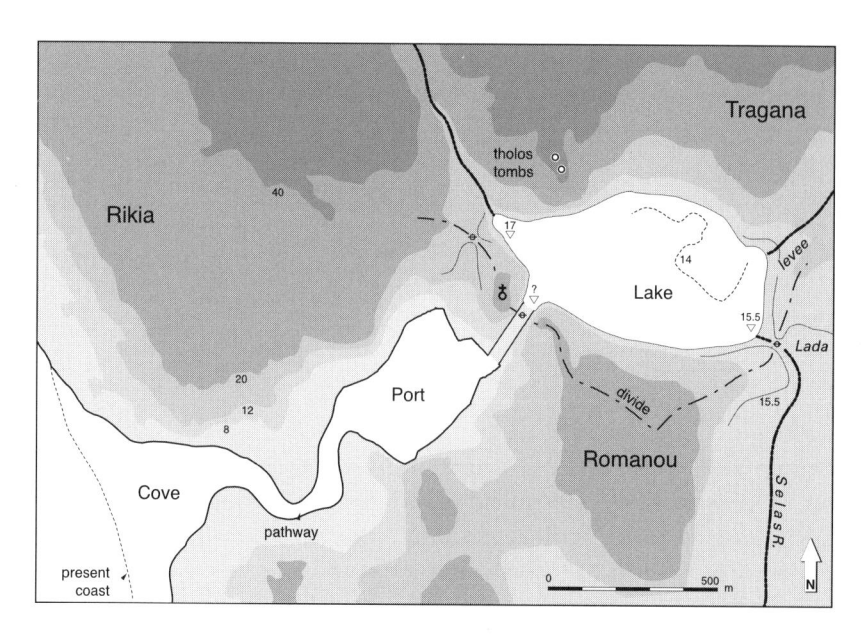

FIGURE 37
*Reconstructed prehistoric topography of the area of the Mycenaean port.
PRAP Archive. E. Zangger.*

(Fig. 37). This rectangular floodplain looks like it might have been a water-filled pool that later became silted up. If this is correct, the remarkably straight boundaries of the floodplain, which measures about 230 by 320 meters, and its location in a dune environment, where natural lakes are unlikely to occur, would have argued in favor of a man-made basin. The only conceivable function of an artificial basin so close to the sea would, of course, be that it served as a protected port. Thus, early on, the working hypothesis was formulated that the rectangular floodplain near Romanou might represent a silted-up port for the Late Bronze Age kingdom.

Determining whether there was once water in the basin is relatively easy—at least in theory. One has to investigate the subsurface deposits to see whether there are sediment layers in the stratigraphy that only form underwater. During the second season of fieldwork, we therefore attempted to take a sequence of cores across the plain using a hand drill or auger. Soon it turned out that theory and practice can be quite different matters. All of our cores terminated at shallow depths in a thick layer of impenetrable gravel. At this stage, we were ready to drop the initial hypothesis and abort the investigation of the basin, but after much encouragement from our archaeological colleagues, who had even secured some extra funding, we returned the following year with a rotary drill truck hired from a local well-driller.

Using this device, we were finally able to reach deeper, despite the continuous threat of collapsing drill holes (Fig. 38). Under the gravel, we discovered a thick layer of clay—a deposit that does indeed only form underwater (Fig. 39). Thus, the initial hypothesis, that the floodplain might conceal a former basin that used to be filled with water, was verified. In the next step, we had to find out whether the water in the basin had been fresh or salty. Microscopic investigations of sediments extracted from the holes revealed shells of many hundreds of organisms that could only have lived in a marine environment. Hence, the water in the basin must have been well connected to the open sea.

This discovery also proved the hypothesis that the basin was—at least in part—constructed artificially, because there is no natural process that would create and keep open this kind of steeply sloping depression so close to the shore. Eventually the basin was filled in, apparently quite rapidly, by the several-meters-thick layer of gravel that had caused us so much trouble. Geologically speaking, the depositional environment changed from one extreme to another. First, the basin had only accumulated wind-blown clay; later, it became quickly filled with coarse gravel carried by the river. These gravel deposits evidently originated after the change in riverbeds. When the Selas River chose its new bed through the basin, it first filled the depression with stream gravel deposits.

Obviously, we wanted to find out when the basin was constructed, how long it was functional, and when the river changed its course, thereby destroying the basin. The well-dated cores taken from Osmanaga Lagoon—mainly to collect pollen samples—aided us in solving this problem. It turned out that the amount of fluvial material deposited in Osmanaga Lagoon dropped to a low rate around 1400 B.C., and then to an even lower level around 1200 B.C. Evidently, Mycenaean engineers did indeed interfere with the course of the Selas River, at first diverting the stream only partially. After 1200 B.C., however, when the palace administration had collapsed, the river permanently chose the shorter course to the Ionian Sea.

Why would Mycenaean engineers want to interfere with the river? This next question turned out to be the most puzzling problem of all, because the port basin and the redirection of the river appeared to us to be mutually exclusive. An artificially constructed basin near the sea that is used as a sheltered port, by itself, makes perfect sense. This kind of construction, called a *cothon* harbor, was even quite popular during the Phoenician dominion of naval trade in the Mediterranean. No engineer, however, should

FIGURE 38
Mechanized drilling equipment at the site of the Mycenaean port. Eberhard Zangger on right. PRAP Archive. J. Bennet.

FIGURE 39
*Eberhard Zangger (left) examining cores extracted by the mechanized drill.
PRAP Archive. J. Bennet.*

want to direct a river through such a basin, because the sediment carried by the stream, mainly during its winter floods, would fill up the basin within just a few years.

Since the basin was undoubtedly man-made, we began to doubt that the change in riverbeds was due to human interference as well. But there were many strong arguments in favor of an artificial redirection, probably the most important one being that the new course of the stream traverses the middle of a bedrock knoll. At this point we felt that advice was needed from an expert in Mycenaean hydroengineering, and we therefore invited Jost Knauss from the Polytechnical University of Munich to participate in our project. Knauss has investigated all the known hydraulic systems created by Mycenaean engineers, for instance at Gla, Tiryns, Mycenae, and in central Arcadia, and has written four books and three dozen articles about the subject.

During the fieldwork, Knauss first noticed sediments of an extensive lake that existed inland of the artificial basin. Lake and basin were separated by the knoll; but they were also connected by the narrow channel that cuts through this knoll. But this new revelation did not really explain the system behind the whole construction either. Maintaining a lake above a man-made port greatly increases the risk that the port might become filled in by sediment when the lake spills over its shores after an unusually heavy rain. With the help of the detailed observations, maps, and diagrams made by Jost Knauss—and a hint by his colleague, Daniel Vischer, from the Eigenoessische Technische Hochschule in Zurich—a plausible explanation for the whole system (and its demise) finally materialized after the end of the 1995 field season.

It all has to do with the epithet "sandy" Pylos. Today, deserted sand beaches several kilometers long stretch north of Romanou. Very likely some, or even much, of this sand used to cover the beach, even during the Late Bronze Age. Under these circumstances, it would have been virtually impossible to keep the entrance to the port basin sediment-free. The seawater that penetrated into the basin would have carried sand with it, and this sand would have soon blocked the port entrance. Thus, the whole construction of the port only made sense when it could be kept free of sediment. In order to achieve this, it had to be flushed with a small but permanent flow of clean water. As long as the basin was filled with so much sediment-free water that there was a steady stream of it flowing out to the sea, no sediment-rich marine water could get into the basin.

Hence, the stream had been diverted simply to flush the port basin. Since river water tends to contain even more sediment than seawater, however, the Mycenaean engineers had to construct a sediment trap first—and that is where the lake comes in. When the sediment-rich river water entered the lake, it lost most of its energy and therefore dropped its sediment. Then, a small current of clean water derived from the surface of the lake ran through the artificial canal into the port basin, while the remaining water left the lake through the original streambed that exited at Osmanaga Lagoon. This system obviously demanded that somebody control how much clean water was directed into the basin and how much dirty water was allowed to escape into Osmanaga Lagoon. When this control was abandoned after the Mycenaean demise, the river was left to itself and chose the shorter course through the former port basin.

This port basin at Romanou not only ranks as the first and thus far only known artificial port in prehistoric Europe, it also—for the first time—demonstrates that Mycenaean hydraulic skills were not limited to domestic drainage and irrigation systems, but also applied to naval installations. This discovery sheds a new light on seafaring and naval trade during the Late Bronze Age. Thus far, many scholars have assumed that during Mycenaean times, vessels were simply pulled ashore, probably because this is the procedure described by Homer. Now we know that we have to look carefully for traces of artificial ports—no matter how concealed they might be under several meters of gravel.

EBERHARD ZANGGER

FOCUS

MYCENAEAN BURIAL *at* PYLOS

Homes of the dead, like homes of the prehistoric living discussed already in this chapter, have been a target of archaeological investigation since the beginning of this century, excavated by a number of the most prominent Greek and foreign archaeologists of their day—Spyridon Marinatos, Carl Blegen, Konstantinos Kourouniotis, and George Korres, to name only the most active. The investigation of tombs has an important tale to tell, since the history of burial in the Pylos region in many regards mirrors the picture we get from the study of prehistoric settlements in the area, and, in a very real fashion, the growth, development, and decline of the Palace of Nestor as a center of political power can be traced in the development of burial customs in its hinterland. In this brief review, five archaeological sites are examined—the Englianos Ridge itself; Volimidia, on the eastern outskirts of the town of Hora; and tombs near three neighboring villages—Myrsinohori, Koryfasion, and Tragana. Each of these sites contributes a piece to the puzzle.

Before the Palace of Nestor was built in the Middle Bronze Age, the most elaborate form of burial was fashioned by building a mound of earth as a memorial (called a *tumulus* by archaeologists), into which would be inserted large jars or boxes constructed of stone slabs containing the remains of the dead. Things begin to change late in the period, when new types of graves were introduced. At Volimidia, a deep shaft in the earth, roofed with wooden beams and stone slabs, was used for burial and follows in style a type much better known from those examples first investigated by Schliemann at Mycenae. Of even greater significance, however, was the emergence in Messenia of an entirely new type of funerary monument, the *tholos*, a stone-vaulted, beehive-shaped tomb probably created with the assistance of masons from Minoan Crete, and consisting of an entrance passage, or *dromos*, leading through an entrance, or *stomion*, to a circular chamber. Indeed, the very earliest tomb of this type yet known on the

YANNOS G. LOLOS

Greek mainland is to be found at Haratsari, near Koryfasion, and there is a near-contemporary tomb only a stone's throw southwest of the Palace of Nestor itself.

The tomb at Haratsari is medium-sized, as tholos tombs go—about 6 meters in diameter. It lies in the middle of a pleasant meadow, about ten minutes south of the village, but it can be difficult to find since it is today wholly underground. It was no doubt used for burial by the inhabitants of nearby contemporary settlements at Portes and Beylerbey (see Chapter 3). On the other hand, associated with the settlement at Englianos and of approximately the same size is the "Grave Circle," as it was called by Blegen, at Englianos, surely also the remains of an early tholos tomb. Inside it, the dead were buried both in pits and in large jars, but the equipment of the burial pits was most lavish—gold, silver, and bronze vessels and weapons were mixed with the ceramic vases that almost always have been found in Bronze Age burials in Greece. Kourouniotis also found a vessel of faience, a silicate-based mixture fired to produce a fused hard lustrous compound that was molded or modeled into various shapes by the Mycenaeans.

The prosperity of Englianos at the dawn of the Mycenaean civilization is also attested by the rich contents of nearby tombs, most significantly Tholos Tomb IV. Tholos Tomb IV lies immediately northeast of the Palace of Nestor, near the parking lot that now serves visitors to the archaeological site, and was discovered in the course of Blegen's excavations at the palace, hidden by a modern workyard for drying currants. Constructed at the beginning of the Mycenaean period and employed for princely or royal burials during the whole of the fifteenth century B.C., the tomb continued to be used for perhaps as long as two centuries. It is larger than earlier tombs in Messenia. The *dromos* is over 10 meters in length; its *stomion* is nearly 5 meters deep and of a similar height; and the diameter of the burial chamber is itself greater than 9 meters. The upper part of the vault, as it appears today, is a recent reconstruction, the original having long since collapsed; but the contents of the tomb were remarkably well-preserved nonetheless. On the floor of the chamber, Blegen found a large semicircular pit cut to hold bones of earlier interments, as well as a stone sarcophagus that presumably held mortal remains not as yet decayed.

Even though the chamber had been severely plundered by tomb robbers in ancient times and most of its contents lay in disarray, sufficient evidence was preserved to allow the deduction that the tholos had once held a minimum of seventeen interments, and that those buried in it had been men and women of high status in the community. For despite the robbery, many items of gold still remained, including items of personal adornment of gold, among them four gold owls similar to those found in tholos tombs at

Peristeria and Kakovatos (Chapter 5); a unique gold seal on which is depicted a winged griffin of emblematic character; and a small gold ring with a representation of a peak sanctuary of Minoan type on its bezel. Among other finds were four sealstones, an astounding 246 beads of amethyst, and even beads of amber imported from the Baltic Sea littoral.

Signs of wealth are now manifested in burials established at many other locations in the Pylos area. There was a Mycenaean settlement at Volimidia, but the site is best known for the substantial number of so-called chamber tombs that have been excavated there, many by the renowned Greek archaeologist Spyridon Marinatos, a third of them built already by the sixteenth century B.C. A chamber tomb, although resembling a tholos in its *dromos* and *stomion*, is generally smaller and lacks a vaulted chamber of stone; in its stead, a similar circular or rectangular chamber was generally hewn from the bedrock itself, into which the tomb was cut. Marinatos argued that Volimidia was Palaipylos, or "Old Pylos," a town that the Roman geographer Strabo claimed had once lain beneath Mt. Aigaleon. In Mycenaean times, some would place here *pa-ki-ja-ne*, a center of religious activity directly dependent on the Palace of Nestor (Chapter 5).

Other monumental burials of the early Mycenaean period point to the power held by the elite of centers well removed from the Englianos Ridge in the centuries when the Palace of Nestor was establishing its hegemony in western Messenia. At Routsi, near the village of Myrsinohori, are two tholos tombs first excavated by Marinatos, both with finds ranging in date from the sixteenth to the fourteenth centuries B.C. The first, like Tholos Tomb IV at Englianos, had been plundered, but still yielded ceramic vases, a bronze pan, a bronze pin, remnants of a silver vessel, and gold ornaments. The second, in contrast, was found almost intact and is, remarkably, one of the few unplundered tholoi discovered on the Greek mainland. A series of well-provided burials were interred in two pits and on the floor of the tomb itself, and among their contents were a variety of weapons, including long swords and two inlaid daggers; many sealstones; jewelery; objects of gold, bronze, stone, and ivory; and much fine pottery. Recently, in 1989, reinvestigation of the burial chamber of the first tomb by Korres found still more treasures in a niche under the tholos wall: bronze objects included a cup, a bent sword 80 centimeters long, and the inner framework of a ceremonial helmet or crown.

There are two more tholos tombs at Viglitsa, near the village of Tragana, one built in the sixteenth century, the other slightly later. Several of the finds from the first tomb are spectacular: a large bronze two-handled vessel; three large jars with ivy sprays, chains of ivy leaves, and lilies; a seal depicting a stylized winged griffin, a mythical animal especially popular in

---

MYCENAEAN BURIAL *at* PYLOS

Mycenaean art; and a clay box of the twelfth century B.C., with a rare representation of a prehistoric Greek warship.

By the later thirteenth century B.C., the Palace of Nestor had been established as the center of power in the region (Chapter 5), and the lavishness of the burials in its vicinity reflects this position. Indeed, at least one, Tholos Tomb III, southwest of the palace on a lower part of the Englianos Ridge, was certainly used for interments of members of the royal dynasty or court, while groups of chamber tombs, cut into soft bedrock on the slopes of the ridge, served the more common folk of the community. Tholos Tomb III appears to have been built in the first half of the fifteenth century B.C., but remained in use well into the thirteenth century B.C. Its chamber, although much disturbed by the collapse of the vault of the tomb, must once have held at least sixteen dead, and, although systematically looted prior to excavation, it yielded gold jewelery, a three-sided sealstone, beads and other small objects of faience and glass paste, and fragments of ivory boxes with finely carved decoration. A two-handled storage jar imported from somewhere along the eastern coast of the Mediterranean in the area of modern Syria or Israel carries a sign of a type used in writing systems employed on the island of Cyprus.

With the destruction of the Palace of Nestor, the use of monumental tholos tombs largely ceased, both on the Englianos Ridge and elsewhere in the region where older tombs had been reused. Chamber tombs, too, were no longer employed. The evidence from Volimidia shows this clearly: there, after 1200 B.C., burials were no longer made. These two forms of burial, so characteristic of the Mycenaean civilization, were products of that civilization, and their passing is a fitting marker of its collapse and the onset of the ensuing Dark Ages of Greece.

FIGURE 40
Oil-storage magazine at the Palace of Nestor with the Throne Room, hearth, and modern olive trees behind. PRAP Archive. R. J. Robertson.

CHAPTER 4

The PALACE and Its OPERATIONS

The story of the discovery of the Palace of Nestor, at the end of a ridge overlooking Navarino Bay, is told in Chapter 2 (Focus). The remarkable success of the very first trench laid out on April 4, 1939, is captured by a typically laconic telegram that Carl Blegen sent on April 21 to a friend in Athens:

> Suggest you come straight here visiting Olympia afterward Kalamata road now practicable Found Mycenaean palace with column bases remains fresco over fifty inscribed clay tablets Love Carl

The physical history of this palace and the various operations it housed are the subject of this chapter.

In the Mycenaean heyday of the early thirteenth century B.C., two impressive palatial buildings stood on the ridgetop crowning the town (see plan, Fig. 41). The larger of these, the Main Building (as it is now prosaically called), stood two stories high near the narrowing southwest edge of the ridge. At the very edge of the hill was the smaller Southwestern Building, whose purposes are less well understood. These were not the first structures to be built here. A settlement occupied the site during the Middle Bronze Age, which begins about 2000 B.C. Near the beginning of the Late Bronze Age (ca. 1700 B.C.), inhabitants built a fortification wall around the area of the later palace; the gateway and stretches of wall still remain in place (see Chapter 3). The architectural history of the citadel remains uncertain, but it is clear at least that an earlier palatial building lay directly under the Main Building. Several segments of stone wall foundations have been found, made of the same large, well-shaped blocks as the Main Building itself, and covering an area of equal size. But this construction was razed at the start of Late Helladic IIIB, at the end of the fourteenth century, and the new palace that replaced it is the one visitors see today.

CYNTHIA W. SHELMERDINE

FIGURE 41
Plan of the Palace of Nestor at the end of excavations by Blegen. J. C. Wright, with permission.

There were two ways to enter the Main Building. The southeastern entrance was fronted by a shaded porch (Propylon 1), its roof supported by a single fluted column. Once inside, visitors found themselves not indoors, but in another porch leading to a courtyard open to the sky (Court 3; Fig. 42). A similar porch and doorway on the northeastern side of the building (Room 41) seem more private; they provided access for those coming from the northeast, through the town and past the domed shape of Tholos Tomb IV, 145 meters from the palace. This doorway led to the more secluded areas on this side of the palace, or, by a short turning route, to the inner courtyard.

Two columns on the northwestern side of Court 3 marked the way to the very core of the palace, the megaron complex (Rooms 4–6). Visitors with business there passed through two porches into the megaron proper, a large room dominated by a round central hearth. Above the hearth, the room was open to the second floor; four columns supported a clerestory around the sides. On the northeastern wall, a rectangular depression in the painted plaster floor is all that remains to show where the king's throne once stood. Next to it, a channel in the floor linking two circular depressions is a unique feature that may have served for the pouring of libations. A preserved fresco of a lion and a griffin comes from the wall to the left of the throne; it was probably matched by another pair to the right. Further to the viewer's right, on the same wall, was a banquet scene, perhaps the culmination of a procession of men and women leading a bull to sacrifice, whose depiction begins in Room 5 (Fig. 43).

FIGURE 42
Artist's reconstruction of Court 3 of the Palace of Nestor, as seen from the southwest. The southeast entrance to the palace is at the right; the entrance to the megaron complex is at the left. P. de Jong. (= C. W. Blegen and M. Rawson, The Palace of Nestor at Pylos in Western Messenia, *vol. 1:* The Buildings and Their Contents *[Princeton: Princeton University Press, 1966], frontispiece.) Archives of the Department of Classics, University of Cincinnati, with permission of Princeton University Press and the Department of Classics, University of Cincinnati.

FIGURE 43
*Procession fresco with bull, from Room 5 of the Palace of Nestor. P. de Jong.
(= M. L. Lang,* The Palace of Nestor in Western Messenia, *vol. 2:* The Frescoes
*[Princeton: Princeton University Press, 1969], pl. 119.) Archives of the Department
of Classics, University of Cincinnati, with permission of Princeton University Press
and the Department of Classics, University of Cincinnati.*

This megaron complex, together with a second suite of rooms also centered on a room with a hearth and paintings of lions and griffins (Rooms 45–53), embodies the power and splendor of a palatial center. The central megaron, at least, certainly had a public function. Access to it from the southeastern entrance is very straightforward, and fresco remains from the outer porch suggest that the ceremonial procession observed in Room 5 may actually have begun here, so that the procession on the wall guided and accompanied a visitor to the throne room. The iconography here, as well as the libation channel next to the throne, suggest that the king played a significant role in the religious affairs of the kingdom. We know from textual evidence that he also presided over secular matters. Pantries near the throne room (Pantries 19–22) contained startling quantities of ordinary household pottery, suggesting the regular entertainment of a large number of people. 2,854 wine cups were found in Pantry 19 alone (Fig. 44). Communal feasting is a way in many cultures of demonstrating and maintaining authority, and this may have been so at Mycenaean Pylos as well. The practice may also have had a ritual dimension; several Pylos texts list foods that are apparently earmarked for such feasts. It has even been suggested that the spacious open area (Court 88) between the Main and Southwestern buildings would have been a good space for large banquets.

CYNTHIA W. SHELMERDINE

The megaron complex embodies the political and religious importance of the palace, but the structure also served a variety of other purposes. The archives complex to the left of the main entrance (Rooms 7–8) identifies the building as the administrative heart of the Pylian kingdom. Storage facilities have already been mentioned. It was also surely a residence—the ground floor boasts not only a possible bathroom (Room 53), with suitable drainage, but a fine bathtub in Room 43, with spiral decoration around the inside (Fig. 45). Two staircases on the northeastern side of the building (36 and 54) led to the upper story. It is impossible to tell much about what went on there, but a few clues exist. Fallen fresco fragments suggest a

FIGURE 44
Broken drinking cups on the floor of Pantry 19 of the Palace of Nestor. (= C. W. Blegen and M. Rawson, The Palace of Nestor at Pylos in Western Messenia, *vol. 1:* The Buildings and Their Contents *[Princeton: Princeton University Press, 1966], fig. 98.) Archives of the Department of Classics, University of Cincinnati, with permission of Princeton University Press and the Department of Classics, University of Cincinnati.*

FIGURE 45
Bathtub in Room 43 of the Palace of Nestor. (= C.W. Blegen and M. Rawson, The Palace of Nestor at Pylos in Western Messenia, vol. 1: The Buildings and Their Contents *[Princeton: Princeton University Press, 1966], fig. 140.) Archives of the Department of Classics, University of Cincinnati, with permission of Princeton University Press and the Department of Classics, University of Cincinnati.*

sizable room over Room 46, and objects of gold and ivory fell from above into the area of Rooms 30–32. Perfumed-oil inventories point to the presence of an oil storeroom over Room 38, and tablets dealing with textiles fell into the megaron itself. Thus we can imagine that the same mixture of private apartments, storerooms, and business areas observable on the ground floor prevailed upstairs as well.

So much for the character of the palace when it was constructed at the beginning of Late Helladic IIIB. However, during the course of the thirteenth century B.C., the building underwent several phases of remodeling, and it is of course the final stage that we see today. The effect of these alterations was to restrict access from outside the Main Building and circulation within it, and to increase storage and workshop space. Among the most significant changes were the creation of Courts 42 and 47, blocking access to the northeastern entrance mentioned above, and the construction of the Northeast Workshop, which postdates Courts 42 and 47. The construction of Court 47 also closes off direct exterior access to Room 46 and the suite of rooms surrounding it. When excavated, Court 42 was full of pottery that had been broken and discarded, including at least 348 shattered drinking cups, suggesting it was used partly as a refuse dump in the final stage of the life of the palace. Court 47 contained pottery that was still in use when the palace was destroyed. Finds included thirty-five stirrup jars, a shape used for storing plain and perfumed oil. These examples are mostly of the small size associated with personal quantities of scented oil. With other finds, they have raised the possibility that perfume manufacture was one of the uses to which this court might have been put, though this is by no means certain. The Northeast Workshop was certainly used for industrial purposes. Tablets found in Room 99 show that chariot repair took place here, among other activities (see below, this chapter).

Much of the ground floor of the Main Building itself was given over to storage in the final years of Mycenaean occupation. Several rooms were devoted to the storage of olive oil. Of these, Rooms 23 and 24 are as old as the palace, but Room 27 was certainly an addition to the original plan, and Room 32 was probably converted to storage use, for its carefully plastered walls and floor are nicer than the treatment storerooms usually receive. Rooms 23 and 32 contain tablets and storage jars that show these rooms to have been repositories for perfumed oil, a commodity of great economic importance to Pylos (see Focus in this chapter).

Such modifications make it clear that the Main Building and its immediate vicinity were increasingly converted for the storage, repair, and perhaps manufacture of important goods in the later part of the thirteenth century. Apparently the authorities anticipated trouble, either locally or from further afield. This was true at other palatial centers as well. Outlying houses at Mycenae were attacked and burned in the middle of the thirteenth century, and a massive construction project followed, in two phases, to extend and strengthen the fortification wall and to provide access to water from inside. Tiryns and Athens also expanded their defenses about the same time. The response to a perceived threat perhaps took a different form at Pylos, since evidence for fortification walls is so far lacking, but the bringing of important goods and activities closer in to the center, and the restricting of traffic to and through the palace, clearly indicate the concerns of the inhabitants.

It is clear, however, that under evidently changed circumstances, the ruler continued to maintain his authority in long-established ways. Like nearly all the tablets from Pylos, those connected with ritual feasting, already alluded to, date to the last year of the palace's existence. There are also other signs that this activity continued. It is very interesting, for example, to see how access to the pantries had changed by the late thirteenth century. In the western corner of the Main Building, Corridor 18 was sealed off by blocking walls at each end, cutting off normal access to Pantries 19 and 20 with their vast quantities of drinking cups. Instead, a doorway was cut in the exterior wall of Pantry 20. Thus, people in the postulated feasting area (Court 88) could reach these stores without gaining entry to the rest of the palace. Pantries 60–62 were also added, providing more storage for tableware and controlling access to the feasting area. The wine-storage building, Rooms 104–105, may be another late addition to the original plan. I think its construction was connected to this need to restrict palace access while continuing to accommodate a large number of guests at banquets.

This is the only explanation that seems to make sense of the otherwise curious placement of the building. It is at the northern corner of the palace complex, almost at the northwest edge of the ridge, which drops off sharply just behind it. Moreover, the only entrance is on this back side. In the early days of the palace, it would have made more sense to put a door on the southeastern side, readily accessible from the northeastern entrance to the palace. A door on the northwest only makes sense if it was meant to be used by people passing from the feasting area around the back side of the Main Building, endlessly refilling the wine cups of elite subjects on whose support the king depended, and over whom he needed to maintain control.

All these measures to control activities and palace access may have postponed disaster, but in the end they could not avert it. Like the citadels of Mycenae and Tiryns in the Argolid, the Pylos palace was destroyed in a violent fire around 1200 B.C. We do not know who, or what, was responsible; even the timing is still under debate. Recent work at the site and restudy of the excavation notebooks suggest that the site was reoccupied at least in the Protogeometric period, contrary to the excavator's original view (see Focus in this chapter). The fire brought the Mycenaean kingdom of Pylos to an end, but there is one consolation for the archaeologist, at least: it was also responsible for preserving some of the most important evidence at the site.

Among the artifacts that came to light in the excavation of Pylos, no single type has made a greater contribution to Mycenaean studies than the tablets that were among the very first finds in 1939. They were inscribed with writing in a curious script that was already known from Knossos on Crete. It was clearly derived from an earlier linear writing system used by the Minoan culture of Crete; hence the names Linear A for this earlier script, and Linear B for the later Mycenaean one. But the tablets could not be read until 1952, when the young British architect Michael Ventris made the surprising discovery that the language written in Linear B was not Minoan, as many had expected, but Greek.

These documents have added a new dimension to our understanding of the Mycenaeans. From them, we know that the Mycenaeans manufactured cloth on an impressive industrial scale, as well as perfumed oil, chariots, and objects of bronze. They worshiped many of the gods we know from Classical Greece, including Zeus, Poseidon, Hera, Ares, and Dionysos. Tablets listing oxen describe several breeds, which read like a Bronze Age version of the Seven Dwarfs—Dappled, Dusky, and Winefaced. At Pylos there was a large labor force, paid in figs and barley by the palace: shepherds and weavers, perfume boilers, bronzesmiths, and bath attendants, all present and accounted for on clay. The administrative hierarchy is also documented, from the king himself, called by the term *wanax*, down to the governors and vice-governors of individual districts.

The Linear B tablets are nothing like the voluminous and varied records known from the Near East. They preserve no laws, no literature, no diplomatic or private correspondence. They are just administrative aides-mémoire: lists of taxes and payments, goods stored, and goods offered to the gods. Furthermore, the tablets only refer to the business of a single year; they were never intended as permanent records. They were not even intentionally baked; we possess only those which were accidentally preserved when a fire destroyed the building that housed them. Thus we have records only of the final year of any palace administration. There are month names but no year dates, only occasional references like "last year's debt," or "the bronzesmiths will pay another year." It seems clear that tablets were not kept after the current year was up; any information worth retaining longer was probably transferred to a less bulky material like leather, as we know was the Minoan practice. These documents of lasting value of course perished in the fire that baked the tablets; it is rather like salvaging one's shopping list while losing the library. For those of us who work with Linear B texts, all this means that our information is limited, both in time and in variety. We do, on the other hand, know that any topic appearing in these records is sure to be palace business. Tablets have so far been found only at palatial centers, and literacy in the Mycenaean world was confined to a rather small number of people. Thirty-three scribes have been identified by their handwriting at Pylos, and about sixty-six at the palatial center of Knossos on Crete. Writing does not appear to have been used for any purpose other than economic administration, and it seems that all (or very nearly all) of that administration was palatial.

So, despite the limitations of this written evidence, by considering what the tablets say, where they were found, and what was found with them we can retrieve a good deal of information about the activities a palace administration controlled. These include land tenure and personnel management, industries such as the manufacture of cloth and perfumed oil, taxation, and religious offerings. The documents from Pylos take the form of short, wide, leaf-shaped tablets and page-shaped tablets with somewhat longer texts, and also small inscribed nodules used as labels or certificates. One recently came to light at Pylos (Fig. 46) that had been used to secure a consignment of javelin handles; the word "javelins" appears on one side, the word "handles" on another, and on the third is the sign *wa*, known as an abbreviation for *wanax*, king. Tablets and nodules have survived from all the Mycenaean palaces so far excavated, but Pylos, with 1,106 tablets, has the lion's share of longer and more complete texts, and these give us some of our best information about Mycenaean administration. Eighty-nine percent of the Pylos tablets come from the archives complex, Rooms 7–8. However, some were found in other parts of the palace; these provide important information about the system of administration, particularly for the textile and perfumed-oil industries (see Focus in this chapter), and for activities in the Northeast Workshop.

Who ran this system, and what can we tell about the haves and the have-nots within it? I have several times mentioned the king: his Mycenaean title, *wanax*, is the same word for "king" used in the Homeric *Iliad* and *Odyssey*. The Linear B tablets are particularly valuable in confirming his existence, for unlike Egypt and most Near Eastern cultures, Mycenaean Greece gives us very little in the way of artistic images of a king. But from the texts we know that the *wanax* was the highest-ranking member of a ranked society. This is particularly clear from landholding documents. Pylos tablet Er 312 shows land held by the king and other officials, giving us some idea of their relative importance:

Er 312
.1   plot of land (*temenos*) of the king (*wanax*)
.2   of so much seed WHEAT 2,880 liters
.3   plot of land of the *lawagetas* WHEAT 960 liters
.4   [line empty]
.5   of the *telestai* [ ]so much seed WHEAT 2,880 liters
.6   and so many *telestai* MAN 3
.7   ? land of the ?
.8   of so much seed WHEAT 576 liters

The size of each plot, or *temenos*, is expressed in terms of the amount of seed grain that would be needed to sow it. The royal plot is three times the

FIGURE 46
Nodule Wr 1480 from the Palace of Nestor: face .α, facet .β. Corpus der minoischen und mykenischen Siegeln *archive. Courtesy of I. Pini.*

size of that owned by the *lawagetas*; his name should mean that he leads the people, and his position here in second place is thought to reflect his standing in the community, but his functions are unclear. Third come the *telestai*; each has a plot equal to that of the *lawagetas*. These officials appear on other landholding tablets; they seem to receive the benefit of this land in return for service of some kind, and they rent out shares in turn to other individuals. The final group has a smaller holding still; the broken figure is probably a 6, and cannot be larger than a 7.

When it comes to the king's functions, however, we have very little evidence. We have already noted that he has a presiding role in religious affairs. He also plays an important part, as one would expect, in the administrative bureaucracy of his kingdom. One sector of palatial industry is under the king's control; the adjective "royal" is applied in tablets from several palatial centers to various types of craftsman and to textiles. But only one text shows the king actually doing anything: on Ta 711, he seems to appoint another man to an administrative post. We cannot on this meager evidence demonstrate for the king a judicial role, or a military one, or that of an international statesman. Indeed, two other sectors of society seem to stand in authority parallel, if not equal, to his: the divine and what we might call the civic sectors.

The king is listed with deities as a recipient of offerings—for example, of perfumed oil at Pylos. This has led some to wonder if the term *wanax* applied to gods as well as men, like the English "lord," or if the king himself had divine status. I do not see a good case in the tablets for a divine *wanax*, whether equated with the king or not. Though most of the perfume allocations are religious, some also go to servants, and to the king. The king here is parallel to the gods, but is not one of them. Another parallel between royal and divine authority concerns craftsmen: alongside the royal artisans are others who in some sense "belong" to a god or goddess. This is true in the Mycenaean kingdoms of Knossos and Thebes, as well as Pylos. The third body with administrative authority is the *damos*, a word that continues in use in Classical Greece and refers to the body politic as a governmental entity. It is most visible to us in the landholding records of Pylos, where all three authorities appear. Indeed, it is a dispute between the *damos* and the religious sphere that gives us our longest extant sentence in Mycenaean Greek:

Ep 704
.3 Eritha the priestess holds a leased plot of civic land from the body politic (*damos*), so much seed WHEAT 38.4 liters

.4 the barley-women hold a leased plot of civic land from the body politic (*damos*) so much seed WHEAT 182.4 liters
.5 Eritha the priestess holds a leased plot and claims to hold a freehold? (*etonijo*) for the god but the *damos* says she
.6 holds a leased plot of civic lands, so much seed WHEAT 374.4 liters
.7 Karpathia the key bearer has two public (leased plots); being obligated with two to perform (service) she does not perform
.8 so much[seed WHEAT]? liters

This document lists holdings of public or civic land, and other kinds of plots. The dispute concerns a priestess called Eritha (lines .3, .5–.6). She has one small share of land in line .3. The share of land in lines .5–.6 is much larger; she claims it has a special status because it is "for the god," but the *damos*, unimpressed, says it is a perfectly ordinary holding. The reason this matters is clear from the entry in line .7. In return for the benefits they derive from this land, the shareholders are obligated to perform some service for the *damos*. The *damos* complains in line .7 that Karpathia the key-bearer (perhaps a religious title) has such a share, but fails to fulfill her obligation. Thus there appear to be three competing authorities in Mycenaean society: the royal, the religious, and the civic. More work needs to be done exploring the role of each; the frictions that arise when they intersect can be very enlightening.

Another important sphere of palatial operations illuminated by the tablets is its industries. There are hints in the tablets that the palace hired some otherwise independent workers, and paid them on contract for their services. It was much more common, however, for those working for the palace to be fully or partially dependent on it. We have records of the food rations, chiefly figs and barley, that such workers received. The palace also collected raw materials and distributed them to craftsmen, and in due course recorded the receipt of the finished products. The perfumed-oil industry is a very good example of how this system worked (see Focus in this chapter). The same organizing principles also applied to bronze and cloth workers at Pylos, and to an extensive woolen industry at Knossos.

At Pylos, some industrial work areas were at the palace itself, while other craftsmen were stationed at other places in the kingdom. Bronzesmiths worked at several towns in both the Hither and the Further Provinces, the two major administrative sections of the kingdom (see Chapter 5). Some smiths are named on the tablets as receiving an allotment of bronze from the palace; other entries record the number of smiths without an allotment. The allotments range in size from 1.5 to 12 kilograms; 1.5 kilograms and 5 kilograms are the two most common amounts. It has been estimated that 1.5 kilograms of bronze would be enough to fashion 1,000 arrowheads; but since we have only the final year's records, we do not know if such amounts were normal or not, or how frequently allocations were made. The intended use of the bronze is not specified, but another tablet, Jn 829, records the collection of bronze from the major economic districts of the kingdom, to be made into javelin and spear points. Some of the smiths are designated as "Potnian," thus associated in some way with the goddess Potnia; nevertheless, they are listed and receive bronze from the palace just like the other smiths. Here again, the religious and secular spheres of influence overlap in an interesting way.

If bronzesmiths were dispersed around the kingdom they worked for, the Northeast Workshop, which as we saw was a late addition to the palace complex, housed artisans working at the center itself. Tablets and other artifacts found here together give a fairly good picture of the variety of tasks they performed. Leather-working was clearly one activity. Tablets in the Ub series (found in Room 99 of the workshop) count animal hides, their allocation to individuals, and the various uses to which they were put, including reins for horses. Some of the products were to be colored red. This makes sense of one otherwise puzzling discovery next door in Room 98: two deposits of apparent dye materials, one red and the other yellow. Another tablet, found in Room 99 of the workshop (An 1282), lists groups of men assigned to chariot manufacture: some are to work on chariots as a whole, others on halters, others on wheels. The mention of wheels is interesting, because another tablet found in the room next door lists chariot wheels "ready for service" (Sa 1313). Further, a long curved strip of bronze from Room 99 looks very much like the rim of a chariot wheel (Fig. 47), since a tablet from Knossos describes wheels as being "bound with bronze."

It makes sense that tablets found in the workshop should record the jobs done there, and the people who performed them. Yet texts kept in the archives complex also seem to refer to activities in the Northeast Workshop; the reason for their storage in a different place will become clear below. One such tablet is Vn 10:

Vn 10
.1   thus the woodcutters give
.2   to the chariot workshop saplings 50
.3   and axles 50
.4   so many saplings the Lousian fields [give]
.5   100 so many saplings 100

FIGURE 47
Curved strip of bronze (top) from Workshop Room 99 of the Palace of Nestor. (= C. W. Blegen and M. Rawson, The Palace of Nestor at Pylos in Western Messenia, *vol. 1:* The Buildings and Their Contents *[Princeton: Princeton University Press, 1966], fig. 316.) Archives of the Department of Classics, University of Cincinnati, with permission of Princeton University Press and the Department of Classics, University of Cincinnati.*

Here we learn about the delivery of wood that is to be used for chariots: the evidence from the Northeast Workshop itself for chariot-working makes it extremely likely that this is the "chariot workshop" referred to in the tablet. Finally, a set of thirty-four Sa tablets also found in the archives complex inventories chariot wheels. As we saw, one of this set was found in the workshop itself. Some of the wheels recorded in the archives complex are listed as "ready for service," and others as "not ready for service." The distribution gives a clue to how the activities of the workshop were monitored. Materials coming in were so noted in records stored in the regular archive. Chariot wheels coming in for repair were also listed there. Tablets relating to the intermediate stages of workshop activities, like personnel records and the allocation of supplies, were written and kept on the spot in Room 99. Each time a task was finished, as with the chariot wheels "ready for service," a tablet was written to record the fact. Ultimately, these records were transferred to the central archive; at the moment the palace was destroyed, several wheel tablets were lodged in the archives complex, but one still remained in the workshop—perhaps the last job those workers completed before the fire that destroyed the palace drove them out of business.

The case of the Northeast Workshop shows how the interplay between archaeological data and the words of the tablets far outstrips what can be learned from either source in isolation. Together, these two sources of evidence give considerable insight into the range of activities that went on at Pylos, and how they were monitored by scribes. They also refer to interactions between the palace and the large kingdom it controlled; this relationship is explored in Chapter 5.

FOCUS

The ANO ENGLIANOS HILLTOP
after the PALACE

After the destruction of the palace at Ano Englianos near the end of Late Helladic IIIB (ca. 1200 B.C.), a thin layer of dust settled over its remains, putting the once-great palatial center to rest. Carl Blegen, the original excavator, came to the conclusion that the hilltop was never again reoccupied. When excavated, the debris from the palace's collapsed walls and ceilings and the bulk of retrieved Mycenaean artifacts covered most areas of the site. Taken alone, these remains confirm Blegen's assessment. Yet, sometime in the Dark Age (ca. 1100–900 B.C.), people resumed domestic activity on the hilltop, leaving behind clear traces of their presence: pottery, tools, and remnants of their homes.

Distinctly indicative of post-Mycenaean activity was a dark black layer of soil that contained Geometric potsherds and iron utensils. This layer covered nearly 20 percent of the palace area (Fig. 48), and further traces of it were found spreading out northeast of the Northeast Workshop and on the eastern slopes of the hilltop just above the modern parking lot. In the agglomerated Rooms 83 to 86, Rooms 88, 89, 90, and Area 63, the black earth rested directly on Mycenaean floors. Here, the later occupants cleared away the debris and utilized the extant Mycenaean walls and floors in their own structures.

The most complete Dark Age construction survives in the broad plaster court separating the main palace building from the Southwestern Building (Fig. 49). Two small rooms, 89 and 90, were built with rubble walls that connected the partially standing southwestern facade of the palace with the northeastern wall of the Southwestern Building. These walls sit on a thin layer of earth resting directly on the Mycenaean plaster floor of Courts 63 and 88. Room 89, approximately 5 meters square, appears to have been the first construction: blocks taken from the palace were reused in the northwest, northeast, and southeast walls, with a stretch of palace facade forming the fourth side of the room. The entrance was likely in the north wall.

CHARLES G. GRIEBEL *and* MICHAEL C. NELSON

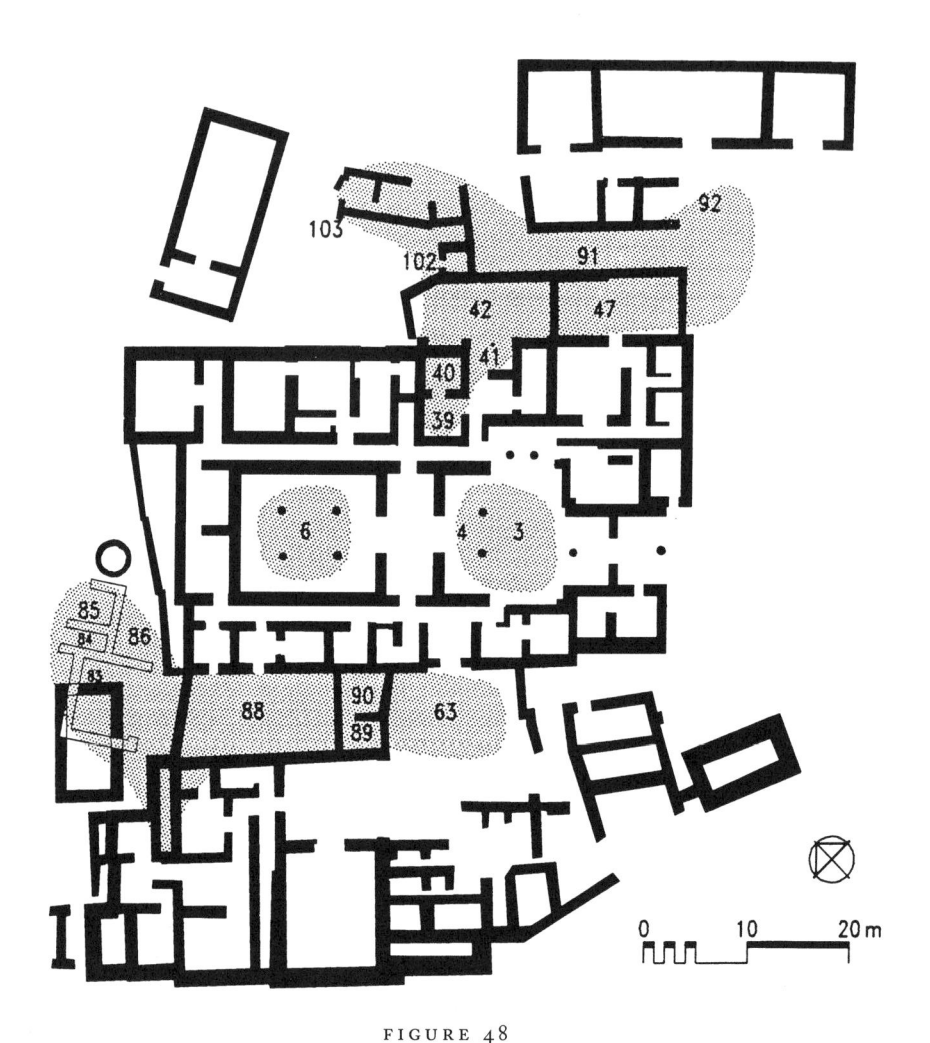

FIGURE 48
*Areas of Dark Age activity within the ruins of the Palace of Nestor (shaded).
M. C. Nelson. Minnesota Archaeological Researches in the Western Peloponnese Archive.
Courtesy of F. A. Cooper.*

A small construction built of upright flat slabs forming a small box or cupboard abuts the northwest wall of this room. Blegen found the box filled with ash and dubbed it a "firebox." Later, Room 90 doubled the size of the house by extending the northwest and southeast walls to the flank wall of the palace. Finally, in a third remodeling, the door that originally opened into Room 90 from Room 89 was blocked, the dividing wall demolished, a flagged floor of rough, flat stones laid in Room 90, and a new door opened at the southeast corner, as indicated by a threshold block.

CHARLES G. GRIEBEL *and* MICHAEL C. NELSON

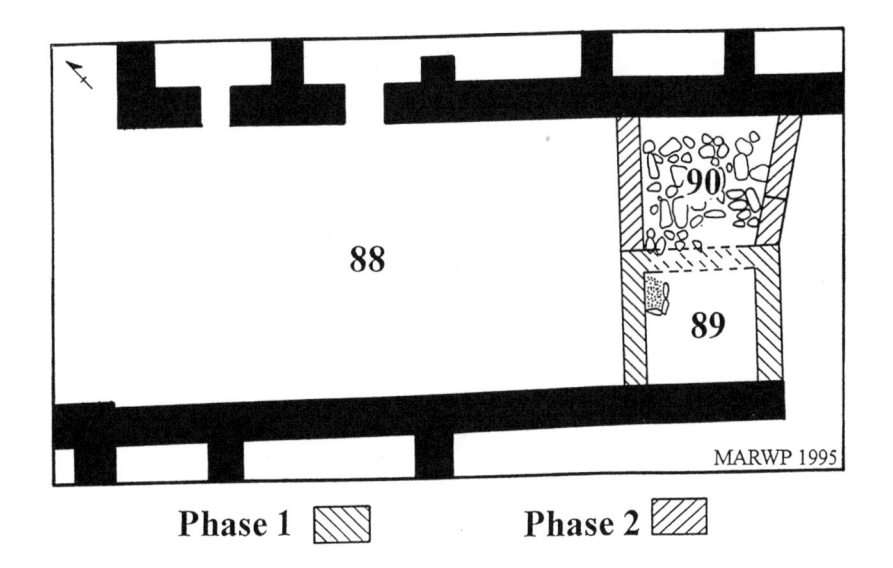

FIGURE 49
Court 88 and Dark Age structures 89 and 90 within the ruins of the Palace of Nestor. M. C. Nelson. Minnesota Archaeological Researches in the Western Peloponnese Archive. Courtesy of F. A. Cooper.

Blegen explained the darkness of the black soil as olive-oil residue, and thus he concluded that this small construction, along with the numerous Geometric potsherds and scraps of iron, comprised a small olive-oil press established on the hilltop at some point in the seventh century B.C. This seems unlikely, given that all the reconstructed Dark Age vessels recovered from this area are domestic wares; no remains of large jars for the storage or transport of olive oil are reported from this later period.

Other signs of Dark Age building activity appear in Area 103. This broad space, surrounded by the northeast palace wall, the Northeast Workshop, and the Wine Magazine, is cluttered with structures of various periods. A building of the palatial period described by Blegen as "barracks-like" is actually composed of different sets of walls with dates possibly beginning as early as the Middle Bronze Age. A section of these walls dates to the Dark Age and rests on a thin layer of earth similar to the walls of Rooms 89 and 90. However, their fragmentary condition prohibits a clear reconstruction.

In Rooms 39 through 42, 47, 91, 92, 102, 103, and portions of Rooms 3, 4, and 6, the black earth rested on top of the Mycenaean debris. Notable among the finds from the northeast area of the palace are four complete

Dark Age vessels, along with six pieces of iron implements, which include four possible cooking spits, one of which measures over 16 centimeters in length; a ring with a hook attached; and a flat piece of iron with a concave edge. These finds and the black soil indicate that inhabitants here settled directly above the Mycenaean remains, though little or no recognizable building activity survives.

Despite the heap of charred wreckage of the palace, the site's small, isolated hilltop and the protection it affords provided the setting for a Dark Age settlement similar to that found at nearby Nichoria. The ruins themselves became an ample source of building supplies, particularly the well-cut limestone blocks fallen from the palace's facades. These benefits did not go unnoticed, and sometime around the turn of the first millennium B.C., a small community of inhabitants utilized the hill and its Bronze Age palatial remains to build a new settlement.

FOCUS

The PERFUMED-OIL INDUSTRY

In many ancient cultures, before distillation, perfume was a greasy business. It consisted of animal fat or some ordinary oil, like olive or sesame oil, scented with various aromatic plants. Perfumed oil was a common offering to the gods, and was also used for medicinal and cosmetic purposes. It was particularly valued in a world without soap, as texts from Greece, Egypt, and Assyria, as well as the Bible, tell us. A recipe for anointing oil is given at Exodus 30:22–23: it contains liquid myrrh, fragrant cinnamon, fragrant cane, and cassia. The Mycenaeans made their perfumes with olive oil. The jars that contained this oil are distinctive in shape. They are sometimes called stirrup jars, because the handle resembles a stirrup, and they have an off-center spout with a narrow mouth, suitable for the small quantities used and easy to stopper with a lump of clay. Such jars come in two sizes. A large transport and storage size, with a capacity of 12–14 liters, is found in settlement contexts (Fig. 50). Much smaller stirrup jars, for personal amounts of perfume, turn up as offerings in tombs, but more important, they are by far the most common type of Mycenaean pottery found outside Greece (Fig. 51). Thus the manufacture and export of perfumed oil was big business for Mycenaean palaces, and there is a good deal of information about it in the Linear B tablets. These give us clues to the various types of perfumed oil and how they were made, as well as the uses to which they were put.

These records belong to several different stages in the process of manufacturing perfumed oil and allocating it for various purposes. Knossos gives us collection records of some aromatic herbs used in perfumery; Pylos does not, perhaps because the collections had not been made at the time of year when the palace burned down. Four Pylos tablets do, however, record the allocation of aromatics and other raw materials to perfumers. These manufacturing records were found, like 89 percent of the Pylos tablets, in the

CYNTHIA W. SHELMERDINE

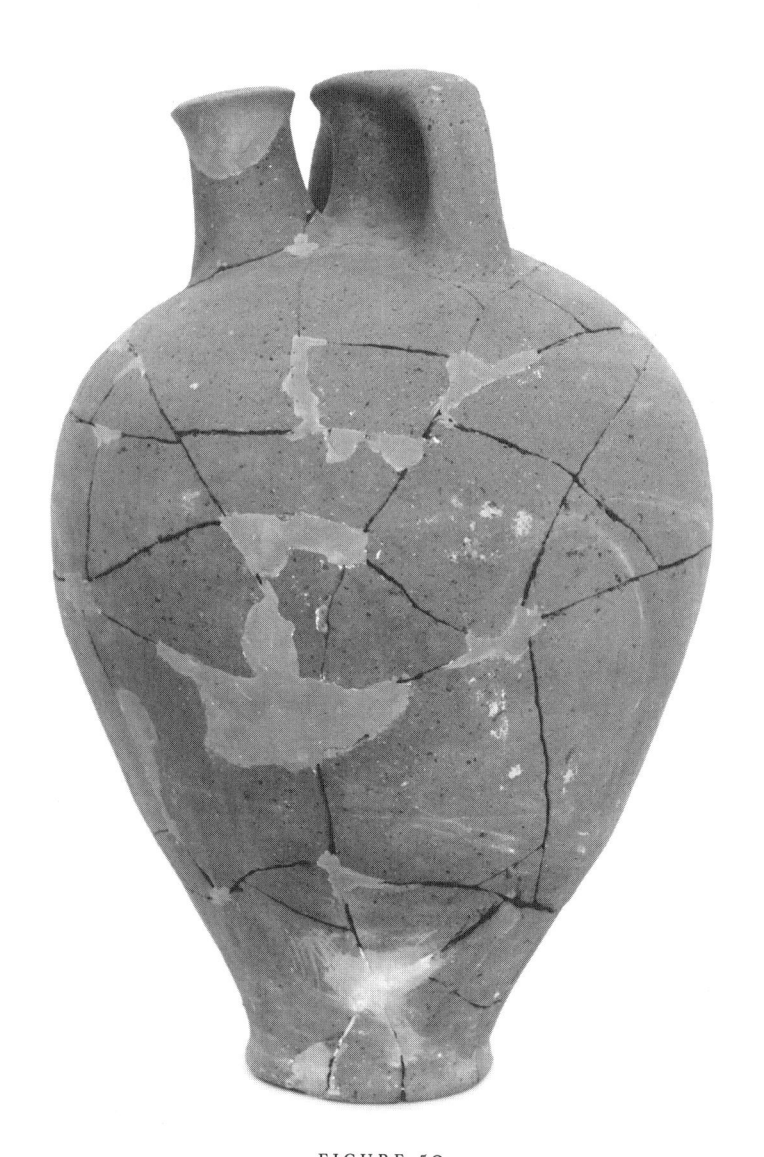

FIGURE 50
Storage-sized stirrup jar from the Palace of Nestor. (= C. W. Blegen and M. Rawson, The Palace of Nestor at Pylos in Western Messenia, *vol. 1:* The Buildings and Their Contents *[Princeton: Princeton University Press, 1966], fig. 389, no. 402.) Archives of the Department of Classics, University of Cincinnati, with permission of Princeton University Press and the Department of Classics, University of Cincinnati.*

FIGURE 51
Individual-sized stirrup jars from the Palace of Nestor. (= C. W. Blegen and M. Rawson, The Palace of Nestor at Pylos in Western Messenia, *vol. 1:* The Buildings and Their Contents *[Princeton: Princeton University Press, 1966], fig. 391, nos. 411, 412.) Archives of the Department of Classics, University of Cincinnati, with permission of Princeton University Press and the Department of Classics, University of Cincinnati.*

archives complex, Rooms 7–8, just to the left of the main entrance. Tablet Un 267 is the fullest and most explicit:

- .1 Thus Alxoitas gave
- .2 to Thyestes the unguent-boiler
- .3 aromatics for unguent
- .4 destined for boiling
- .5 coriander AROMATIC 576 liters
- .6 cyperus AROMATIC 576 liters *157* 16
- .7 FRUITS 240 liters WINE 576 liters HONEY 58 liters
- .8 WOOL 6 kilograms MUST 58 liters

Oil is notably absent from the list, as are the aromatics that will give the oil its final fragrance, such as roses and sage (see below).

The PERFUMED-OIL INDUSTRY

Perfume recipes preserved in the writings of first-century A.D. author Dioscorides give us a clue as to how each of the substances listed, at least those we can identify, might have been used in Mycenaean perfume-making. Since olive oil by nature is resistant to absorbing odors, classical perfumers pretreated it by boiling astringent herbs in it. The astringents were chopped or ground, then soaked in wine or water and heated in the oil. After they were strained out, the aromatics that would give the oil its final fragrance were steeped in it for several days; a fresh batch was added every twenty-four hours. Such recipes breathe life into the Mycenaean lists of ingredients. Coriander and cyperus are astringents, and Un 267 makes it clear that boiling will take place. Wool could be used for straining, and even honey was used by classical perfumers, to coat both their hands and the insides of the jars that would hold the oil during the steeping process.

Fr 1184, another tablet from the archives complex, documents the transfer of oil from one perfumer to another; the verb is part of the technical vocabulary of palace transactions, and indicates the delivery of oil into the palace (Fig. 52a):

.1   Kokalos delivered so much olive oil
.2   to Eumedes OIL 518 liters
.3   from/with Ipsewas oil jars 38

FIGURE 52
Linear B tablets:
a. Pylos Fr 1184. Program in Aegean Scripts and Prehistory, University of Texas at Austin Archive. Courtesy of T. G. Palaima, with permission from the University of Cincinnati and E. L. Bennett Jr.

CYNTHIA W. SHELMERDINE

b. Knossos K 778. Program in Aegean Scripts and Prehistory, University of Texas at Austin Archive. Courtesy of T. G. Palaima, with permission of J.-P. Olivier.
c. Knossos K 700. Program in Aegean Scripts and Prehistory, University of Texas at Austin Archive. Courtesy of T. G. Palaima, with permission of J.-P. Olivier.

These oil jars are the stirrup jars we know from archaeological finds; a picture of one, with the distinctive off-center spout, appears as an ideogram on two Knossos tablets, once accompanied by the word for "oil jars" (*ka-ra-re-we*) and once by its abbreviation *ka* (Figs. 52b, 52c):

KN K 778
   .1]oil jars **210*^{VAS} 180

KN K 700
   .1] 300 **210*^{VAS}+*KA* 900[
   .2] 300 **210*^{VAS}+*KA* 900 ?[

The jars on PY Fr 1184 were likely intended to hold the oil recorded there. If so, at 518 liters to thirty-eight jars, each jar would contain 13.6 liters of oil. This is within the range of the large-size oil-storage jars that have actually been excavated; several from Mycenae have been measured at a capacity of 12 to 14 liters of oil.

Unlike the manufacturing tablets, fifty-plus records of finished products come not from the archives complex but from storerooms in other parts of the palace. These tablets of the Fr series describe treated oil both by variants of the oil ideogram and by adjectives that specify oil treated with rose, sage, or henna. The latter probably refers to a dye, since henna is not native to Greece: the dried henna leaves used for dyeing could readily be imported from Egypt, but the quantities of fresh flowers (which smell like lilacs) necessary to scent the oil could not—they would spoil before they could be used. Some Classical perfumes were colored red, and this is true of some Mycenaean perfumes also, at both Pylos and Knossos. The majority of the Fr tablets (32) were found in Room 23 (Fig. 53), one of two oil storerooms behind the megaron (Room 6). Large storage jars set into benches along the walls contained oil, as is clear from the greasy residue found in them and from the intensity of the destruction fire in this area. A wad of clay also preserved by the fire shows that tablets were actually fashioned and written here.

Other perfume tablets come from Room 32 and from a storeroom upstairs, above Room 38. Some are inventory records; others list allocations. Many of these are for religious purposes; for example, oil is sent to the goddess Potnia "as an ointment for robes." However, the king also receives allocations, as do some unspecified servants or attendants. Several different scribes wrote the tablets concerned; as a rule, each worked in a certain room, with a certain kind of oil, and each laid out information in a differ-

FIGURE 53
Storerooms 23–24 behind the megaron of the Palace of Nestor. (= C. W. Blegen and M. Rawson, The Palace of Nestor at Pylos in Western Messenia, *vol. 1:* The Buildings and Their Contents *[Princeton: Princeton University Press, 1966], fig. 22.) Archives of the Department of Classics, University of Cincinnati, with permission of Princeton University Press and the Department of Classics, University of Cincinnati.*

ent way. This is clear from a comparison of tablets by three different scribes (Fig. 54):

Hand 2:
PY Fr 1226
.1   to the Lousian field for the gods, sage-scented OIL
        4.8 liters
.2   [line empty]

PY Fr 1205
to the attendants, for anointing OIL 25.6 liters

The PERFUMED-OIL INDUSTRY

Stylus 1217, Class ii:
PY Fr 1225
.1 olive oil to *hupoio* Potnia
.2 as ointment for robes OIL 9.6 liters

Stylus 1203, Class ii:
PY Fr 1201
in all so much RED OIL 406.4+ liters

PY Fr 1203
cyperus-scented rose-scented RED OIL 44.8 liters

Hand 2 puts the destination of the oil first, and ends with an adjective describing the oil. The scribe of Stylus 1217 begins with the word "oil," and uses the expression "as ointment" instead of "for anointing." The tablets by

FIGURE 54
Linear B tablets:
a. Pylos Fr 1226. Program in Aegean Scripts and Prehistory, University of Texas at Austin Archive. Courtesy of T. G. Palaima, with permission from the University of Cincinnati and E. L. Bennett Jr.
b. Pylos Fr 1225. Program in Aegean Scripts and Prehistory, University of Texas at Austin Archive. Courtesy of T. G. Palaima, with permission from the University of Cincinnati and E. L. Bennett Jr.

CYNTHIA W. SHELMERDINE

the scribe of Stylus 1203 are inventories, not allocations, so they contain only descriptions of the oil being counted. Thus scribes in this administrative department had very specific responsibilities, and each could be held readily accountable for the oil he reported on. The only exception is Hand 2, whose tablets appear in all the rooms concerned, and who seems from the range of his contributions to have been the head of this administrative department. (He also wrote the transaction tablet Fr 1184.)

The mention of oil with textiles on Fr 1225 is especially interesting. Homer often refers to cloth as "shining" or "fragrant," and the young men's chitons on Achilles' shield in *Iliad* 18 are "shining with olive oil." Such references were thus once thought to be poetic exaggeration, but treating wool and especially linen with oil does soften the fabric and make it shine. The practice is attested in modern times, and this Pylos tablet shows that the Mycenaeans knew it as well. In the epics, scented clothing belongs chiefly to the divine sphere, and it is the gods who use perfumed oil as a body ointment. In the Mycenaean period, perfume is much more common in the human world. Several real Bronze Age practices are transferred from the human to the divine sphere in the Homeric epics, and this is one example. Most important for our appreciation of Mycenaean kingdoms, though, is the real economic importance of scented oil in the Late Bronze Age. The 1,800 oil jars counted on tablet K 700 from Knossos (see above) represent big business, as do the hundreds of stirrup jars found outside Greece—silent witnesses to the commercial success of the Mycenaeans.

FIGURE 55
Mt. Aigaleon from the southwest, near the Museum of Hora, with Volimidia in the foreground. PRAP Archive. R. J. Robertson.

CHAPTER 5

The LINEAR B ARCHIVES *and the* KINGDOM *of* NESTOR

At the beginning of this book, we read how a Roman land surveyor in A.D. 78 verified the boundaries between Laconia and Messenia. That boundary was a bone of vigorous contention because of the centuries of domination Messenia had experienced at the hands of its neighbor to the east, Sparta, even though at the time, both areas were subject to a much larger authority—Rome. The contested boundary on Taygetus is one example of how political territories change through time, both in size and in shape, making it difficult to define regions for archaeological study that are coextensive with ancient political boundaries in all periods. In the Bronze Age, some 1,300 years before Monomitos, when political territories in Greece were often larger than in later periods, there was a similar boundary to that defined by Monomitos *within* Messenia, along the Aigaleon Ridge that runs from northwest to southeast, from near Cyparissia to Mt. Lykodimos, crossing the northeastern corner of PRAP's survey area. As far as we know, this boundary was not physically marked on the ground, but it is embodied in a few of the earliest texts written by Messenians, the Linear B documents found at the Palace of Nestor. These texts and others, as we shall see, allow us to determine the size and shape of the territory controlled by the palace. They allow us to take the palace's activities outside the immediate area of the palace structures themselves into its territory, the territory on which it depended for its continued existence. In combination with the archaeological remains, they also allow us to see how the site of Pylos expanded its power and influence. Originally the core of a small political unit, its control extended first to the Aigaleon Ridge, then to the very foothills of Taygetus, forming a Bronze Age political unit somewhat similar in shape to that demarcated by Monomitos over a thousand years later.

The subject of this chapter is, therefore, the palace's territory. How large an area did it control? How was its control structured? How did the palace

JOHN BENNET

expand its interests over this large area? What activities did it monitor in this area? Yet, this goal leaves us with the problem of how we are to extend our scope beyond the known center and equate other place names with specific sites. It is clearly impossible to achieve total success in such an enterprise—matching every place name with known archaeological remains—since we would have to identify on the ground all the ancient settlement sites within the likely region of the Pylos polity, and archaeological sites are rarely preserved to these levels (see Focus in this chapter). If we take a regional rather than a site-by-site perspective, however, we can begin to discern patterns that allow some general comparisons from the textual data to the archaeological, and to draw interesting conclusions about the structure of the territory and the process by which it was acquired. We begin our exploration with the Linear B documentary evidence from Pylos itself.

Un 2
   .1 At Sphagianes, on the occasion of the king's "initiation,"
   .2 the man in charge of the establishment? released:
   .3 1,575 liters of barley; 14.5 liters of cyperus; 8 liters of "O" [another type of cyperus?]
   .4 115 liters of flour; 211 liters of olives; 19 liters of *132; 10 liters of honey
   .5 96 liters of figs; 1 ox; 26 rams; 6 ewes; 2 he-goats; 2 she-goats
   .6 1 fattened pig; 6 sows; 586 liters of wine; 2 pieces of *146 cloth

This document was compiled to record the supplies necessary for a festival held at Sphagianes, a cult place near the palace. The most likely interpretation of the occasion is the "initiation" of the king (called the *wanax* in Mycenaean Greek), perhaps actually the coronation of the new ruler. It is in connection with such an event that scenes like those depicted on the walls of the central megaron of the palace might have occurred and the thousands of drinking vessels kept in storerooms next door might have been used (see Chapter 4).

Where did these supplies come from? By what mechanism were they collected? What ideological basis lay behind their collection and use? The short answer is that they came to the palace from the territory it controlled in its latest phase by means of a complex system of taxation and economic management that functioned not just to channel commodities to the palace center, but also—through rituals such as that described—to integrate the population within the palace's territory.

Fortunately, we are able to observe this procurement of commodities more clearly from the Linear B documents preserved in the final destruction of the palace at Pylos than from the other major Linear B archive of the Bronze Age Aegean at Knossos on Crete. We can also develop from these same documents an understanding in some detail of the geographical structure of the Pylian polity and the mechanisms of control adopted.

In the first place, we know the name of the Bronze Age center on the Englianos Ridge. It was called Pylos, and this name appears fairly frequently—as *pu-ro*—on the Linear B documents found in the palace. In Classical times, the name was applied to Coryphasion (and—more recently still—to Navarino), but the ancient geographer Strabo, writing in the early first century A.D., was aware of a tradition that another site had borne the name before the Classical period: "The ancient Messenian Pylos was a city under Aigaleon, and, when this city was destroyed, some of its inhabitants settled on Coryphasion [the site of the Classical city-state: see Chapter 6]" (Strabo 8.4.2). The same author also quotes a hexameter proverb about the abundance of places named Pylos in the Peloponnese: "There is a Pylos before Pylos; and there is yet another Pylos" (Strabo 8.3.7). This tradition, together with the references to Pylos in the Linear B texts, allows us to give a name to the center of the kingdom, with its palatial center on the Englianos Ridge. But can we say more about the area controlled from that center, and about how those controlling that territory conceptualized it as a geographical unit?

The first point that has struck scholars is that the Pylian administrators maintained in their records an explicitly geographical distinction between two sectors in the polity. These were called "This-side-of-Aigolaion" and "Beyond-Aigolaion," and Linear B scholars customarily refer to these as the Hither and Further provinces.

Ng 319
.1   This-side-of-Aigolaion: 1,239 units of flax
.2   and 457 units not provided

Ng 332
.1   Beyond-Aigolaion: [at least] 200 units of flax
.2   and [?] units not provided

These two texts exemplify the distinction, totaling contributions of flax by the two major sectors. (It is unfortunate that the figure for the Further Province is not preserved, since it would be interesting to compare it with that preserved for the Hither Province.) The rationale for this division is similar to the later Roman distinction between the north Italian provinces of *Gallia Cis-* and *Trans-alpina*, "Gaul this-side-of-the-Alps" and "Gaul across-the-Alps." This distinction implies a "mental map" of the polity, separated into two zones by a distinct topographic feature, as distinct from the "itinerary" form of organization of place names in lists, a type familiar from other contexts in the later ancient world, and used elsewhere in the Pylos documents.

The feature to which "this-side-of" and "beyond" refer seems almost certainly to have been the mountain range known in Strabo's day—and even today in learned circles—as Aigaleon. Although the equation is not perfect, it has been widely accepted and makes a great deal of sense, since the range is the most prominent feature of the eastern horizon from almost any spot within the vicinity of Bronze Age Pylos (Fig. 56). Interestingly, the chain is not so distinctive further south, where it shades into Mts. Maglavas and Lykodimos, with low-lying topography in between (Fig. 57). To the north, on the other hand, the northern end of the Aigaleon chain towers over modern Cyparissia and reaches almost to the coast, leaving virtually no room for a Hither Province at all (Fig. 58). The boundary preserved in the texts is therefore highly distinctive on the ground and is a feature most notable from the vicinity of Pylos itself.

The geographical structuring within the documents is not confined to this major bipartite division. A series of texts contains lists of place names in fixed order. One of these—On 300—separates the list into two paragraphs, the second headed *pe-ra-a-ko-ra-i-jo* ("Beyond-Aigolaion," the Further Province), assigning the two groups of place names to their respective sectors of the polity. The longest fixed list (Jn 829) contains sixteen place names (Fig. 59). Each contributes bronze, apparently for the manufacture of arrow tips and spearheads, in the names of officials, the *ko-re-te* and *po-ro-ko-re-te*, perhaps "mayor" and "vice-mayor." The first nine place names—all those within the Hither Province—turn up in identical order on two additional complete texts: Cn 608, where the inhabitants of each locality will fatten a small number of pigs (presumably for a public festival, such as that on Un 2 above), and Vn 20, which records distributions *from* the palace of considerable quantities of wine—the lowest assignment is close to 2,000 liters (Fig. 60 [showing all three texts]). What is more, most of these names appear on a series of single-entry texts (the Ma series)—one for each place name. These documents record tax assessments (and some returns, marked *a-pu-do-si*) on six commodities, always in a fixed proportion to each other, for the nine Hither Province place names and for eight others, six of which match place names attested on Jn 829. It seems that, for taxation purposes, one of the districts attested on Jn 829—

JOHN BENNET

FIGURE 56
Aigaleon range (in distance) from the Cave of Nestor. The range slopes down toward Mts. Maglavas and Lykodimos (out of the picture to the right). PRAP Archive. J. L. Davis.

FIGURE 57
Mts. Maglavas and Lykodimos from the north. PRAP Archive. J. Bennet.

FIGURE 58
North end of the Aigaleon chain at modern Cyparissia. The medieval kastro *(fort) is perched on a spur (center) jutting out from the ridge. PRAP Archive. J. L. Davis.*

e-re-i—is split into two in the Ma series. The commodities required by the Ma series are not all identified, but seem to include hides, a basic type of cloth, and perhaps honey (the latter two are mentioned on Un 2).

These documents not only offer a glimpse into geographical structure, but also imply that these place names had important status within the Pylian administration, perhaps as places where taxed commodities would be assembled before transshipment to the center. Further confirmation of their status is suggested by the fact they had named officials (Jn 829; On 300) or were assigned considerable supplies of wine (Vn 20). However, their subordination to the palace is made clear by the fact that Pylos itself does not turn up in these lists, although it does appear on other documents. It is not difficult to see why a center would not figure in lists of subordinate places (for the most part) making contributions. It is logical to assume that those places in the lists are the chief subordinate settlements of the polity and, further, that the fixed order of their grouping has some sort of rationale.

There are a number of possibilities for that rationale. In theory, the place names could be listed in rank order by the quantities of commodities assigned to them or required from them. This is clearly not the case, because the quantities seem to vary randomly (e.g., those on Cn 608 run [in order] 3—3—6—2—2—2—3—2—2 [see Table 1]). We can also exclude the possibility that the places might have been ordered in a pseudo-alphabetical order, just like our A, B, C, etc. That this is not the case can be demonstrated by the fact that an initial /a-/ sign occurs in the fifth and sixth positions on Jn 829, and then again in the thirteenth (see Fig. 59). Similarly, initial /e-/ occurs twice, in the fourteenth and sixteenth positions, with another initial sign in-between. A further peculiarity of the lists cannot be explained in this way. The place name *ro-u-so* occurs on Jn 829, but in the same position on Cn 608 and Vn 20, we have *e-ra-to*. (The explanation is likely to be that they were two different names for the same area.) If the rationale were pseudo-alphabetic, then the order ought to have changed depending on which name was used.

This leaves us with a third possibility: that the organizing principle is geographical and in some way reflects a geographical structure within the polity. Two pieces of evidence support this conclusion. First, the fourth place name (*pa-ki-ja-ne*) has close links in other documents—such as Un 2 at the beginning of the chapter—with the center at Pylos. This suggests that Pylos lay roughly in the middle of the Hither Province group, and that the lists do not begin (or end) with the center and follow an unpredictable route through the polity. Second, there is another group of documents (the so-called *o-ka* tablets, after a term that occurs frequently on them) that records detachments (*o-ka*) of personnel assigned to coastguard duties. Because these texts deal with groups detailed to watch the coast, the places they list ought to be on or near the coast. In a few cases, the places to which coast guards are assigned also appear as place names on the fixed-order lists. In particular, the last tablet in the *o-ka* series (An 661) lists in close proximity *ka-ra-do-ro* (the eighth Hither Province place name) and *ti-mi-to-a-ke-e* (the first Further Province name), suggesting that the two provinces had a contiguous coastline, and that the Further Province's was quite short.

It seems likely, therefore, that the order embodied in the lists does reflect a geographical structure. The most plausible reconstruction would see the Hither Province list running along the western coast of Messenia, from north of Cyparissia, around the Akritas Peninsula, then up the western shore of the Messenian Gulf, to the area of Nichoria (Fig. 61). The spatial arrangement of the Further Province place names is more problematic, but it seems that this province would begin in the southwestern section of the Messenian Valley, and its relatively short coastline would have comprised the north coast of the Messenian Gulf. The Further Province place names would fall mostly inland, within the Messenian Valley system, rather than running along the linear feature of a coastline. The fact that the ordering of

Official Pylos Serial Number — **Jn 829**

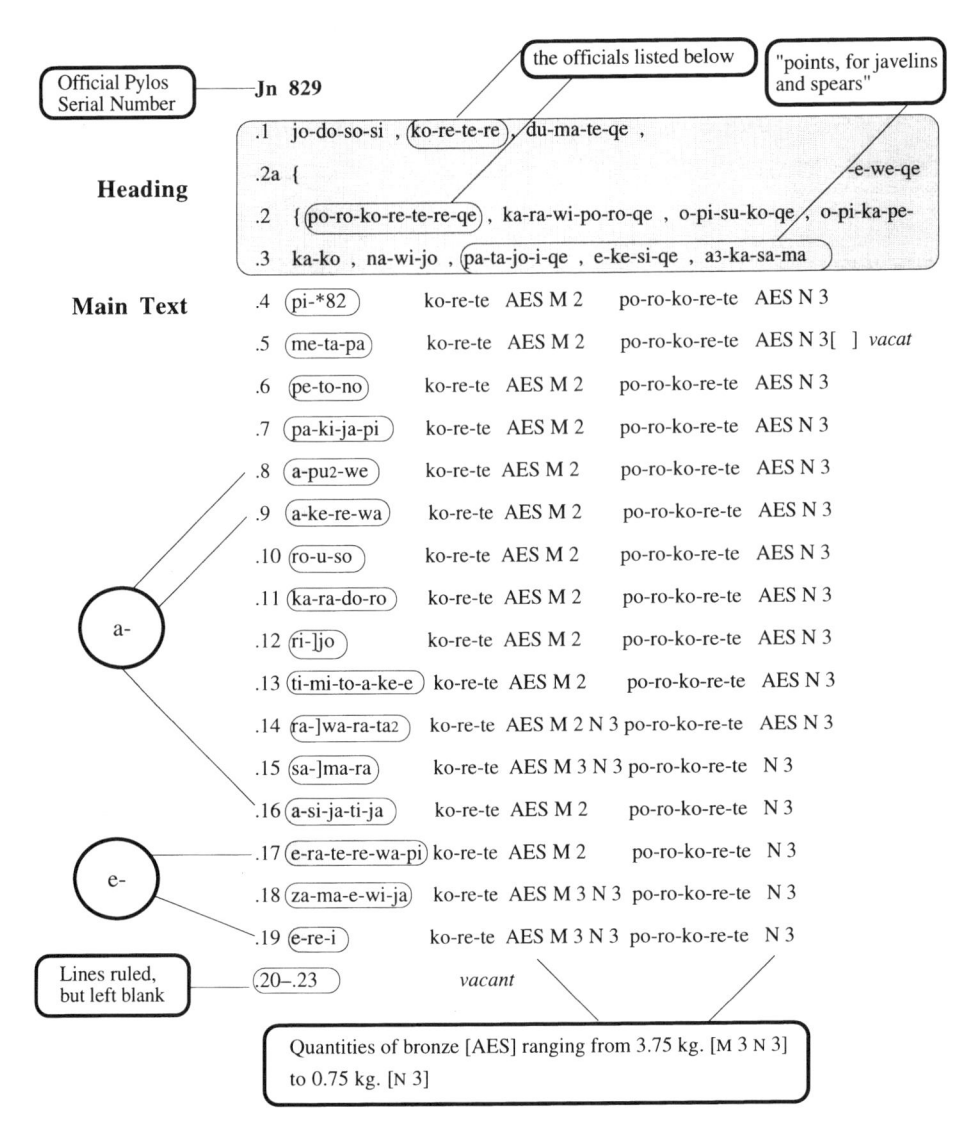

"the officials listed below" "points, for javelins and spears"

Heading

.1 jo-do-so-si , (ko-re-te-re) , du-ma-te-qe ,
.2a {   -e-we-qe
.2 { (po-ro-ko-re-te-re-qe) , ka-ra-wi-po-ro-qe , o-pi-su-ko-qe , o-pi-ka-pe-
.3 ka-ko , na-wi-jo , (pa-ta-jo-i-qe) , e-ke-si-qe , a3-ka-sa-ma

Main Text

.4 (pi-*82)   ko-re-te AES M 2   po-ro-ko-re-te AES N 3
.5 (me-ta-pa)   ko-re-te AES M 2   po-ro-ko-re-te AES N 3[ ] vacat
.6 (pe-to-no)   ko-re-te AES M 2   po-ro-ko-re-te AES N 3
.7 (pa-ki-ja-pi)   ko-re-te AES M 2   po-ro-ko-re-te AES N 3
.8 (a-pu2-we)   ko-re-te AES M 2   po-ro-ko-re-te AES N 3
.9 (a-ke-re-wa)   ko-re-te AES M 2   po-ro-ko-re-te AES N 3
.10 (ro-u-so)   ko-re-te AES M 2   po-ro-ko-re-te AES N 3
.11 (ka-ra-do-ro)   ko-re-te AES M 2   po-ro-ko-re-te AES N 3
.12 (ri-]jo)   ko-re-te AES M 2   po-ro-ko-re-te AES N 3
.13 (ti-mi-to-a-ke-e) ko-re-te AES M 2   po-ro-ko-re-te AES N 3
.14 (ra-]wa-ra-ta2)   ko-re-te AES M 2 N 3 po-ro-ko-re-te AES N 3
.15 (sa-]ma-ra)   ko-re-te AES M 3 N 3 po-ro-ko-re-te N 3
.16 (a-si-ja-ti-ja)   ko-re-te AES M 2   po-ro-ko-re-te N 3
.17 (e-ra-te-re-wa-pi) ko-re-te AES M 2   po-ro-ko-re-te N 3
.18 (za-ma-e-wi-ja)   ko-re-te AES M 3 N 3 po-ro-ko-re-te N 3
.19 (e-re-i)   ko-re-te AES M 3 N 3 po-ro-ko-re-te N 3

a-
e-

Lines ruled, but left blank — (.20–.23)   vacant

Quantities of bronze [AES] ranging from 3.75 kg. [M 3 N 3] to 0.75 kg. [N 3]

FIGURE 59
Explanatory diagram, showing structure and content of Linear B tablet Jn 829.
J. Bennet.

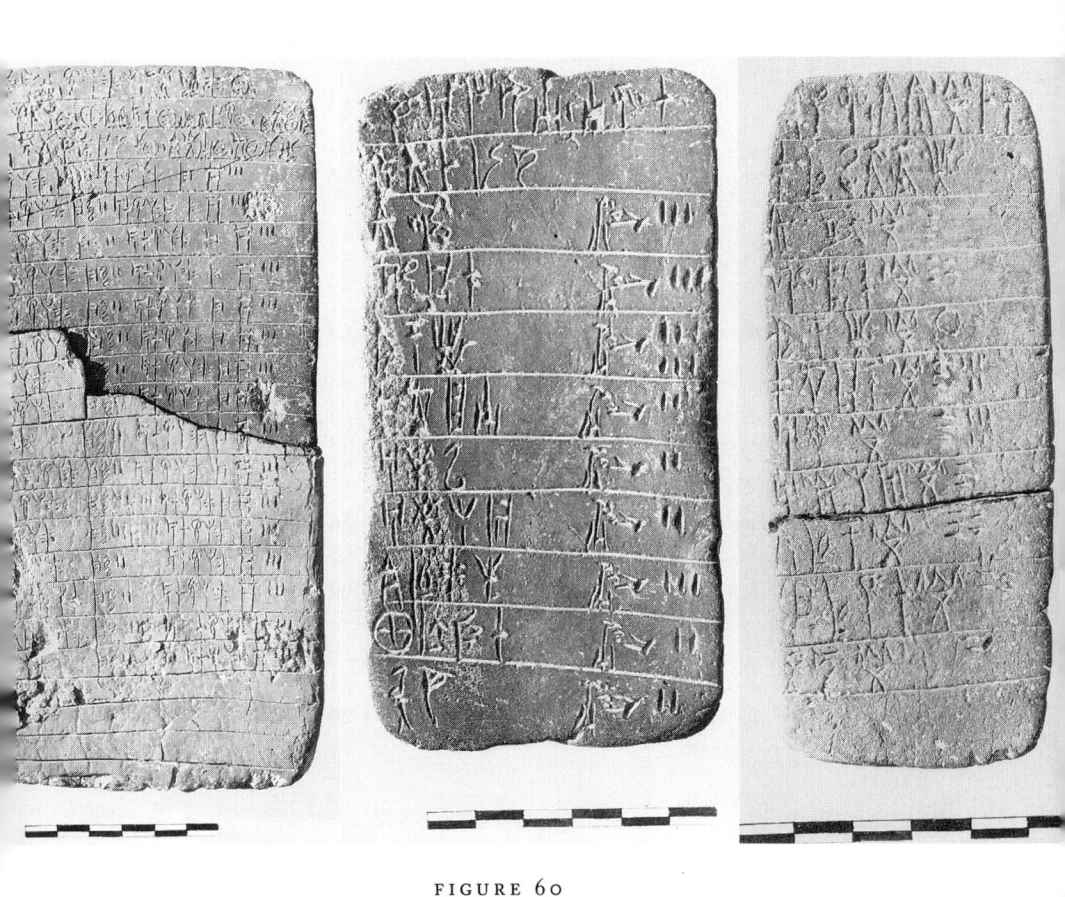

FIGURE 60
The major Linear B texts relevant to the Hither Province lists of place names: Jn 829, Cn 608, and Vn 20. Archives of the Department of Classics, University of Cincinnati. With permission of E. L. Bennett Jr. and the Department of Classics, University of Cincinnati.

Further Province place names is less stable than those of the Hither Province probably reflects this less clear geographical structure.

The Linear B texts can be made to yield still more information about the structure of the Pylian polity. The Hither Province list can be broken down—merely by subdivision, not by changing the list order—into four groups of place names, which contribute or receive approximately equal amounts of various commodities (see Table 1). This pattern suggests that there may have been a grouping of these places for fiscal purposes. The same is true of the Further Province place names: they can be grouped—only by their assessments or contributions in the Ma series, since they do not appear on Cn 608 or Vn 20—into four units that, again, seem to have a

TABLE I

FISCAL GROUPINGS AMONG MAJOR PYLIAN CENTERS

GROUP	PLACE NAME	Cn 608	Vn 20	Ma SERIES	LOCATION?
	Hither Province				
1	pi-*82	3	50	28	[N]
	me-ta-pa	3 = 6	50 = 100	28 = 56	
2	pe-to-no	6 = 6	100 = 100	63 = 63	[C]
3	pa-ki-ja-ne	2	35	22	
	a-pu$_2$-we	2 = 6	35 = 100	23 = 68	[SW]
	a-ke-re-wa	2	30	23	
4	ro-u-so / e-ra-to	3	50	17	
	ka-ra-do-ro	2 = 7	40 = 110	18 = 52	[SE]
	ri-jo	2	20	17	
				Total = 239	
	Further Province				
I	ti-mi-to-a-ke-e	—	—	24	
	sa-ma-ra	—	—	24 = 72	[SW]
	a-si-ja-ti-ja	—	—	24	
II	ra-u-ra-ti-ja	—	—	70 = 70	[SE]
III	e-ra-te-re-we	—	—	46	
	a-te-re-wi-ja	—	—	23 = 69	[NW]
IV	za-ma-e-wi-ja	—	—	28	
	e-sa-re-wi-ja	—	—	42 = 70	[NE]
				Total = 281	

broadly geographical rationale. However, unlike those of the Hither Province, the place names that belong to the same fiscal units in the Further Province are not listed together on Jn 829.

We can make the deduction, then, that the Further Province was organized in a very similar fashion to the Hither Province for the purposes of these taxation documents. In each province, there were four fiscal units, one consisting of a single place name. Since this one place could meet the full tax burden alone, its territory must have been larger than that of other

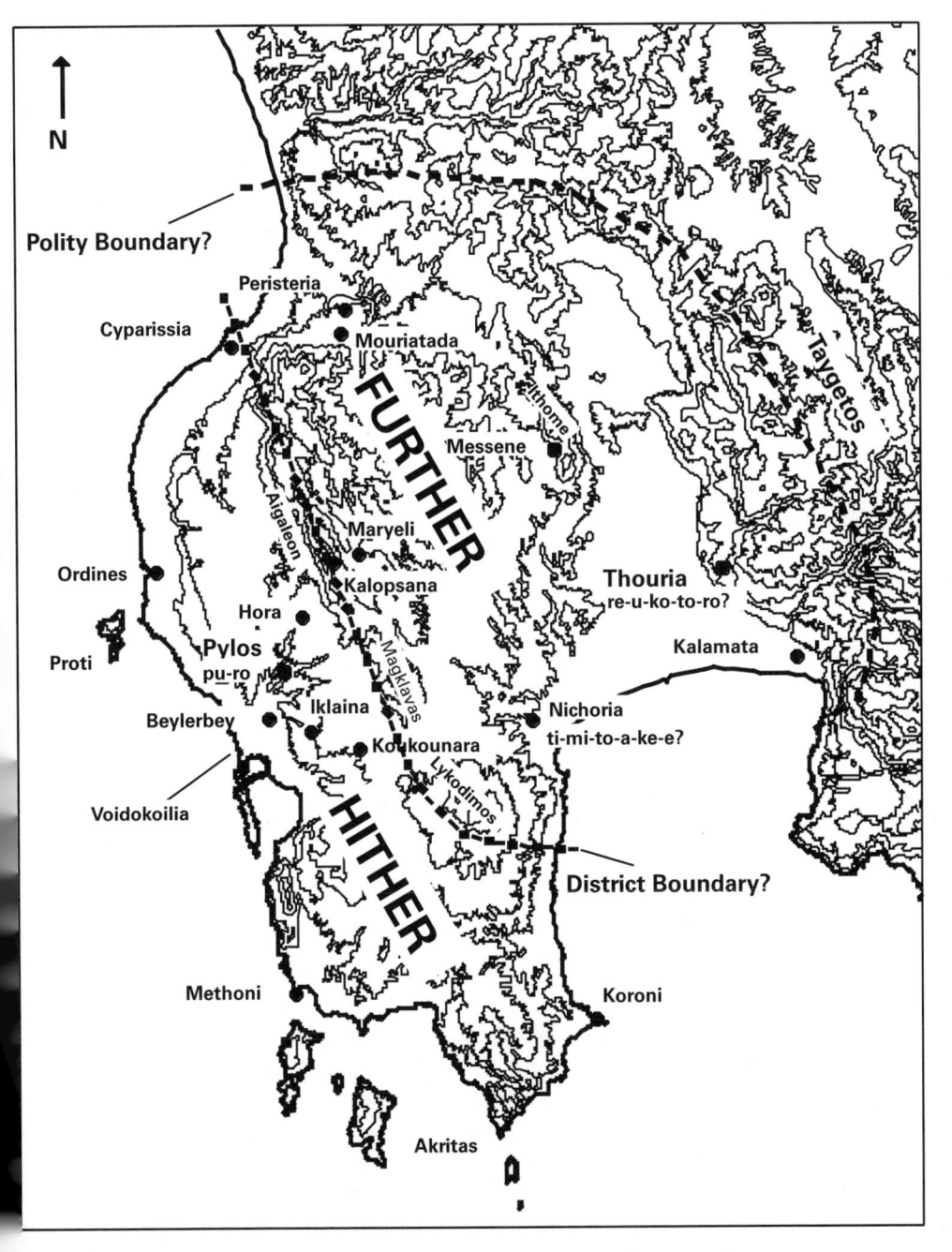

FIGURE 61
The Mycenaean geography of Messenia. PRAP Archive. J. Bennet.

places in the province. In addition, the four units of the Further Province were assessed a 17 percent greater total than those in the Hither Province, as the total assessments in the Ma series indicate (see Table 1).

These taxation documents also provide the best clue to the overall size of the polity controlled from the palace. Since the tax burden on the Further Province is only slightly larger than that imposed on the Hither, and the total number of subordinate centers roughly equal (nine in the Hither Province, as opposed to seven or eight in the Further), it is very likely that their overall sizes were similar. If we are correct in defining the physical boundary of the Aigaleon Ridge as the boundary between the two regions (both from its physical appearance and from its name), then it must have divided the polity roughly in two. The above reconstruction fits with such a division, and renders most implausible any suggestion that Pylos's power extended further east, beyond Taygetus, or up into Arcadia to the northeast. Some independent confirmation of this is offered by the fact that it is no more than a day's walk from Englianos to Cyparissia in the north or Methoni in the south, or to Nichoria, apparently on the western edge of the Further Province.

Is there any other way in which the Further Province resembled the Hither? A group of documents—the Aa and Ad series—lists twenty-eight female work groups at the center, Pylos (comprising a preserved total of 377 women), and six (67 women) at another place, *re-u-ko-to-ro*, or Leuktron. The purpose of the texts seems to have been to assess the quantities of rations the palace needed to provide for these dependent workers. One group of texts, Aa 60–98, by one scribal hand, including the workforce at Leuktron, was found together in the archives room with the label that marked the basket in which they were filed (Wa 114), on which is written *pe-ra-a₃-ko-ra-i-jo*, demonstrating that the texts deal with the Further Province. The second group, Aa 240–1182, by another hand, deals with the Hither Province, including the more substantial workforce at Pylos. The presence of this workforce at Leuktron, plus Leuktron's absence from Further Province lists, has led scholars to suppose that Leuktron in some way holds a parallel position in the Further Province to Pylos in the Hither: namely, that it in some way functions as the capital of the Further Province.

The Linear B texts allow us to reconstruct the structure of the Pylian polity in the following manner. There was one center for the whole polity at Pylos: Linear B *pu-ro*, the palace site at Ano Englianos. The polity was divided geographically into two parts, distinguished as "This-side-of-" and "Beyond-" Aigolaion (modern Aigaleon). The Hither Province had nine places functioning as subcenters of some sort, while the Further Province had seven, or possibly eight (if all the places with entries on the Ma tablets are counted). To some extent, the two sectors mirror one another: both have four basic subdivisions for fiscal purposes, one very large; and that "Beyond-Aigolaion" appears to have had its own parallel capital—presumably subordinate ultimately to Pylos itself—at a place called Leuktron.

Such a reconstruction, although it takes into account in a general sense the topography of Messenia, does not allow us to look at any particular archaeological sites and compare this text-based picture with the material world. In order to be able to do so, we must be able to identify the specific locations of at least some of the Linear B place names. Pinning down the location and nature of the center itself is not a problem; it lies at the palace site on the Englianos Ridge, just to the southwest of the modern town of Hora, and we have seen already in Chapter 4 what activities we can reconstruct for it, and, in Chapter 3, what was going on in the immediate vicinity. To go beyond the center itself, however, one needs to take a larger view, applying regional survey data to the question by combining the general geographical information from the Linear B tablets relating to the major place names within the Pylos polity with regional settlement data for the whole of Messenia. Using estimates of the sizes of Late Helladic IIIB settlement sites, it is possible to show that the eighteen largest sites documented in the region (including the palace itself) lie generally where we would expect them. Ten—the nine of the fixed lists, plus Pylos itself—lie west of the Aigaleon range, in the likely territory of the Hither Province. The other eight—the seven of the fixed lists, plus Leuktron—lie to the east, in the likely territory of the Further Province. It is remarkable that eighteen sites—approximately the correct number for what we must assume to be the most significant sites within the polity—stand out in the archaeological data.

The picture suggests that there may have been a four-tier settlement hierarchy, a situation that fits well with the textual information:

(1) the two "capitals": Pylos and Leuktron;
(2) a small number of large sites, the sixteen or seventeen major sites in the fixed lists and the Ma tablets (sites such as Gargaliani *Ordines*, Hora *Volimidia*, Koryfasion *Beylerbey*, Koukounara, Iklaina *Traganes*, or Rizomylo *Nichoria*);
(3) an intermediate tier of medium-sized sites (2 hectares or smaller), the "bottom end" of the site-size hierarchy defined by the University of Minnesota Messenia Expedition (see Chapter 2, and Focus in this chapter), perhaps reflecting the forty places mentioned in the tablets that function in three or more areas of the overall palatial economy; and

(4) a large number of small sites, mostly occurring in the documents in only one area of the palatial economy, many of them perhaps not detected by the extensive techniques employed by the University of Minnesota Messenia Expedition.

We can be more specific in a few other cases. First, the division of the Further Province place names into four groups in the Messenian Valley suggests that the groups may have been divided into four sectors in the southwest, southeast, northwest, and northeast. By links within documents, we can propose that *ti-mi-to-a-ke-e* lay in the southwest, closest to the Hither Province, and it can convincingly be identified with the archaeological site of Rizomylos *Nichoria* (see Focus in this chapter). The district of *ra-u-ra-ti-ja*, then, probably lay in the southeast, a region in which there exists a very large and spectacularly situated archaeological site, known as Thouria in later times (Figs. 61 and 62). This site can be plausibly identified with Linear B Leuktron. Its parallel situation to Pylos is striking: it dominates its region, commands a route through the Taygetus range to the Eurotas Valley of Laconia, and from the site one can even see the highest peak of the Aigaleon Ridge, the peak known today as Ayia Kyriaki. It is just possible that this parallelism is reflected in the documents, because

FIGURE 62
From the acropolis of ancient Thouria (possibly Linear B Leuktron) east toward the Taygetus range and Laconia. PRAP Archive. J. Bennet.

there is a place name *pu-ro ra-u-ra-ti-jo*, perhaps "Lawastian Pylos," so-called to distinguish it from *the* Pylos, but also possibly to point out its parallelism with *the* Pylos as capital of the Further Province. Even in the Bronze Age, as in Strabo's day, it seems there were multiple Pyloi.

Perhaps this place had previously been known as Leuktron, but—during the period of Pylian domination of the Further Province—it came to be known as another Pylos. This raises the question of how Pylos extended its control over the 2,000 square kilometers it controlled by the time the palace was destroyed at the end of Late Helladic IIIB, around 1200 B.C. Can we draw any conclusions about prior stages in the development of the Pylian polity? The division of the polity into "This-side-of-" and "Beyond-Aigolaion" and the subdivision of each of these sectors into relatively fixed subdistricts was established by the time of the documents. But for how long?

Because the texts belong to the very last year of the Pylos polity, there is no time depth in them beyond "last year's," a term that appears on a handful of examples. Nevertheless, there are some clues implicit in the place-name evidence already discussed. The existence of the fixed list of nine and seven/eight place names might reflect places that, although subordinate to Pylos at the time of its destruction, had been—at some prior period—independent centers. Similarly, the Hither/Further Province division, although geographically defined by Pylos's position west of ("this side" of) Aigaleon, at least suggests that there had not always been a Further Province and that expansion had proceeded from west to east at some earlier time. The Linear B documents—confined to one year in the life of the palace—cannot help to calibrate the time scale of such developments. In order to do this, we depend on archaeological data that offer a diachronic perspective.

In many places in Messenia, Middle Helladic settlement is marked by the construction of tumuli, which represent the visible burial locations of local elites. (Later in the region's history, long after their actual occupants' names were forgotten, these visible markers had power for the local inhabitants: see Focus in Chapter 7.) Late in this period and in the early Late Helladic I period, there is an intensification of such status display in the form of the construction of tholos tombs, a phenomenon that appeared earlier in this region than elsewhere in Greece. The investment of labor in the construction of tholos tombs and the fact that they form visible markers on the landscape and can be repeatedly reused suggests that such structures again mark the burials of elites. These tombs can be seen as a logical extension and intensification of Middle Helladic status-marking in the region. This is perhaps most vividly demonstrated at Petrohori *Voidokoilia* (see

Fig. 61), where a tholos tomb was constructed within an existing Middle Helladic tumulus (see Chapter 3), perhaps implying a claim by the Late Helladic I elite to the territory marked by the 400-year-old tumulus. These tholos tombs mark the location of emergent power centers—chiefdoms, perhaps—within the Late Helladic I period, potential rivals to the settlement on Englianos. It is attractive to think of these centers of power as the predecessors of those places mentioned in the Linear B fixed-order lists.

We have already seen in Chapters 3 and 4 how the immediate area of the palace reflects the emergence of a major center from Middle Helladic times onward, with its group of early tholos tombs (IV, the "Grave Circle," and III), an early fortification wall, and the Late Helladic IIIA monumental structures beneath the latest palace. The nearby site at Hora *Volimidia* appears not to have had a tholos tomb, perhaps suggesting that it had already come under the influence of the ruling elite at Ano Englianos by the late Middle Helladic period. The expansion of power centered on the site of Ano Englianos seems to have culminated in the construction of the main palace complex essentially in the form in which it is now preserved at the beginning of Late Helladic IIIB. If Blegen's dating is correct, then it was destroyed late in Late Helladic IIIB (perhaps ca. 1200 B.C.), a century (four generations) later.

The concentration of power on the palace site seems to have been complemented by a "demotion" of sites in its vicinity, since most of the tholos tombs at other nearby sites go out of use in Late Helladic IIIA, at a period when the first Linear B documents and monumental structures are attested at the palace. It is interesting that most of these sites lie south or southwest of the palace site, rather than to the north, a fact that might suggest that the site already acted as a focal point for an extensive territory to the north and northwest along the coast. Among the advantages of the site was its superb location, situated on one of the ridges extending northeast-southwest from the Aigaleon range, with excellent views to the coast, difficult approaches by land (except along the line of the ridge), and—importantly—a location visible from many points around in all directions. Not only did the palace come to dominate its region politically, but it was a widely visible presence in the landscape. The route along the ridge controlled by the palace must have been an important one, allowing access through the area of modern Hora over a low saddle in the Aigaleon range into the Metaxada Valley, which housed the important Middle Helladic and early Mycenaean site of Kalopsana (Fig. 63).

Can we take this local reconstruction beyond the immediate region of the palace and chart the expansion to include the entire area known to have been controlled from the Englianos site by the Late Helladic IIIB period?

FIGURE 63
*Metaxada Valley from the south (Kalopsana lies to the left in the distance).
PRAP Archive. J. Bennet.*

Fortunately, we have excellent data from the site of Rizomylo *Nichoria* (see Focus in this chapter). The settlement at Nichoria reached its maximum size (about 5 hectares) in the Late Helladic IIIA2–B1 phase, about 1350–1250 B.C., clearly the largest site within its region and comparable in size to major sites within PRAP's survey area (see Focus in this chapter). At the beginning of this phase, there is some discontinuity at the site. The focal point of the settlement—a megaron, similar in plan, though not as large and well appointed as that at Pylos—went out of use and was not rebuilt, suggesting the site's subordination. Within the same time period, a new monumental tomb structure, the tholos tomb at the western edge of the site, came into use, replacing an earlier tholos tomb, which had been in use from Late Helladic I to IIIA2. The argument here is that tholos tombs were now intimately linked to ruling families, and were not merely sites of conspicuous display. Such display seems to have taken place in other contexts. The construction of a new tholos tomb at Nichoria would, therefore, imply the establishment of new rulers.

Both of these changes, it can be argued, indicate the presence of a new authority at Nichoria and the establishment of a new ruling elite at the site, under the sponsorship of an external power not located within the site itself. The location of this authority might have been the Palace of Nestor. If this is so, and we are observing the incorporation of Nichoria into the Pylian polity, then it is interesting that it seems to take place in Late Helladic IIIA2, the phase immediately before the construction of the final palace on the Englianos Ridge. In this context, it is interesting that one possible reconstruction of the Linear B name for Nichoria is "glen of the frontier," suggesting that it lay at one time on the edge of the Pylos polity. It is also possible that the site was linked by road to the area southeast of the Palace of Nestor at the same time. Remains of a road of probable Bronze Age date have been detected, zig-zagging up the slope west of Nichoria—above the modern asphalt road and its Turkish predecessor.

From this state of affairs, we can draw the likely conclusion that it was only after the incorporation of Nichoria that the rest of the Further Province—*pe-ra-a$_3$-ko-ra-i-ja*—was incorporated, and that this took place in the period when the final palace was constructed, around 1300 B.C., only a century before the destruction that preserved the Linear B texts. The incorporation of *pe-ra-a$_3$-ko-ra-i-ja* would then have been a relatively recent event within the history of the polity, maybe three to four generations in the past, whereas power relations between the palace and the nine settlements of the Hither Province might have been established twice as long before.

The fact that the Further Province had only recently been incorporated may be reflected in the relative instability in the geographical listing of its place names. Similarly, of the nine names we have preserved for Further Province district centers, only four (*e-ro*, which itself apparently corresponds to two district names, *a-te-re-wi-ja* and *e-sa-re-wi-ja*; *sa-ma-ra*; *e-ra-te-re-we*; and *ti-mi-to-a-ke-e*) are not apparently formed with an adjectival suffix (*ra-u-ra-ti-ja* [with its center perhaps distinguished specifically as *pu-ro ra-u-ra-ti-jo*], *a-si-ja-ti-ja*, *za-ma-e-wi-ja*, *a-te-re-wi-ja*, and *e-sa-re-wi-ja*), meaning "district of X," or something similar. This is in striking contrast to the Hither Province place names. Are these place names perhaps (artificially coined?) district names created to describe the districts of the major centers east of Aigaleon incorporated into the Pylos polity? And is the fourfold division into taxation groups perhaps imposed on the basis of the long-established—essentially geographical—division of the Hither Province? And, finally, is the 17 percent larger assessment on the Further Province perhaps an exploitative or punitive measure, rather than merely a reflection of its slightly larger land area or productive capacity?

The dynamics of change within the polity are also reflected near its northern boundary. There, a new settlement is founded at Mouriatada *Elliniko* (see Fig. 61), a site with a fortification, a megaron, rooms with painted plaster decoration, and a nearby tholos tomb. The site belongs entirely within the Late Helladic IIIB phase, almost exactly contemporary with the final phase of the palace at Ano Englianos. The significance of Mouriatada's foundation is that it seems to have replaced one of the most spectacular early Mycenaean sites in Messenia—Myron *Peristeria*—a relatively short distance to the north. Peristeria, the site of three early Mycenaean (Late Helladic I–II) tholos tombs and, for that reason, clearly a site of considerable importance in the region at that time, may have been eliminated and superseded by Mouriatada within the Late Helladic IIIB period. If we are reading the archaeological record correctly, then we seem to have an instance of considerable intervention by the palace in this region. Apparently the center at Pylos sponsored a newly emergent center at the expense of the "traditional" center of power in the region.

It is just possible that the Linear B textual data also offer some reflection of this situation. A Further Province place name, *a-te-re-wi-ja*, and the Hither Province place name *me-ta-pa* are linked on Aa 779, a tablet recording a work group at *me-ta-pa*, which appears on its front; *a-te-re-wi-ja* is written on its lower side. Another text, An 830, implies a link between *a-te-re-wi-ja* and another Hither Province place name, *pi-*82*. Clearly, any link between the Hither and Further provinces at their northern extremes is likely to have been through the Cyparissia Valley, which implies that *a-te-re-wi-ja* may have lain in the western part of this valley. Might the work group on Aa 779 originally have been at *a-te-re-wi-ja* (Peristeria), but have been moved to *me-ta-pa* to be under closer supervision within the recent recorded past? *E-re-i*—the place name used on Jn 829, but not in the Ma series—might therefore represent the new site of Mouriatada with its "mayor" and "vice-mayor," and *a-te-re-wi-ja* might have been used on the Ma tablets to refer to the district over which *e-re-i* now stood. (An alternative reading, if *e-re-i* is actually "split" into two for the Ma texts, is that *a-te-re-wi-ja* represents Mouriatada, the westernmost of two settlements newly favored at the expense of Peristeria, the other going by the name of *e-sa-re-wi-ja*.) There is support for linking *a-te-re-wi-ja* with the list on Jn 829 with its status terms (the *ko-re-te* and *po-ro-ko-re-te*) in the fact that An 830 records "mayoral" (*ko-re-te-ri-jo*) land within (the territory of?) *a-te-re-wi-ja*.

It was from this extensive territory—twice the size, for example, of that of the later Classical city-state of Athens, itself one of the largest in Greece at the time—that the center on the Englianos Ridge drew its lifeblood in terms of the raw materials and people that ensured the continued success of the system. We have seen something of the taxation system, designed to ensure compliance by requiring basic, transportable commodities according to fixed proportions and fiscal groupings. What other activities did the palace control? We have already seen (Chapter 4) those activities that were confined to the immediate area of the palace (land), or even the palatial structures themselves (perfume manufacture; production and repair of military equipment; the making of wool cloth). What other activities can we document for the rest of the polity?

Throughout the polity, the production of flax—ultimately for linen cloth—was an important and carefully monitored activity. We have seen already the totaling documents for flax production by major district of the polity. There is an extensive series of documents that records flax assessments at about fifty locations, some apparently small settlements only recorded by the palace in this context. These documents even go to the length of including exemptions from production for various groups. From this flax, linen cloth was produced—at a more restricted number of places, including Pylos itself, Leuktron, and some of the major subcenters—by the work groups alluded to above, for which the palace provided rations from its extensive landholdings. The cloth was used within the polity—for armor for the elite, and clothing for dependents—and, we presume, exchanged beyond its boundaries for other valuable commodities not locally available.

Unlike Knossos on Crete, Pylos apparently did not have a large woolen-cloth industry to go alongside its extensive production of linen. Yet there are signs of such an industry, particularly in the large number of flocks that were managed, probably in the central uplands of the Aigaleon range, between the two sectors of the polity. These were composed not only of sheep, but of goats as well. These animals had usefulness beyond their wool—a renewable resource; they would also find their way onto the table at festivals, as we have seen. To the basic ovicaprid diet at such festivals would be added pigs and oxen. The oxen would, of course, have been of great value while alive as traction animals, drawing plows on palace-controlled land and pulling carts to transport commodities over the roads that have been detected in at least one area.

More intrinsically valuable commodities were also produced, or at least worked, throughout the polity. The fact that each district was required to contribute quantities of bronze on tablet Jn 829 suggests that bronze-working was widespread. Some of the Ma texts also document a tax exemption for bronzesmiths, suggesting their importance to the overall economy. The care taken in managing the system is demonstrated by a series of about twenty texts that detail amounts of bronze assigned to teams of smiths, noted by name. The documents even list those smiths without an assignment of bronze. Interestingly, few of the important place names occur among these tablets, suggesting that bronze-working—a smoky, smelly process requiring extensive supplies of wood fuel—might have taken place at out-of-the-way locations, away from habitation sites.

Unfortunately, we can be far from certain what happened to the finished goods produced in and around the palace from commodities that reached it through this complex procurement system. Analogies from other Mycenaean centers, particularly Knossos on Crete, suggest that valuable goods—for which read "goods into which a great deal of labor had gone"—would have been circulated among the local elites to ensure loyalty and traded with other states within and beyond the Mycenaean world, as was the case with perfumed oil (see Focus in Chapter 4). There is, however, little textual evidence to attest to such exchange beyond the boundaries of the Pylian state. It may have happened less frequently, and therefore not found its way into the documents preserved by the final destruction, or it may not have been recorded systematically on clay tablets. One Pylos text (Un 443), however, appears to record payment in supplies to an individual for the mineral alum, presumably an import, useful in the dyeing industry. For evidence of such trade, we need to look at its reflection in the archaeological record beyond the Peloponnese in the Uluburun wreck, a ship containing large quantities of copper, tin, glass, and other commodities that went down off the southern coast of Turkey perhaps a century before Pylos fell.

We can see something of the ideological function fulfilled by such a collection system in another "recipe" for a festival, this time at Pylos itself.

Un 138
.1 At Pylos, owed [to the palace] from Dunios
.2 1,776 liters of barley, 421 liters of eating? olives
.3 374 liters of wine, 15 rams, 8 yearlings?, 1 ewe, 13 he-goats, 12 pigs
.4 1 fattened pig, 1 cow, 2 bulls
.5 from Mezawon 462 liters of barley, 672 liters of olives for pressing?

Here, the agricultural commodities produced on palace land (grain, olives, wine) and the livestock (sheep, goats, pigs, oxen) appear in a context where their function is display, conspicuous consumption by the center for the enjoyment of a large number to demonstrate the success of the state and to ensure its continuity. It is likely that in such rituals we see the continuity of those rituals previously associated with the early Mycenaean tholos tombs that acted as the focus for emergent chiefdoms. By the Late Helladic IIIB period, the tholos tomb may have been more or less the private domain of the ruling family, and it is conspicuous display centered on the abode of the living elite that has taken its place as an integrating force in society.

Providing a historical reconstruction of the structure and expansion of power centered on a Late Bronze Age palace is no easy enterprise. However, with the uniquely rich archaeological and textual record offered by the Palace of Nestor and its surrounding territory, such a reconstruction becomes feasible, and we can begin to understand how the Bronze Age inhabitants understood the land in which they lived and how their rulers ensured their loyalty. This chapter has, however, focused almost exclusively on the higher branches of the tree: the ruling elite and their patterning over the Messenian landscape. A final Pylos document offers a tantalizing, if uncertain, glimpse of other groups within (or on the fringes of) the Mycenaean state:

Cn 3
.1 How Mezana are sending
.2 oxen to Diwieus, the "inspector"?:
.3 The Okarai at a_2-ra-tu-a   1 ox
.4 The *Ku-re-we* at *pi-ru-te*   1 ox
.5 The Iwasiotes at *e-na-po-ro*   1 ox
.6 The Ulumpiaioi at Orumanthos   1 ox
.7 The Ulumpiaioi at a_2-ka-a_2-ki-r-i-ja-jo 1 ox

This document lists a series of contributions of an ox to a man Diwieus, an important member of the Pylian elite, whose title probably means "inspector." The names seem to be groups associated with particular places, groups that occur elsewhere as members of contingents on the *o-ka* (coastguard) tablets. An intriguing aspect of the text is the fact that two groups seem to be called "Ulumpiaioi," very close in form to that of the place name Olympia, later attested in the northwest Peloponnese; one group may be at Orumanthos, again similar to a later Peloponnesian mountain name, Erymanthos. To some extent controversial is the interpretation of the word *me-za-na* in the first line. If this is a collective name for the groups listed below it, then it is tempting to see a link between it and Messana, the local form of Messene, the ancient place name traditionally associated—after the Bronze Age—with Mt. Ithome, and chosen as the name of the newly founded capital of the region in 369 B.C. The fact that these groups were contributing oxen to an official of the Pylian state suggests that they might have been recognized as semi-independent corporate groups, either within or on the boundaries of the Pylian state, distinct from the population within the state, which seems to have been referred to as the *damos*.

JOHN BENNET

If this is the case, then it is interesting that the name Mezana/Messana came to be associated with the whole region after the Bronze Age. Is it too fanciful to imagine a subordinate group expanding into the power vacuum left after the collapse of Pylos and giving its name to the region, only to be themselves overrun by the Spartans, whose domination was the source of a bitter rivalry reflected over a thousand years later in the Monomitos inscription? If the Mezana are ethnically related to the historical Messenians, then our first texts from the region—the Linear B documents—ironically may *not* have been the first documents written by Messenians. Their authors were Mycenaean speakers, who fled the region after Pylos's collapse, perhaps ending up in Arcadia, the mountainous region of the Peloponnesian interior, the region of historical Greece that shows the closest linguistic affinities with the language of the Mycenaean elite preserved in the Linear B tablets.

FOCUS

The PRAP SURVEY'S CONTRIBUTION

PRAP's contributions to our understanding of the territory of the Late Bronze Age Palace of Nestor can be summarized by a visual metaphor. The picture now has a greater magnification and the focus is better.

In terms of magnification, we have increased the number of known sites in the region. The work of the University of Minnesota Messenia Expedition (UMME) in the 1960s revealed about 102 sites of Late Helladic IIIB date within the likely territory of the Pylos polity. However, the Linear B documents list a total of about 240 place names. This is a major discrepancy, and is, in fact, contrary to what one might expect. One might expect the palace center only to document interests at a relatively small number of quite important sites. (This is certainly the case with the only other comparable polity, that based at Knossos in central Crete.) It seems difficult in the case of Pylos to resist the interpretation that the palace documented an interest at almost all sites within its territory, a staggering achievement, given its size and the transport and information-processing technology available.

Can we explain the large discrepancy between the settlement figures attested archaeologically and those attested in the Linear B texts? First of all, the UMME project seems consistently to have underestimated the number of small sites. Of the 102 identified, only about forty are smaller than 1 hectare in size, whereas we might expect smaller sites to make up the largest class of settlements within the overall settlement hierarchy. PRAP has succeeded in documenting some of these smaller sites and has increased the number of known Mycenaean sites within the area surveyed by about 50 percent. If we apply this factor to the total known sites within the territory of the palace, we arrive at a possible total of about 150 sites that might be observed archaeologically, rather than 102. The discrepancy is still large, but is approaching the same order of magnitude. A second contributory factor to the underrepresentation of archaeological sites might well be the

JOHN BENNET

geomorphological instability of some regions of our area that might have led to the disappearance of sites from the archaeological record (see Chapter 1).

PRAP's work has also thrown this picture into much sharper focus. The careful study of sites has enabled us to define their sizes with greater precision than prior research achieved. As a result, large sites now stand out much more clearly, and the overall settlement hierarchy is better focused. Our work at the palace (see Chapter 3) has demonstrated that the settlement around the central palatial buildings probably extended over 20 hectares, or three times its previously estimated size. This makes the settlement comparable in area to that at Mycenae (perhaps 30 hectares, including the walled citadel) and makes the influence exerted by the palace site more understandable. Subordinate to the palace in the settlement hierarchy were some sites of considerable size, such as Koryfasion *Beylerbey* and Gargaliani *Ordines*, respectively one-quarter and one-sixth the size of the palace settlement. The clear definition of these second-order sites fits well with the picture offered by the Linear B documents, where sites of this rank appear in lists as the major subordinate places at which contributions to the palace were collected and activities associated with the industries centered on the palace were located (see the main text of this chapter). Around these second-order places, there seems to have been a clustering of smaller sites at a third level—their size now more clearly defined by PRAP.

PRAP's work allows us to go beyond improvements in our understanding of the number of settlements and their relative size—essentially quantitative conclusions—to more qualitative evaluations of the nature and dynamics of settlement change in the region. The PRAP survey area is clearly much smaller than the total area controlled by the Late Bronze Age polity centered on the so-called Palace of Nestor. However, the area was carefully chosen to straddle the prominent boundary between the two sectors of the polity (see the main text of this chapter) and to examine areas that lay "beyond Aigaleon." In those areas, an interesting story can be told. The specific units intensively covered by PRAP surveyors contained two prominent sites of the Middle Helladic period, Metaxada *Kalopsana* and Maryeli *Koutsouveri* (Fig. 64), both situated in valleys, both located on and around prominent hilltops. Intensive surveys in the vicinity of both of these sites—and for quite some area around them—revealed almost no palace-period Mycenaean material. Indeed, on those sites, although we found abundant Middle Helladic and early Mycenaean material, palace-period Mycenaean pottery was very scarce.

Thanks to PRAP's intensive survey in these areas, we are able to be more confident than before about the scarcity of Mycenaean settlement there. It seems likely that settlement was affected by its liminal status in the bound-

FIGURE 64
View of the prominent hill of Koutsouveri, dominating the modern village of Maryeli. PRAP Archive. J. Bennet.

ary zone between the two sectors of the polity. There are a number of possibilities—not all mutually exclusive—that might explain this unusual settlement pattern. First of all, these are marginal areas, quite distant from the coast. Their topography militates against extensive agriculture without considerable investment in terracing. It is likely that the appearance of Middle Helladic settlements was a function of the expansion of population that Messenia enjoyed at that time. There would have been sufficient agricultural land to accommodate the relatively small populations of these sites. By the Mycenaean period, there must have been greater attraction to the flourishing centers both to the west, in the Englianos region, and to the east, in the Messenian Valley and its surrounding foothills. Not only that, but the intensive agricultural regime centered on the palace may have—in good years—produced a superabundance of food. In short, the inhabitants of these areas might simply have migrated, attracted by the "good life" to the east or west. The existence of some Mycenaean material at these locations might reflect their continued use as specialist settlements, perhaps associated with herding—an activity well attested in the Linear B documents, and, as far as we can tell, particularly in the uplands bordering both sectors—or with activities like metalwork, for which the necessary large quantities of wooden fuel would have been readily available.

A second possibility is more sinister. The liminal status of these areas—the refuge of revolutionaries in the early nineteenth century of our era—might have posed a threat to the emergent political unity centered on the Palace of Nestor, particularly in the period when it expanded its political control to the east, over into the Messenian Valley. We might imagine that the palace authorities "encouraged" inhabitants to move out of these areas, or those inhabitants might have fallen victim to hostilities associated with the palace's aggressively expansionist regime in its later phase. The small amounts of Mycenaean material demonstrate, however, that the area was not completely abandoned. As with the first possibility, it could be that

FIGURE 65
Section of a Mycenaean road west of Nichoria, with the built retaining wall that supports it. Reproduced from W. A. McDonald, "Overland Communications in Greece During LH III, with Special Reference to Southwest Peloponnese," in E. L. Bennett Jr., ed., Mycenaean Studies: Wingspread, 1961 *(Madison: University of Wisconsin Press, 1961), pl. 15, with permission of the University of Wisconsin Press.*

The PRAP SURVEY'S CONTRIBUTION

specialist activities, under close palatial control, were tolerated in these marginal areas.

A final possibility relates to the changing structures of the polity. It is possible that there were special relations between the Hither Province and the site of Nichoria (Linear B *ti-mi-to-a-ke-e*) before the incorporation of the Further Province (see the main text of this chapter). By the time of the final palace, Nichoria may have formed an important link between the Hither and Further provinces. Some idea of the importance of this link is given by the fact that a road was apparently built running west from Nichoria (Fig. 65), over a pass, to the area west of Aigaleon, the very same route that the modern asphalt road from Kalamata to Pylos takes through this region. The construction of the road not only indicates the importance of the link, but also has implications for the movement of commodities and personnel. Its construction may have facilitated transportation between west and east to such a degree that older routes, such as that running east of the palace over into the Metaxada Valley (in which Metaxada *Kalopsana* is situated), might have become less used. Areas like the Metaxada and Maryeli valleys may have become even more remote in the final period of the Pylos state as a result.

The explanation may well be a combination of all three of these factors, but PRAP's intensive survey in the area allows us to speculate about the phenomenon on much firmer grounds.

In these ways—and a number of others—PRAP's work has improved our vision of the Late Bronze Age, as it has for all other periods throughout the long and fascinating history of Messenia.

FOCUS

UMME *and* NICHORIA

The site of Nichoria commands a ridge that marks the western edge of the fertile Pamisos River Valley, and the northwestern corner of the Messenian Gulf. As you stand on the site, you can look down the coast, past where the small headland of Petalidi (ancient Koroni) curls out into the water. Or you can turn east (Fig. 66) and look across the valley, improbably green even in mid-summer, to the city of Kalamata and the solid mass of the Taygetus mountain range, which forms a backdrop over 2,400 meters high, and snakes off southward to form the tall spine of the Mani. The only good route of access from Kalamata to Pylos climbs from the valley at Nichoria and continues westward across the Messenian Peninsula through a natural break in the Aigaleon range; halfway there, a fork allows you to choose whether to head for modern or Mycenaean Pylos.

Apart from the modern cities themselves, little has happened to make the view from Nichoria today different from what a Mycenaean inhabitant of the town would have seen. The modern village of Karpofora lies one ridge to the west; its houses of mud brick on stone foundations and its curving unpaved streets echo the Mycenaean street and houses uncovered at Nichoria (Fig. 67). Until 1969, when the University of Minnesota Messenia Expedition began its excavation of Nichoria, residents of Karpofora walked forty-five minutes down to the bottom of the ridge to get their water, as the Mycenaeans, too, must have done. (In 1995, a friend who still lives in the village told me she missed, in a way, the enforced sense of community those water trips occasioned.)

UMME was one of the first projects to pay attention to an entire region. The director was an archaeologist, William A. McDonald, the associate director a natural scientist, George R. Rapp, Jr. They spent the 1960s surveying the province of Messenia, and documenting settlement patterns throughout antiquity. Only then did they select Nichoria for closer investigation. The goal, as a pre-excavation report put it, was "to work out for this

CYNTHIA W. SHELMERDINE

FIGURE 66
View east from Nichoria into the valley of the Pamisos River. C. W. Shelmerdine.

particular settlement and its immediate environs a minutely detailed reconstruction of as much of the physical and manmade environment as is possible." The excavation staff was large and interdisciplinary; in addition to recovering and studying archaeological finds, staff members investigated the environmental history and setting of the site, compared ancient and modern vegetation, studied human and animal bones, and conducted geophysical research. By the time I arrived in 1972 as a student member of the team, Nichoria was already on the map. Byzantine remains were plentiful, as were those of the Dark Ages (the twelfth to eighth centuries B.C.; see Chapter 6). The Bronze Age street was emerging; a tholos tomb—the burial choice of the Mycenaean elite—was being explored; and I was soon studying the pottery from a Mycenaean house with storage jars in the basement, several successive strata of habitation, and a lone mud brick preserved in one of the walls (Fig. 68). But to understand the Mycenaeans who lived and died here, it was necessary to explore the relationship of this town to the palatial center of Pylos. This, too, a variety of evidence allowed me to do.

Even before Nichoria was excavated, surface survey by the Minnesota team had shown it to be one of the largest Bronze Age settlements in this region of Messenia, as well as being strategically located. Excavation revealed that its prosperity rose and fell with that of the palace; the tholos tomb was built and used only during the heyday of the Pylian kingdom, and though robbed, its remaining contents show that some in the community had considerable purchasing power and access to prestige goods

FIGURE 67
Mycenaean street in Nichoria Area III. (= W. A. McDonald and N. C. Wilkie, eds., Excavations at Nichoria in Southwest Greece, *vol. 2:* The Bronze Age Occupation *[Minneapolis: University of Minnesota Press, 1992], pl. 7–37), with permission of the University of Minnesota Press. Courtesy N. C. Wilkie.*

FIGURE 68
Balloon photograph of Mycenaean House (center) in Nichoria Area IV. (= W. A. McDonald and N. C. Wilkie, eds., Excavations at Nichoria in Southwest Greece, *vol. 2:* The Bronze Age Occupation *[Minneapolis: University of Minnesota Press, 1992], pl. 7–108), with permission of the University of Minnesota Press. Courtesy N. C. Wilkie.*

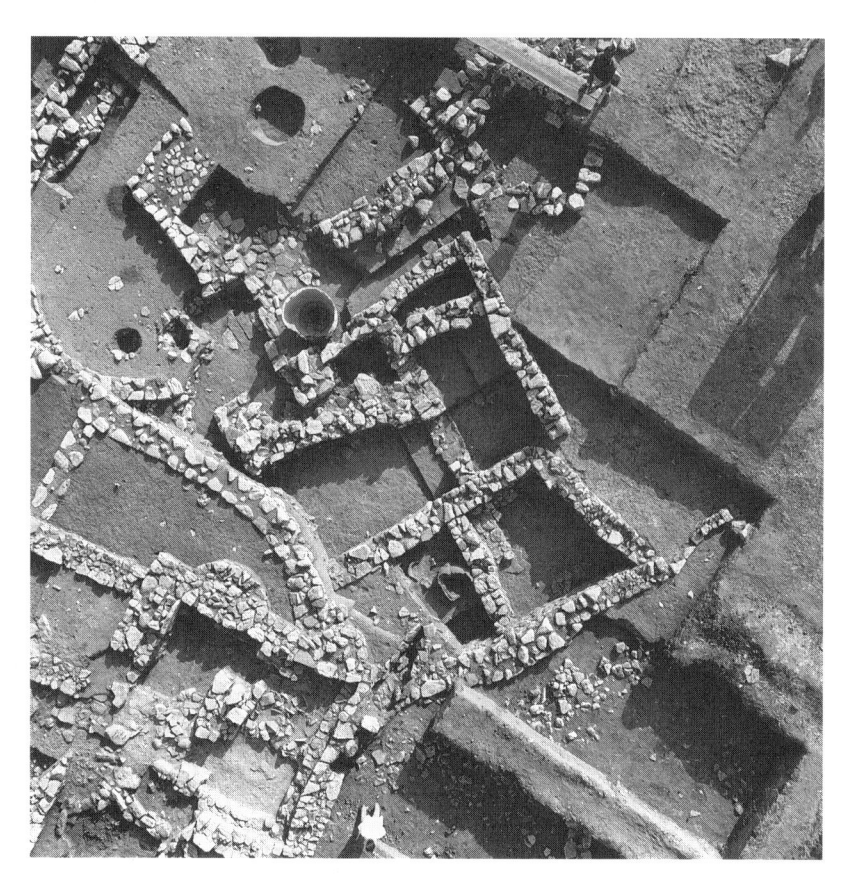

(Fig. 69a, Fig. 69b). The site itself was abandoned as close to the time the palace burned down as ceramic evidence can pinpoint. Further, pottery, spindle whorls, and loomweights at the two places were very similar, suggesting close communication. All these clues suggested Nichoria was important enough to appear in the administrative records of the kingdom. Lying beyond Mt. Aigaleon, it was clearly in the Further Province of the 2,000-square-kilometer Pylian kingdom (see Chapter 5). So as excavation continued, I began to compare what we knew of the site with information in the tablets about district centers in that province. The place usually cited in the form *ti-mi-to-a-ke-e* proved to be a remarkably close match.

First and foremost, *ti-mi-to-a-ke-e* appears in a list of important lookout points overlooking the coast. Nichoria is ideally situated to serve as a lookout; it is the nearest point to Pylos from which both the coastline and the valley are visible, and it lies on the most direct route back to the palace. Moreover, it is the only such site; the Minnesota survey found no other substantial settlement in this vicinity. Then, *ti-mi-to-a-ke-e* was a center for bronze-workers. At Nichoria, a bronze-working establishment was discovered of the same date as the Pylos tablets. Metallurgists were puzzled, though, to note that most of the work done here involved not the alloying of tin and copper, but the melting down and reworking of bronze. The tablets provide the explanation for this: the palace allocated lump bronze to smiths at *ti-mi-to-a-ke-e* and elsewhere, for reworking into spear points, arrowheads, and the like. Finally, *ti-mi-to-a-ke-e* was a major source of flax for the kingdom's linen industry, by far the largest in the Further Province.

FIGURE 69
Finds from tholos tomb at Nichoria:
a. *Carnelian sealstone.* Corpus der minoischen und mykenischen Siegeln Archive. Courtesy of I. Pini, with permission of the University of Minnesota Press. (= W. A. McDonald and N. C. Wilkie, eds., Excavations at Nichoria in Southwest Greece, *vol. 2:* The Bronze Age Occupation *[Minneapolis: University of Minnesota Press, 1992], pl. 5–59).*
b. *Gold beads.* (= W. A. McDonald and N. C. Wilkie, eds., Excavations at Nichoria in Southwest Greece, *vol. 2:* The Bronze Age Occupation *[Minneapolis: University of Minnesota Press, 1992], pl. 5–93),* with permission of the University of Minnesota Press. Courtesy N. C. Wilkie.

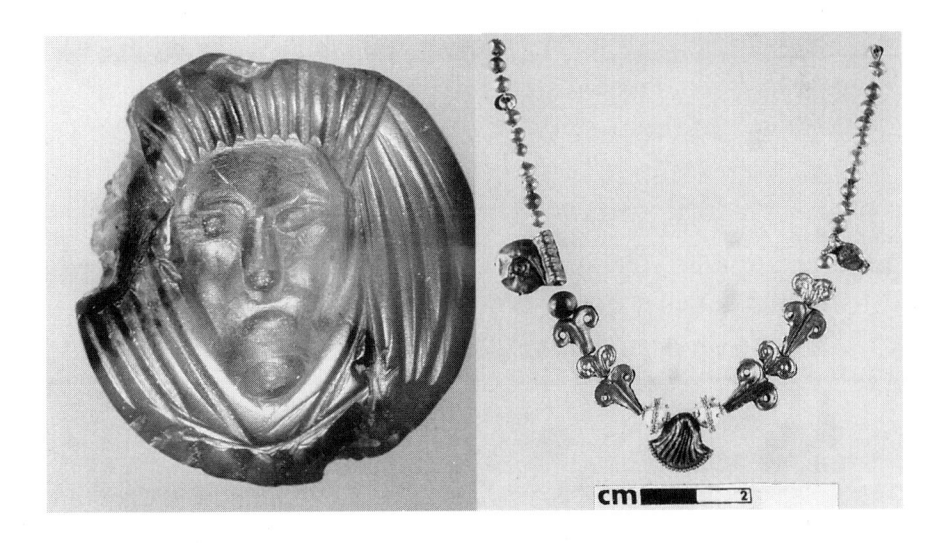

UMME *and* NICHORIA

Flax can only be grown in areas that meet two exacting requirements. They must have very rich soil, since the crop quickly exhausts even the most fertile land; and they must have a good supply of water, for the flax must be thoroughly soaked (retted) before it can be spun. Soil analysis and other environmental studies by the Minnesota team proved that the Nichoria area, unlike most of the Messenian Valley, has all the qualities needed to be a center of flax production: flat bottomlands, rich soil, the water from five nearby rivers for retting, and a convenient road for transporting the flax to Pylos.

It thus seems very likely that Nichoria is *ti-mi-to-a-ke-e*. Many different kinds of scientific and environmental analysis played a role in the identification, but science alone could not name the site. For this, the traditional techniques of excavation and the study of written documents were also necessary. This was for me a nice example of how old and new archaeology might work together to write the history of the Mycenaeans. For the historian, there is an added bonus of a more personal kind, if the identification is correct: when the palace burned down and preserved the tablets around 1200 B.C., we can now say that Nichoria had a mayor named Perimos.

FIGURE 70
Voidokoilia Bay, ancient Coryphasion, Palaionavarino, and the island of Sphacteria, from the north. PRAP Archive. R. J. Robertson.

CHAPTER 6

AFTER *the* PALACE:
The EARLY "HISTORY" *of* MESSENIA

The likely interpretation of their story suggests they [Idas and Lynceus] were buried in Messenia and not here [in Sparta]. But the misfortunes of the Messenians and the length of time they spent in exile from the Peloponnese made much of their past unknown to them, even when they returned. And, because they are ignorant, it is possible now for those who wish to, to dispute their account.

PAUSANIAS *Description of Greece* 3.13.1–2

Even in antiquity, so completely had the earlier historical periods of Messenia's past degenerated into a confusing morass of unsubstantiated myths that even the traveler Pausanias despaired of being able to find out anything approximating the truth. The legends of Nestor's Pylos were still well known; indeed, it was the monuments at Coryphasion, including Nestor's cave and the tomb of Thrasymedes (Nestor's son), that were some of the very few to be pointed out to Pausanias on his travels in the region. But what of later times, and the legendary struggles against the Spartan aggressor? Was there any reliable history of these periods at all?

While the broad outlines of the history of Messenia from the end of the twelfth century B.C. until the liberation from Spartan control in the fourth century can be discerned, a more detailed picture of Messenia after the palace often proves to be elusive. Our shadowy understanding of this period is due both to weaknesses in the literary sources and to the heavy Bronze Age emphasis of most archaeological work in the region (see Chapter 2).

The long expanse of time treated in this chapter can be divided into two distinct chronological periods, each of which presents different problems. The first chronological period, the Dark Age, is a poorly understood historical era throughout Greece. Yet due to the work of the University of Minnesota Messenia Expedition at Nichoria, Dark Age Messenia is less ob-

ANN B. HARRISON *and* NIGEL SPENCER

scure than many other areas of Greece in the same period. The subsequent Archaic and Classical periods, the pinnacle of Greek culture, are marked by the land's complete subjugation to the neighboring Spartans.

For from the late eighth century until the fourth, in the most basic sense, Messenia as an entity did not exist. At the end of the fifth century, the Greek historian Thucydides refers to "what was once the land of Messenia," for by then it had long been merely southwestern Laconia, the territory of Sparta. Indeed, this domination would have been the overwhelming element in the lives of the Messenians, as they were incorporated in the sharply hierarchical structure of Spartan society. Within this system, most Messenians occupied the lowest role, that of helot, a status only slightly different from chattel slavery.

With few reliable written sources for the history of Messenia, the examination of the archaeological data takes on added importance. Archaeology alone has the potential to offer some answers to major questions about the Dark Age, Archaic, and Classical periods in Messenia. What happened after the palace burnt down and the kingdom centered on the palace at Ano Englianos had collapsed? Was there a change after the conquest by the Spartans, in either the location or the types of settlement in which the Messenians lived? Did the Spartans force their Messenian helots to come together in large groups on their estates, working the plots of land now owned by their Spartan masters? Or did the Messenians continue to dwell in towns and villages scattered throughout the landscape, much as they had done in the days of the Bronze Age kingdom? In short, how did the Messenians live?

THE DARK AGE

Following the destruction of the Mycenaean kingdoms, Greece entered a period referred to by scholars as the Dark Age, which lasted until the eighth century B.C. This name reflects both the sharp decline in material culture found throughout Greece at this time, and our limited understanding of this period of Greek history. Literacy was lost, and isolation set in as international contacts ceased. It was a period of intense depopulation overall, and of large-scale population movements. The unifying political and economic systems of the Bronze Age were lost in extreme regionalism.

The effects on Messenia of the destruction of the Palace of Nestor at Ano Englianos were immense. From a situation where the region boasted about 240 settlements in a kingdom organized into two provinces with a highly developed administration, a carefully structured economy, and a ruling elite with an advanced level of culture (see Chapters 4 and 5), there followed almost total desolation. Few signs of activity anywhere in Messenia exist in the succeeding Late Helladic IIIC and Submycenaean periods, and the recovery from the shock of the kingdom's collapse seems to have been extremely slow.

Fewer than two dozen Dark Age sites have been identified in Messenia. Settlement reached a peak in the ninth century, and concentrated in very fertile areas, such as the Stenyclarus Plain and the Pamisos River valley, and in the area of Pylos. Almost all these Dark Age settlements were on sites occupied in the Mycenaean period, but large areas previously occupied in the Mycenaean period were abandoned, including most of the interior of the peninsula.

As for how the Messenians were living in the Dark Age, some general aspects can be determined. By the mid-eleventh century, there may have been new people moving into Messenia from the northwest, as the pottery shows connections with areas such as Ithaca and Aetolia. The mythical tradition of an incursion by outside peoples, the return of the Heraklidai or descendants of Herakles after the Trojan War, perhaps remembers this population movement. In the tenth and ninth centuries, the prosperity of settlements increased, and there was growing contact with other areas in western Greece and with Laconia. Also, the site of the sanctuary at Olympia in neighboring Elis received its first dedications. The site of Olympia would develop into one of the most important Panhellenic sanctuaries in the Greek world, but at this time it had a much more local character, and Messenia played an important role in early activity at the sanctuary.

At the former palace site at Ano Englianos, there was some sporadic reoccupation (see Focus in Chapter 4). The inhabitants even reused some of the ruined palace walls and built a small Mycenaean-style tholos tomb to the south of the palace; but the settlement may have died out again by the later eighth century and never seems to have been particularly significant (Figs. 71, 72).

The most substantial Early Iron Age site detected by the UMME team was at Nichoria, where subsequent excavations revealed that a small group of people had later reoccupied the ridgetop, previously an important Late Bronze Age site named in the Linear B tablets, forming a village that continued to exist for much of the Dark Age (see Focus in this chapter). One of the most important discoveries at Nichoria made through the faunal analysis was the great increase in pastoral practices in the Early Iron Age and the adding of a significant amount of meat (especially deer and cattle) to the diet of the Nichorians.

Furthermore, this change apparent in Messenia subsequently was proposed to explain both the shorter-lived settlement sites in many areas of

FIGURE 71
Dark Age tholos tomb at the southwestern end of the Englianos Ridge. Reproduced from C. W. Blegen, M. Rawson, W. Taylour, and W. P. Donovan, The Palace of Nestor at Pylos in Western Messenia, *vol. 3:* Acropolis and Lower Town, Tholoi, Grave Circles and Chamber Tombs, Discoveries Outside the Citadel *(Princeton: Princeton University Press, 1973), fig. 294. With permission of Princeton University Press and the Department of Classics, University of Cincinnati.*

Greece during the Early Iron Age (possibly the result of more nomadic ways of life associated with pastoralism) and the increase in dedications of animal figurines at Olympia (Fig. 73). Indeed, in light of this alleged new importance in stock-raising and cattle-herding, together with the dedications at Olympia, it is certainly notable that amongst the mythical local traditions told to Pausanias as an explanation for the beginnings of hostilities between the Spartans and Messenians in the mid-eighth century, one concerned a dispute over a herd of cattle owned by the Messenian Polychares, himself an Olympic victor.

The future of Messenia is seen at Nichoria. The last phase of the Dark Age settlement at Nichoria, which was apparently a much smaller, more introverted, and declining community, together with the subsequent violent destruction of the site by fire, may well be an indication of the lengthening shadow Sparta was casting over Messenia. An invasion was imminent, and, resist as they might, the Messenians were about to be subjected to three centuries of serfdom.

THE SPARTAN CONQUEST OF MESSENIA

> To our king, Theopompus, dear to the gods,
> Through whom we captured broad Messene,
> Messene rich for plowing, rich for planting.
> Around it they fought for nineteen years
> Without pause, keeping a strong heart,
> The warriors, fathers of our fathers.
> In the twentieth year, abandoning their rich crops
> The enemy fled from the great Ithomaean mountains.

TYRTAIOS *Fragments* 3 – 5

FIGURE 72
Pottery vessels from the Dark Age tholos tomb at the southwestern end of the Englianos Ridge. (= C. W. Blegen, M. Rawson, W. Taylour, and W. P. Donovan, The Palace of Nestor at Pylos in Western Messenia, *vol. 3:* Acropolis and Lower Town, Tholoi, Grave Circles and Chamber Tombs, Discoveries Outside the Citadel *[Princeton: Princeton University Press, 1973], fig. 298.) Archives of the Department of Classics, University of Cincinnati, with permission of Princeton University Press and the Department of Classics, University of Cincinnati.*

AFTER *the* PALACE: *The* EARLY "HISTORY" *of* MESSENIA

FIGURE 73
Bronze votive statuette of a bull. Museum of Art and Archaeology, University of Missouri-Columbia. Gift of Marie Farnsworth. With permission.

The Spartan conquest of Messenia was a long process that began in the eighth century B.C., and probably was not completed until the end of the seventh. The conquest came about through two Messenian wars, which are sketchily documented, and which in later historical sources took on a legendary or heroic air, creating a noble past for the new Messenian state of the fourth century.

One expects a major historical event such as the virtual enslavement of one group of Greeks by another for several hundred years to be well documented. However, this is not the case. There is a truism that history is written by the victors, and this certainly holds true for Messenia. The Spartans were known in antiquity for secrecy in internal matters, and Spartan authors devoted few words to their society's treatment of a subservient population. As for histories written by other Greeks not directly involved in the conflict, no contemporary accounts have been preserved, only works written at a much later date. The preserved historical sources for the Spartan conquest of Messenia are problematic, reflecting political agendas and propagandistic aims, rather than attempting to be an unbiased presentation of facts.

ANN B. HARRISON *and* NIGEL SPENCER

The Spartan poet Tyrtaios, who lived at the time of the Second Messenian War in the seventh century B.C., provides us with the only preserved contemporary account of the conflict. Yet Tyrtaios's work is preserved only in small fragments, and rather than being a neutral telling of events, Tyrtaios's poems were written as patriotic, inspirational works for Spartan soldiers.

Certainly, the most complete and detailed account of the Messenian wars is provided by Pausanias, writing in the second century A.D. However, Pausanias is not an unimpeachable source—or, more accurately, the earlier writers on whom he draws are not entirely trustworthy. For although these writers may have had access to historical works that have since been lost, they may also reflect a fourth-century rewriting of events with a political agenda. After the liberation from the Spartans and the founding of the city of Messene in 369 B.C., an entire "history" of Messenia appears to have been created for political and propagandistic purposes. From this time on, the Messenians were free to invent stories of the previous heroic defense of their land against the Spartan invader, and Hellenistic and Roman authors may reflect this fabricated history.

Keeping these weaknesses in mind, what do the sources tell us of the Spartan conquest of Messenia? To start with, it would seem that even before the conflict called the First Messenian War began, there was a certain degree of Spartan encroachment into Messenian territory. Strabo mentions in passing that the Spartan king Teleklos, who is believed to have ruled in the mid-eighth century, founded three colonies in Messenia. Also under Teleklos, there is an indication that Sparta may have been active around Pherae (modern Kalamata), in the Nedon Valley, and the Messenian Gulf. Pausanias also describes an initial conflict between Spartans and Messenians at a border sanctuary (see Introduction), which ends in the death of Teleklos. It is indeed such encroachment on Messenian territory on the part of the Spartans that may have led to the Messenian wars.

The First Messenian War began with the Spartans making a surprise attack without declaring war, according to Pausanias, who places this a generation later than the initial conflict. The Tyrtaios passage above states that the war lasted twenty years, and Pausanias describes the war as "carried on with continual small-scale banditry and seasonal raids on each other's territory," with occasional pitched battles. While the conflict may have been "small-scale," it was not isolated, for each side had allies. Messenia was aided by Arcadia, Argos, and Sicyon, traditional enemies of Sparta, while Sparta had Corinthian help. After a large battle in the fifth year of the war, the Messenians withdrew to Mt. Ithome, later site of the postliberation city of Messene, which served as the focus of their resistance. The war finally ended, according to Pausanias, with the Messenian ruler committing suicide, after which, due to attrition and siege, the Messenians abandoned Ithome.

The result of the First Messenian War was the Spartan seizure of the Stenyclarus Plain and perhaps the western Pamisos River valley. The land was annexed and the subjugated Messenians now worked it for Spartans. The settlement on Mt. Ithome was destroyed. Areas of land along the Messenian Gulf were given as rewards for allies; specifically, the inhabitants of Asine in the Argolid, who had been driven from their home by the Argives, were settled at the new site of Asine. At this point, much of western Messenia was probably not yet under Spartan control.

The conflict known as the Second Messenian War is actually the first major rebellion of those Messenians brought under Spartan control as a result of the first conflict. Pausanias places the revolt in the Stenyclarus Plain, and tells the story of the folk hero Aristomenes. The Second Messenian War follows a pattern similar to the first, with raiding, few battles, similar alliances, and the eventual withdrawal of the Messenians to a mountain stronghold (this time Mt. Eira in the northwest). Once again the Spartans were able to wear down the resistance, and to reassert and expand their power. Again a settlement loyal to the Spartans was planted in Messenia, Methoni, with the exiled population from Nauplia in the Argolid. It was probably at this point that all of Messenia, including the west coast and the Pylos area, came under Spartan control. With the loss of the second conflict, Messenia's fate was sealed.

When did this conquest of Messenia occur? Although there is little agreement among scholars as to the precise date of the First and Second Messenian wars, their general chronological placement can be determined. On the basis of literary and limited archaeological evidence, the First Messenian War probably dates to the late eighth century. As for the second war, Pausanias dates it 685–668, but this date is probably incorrect, as it conflicts with the dating of Tyrtaios. Also, Sparta suffered a major defeat at the hands of the Argives in 669, making the subsequent period of Spartan weakness the most likely time for the Messenians to revolt.

The reason for the Spartan conquest of Messenia is quite clear: land. Throughout Greece, the eighth century was a period of intense population growth and a time of expansion for many other city-states. States were faced with the problem of having insufficient arable land under their control. Sparta's main fertile region, the Eurotas Plain, was not large enough to be divided among and support all Spartan citizens. This land shortage presumably led to social tension within the community, and a lost poem by

Tyrtaios, referred to by Aristotle in the *Politics*, may indicate calls for land redistribution in his time.

Indeed, Sparta had already expanded from its original small territory and taken over the rest of Laconia, the inhabitants of which were for the most part turned into a dependent subclass. This shortage of arable land was certainly not unique to Sparta. Most Greek states solved the problem through overseas colonization, which boomed in the eighth century. Sparta sent out few such colonies, instead essentially "colonizing" the territory of neighboring Greek states. Throughout its history, Sparta would be in conflict with the neighboring states of Arcadia and Argos, which, unlike Messenia, managed to drive off the Spartans.

This need for land explains why the Spartans were so interested in Messenia, which was known in antiquity for the fertility of its countryside. In fragments of a lost work, Euripides contrasts the two areas. Laconia has "much arable land, but it is not easy to work, for the land is hollow, hemmed in by mountains, rough and troublesome for hostile forces to penetrate," whereas Messenia is "a land rich in fine fruit, watered by countless streams, with abundant pasture for both cattle and flocks, neither stormy in the winds of winter, nor made overly hot by the chariot of the sun."

SPARTAN SOCIETY

In order to understand Messenia in the Archaic and Classical periods, we must examine the political and economic structure of Sparta. The population of Laconia was organized into three major groups: *Spartiates*, *perioikoi*, and helots. The *Spartiates* were the fully enfranchised citizens of the urban center of Sparta. The adult male citizens of Sparta dedicated their lives to the state, living a unique communal, military life-style. This was made possible by the labor of the two lower subclasses in the social structure, the *perioikoi* and the helots. The *perioikoi* (literally, "those who live around") lived in towns and villages throughout Laconia, had limited political rights, and engaged in trade and manufacture. The helots' primary role was as agricultural labor, although they also fought in Spartan armies. Helots were completely disenfranchised, practically slaves, or, as one writer in the third century B.C. put it, "between free men and slaves."

Although Greece is heralded as the birthplace of democracy, slavery was a constant in the Greek world. Most slavery, however, was chattel slavery, able to be justified through a certain "otherness" on the part of those enslaved—prisoners taken in war, for example. With the helots, a very different situation was created. Entire populations of Greeks were enslaved by other Greeks. The term "enslaved" is problematic, however. Technically, helots were not slaves, although on a realistic level there was little difference between the two. Slaves could be owned by individuals and could be freed by their owner. Helots, on the other hand, were owned by the state and could only be manumitted by the state. Helots were attached to the land and could not be sold. All *Spartiates* received plots of land called *kleroi*, worked by helots, the agricultural production of which was given to the Spartan communal mess. This helot agricultural labor freed the *Spartiates* from the task of producing a living.

When Messenia came under Spartan domination, this sociopolitical template was imposed upon the populace. The land was divided into *kleroi* (owned by *Spartiates*), worked by the mass of the Messenian population, who had helot status. Fertile areas such as the Stenyclarus Plain and the Pamisos River valley were clearly areas for the *kleroi*, and given the fertility of Messenia, most of the Spartan *kleroi* were probably located here rather than in Laconia. A small number of Messenians would have had perioikic status. The precise number and location of perioikic towns in Messenia is uncertain, but a number of towns along the west coast, such as Methoni, Cyparissia, and Aulon, were clearly perioikic.

Ancient sources indicate that Sparta's treatment of the helots in general, and the Messenian helots in particular, was quite harsh:

> The conditions imposed upon the Messenians themselves by the Spartans were as follows. First, they bound them by oath neither to revolt from them ever nor to undertake any revolutionary act. Second, while they imposed no stated tax, nevertheless the Messenians used to bring one-half of all their agricultural produce to Sparta. It was decreed in addition that, for the funerals of the kings and of others in political office, both husbands and wives should come in black clothing from Messenia. And, for those who ignored this order, there was a penalty. Regarding the punishments brutally imposed on the Messenians, Tyrtaios's poetry says:
>
>> Just like donkeys ground down by great burdens,
>> Of deadly necessity carrying to their overlords
>> Fully half of all the fruit the land produces.
>
> And that there was a compulsion on them to join in mourning, he has demonstrated in this way:
>
>> Lamenting their masters, wives and husbands alike
>> Whenever the destructive fate of death came upon one.

PAUSANIAS *Description of Greece* 4.14.4–5

Each year, the Spartans ritually declared war on the helots, and instituted the Krypteia, a practice where a band of Spartan youth would murder helots. Thucydides tells of an episode in which the Spartans promised freedom to 2,000 of the best and bravest helots, and then once these men had been determined, proceeded to kill them, since they would be the men most likely to lead a revolt. It is not surprising that, given this treatment by their Spartan overlords, the Messenians did revolt, frequently.

HELOT REVOLTS AND THE PELOPONNESIAN WAR

Sparta's problem with Messenia was not solved with the Second Messenian War, as further rebellions are documented throughout the fifth century. Plato blames a Messenian rebellion for the Spartans' late arrival at Marathon in 490. This contradicts Herodotos's explanation, but may find some confirmation in archaeological evidence. Around 465, Sparta was struck by a devastating earthquake, and presumably the Messenians again took advantage of this period of Spartan weakness to revolt, starting the Third Messenian War. In this conflict, the helots were joined in the revolt by the perioikic towns of Thouria and Aithaia. Mt. Ithome was fortified and again served as the center of the resistance (Fig. 74). The Messenians withstood a siege by Sparta and its allies. Eventually a deal was worked out, the rebellious Messenians were allowed to go into exile, and the Athenians settled them at Naupactus.

At the end of the century, from 431 to 404 B.C., most of Greece was involved in the Peloponnesian War, a conflict in which the primary combatants were Athens and Sparta, each with its allies. During this war, Athens fully exploited the helot situation by taking the moral high ground over Sparta's treatment of the helots and encouraging helot revolts. The Messenians who had been exiled to Naupactus after the Third Messenian War were used as infiltrators by the Athenians in a sort of internal guerilla warfare against the Spartans, culminating in the Battle of Sphacteria early in the war (see Focus in this chapter). This Athenian foothold in Messenia would remain a constant issue throughout the war, until the Spartans took Pylos in 408.

The Spartan defeat of Athens in 404 did not lead to peace in the Greek world. The early fourth century was marked by frequent warfare, and the Messenians had their role. No longer having the protection of the Athenians, the Messenians were expelled from Naupactus in 402, and Sparta proceeded to reconsolidate its hold over Messenia. It also began a campaign of expansion and punishment against its neighbors. In 398, Sparta again

FIGURE 74
Mt. Ithome as seen from the site of Malthi in the Soulima Valley. PRAP Archive. J. L. Davis.

faced a helot revolt; this time, however, the helots were only part of a larger revolt by several groups with limited rights and status, and the revolt was led by a Spartan named Kinadon. Although this revolt was quickly put down, Sparta faced greater threats from outside its boundaries. For an alliance of Sparta's enemies led by the Boeotians had formed to stop Sparta's aggression, and the Theban general Epaminondas would soon end Sparta's dreams of empire at the Battle of Leuctra (see Chapter 7).

PRAP AND MESSENIAN SETTLEMENT PATTERNS

The acquisition of Messenia was a proverbial double-edged sword for Sparta. On the one hand, it allowed Sparta to grow into a strong and prosperous state, yet at what cost? For one gets the impression from the ancient literary sources that it also created a monster that would dominate all of Sparta's actions for the next few centuries. The Spartans were now vastly outnumbered by an enslaved population, on which they were dependent for their very subsistence. And this was not a docile population, given the revolts. The Spartans had a tiger by the tail. Therefore, let us return to the question asked at the beginning of the chapter: How did the Messenians live? Since the majority were involved in agriculture, were their lives similar to those of other Greek farmers? Or more pertinently, how did the Spartans allow the Messenians to live? Looking at the situation from a Spartan point of view, how do you best control a subject population, by dispersal or by conglomeration?

Here we can turn to the archaeological evidence. Traditionally, archaeological work has focused on urban centers, because archaeological excavations work most effectively when there is a densely settled area. For this reason, the Greek countryside has been poorly understood. Only with the rise of regional survey archaeology have questions of the countryside really been addressed. Survey work in Greece over the last twenty-five years is beginning to clarify the reality of the ancient Greek world, for it must be remembered that only a very small proportion of Greeks lived in the cities.

One of the first regional survey projects in Greece, the University of Minnesota Messenia Expedition, explored Messenia in the 1970s (see Chapter 2). For the period of Spartan domination, UMME documented relatively few sites in the survey area as a whole, and especially few on the west coast. Four areas of settlement density were noted: the Pamisos River valley, the Stenyclarus Plain, the southeastern coast of the peninsula near Koroni, and the area immediately around Pylos. As subsequent regional surveys were done throughout Greece, a certain standard settlement pattern emerged, and the small number and the types of site identified by UMME seemed anomalous. However, it was presumed that this low count was due to a number of factors, including UMME's emphasis on prehistoric periods, and on a less-intensive survey method, which would miss many small sites.

Since UMME ended, numerous surveys have set these "normal" settlement patterns for the Archaic and Classical periods in Greece. One of the better known of these surveys centers on Boeotia, also a heavily agricultural area. The Cambridge-Bradford project intensively surveyed an area of western central Boeotia and showed a countryside densely filled with small, independent farmsteads. For the Archaic to Early Hellenistic periods, that is, around 600–200 B.C., the striking feature of the Boeotia survey is the heavy density of small sites; approximately two-thirds of those sites can be interpreted as farmsteads. This pattern is repeated throughout Greece. In the Peloponnese, the Nemea Valley Archaeological Project found that the settlement pattern in the Archaic through Hellenistic periods consisted of small sites, probably farmhouses, and a few large town sites. Without going into details, this pattern holds true for the southern Argolid, Arcadia, the island of Ceos, Laconia, and to a certain extent, Attica.

So was settlement in Messenia actually different from the rest of Greece, or had UMME just missed sites? The general assumption had been the latter, given UMME's methodology. One of PRAP's goals was to identify these missing Archaic and Classical sites, in essence to fill in the holes on UMME's map of Messenia, specifically in the "empty" west. This, however, was not the outcome. PRAP found very few sites of this period not already documented by UMME, and specifically, PRAP did not find the farmsteads so common in other areas in this period. The Messenians of our survey area in the Archaic and Classical periods appear to have lived in a few fairly large towns or villages, not dispersed on farmsteads. Perhaps more enlightening is the change from this pattern in the early Hellenistic period. After the liberation from Sparta, there appear to have been many more settlements, and there is now evidence for farmsteads, a pattern in keeping with other areas of Greece. This pattern echoes the results of a small survey connected with the Nichoria excavations, the Five Rivers Survey, which identified few Archaic-Classical sites and was not able to document any farmsteads of this period, but did identify Hellenistic farmsteads.

The PRAP survey results indicate that Messenia was indeed different from other areas of Greece, in terms of both number and types of settlements. More important, the results show that this settlement pattern changes when Spartan domination ends, linking this unusual settlement pattern specifically with Messenia's subjugated role. Therefore, issues of both the number and the types of settlements need further examination.

First, let us address the question of the absence or presence of settlements in the Pylos area. There is a strong tradition, both ancient and modern, that the area around Pylos was sparsely populated. In his discussion of the Pylos campaign, Thucydides refers to the area as deserted. Historians have tended to follow Thucydides' lead, believing the area to have been sparsely populated. The PRAP results now provide archaeological evidence to support this view. While clearly not deserted, the PRAP survey area had limited settlement during Archaic and Classical times.

As for the types of settlement, what sort of people lived here? Was their status perioikic or helot? Perioikic communities are documented along the coast to the north and south of the survey area at Cyparissia and Methoni. But with no further literary evidence, the question arises whether every nucleated settlement in Messenia should be interpreted as perioikic. There has been a tendency among scholars studying Messenia to assume that this would be the case, because the assumption was that helots would be dispersed. This idea of helot dispersion has a strong hold on the study of Messenia under Spartan domination. A passage from the publication of the Five Rivers Survey clearly expresses this:

> Given its fertility, the Five Rivers area was probably among those lands initially divided into helot farmsteads. Indeed, under the helot system, it

was to Sparta's advantage to keep the helot population scattered throughout the countryside, perhaps even restricting the size of helot communities to an extended family of ten or fifteen members; ideally this would inhibit the Messenian proclivity to resist and revolt against their Spartan overlords.

Yet it must be remembered that this is a survey that identified no farmsteads.

The idea that helots must be divided appears to arise both from our modern ideas of controlling large, potentially rebellious populations (if people are kept separated, they can't be plotting against you) and from Spartan actions in other situations. For example, in the early fourth century, Sparta destroyed Mantinea in Arcadia and required its population to disperse. However, the opposite method, that of bringing people together so they can be watched and guarded, is also quite effective in controlling groups and may find support in the archaeological data from Messenia.

A site in the Soulima Valley in northern Messenia represents a possible clue to the answer to our question. In the early 1980s, utility work exposed part of a large structure in the village of Kopanaki (Fig. 75). Subsequent

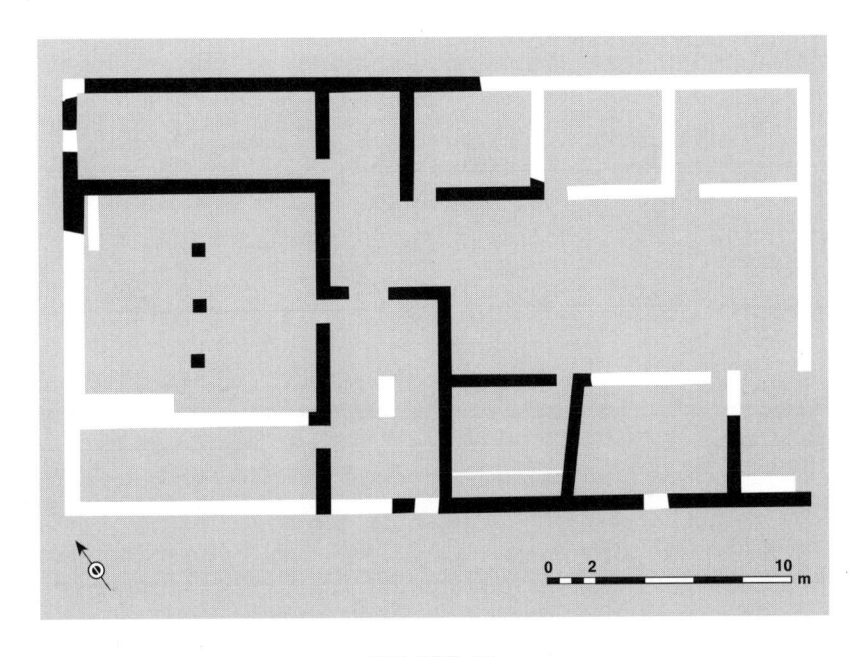

FIGURE 75
The house at Kopanaki. After N. Kaltsas, "Ἡ ἀρχαϊκὴ οἰκία στὸ Κοπανάκι τῆς Μεσσηνίας," Ἀρχαιολογικὴ Ἐφημερίς (1983): 218, fig. 2. R. J. Robertson.

excavation revealed a large eleven-room structure built around a central courtyard. The pottery from the site indicates a date from the second quarter of the sixth to the end of the first quarter of the fifth century, at which point the structure suffered a violent destruction. As for scale, the building measures approximately 30 meters by 17 meters, and the thickness of the walls implies a second story.

This is very large—so large, in fact, that initially it was taken to be a Roman villa. To put it into context, this structure is almost twice the size even of large Classical farmhouses like that at Vari in Attica, dating from the fourth century. It is on a scale with the biggest wealthy Hellenistic houses at Priene in Asia Minor. It was unimaginable that an Archaic farmhouse would be this large. A structure of this magnitude implies that the Messenian countryside was not dotted with helots on independent farmsteads working individual fields; instead, huge estates were presumably farmed by groups of helots under Spartan supervision. The Spartans appear, at least in some cases, to have preferred nucleation over dispersal as a control strategy.

Although such evidence does not tell us the status of the nucleated settlements in the Pylos area, it does indicate that they do not have to have been perioikic. The unusual settlement patterns of Messenia in the Archaic and Classical periods, as well as the change of these patterns in the Hellenistic, reflect the unique social and economic conditions of Spartan domination.

FOCUS

CERAMIC TYPOLOGY *for* BEGINNERS

When most people think of the excitement and romance of archaeology, the buried cities and temples, the gold and precious objects, the shining marble statuary, they rarely think of pottery. Perhaps the more knowledgeable will recall the elaborate decorated vases on display in museums throughout the world. But few would think of the relatively plain and unattractive pottery that is the backbone of most archaeological work.

The study of pottery is essential in archaeology. Imagine a world in which every container in your home currently made out of plastic or glass was made of clay. Imagine the huge storage needs for food, and especially for water in a world without our plumbing. Now you begin to have an idea of the importance and the quantity of pottery found in the ancient world. This sheer quantity is one of the reasons that pottery is the most common class of object found in archaeological work; most archaeological projects find themselves with literally tons of it (Fig. 76). It is virtually indestructible: Of all the various types of artifact created by ancient societies, pottery is the most likely to survive, if for no other reason than it has no reuse value. Objects made of metal were often melted down for the value of their material. There are numerous examples in history of bronze statues being melted down for cannonballs, or gold statues melted down for coinage. Marble statues, as well, often met an indecorous fate, being burned to make lime. As for the great architectural monuments, they, too, often ended up in the lime kiln, or had their blocks reused for later architecture. Therefore, the small broken potsherd can be one of the most important elements in an archaeological project, because it remains while other types of evidence disappear.

For archaeologists, pottery points to trade and cultural contacts, to status and affluence, and it is probably the most consistently used chronological indicator. In survey archaeology, the surface scatters of pottery

ANN B. HARRISON

FIGURE 76
*Tins of pottery awaiting study in museum. PRAP Archive.
R. Dupuis-Devlin and E. Dallagher.*

FIGURE 77
*Table of sherds of pottery being analyzed. Ann B. Harrison in foreground.
PRAP Archive. R. Dupuis-Devlin and E. Dallagher.*

sherds are the primary evidence of ancient occupation of a site. Archaeologists generally separate pottery into two categories (Fig. 77): fine, decorated wares, the ancient equivalent of your best china; and plain or coarse wares, that is, the sorts of everyday vessels found in your kitchen. Of these two classes of pottery, the fine wares have received much more attention, both from specialized scholars and from museum curators, who regularly display them. The coarse wares have been much less thoroughly studied, yet they comprise the majority of pottery found in archaeological work. It also should be pointed out that pottery production in antiquity was highly regional, with various localities producing different "styles" of ceramics.

The most important role of pottery in archaeology is as a chronological indicator. Archaeologists work with both relative chronologies—the creation of a sequence in which it can be said that one object is older or more recent than another—and absolute chronologies—the linking of an object to a real date. The dating of pottery and its use as a chronological indicator involves both types of chronology. By studying and sorting thousands of pots, archaeologists have created relative, stylistic sequences for most regional styles of Greek fine wares and some coarse wares, which are even more localized in their production. Then, through archaeological discovery of pottery in a securely dated context—say, for example, a sealed destruction layer that is firmly dated in historical sources—the relative chronology can be linked to the absolute chronology. Pottery can also be tied to absolute chronology through synchronisms. Finding a well-dated regional ware in a closed context with an undated regional ware allows the latter to be dated. Through these methods, an absolute chronology has been set for most Greek pottery. Using this chronology, the archaeologist in an excavation can date the layers of his stratigraphy, or in a survey can date the various sherd scatters.

The finding of imported pottery at a site indicates trade on some level, either direct or through intermediaries, with the production center. Along with trade comes the idea of cultural contact. The degree of cultural contact implied by imported pottery varies in each instance, but a general principle exists that the degree of contact increases with the frequency of the imported pottery. Fine wares are the main pottery trade commodities, as most coarse-ware production was local. The exceptions are the pots created specifically to travel, that is, the transport vessels designed to ship commodities throughout the Mediterranean.

Pottery may also reflect the status or affluence of its owner, to a certain extent. There has been argument recently in archaeological circles over whether clay vessels can definitionally be considered a luxury or status item, in the way a gold or silver vessel might. Clearly not, but in the long continuum between the coarsest clay bowl and the most elaborate gold cup, there is a definite differentiation between various types of pot. Some types of pottery were much more difficult and time-consuming to produce; hence, presumably, they would be more "expensive." It is assumed that a large, elaborately decorated painted vase such as an Attic red-figure work in a museum display would cost more than an undecorated water jug. Also, imported pottery was presumably a luxury or status item, costing more than locally produced pottery. Therefore, the proportion of such relatively high-cost items can be used to try to determine the degree of affluence of the inhabitants of an archaeological site.

FOCUS

NICHORIA: *An* EARLY IRON AGE VILLAGE *in* MESSENIA

At the site of Nichoria on the narrow, winding ridgetop near modern Rizomylo, above the northern coast of the Gulf of Messene, the change from the thriving Bronze Age settlement in the Further Province of the Pylian kingdom to the small early Iron Age village that succeeded it was as striking in its scale as the transformation apparent elsewhere in Messenia. In place of the substantial Mycenaean site laid out on the hill, complete with streets, stone-built drains, and formal entranceways, the initial Iron Age group of approximately sixty or seventy people who were scattered along the ridgetop from the eleventh century lived in structures so flimsy that they left no physical trace of their occupation beyond a scatter of their broken pottery vessels.

Slowly this meager population grew, forming a settlement focused in the saddle of the ridge and possibly reaching as many as 200 people a century later. But although use was made of the ruined walls of the previous Bronze Age houses, gone were the paved courtyards outside well-fashioned rectangular (sometimes two-story) buildings of two to three rooms, replaced by generally one-roomed oval or apsidal structures of wattle and daub built on stone socles with pitched, probably thatched, roofs (Fig. 78). Gone, too, was the largely cereal-based economy that the inhabitants had practiced in the late Bronze Age (clear from the Linear B tablets, which refer to the produce from the site, then known as *ti-mi-to-a-ke-e*). In its place, the Iron Age dwellers relied much more on a mixed diet that incorporated not only cereals, grapes, olives, and pulses, but also a high proportion of meat. Cattle and deer, especially, were favorite foods, and the intensive hunting for deer is clearest during the first Iron Age settlement phase, as if an initial culling of local herds in the nearby coastal valleys and plains preceded a subsequent scarcity after these herds were decimated and driven away, necessitating searches for alternative food sources.

NIGEL SPENCER

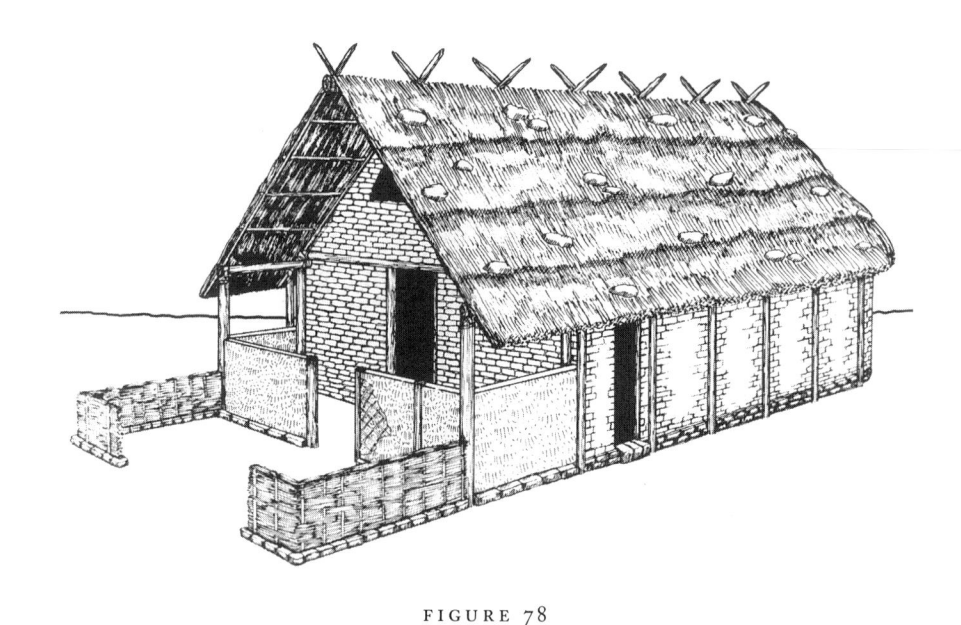

FIGURE 78
Reconstruction of Unit IV-1, phase 2, at the site of Nichoria. Reproduced from W. A. McDonald, W.D.E. Coulson, and J. Rosser, Excavations at Nichoria in Southwest Greece, *vol. 3:* Dark Age and Byzantine Occupation *(Minneapolis: University of Minnesota Press, 1983), fig. 2–23, with permission of the University of Minnesota Press.*

But amongst these Iron Age practices, which contrasted (especially in their scale) with many of the previous habits of the Bronze Age, there were clearly traditions preserved from the earlier way of life in the Pylian kingdom. Almost as if groups of refugees had abandoned the Nichoria hilltop and survived the collapse of the kingdom, lived nearby (in a place as yet undiscovered), and then returned to the site, some of the pottery and metalwork in use at Nichoria in the eleventh century B.C. exhibited close similarities with the earlier Mycenaean items. The Mycenaean cemetery was reused also, and in the tenth century the dwellers at the increasingly substantial Iron Age village decided to build a Mycenaean-style tholos tomb in which to bury four members of their community.

It was in this "middle" phase of the village's life, from the later tenth to ninth centuries (before the decline and end of the village in the eighth century), that the contacts were most broad. The potters at Nichoria were making vessels similar to those as far away as Achaea and Ithaca in the north and west, and to the east contacts were clear with the practices of those dwelling beyond the Taygetus range in Laconia. This knowledge of Spartan wares quite possibly came through interaction at mediating locations such as Volimnos, a site high on the mountain pass between the two regions, where material of this early date suggests early contact, possibly in the context of a shrine visited by both Messenians and Laconians. At Nichoria, spindle whorls and loomweights were found also amongst the Iron Age houses, indicating that textiles were produced; leatherwork was fashioned, too. There were homemade metal items smelted by members of the community skilled in metallurgy, with the working of copper, tin, and iron taking place in the village itself (Fig. 79). Indeed, the large amount of tin used by the Nichorians suggests that, given the lack of any locally known sources, contacts may have been especially wide; and a piece of twisted gold wire underlines the desire on behalf of at least some members of the village to acquire luxury items of precious metal for personal adornment or cult purposes.

But this relative prosperity was not to last. A third and final phase of the site in the early eighth century showed a clear decline from the outward-looking previous generations. The population fell, possibly by as much as a half, to around 100 people, and only the central area of the ridge, the focus of the previous, more expansive settlement, remained occupied. Contacts with areas abroad were broken, and the material culture (such as the ce-

FIGURE 79
Metal shield boss from Nichoria. Reproduced from W. A. McDonald, W.D.E. Coulson, and J. Rosser, Excavations at Nichoria in Southwest Greece, vol. 3: Dark Age and Byzantine Occupation *(Minneapolis: University of Minnesota Press, 1983), fig. 5-3, with permission of the University of Minnesota Press.*

ramics) became more introverted, with the Nichorian potters producing wares with little sign of contact with any region beyond the bounds of Messenia. This final phase was marked also by an intensification of storage facilities in the most impressive known structure of the final village, a long apsidal building in the central saddle of the ridge.

Whether or not this last feature of centralized storage was a sign of growing insecurity among the villagers, perhaps indicating the threat from increasingly expansionist policies at Sparta, whose designs upon Messenia were soon to be clearly stated, the last small settlement was destroyed in an intense conflagration toward the middle of the eighth century. Fire swept over the whole central area of the ridgetop where the last houses of the Iron Age village had stood, collapsing the long apsidal building and scattering fragments of burnt mud brick and charcoal across the whole settlement area. The villagers fled and, perhaps for the first time since the site had formed one of the major regional centers of the Bronze Age kingdom, the hilltop of Nichoria lay silent and uninhabited.

FOCUS

The BATTLE of SPHACTERIA
(425 B.C.)

The Peloponnesian War, which had begun in 431 B.C. between the two sets of allied forces under the command of Athens and Sparta, dragged on with no end in sight. Every year the forces of the Spartans with their Peloponnesian allies invaded Attica, wreaking extensive and regular devastation of crops and forcing the Athenians to abandon their rural settlements and retreat into the walls of Athens itself. Such were the cramped living conditions that ensued that a plague had already occurred in 430 B.C., decimating the sheltering Athenian citizens (and claiming the life of Pericles himself and his two sons).

In response to these regular invasions of their own land, the Athenians formed a plan for retaliatory action and decided to bring into play their superior navy and strike close to the heartland of the enemy in the Peloponnese itself. Ships were dispatched around the coast of the Peloponnese, attacking strategic places that included Methoni in Messenia; but no permanent bases had been established until 425 B.C., at which point one of the generals experienced from earlier missions, Demosthenes, requested forces in order to continue harassing these southern coastlines. The Athenian Assembly agreed, and the fleet set sail, but the mission was distracted on hearing that Peloponnesian ships had arrived at Corcyra (modern Corfu), and two of the other generals sailing with Demosthenes urged that the Athenian vessels should hurry northward to the area immediately. Demosthenes, however, was adamant that the initial Athenian raids upon Spartan-occupied Messenia, aided by the Messenians exiled after their failed revolt in the 460s and now living at Naupactus, should be followed up. The chance should not be missed, he argued, of now establishing a more permanent base for guerilla-style operations in the south, and Demosthenes considered the most logical place to establish this base to be the large, natural harbor at the Bay of Sphacteria, with its rocky, defensible promontories and the long, narrow island on its seaward side.

NIGEL SPENCER

FIGURE 80
Fort of Neokastro with the island of Sphacteria and Palaionavarino in the distance. PRAP Archive. J. L. Davis.

This choice was certainly a shrewd one based on the topography of the bay and its strategic importance (Fig. 80). Both the island of Sphacteria (which formed the western limit of the bay, lying offshore with a north-south orientation) and the high rock known in antiquity as Coryphasion, and later in history as Palaiokastro (because of its ruined medieval castle), were sheer outcrops, easily fortified and defensible with even a small detachment of hoplites. Much later, the Arabs and Turks recognized the importance of both spots to the defense of the settlement at modern Pylos on the eastern side of the bay during the Greek War of Independence in 1825. In this campaign, the task of overwhelming the Greek garrison on Sphacteria became their chief aim, since they knew that the town opposite was untenable once the stronghold had fallen.

Initially, however, the Athenians were unimpressed with Demosthenes' decision. Why was time and money being spent on fortifying Coryphasion? After all, they mocked, there were many more deserted headlands in the Peloponnese that Demosthenes could fortify if he so wished. Nevertheless, a storm that kept the fleet sheltering in Sphacteria Bay gave Demosthenes the opportunity to start putting his plan into action, and his Athenian troops spent six days constructing defenses on the less naturally fortified spots of the Coryphasion promontory (at its southern end). Demosthenes stayed behind with a garrison of five ships when the weather became better, and the rest of the Athenian fleet set sail for Corcyra.

The response from the Peloponnesian army was swift. Its forces immediately retreated from Attica, and orders were sent out to all available troops in the Peloponnese to proceed to the Pylos area as quickly as possible to face the Athenian garrison. The Peloponnesian fleet at Corcyra was also recalled, and escaped the notice of the Athenian ships sailing northward to meet it when the Peloponnesians dragged their boats over the narrow isthmus at Lefkas; thus the small detachment under Demosthenes could be blockaded within its hastily constructed walls at Coryphasion. In order to make the blockade effective, the Peloponnesians set up a camp on land to the north, blockaded the bay to the west and east with their ships, and occupied the mostly wooded island of Sphacteria to the south. An assault was imminent.

Demosthenes, still awaiting reinforcements from the fleet in the north, to whom he had sent messengers warning of the impending danger to the garrison, exhorted his men to defend their post, which they did in the face of repeated attacks by land and sea from the Peloponnesians. The irony of the situation was not lost on the main ancient source for the episode, Thucydides, who pointed out that here were the Peloponnesians, normally seeking to wage war by land, forced to attack by sea against the blockaded Athenians, who themselves were in an unusual position, since it was they who normally relied upon their superior navy to win the day. Their vast superiority in number proved insufficient for the Peloponnesians, however; Demosthenes' men could not be dislodged from Coryphasion, Athenian reinforcements arrived, and the tables were about to be turned.

The Athenian fleet arrived suddenly, catching the Peloponnesian ships off-guard, absent from their blockading positions around Coryphasion and Sphacteria; in the ensuing battle inside the bay, many of the Peloponnesian ships were wrecked or boarded, leaving the Spartan garrison on the island of Sphacteria effectively cut off from its land army, which had now arrived in force and was camped to the northeast of Coryphasion. Thus the situation had been reversed completely, with the Athenians now able to hold off the Peloponnesian land army and establish their own blockade on the remaining garrison of 420 men on Sphacteria, a situation that so concerned the Spartan government that peace was sought with Athens in return for the safe conduct of the hostages. When the Spartan envoys presented their proposals to the Athenian Assembly, however, the demagogue Kleon encouraged the citizens to refuse their offer of peace. No settlement was agreed upon, and the Spartans returned home empty-handed.

With this failure to peaceably reconcile the situation, the blockade of the Spartans on Sphacteria continued, but the situation was becoming difficult, and not just for the trapped Spartan hoplites. The Athenians, too, had little food and water, and supplies were being secretly smuggled to the Spartans by swimmers from the mainland, ensuring that there was no immediate surrender by the garrison. At this point in Athens, with frustration growing at the continuing stalemate, Kleon boasted that he himself would swiftly remove the garrison from Sphacteria. No doubt to his shock, his archrival Nikias then resigned from the post of general and, together with the Assembly of Athens, granted him the opportunity to do exactly this!

Kleon traveled south and began to plot the assault with Demosthenes, who had been especially apprehensive about moving any forces against the Spartans because of the wooded nature of the island of Sphacteria, which could conceal the enemy's movements and true numbers. At this point, however, by a stroke of good fortune (and no doubt helped by the intense heat of early August), one of the Athenians put in on the shore of the island and by chance set the forest alight. Fanned by a strong wind, the flames burnt much of the cover that had added to the security of the Spartan garrison, and thereby made an attack much more feasible.

A day after the fire, just before dawn, a force of 800 Athenian troops landed at two points near the southern end of the island, surprising and putting to the sword the advance guard of Spartans in this area (Fig. 81). The main Spartan contingent fell into ranks, moving south along the rough terrain to face the large number of troops from the Athenian ships that had landed. After bitter exchanges, with a number of the Spartans wounded by the volleys of arrows and javelins from their opponents, the defenders, heavily outnumbered, fell back northward to their fortified position near the summit of the island. Here, they held out with great bravery, but their position near the summit was turned by a group of Messenians, who informed Kleon and Demosthenes that there was a natural stairway in a gorge on the northeast side of the island that would allow the Athenians to assault the Spartan position from the rear. The Spartan position was now untenable, and at this point the Athenians offered the defenders the opportunity to surrender, Kleon cleverly realizing that there was far more political capital to be gained from bringing back the remaining Spartans alive to Athens if possible. With little choice but to accept, the 292 surviving defenders (120 of whom were Spartan citizens) were disarmed and taken to Athens.

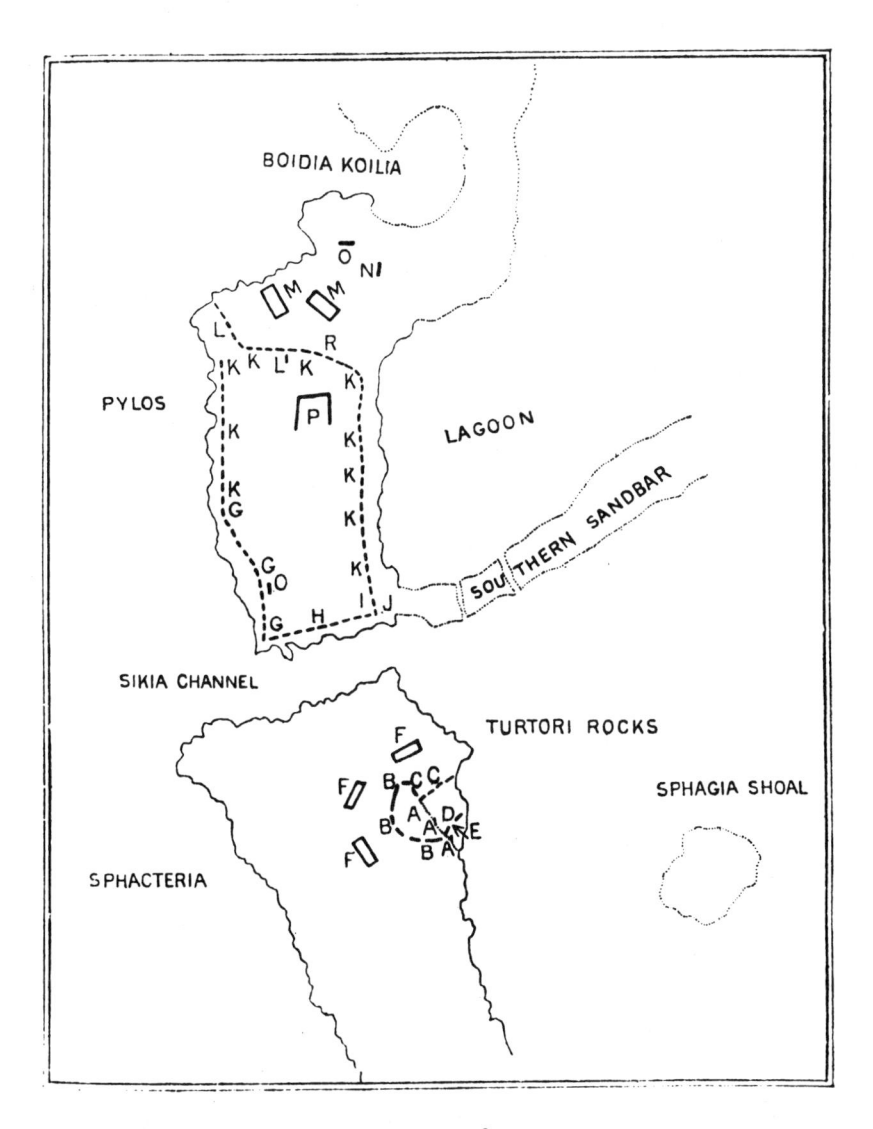

FIGURE 81
Map showing the conjectural positions of Spartan and Athenian military contingents stationed in defense and blockade of Coryphasion. B-C-D represent Spartan positions on Sphacteria; F, the body of the Athenian attack. G-H-I-K represent the Athenian line of defense at Coryphasion; M, the Spartan attack. Reproduced from R. N. Burrows, "Pylos and Sphacteria," Journal of Hellenic Studies *16 (1896): 56.*

For Kleon, the mission was a spectacular political success. The army of the Spartans, previously considered invincible, had surrendered to an Athenian land force, the Athenians now had hostages whose lives could be threatened if there were any more Peloponnesian invasions of Attica, and Pylos could be firmly garrisoned with a detachment of Messenians from Naupactus to wage more frequent guerilla-style raids on their enemy. The Messenians rejoiced at the opportunity to return to their former homeland, helots who lived nearby and had been under the Spartan yoke deserted to their cause, and the Naupactan Messenians dedicated a statue of Victory in the sanctuary at Olympia to celebrate the campaign. The Athenians themselves set up a trophy on the island of Sphacteria and another statue of Victory on the Acropolis in Athens, and with such a display of military prowess and with Kleon preeminent politically, the way was clear to swell the treasuries in Athens by vastly increasing the tribute paid to the city by its allies.

FIGURE 82
The coast at Dialiskari, as seen from southwest near the church of Ayios Nikolaos, with modern fishing boats in the foreground and new summer villas in the distance. PRAP Archive. R. J. Robertson.

CHAPTER 7

LIBERATION and CONQUEST: HELLENISTIC and ROMAN MESSENIA

In July 371 B.C., a battle was fought that, although it took place many hundreds of miles away to the north in central Greece, irrevocably altered the relationship of Sparta and Messenia. At the plain of Leuctra in Boeotia, troops led by the Theban general Epaminondas soundly defeated Spartan forces—their first major defeat in open combat for some three centuries. Soon after, in 370 B.C., Epaminondas led an unprecedented invasion of Sparta's own home territory. As soon as Epaminondas crossed into Spartan lands, many Messenians rose up in revolt against their overlords. Their rejection of Spartan domination was sealed by Epaminondas's liberation of the Messenians and his foundation of the polis (city-state) of Messene.

Pausanias, the second century A.D. traveler, offers the following account of this foundation:

> Since the place where the Messenians now have their city seemed most suitable for settlement to Epaminondas, he ordered enquiries to be made of the seers as to whether the divine world, too, would give him their consent here. When they gave the word that the rituals were auspicious, he made preparations for the foundation in this way, ordering stone to be fetched, and sent for craftsmen, whose skill was in laying out streets, building houses and temples, and constructing circuit walls. When everything had been made ready, at that point—once the Arcadians had provided sacrificial victims—Epaminondas himself and the Thebans made sacrifices to Dionysus and to Ismenian Apollo in the customary way; the Argives sacrificed to Argive Hera and Nemean Zeus; the Messenians to Zeus of Ithome and to the Dioscuri, and their priests to the Great Goddesses and Caucon. In common, they then called upon the heroes to return to them and live with them: particularly Messene the daughter of Triopas, but after her Eurytus, Aphareus and his chil-

---

SUSAN E. ALCOCK

dren, and, from among the children of Heracles, Cresphontes and Aepytus. However, the loudest invitation, from everyone, was for Aristomenes. That day was spent in sacrifice and prayer, but for the days following they raised the circuit of walls and built houses and sanctuaries within them....

The Messenians reentered the Peloponnese and rescued what was theirs 287 years after Eira's capture, when Dyscinetus was archon at Athens, in the third year of the 102d Olympiad, when Damon of Thurii won his second victory.

PAUSANIAS *Description of Greece* 4.27.5–9

The foundation of Messene, named after the early queen of the region, made good sense. Providing the Messenians with a fortified urban center of their own strengthened their ability to check any future expansionist tendencies on Sparta's part. Indeed, Epaminondas also founded Megalopolis (literally "Great City") in Arcadia in 369 B.C. to create yet another hostile presence on Sparta's borders. Yet as Pausanias's account makes clear, this city foundation was more than a smart political and military ploy. Invoking the gods and summoning the heroes (including the legendary freedom-fighter, Aristomenes) transformed the creation of Messene into a highly charged symbolic event, marking this stunning reversal of fortune. With liberation, Messenian exiles from as far away as Sicily and North Africa returned to their land, the despised helots became citizens of their own state, and a dispossessed people were finally given a home.

The site chosen for Messene—incorporating Mt. Ithome—was symbolically as well as strategically appropriate, for Ithome, and Zeus Ithomatas, had long served as the refuge and "heart" of Messenian territory. The walls of Messene embraced not only the acropolis of Ithome and the "built-up" town, but also a considerable area of countryside—the wall line is some 9 kilometers long (Fig. 83). Such an "enceinte" walling system became popular in the fourth century B.C., for it allowed natural defenses to be exploited (in this case, the heights and ridges of Ithome) and protected agricultural lands that could feed an urban populace in case of siege. The walls of Messene, all stone-built to a height of some 7 to 9 meters, are agreed to be among the most sophisticated defenses, and certainly the most spectacular to view, in all of Greece (Fig. 84). Later sources claim that the city and its walls were built with incredible rapidity—in eighty-five days, according to one author. Modern-day viewers of the immense and carefully constructed wall circuit find this hard to believe, and it probably is an exaggeration. On the other hand, it has been found that communal build-

FIGURE 83
*Mt. Ithome with the fourth-century wall line of Messene visible on its slopes.
S. E. Alcock.*

FIGURE 84
*Arcadian Gate, one of the massive gateways in the fortifications at Messene.
J. F. Cherry.*

ing projects, done to a tight time schedule, can serve as one means to bind a population together, to teach them a sense of common purpose. The rapidity of the creation of Messene was, again, not only strategic, but a way for the Messenians, with the help of their allies, to renew their sense of self and of purpose.

With the foundation of Messene, the "tale of the Messenians" reached an almost storybook happy ending. That neat conclusion to the struggles and pain of this people may be one reason why Messenia's postliberation history has been little explored by classical scholars. Yet it is not enough to say that the people of Messenia lived "happily ever after"—what happened to them after they were freed?

As might be expected, relations between Sparta and the new state of Messenia remained deeply hostile. Sparta resisted any public acknowledgment of its losses and refused to accept the existence of Messene, instead plotting various ways to retrieve its "ancestral" territories. A speech attributed to a Spartan king at this time bitterly commented: "The most irritating thing is not that we shall be unjustly deprived of our land, but that we shall witness our slaves as masters of it." Messenia's loathing, and fear, of Sparta appears to have influenced many of its postliberation political friendships. For example, Messenia allied itself with Philip II of Macedon, father of Alexander the Great, as a protector against Sparta, despite the remonstrances of Demosthenes of Athens, Philip's great enemy. In spite of embassies from Athens, Messene (together with many other Peloponnesian cities) remained neutral in the Battle of Chaeronea (338 B.C.)—the encounter that would seal Greece's fate as a secondary player in the power politics of the Hellenistic world. To reward his allies, the victorious Philip subsequently marched south to Sparta, stripping it still further of both pride and territory (some of which was given over to Messenia).

As the alliance with Philip suggests, the cities of Messenia, under the leadership of Messene, were now fully involved in the political and military machinations of the age. In other words, after liberation Messenia resumed a more "normal" role in Greek politics and warfare. The saga of alliances and betrayals among the Greek cities during the Hellenistic period (beginning in the later fourth century B.C.) is too complicated to rehearse in detail. One development to note, however, is the increasing political and military intervention of larger and more powerful states, especially the Antigonid kingdom in Macedon to the north. When such external powers became involved in Greek affairs, they identified Messene as a crucial point to control, given the strength of Mt. Ithome and its strategic location in the southern Peloponnese. At the end of the third century B.C., King Philip V of Macedon was advised, when contemplating the invasion of the Peloponnese, to seize both Acrocorinth (the fortified citadel of Corinth) and Mt. Ithome: "If you grab both horns, you will hold the ox fast"—or hold, in other words, the entire Peloponnese.

Messenia resumed its place in the world of Greek social and cultural life as well, not least by its production of notable talented individuals. One such person was Damophon, a citizen of Messene whose family tree can be traced back through inscriptions found by excavations in the city. Damophon was a celebrated artist whose career seems to have peaked in the late third/early second century B.C. He is known for working in what is called the "neoclassical" style; that is, his sculptures deliberately evoked the artistic styles of the Classical age of the fifth century B.C. His best-preserved sculptural group comes from the sanctuary of Despoina at Lycosura in Arcadia; the group includes Despoina (the "Maiden," or Persephone), her mother Demeter, Artemis, and the Titan Anytos (Fig. 85). In antiquity, Damophon was also famous for repairing Pheidias's statue of Zeus at the great Panhellenic sanctuary at Olympia, a task for which he was publicly honored.

So far, this account has dwelt primarily upon the city of Messene, which lies some 15 kilometers to the northwest of the Pylos region. From documentary sources, we know little specifically about our study region during this era. Liberation may have come slightly later to the western reaches of Messenia; some Messenian towns, possibly because of the presence of Spartan garrisons, appear to have remained loyal to Sparta. Only in 365 B.C., for example, was Pylos/Coryphasion, together with Cyparissia to the north, captured by the Argives and given over to Messenia. Indeed—although our sources are unclear—it may be only now that a proper settlement, rather than just a fortified site, was founded on the headland at Pylos/Coryphasion, and a true polis constituted in this area.

One preliminary archaeological observation that we can make about our study region, however, is that there appears to be an increase in settlement and land use in the period *after* the liberation from Sparta. Just as the Messenians resumed their place in Greek political, military, and cultural activities, so—with freedom—they reorganized their lives within the countryside, which they now farmed for themselves and not for their Spartan masters.

That state of autonomy, of freedom, would not, however, last long. At a peace conference ending just one of the innumerable Greek conflicts that scarred the last three centuries B.C., one far-sighted speaker reminded the assembled powers of "the clouds now appearing from the west"—the growing power of Rome. It was not long before Rome and Messenia came in contact, with Messenia siding with Rome against Philip V of Macedon,

FIGURE 85
Reconstruction of the cult group at Lycosura in Arcadia; sculpted by Damophon of Messene (200–150 B.C.). Left to right: Artemis, Despoina, Demeter, Anytos. Reproduced from G. Dickens, "Damophon of Messene II," Annual of the British School at Athens 13 (1906–7): pl. xii. With permission of the British School at Athens.

the king who tried to seize Ithome at the end of the third century B.C. Rome increasingly intervened in Greek affairs, for example in forcing Messenia, much against its will, to join a larger confederation of states, the Achaean League (191 B.C.). Despite this, Messenia did not fight with the league against Rome in the Achaean War (146 B.C.), when several cities, including Corinth, were sacked mercilessly in the Roman victory. Bad times for much of Greece continued for the next century or so, as the peninsula became one theater for a series of bloody Roman civil wars. Most of the devastation occurred to the north of Messenia, which, it is worth noting, seems largely to have escaped these traumas. In the last of these civil conflicts, however, the Messenians chose to side with Antony and Cleopatra against Augustus—as did most of Greece, with the notable exception of Sparta. After his decisive victory in the sea battle at Actium (off the coast of northern Greece), Augustus punished his opponents, including Messenia, and rewarded the Spartans, not least by assigning them certain Messenian cities.

Augustus is responsible for creating the Roman province of Achaea, a province of roughly the same size and shape as modern mainland Greece; the provincial capital probably lay at a newly refounded Corinth. With this formal annexation, Messenia joined the Roman empire, becoming subject to imperial rule, imperial laws, and imperial taxes. Apart from episodes such as Nero's short-lived declaration of freedom for all the Greeks in 67 A.D. (rescinded almost immediately by Nero's less profligate successor, Vespasian), Messenia would remain part of a larger empire from the early first century B.C. until the early-nineteenth-century War of Greek Independence, almost two thousand years later.

The Messenian region possessed certain advantages that allowed the Roman period (at least until the fifth century A.D.) to be an era of apparent prosperity. Compared to many other parts of the Greek peninsula, Messenia is a fertile zone; given the imposition of regular Roman tax demands, this agricultural productivity was a great boon for the region's inhabitants. About the time of Augustus, the geographer Strabo remarked, "One should accept what Euripides says, that Messenia is a land rich in fine fruit, watered by countless streams, with abundant pasture for both cattle and flocks, neither stormy in the winds of winter, nor made overly hot by the chariot of the sun . . . a land indescribably productive." Admittedly, Strabo is here quoting a fifth-century playwright; it is also true that this admirable reputation better fits the plains close to modern-day Kalamata and the Taygetus mountain range than the "sandy Pylos" area. Nevertheless, the fertility that made Messenia an attractive target for Spartan expansion clearly was also a positive factor in its Roman development. A second advantage for the region was its western location and orientation. If Messenia had previously been something of a remote and inaccessible backwater in a Greek world looking to the Aegean and the east, now places "facing west"—places such as Patras, Corinth, Nicopolis, Olympia, and Messenia—thrived owing to their greater proximity to Italy and Rome (see Frontispiece).

The attractions of Messenia were perceived even before Greece became a Roman province. In the course of the second and first centuries B.C., *negotiatores* (businessmen) settled in various parts of the Greek mainland and islands. *Negotiatores* were often referred to as *Rhomaioi*, though many of them were actually of Italian origin. These men, in the first instance, were interested in commerce and trade, but they often soon invested in land as well: it is not surprising that groups of *Rhomaioi* are especially prominent in the more fertile parts of Greece, such as Boeotia and Messenia. Evidence of their presence in Messene comes from an inscription recording a special tax collection in the early first century A.D. *Rhomaioi* were liable to this tax, though they were also apparently late in their payments; the amounts owed suggest that these individuals owned a substantial amount of land in Messenian territory. Though the appearance of *Rhomaioi* as the possessors of such sizable estates might in some cases indicate the dispossession of native landowners, their presence could also have contributed to the economic well-being of the area and its positive treatment by Rome.

Rome's rule of its provinces tended to remain at a fairly "hands-off" level, with an estimated ratio of one Roman official for every 350,000–400,000 provincials. Yet Rome could also become directly involved in disputes between Greek cities. This included the endless, if now nonviolent, bickering between Sparta and Messenia over their respective boundaries. One particularly long-running argument concerned an area called the Ager Dentheliates in the Taygetus mountain range, the site of an important sanctuary to Artemis Limnatis. According to Pausanias, this sanctuary had been, somewhere far back in time, the scene of the very first hostilities between Messenians and Spartans. The tug-of-war over the Ager Dentheliates lasted for centuries; the Roman historian Tacitus tells us that the dispute was carried on and argued "according to the testimonia of poets and historical records." At least six separate arbitrations are known over this issue, the last of which was made by the Roman governor of Achaea and confirmed by no less a body than the Roman Senate—in favor of the Messenian claim (see also the Introduction to this volume).

The apparent prosperity and relative good fortune of Roman Messenia can also be measured by examining its most important (and best explored) city—Messene. Inscriptions reveal a major episode of rebuilding and town improvement during the Augustan Age, a sign perhaps of better and more peaceful times following the difficult preceding decades. Pausanias, who visited the city some five centuries after its foundation by Epaminondas, gives us a remarkable description of its state in the later second century A.D. A translation of his tour through the city (as abridged by Christian Habicht to exclude historical digressions and explanations) runs as follows:

> Around Messene there is a wall, the whole circuit of stone, with towers and crenellations built onto it.... In their marketplace, the Messenians have a statue of Zeus the Savior and a fountain called Arsinoe ... it is fed by water from a spring called Clepsydra. Of the gods, there are sanctuaries of Poseidon and Aphrodite. Particularly worthy of note is a likeness made of Parian marble of the Mother of the Gods, a piece by Damophon.... Also by this Damophon is what the Messenians call the

Laphria. . . . Also built for the Messenians is a temple of Eileithyia, with a statue of stone. Nearby is a hall of the Curetes. . . . The Messenians also have a sacred shrine to Demeter and statues of the Dioscuri, carrying the daughters of Leucippus. . . . But the sanctuary of Asclepius offers the greatest number of statues and those particularly worth viewing. For, apart from statues of the god and his sons, and of Apollo, the Muses, and Heracles, there is a representation of the city of Thebes, of Epaminondas the son of Cleommis, of Luck, and of Artemis, the bringer of light. Those made of stone were sculpted by Damophon—I know of no other Messenian sculptor whose work is worthy of mention other than him. The image of Epaminondas, however, is of iron, and the work of another craftsman, not him. There is also a temple of Messene, containing a statue of gold and Parian marble. In the rear of the temple are representations of the kings of Messenia. . . . Asclepius is also painted. . . . Omphalion, a student of Nicias, Nicomedes' son, painted these pictures. . . . The area called "the place of sacrifice" by the Messenians has images of all the gods the Greeks acknowledge, and, in addition, a bronze statue of Epaminondas. There are also ancient tripods. . . . The statues in the gymnasium are the works of Egyptians: representations of Hermes, Heracles, and Theseus. . . . There is also a tomb of Aristomenes here. . . . In the stadium of the Messenians there is also a bronze statue of Aristomenes. Not far from the theater is a sanctuary of Sarapis and Isis. As you ascend to the summit of Ithome, which is the Messenians' acropolis, there is a spring called Clepsydra. . . . They carry water from the spring to the sanctuary of Zeus of Ithome every day. Zeus's statue is a piece by Ageladas. . . . In addition, they maintain an annual celebration, "the Ithomaea." . . . As you take the road for Arcadia leading to Megalopolis, at the gates, there is a Hermes of Attic craftsmanship.

PAUSANIAS *Description of Greece* 4.31.5–33.3

This impressive range of civic buildings (walls, marketplace, theater, gymnasium, stadium, public fountains) and sanctuaries (to Poseidon, Demeter, Artemis, Zeus, and many others) testifies to an active and thriving community. A stress on the city's legendary heroes and historical founders (Messene, Aristomenes, Epaminondas) remains very pronounced, as the Messenians turned to their past as a source of local identity and of pride (see Focus in this chapter).

Excavations at Messene since the 1950s (under the direction of the Greek archaeologists Anastasios Orlandos and Petros Themelis) have revealed many traces of the city Pausanias visited, most notably a large square complex, probably to be identified as the sanctuary of Asclepius (Fig. 86). The colonnaded complex, which measures 60 by 65 meters, held within it the temple and altar to Asclepius, as well as shrines to Artemis, Fortuna, Epaminondas, and the Muses. A small theater is attached to the eastern side of the sanctuary complex, which has been dated on various grounds to the Hellenistic era. The Asclepiea is the best-known portion of the city; other elements located by archaeologists include a larger theater to the northwest, a stadium and hero shrine to the southwest, the Clepsydra spring to the north (within the present-day village of Mavromati), and the high acropolis sanctuary of Zeus Ithomatas. The marketplace, or agora, of the city seems to have lain immediately to the north of the Asclepiea. Everywhere in the excavations, finds such as statue bases, coins, pottery, fragments of sculpture, and inscriptions add to our impression of a flourishing community.

One other major civic monument remains to be mentioned. An important sign of the Roman conquest, and of its acceptance within Greek lands, was the appearance of the imperial cult—the worship of the Roman emperor and his family. At Messene, a Sebasteion (as imperial cult places were called in the Greek East) dating to the Augustan Age was located within the Asclepiea, in a long raised hall running along the north side of the complex. After climbing an imposing monumental staircase, individuals worshiping at the Sebasteion could look down on the shrines below and out over the territory of Messene sloping away to the south. With its central and raised position, the imperial cult became a dominant element in the Messenian cityscape, as it did in most major cities of the Roman empire.

Messene was by no means the only city in Roman Messenia, as Pausanias's narration of his travels makes clear: he also mentions, for example, Abia, Koroni, Asine, and Mothone (which the emperor Trajan made a "free city" in the early second century A.D.). As for the area of Pylos specifically, Pausanias has unfortunately little to say; moreover, he speaks only of coastal settlements. He reaches the area as he travels northward from Mothone (today, Methoni):

> From Mothone to the promontory of Coryphasion is a journey of about 100 stades [19–21 kilometers]. On this promontory lies Pylos. Pylos, son of Cleson, settled it, bringing the Leleges from Megara, which they occupied at that time. But he got no benefit from it, being expelled by Neleus and the Pelasgians from Iolcus. So, he left for the neighboring area, where he took possession of Pylos in Elea. Neleus, on becoming king, so increased the reputation of Pylos that Homer in his epic poetry named it the city of Neleus. There is there a sanctuary of Athena, with

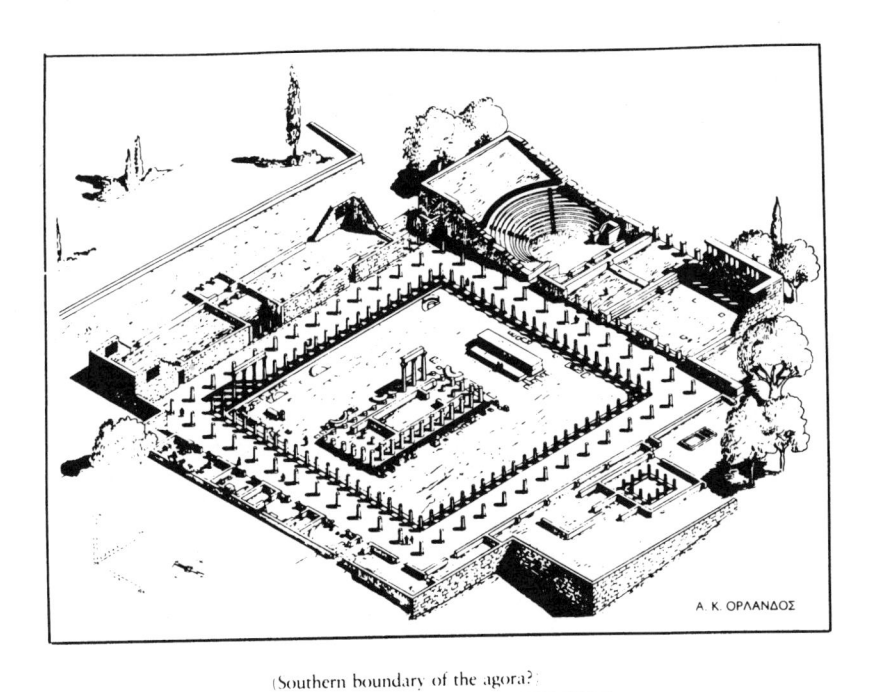

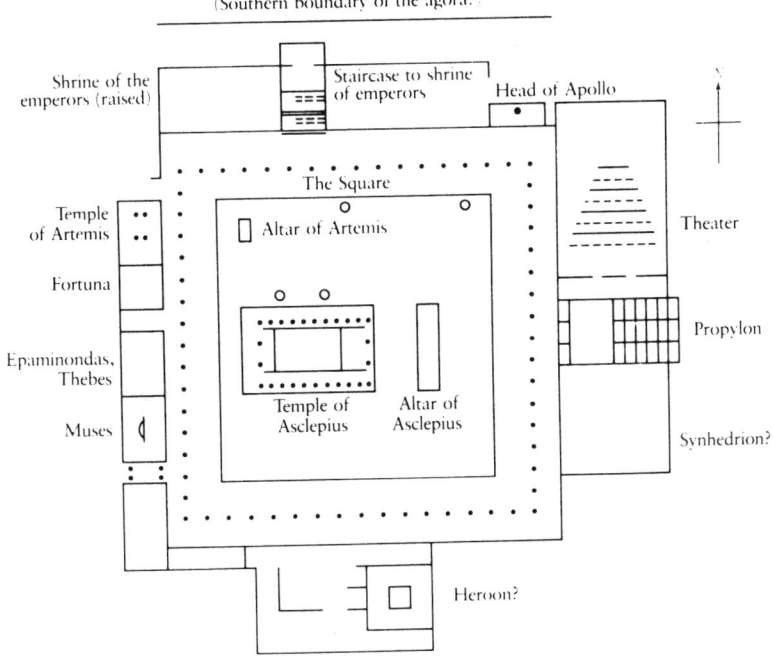

FIGURE 86
Reconstruction and schematic plan of the Asklepieion at Messene. Top, with permission of Archaeological Society of Athens; bottom, with permission of A. S. Bradford. Ensemble reproduced by permission of C. Habicht.

the epithet "Coryphasian," and a building called the house of Nestor, in which Nestor has actually been painted. His tomb is within the city, while that a short distance away they say is the tomb of Thrasymedes. Within the city there is also a cave; they say that Nestor, and before him Neleus, used to stable their cattle there. These cattle would have been of Thessalian breed, having once belonged to Iphiclus, the father of Protesilaus. Neleus asked for these cattle as a bride-price from his daughter's suitors, and because of them Melampous arrived in Thessaly as a favor to his brother Bias, but was bound by Iphiclus's cattlemen. He got them as a reward for the prophecies he made for Iphiclus at his insistence. So men of those times made great efforts to assemble this sort of wealth—herds of horses and cattle—if indeed Neleus desired to get hold of Iphiclus's cattle and Eurystheus instructed Heracles to steal away the herd of Geryon on account of the reputation of the cattle in Iberia. It seems that Eryx, too, who ruled in Sicily at the time, had such a strong desire for the cattle from Erytheia that he wrestled with Heracles, with these cattle and his kingdom as the prizes. Homer, too, has told in the *Iliad* how Iphidamas, the son of Antenor, offered 100 cattle as the first of the bride gifts to his prospective father-in-law. These stories support the argument that people in those days took particular pleasure in cattle. However, in my view, Neleus's cattle were pastured for the most part in the area beyond the border. For the country of the Pylians is generally sandy and not suitable to provide that much grazing land for cattle. Homer, too, supports me as a witness, since whenever he makes mention of Nestor, he adds repeatedly that he was king of "sandy" Pylos.

In front of the harbor lies the island of Sphacteria, just as Rheneia lies off the anchorage of Delos. The ups-and-downs of humans seem to elevate even places previously unknown to fame. The name of Kaphereus in Euboea is famous because of the storm that hit the Greeks with Agamemnon there as they were traveling back from Troy; Psyttaleia near Salamis we know because of the Persians who fell there. In this same manner, the Lacedaemonian rout made Sphacteria well known to everyone. The Athenians set up a bronze representation of Victory also on the acropolis as a monument to the events on Sphacteria.

PAUSANIAS *Description of Greece* 4.36.1–6

Pausanias then moves on briefly to describe Cyparissia to the north and, in no more than three lines, has reached the border between Messenia and Elea.

This passage of Pausanias has been quoted in full to give some notion of his emphasis on "ancient history"—on Neleus, Nestor, and their doings, and on mythic history generally. Such an emphasis is typical of Pausanias, who is nowhere very interested in describing the Greece of his own, Roman age, preferring instead to look for traces and tell stories of the prehistoric or classical past. His Book 4, on Messenia, however, is especially rooted in the region's mythic age. Where most books are a fairly even mixture of what Pausanias terms *logoi* ("things spoken," such as traditions or history) and *theoremata* ("things to be seen," such as monuments of the area), some 80 percent of his description of Messenia deals with *logoi* only, and largely with tales of the Messenian resistance to Sparta at that. In Pausanias's eyes, there was not much to "see" in the region, thanks to the years lost to Spartan domination.

Such a biased perspective can be offset by a very different view of Roman Messenia, a view that depends upon archaeological evidence for the countryside. A survey around the site of ancient Nichoria, in the so-called Five Rivers area, revealed a decided increase in Roman settlement numbers, a very different trend from elsewhere in the Greek landscape at this time. This survey also claimed to have found several villa sites, a villa being normally identified as a large establishment, with accessories indicating an affluent, even luxurious, life-style for its occupant (such as mosaics, marble decorations, sculptures, baths). Five of the Five Rivers villas, for example, boasted associated bath structures. Well-to-do residences were also found by PRAP, notably at the site of Bouka (see Focus in this chapter) and the Late Roman villa site of Dialiskari (see Focus in this chapter). Though all these villa sites second the evidence of Messene in suggesting that Roman Messenia was a prosperous place to live, we must be cautious. Roman rule and Roman taxation, it is very clear, ultimately led to growing disparities in wealth and status between the "haves" and the "have-nots" in provincial society. As always, the "haves" show up much more clearly in the archaeological record, but the poor and underprivileged—by far the majority even in a region such as Messenia—also appear, as the people who farmed and worked the land to make it prosper, who paid their taxes, who visited the marketplace at Messene, who honored the emperor in public festivals, who kept the villa sites of the rich running and beautiful.

Bouka and Dialiskari, as well as other villas in Messenia, are in coastal, or near-coastal, locations. In general, one very clear pattern discovered by our survey is a predilection for coastal settlement in Roman times. This suggests still further that the region was interested now in reaching "outward," in becoming part of the Roman world system. What happened when that world system, that empire, began to fracture, and finally to break apart, is the subject of the next chapter.

LIBERATION *and* CONQUEST: HELLENISTIC *and* ROMAN MESSENIA

FOCUS

DIALISKARI: *A* LATE ROMAN VILLA *on the* MESSENIAN COAST

In 1993, one of the PRAP fieldwalking teams was assigned to survey a band of territory along the Messenian shoreline, between the modern towns of Marathoupolis and Romanou (Fig. 87). Until recently, olive trees spread uninterrupted from below the steep Gargaliani Ridge to the edge of the Mediterranean in this coastal plain. Today, however, this land is rapidly being converted from olive groves to vacation homes. Here, perhaps more than in any other part of the study area, there was an immediate need to note and record antiquities before their possible destruction; this is a case of archaeological surface survey acting as a kind of "rescue" archaeology.

As our work brought us closer to the small chapel of Ayios Nikolaos (patron saint of sailors), set on a small promontory across from the island of Proti, we were aware we might well be nearing an important, previously known site. In 1930, the Swedish scholar Natan Valmin had reported seeing notable antiquities here, and claimed it as the location of ancient Erana, one of a very few settlements named by ancient authors in this part of the Peloponnese. Just as Valmin might have predicted, as fieldwalkers moved into the vicinity of the church, they noted a distinct increase in the density of sherds observed. Then, while taking a water and cookie break beside an unoccupied summer home, they suddenly realized that the roof above them was supported by four ancient columns, now heavily whitewashed. The team later discovered these very columns had been noted and photographed by Valmin—some sixty-three years before (Fig. 88). Valmin had also reported another nearby modern home that incorporated a Roman mosaic into its courtyard; this mosaic, too, we "rediscovered" (Fig. 89).

More pottery and architectural fragments were encountered in this location, known today as Dialiskari, as we continued to move across the site. Other column drums, the foundation of a polygonal building, and several walls were found. In the rocky coastline, a large basin and two long channels had been cut; their lines are still remarkably clear today. It seems prob-

---

DAVID STONE *and* AXEL KAMPKE

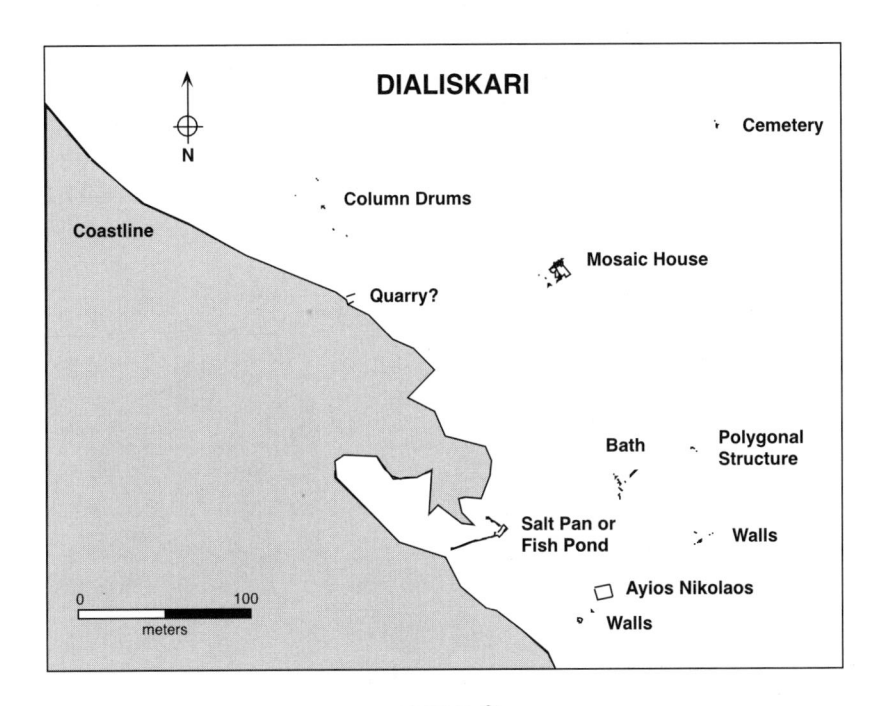

FIGURE 87
Plan of Dialiskari produced by TotalStation. PRAP Archive. D. Stone and S. Heath.

able that the resulting structure was used as a fish pond or salt pan. A quarry also had been opened in the coastline to the south of the site. More disturbingly, an apparent bulldozer slash into the side of a field exposed part of a hypocaust, the heating system used in Roman bath buildings (Fig. 90). At the edge of the site, small rock-cut tombs were also found. Finally, in addition to all these architectural or rock-cut features, fieldwalkers discovered a high density of potsherds and tile across the site, many of which appeared at first examination to be of Late Roman date.

Although Valmin's observations, combined with our initial fieldwalking, told us a fair amount about Dialiskari, a second stage of more intensive examination was clearly necessary, not least to try to determine the character of the site. Was it a large town with numerous inhabitants? Or might it have been a private villa, the home of a wealthy and influential individual? To gain a better understanding of the chronological range of the site, and a more detailed spatial control of possible functional variation across it, gridded collection of surface material within restricted areas was undertaken in 1994 (Fig. 91). The results of this work indicate that most human activity at Dialiskari can be dated to the fourth to seventh centuries A.D. (the Late Roman period), though some earlier Hellenistic and Roman material was also observed. Finds included imported fine wares for the table (including African Red Slip ware), support tiles for a bath hypocaust system, mosaic tesserae (including a blue glass tessera), fragments from glass vessels, pieces of marble wall revetment, a fragmentary dedicatory inscription, and several pieces of imported millstones. For all its richness, the edges of the site at

FIGURE 88
"Column House" at Dialiskari in the 1930s and in the 1990s. Top, reproduced from M. N. Valmin, Études topographiques sur la Messénie ancienne *(Lund: C. Blom, 1930), 139, fig. 25. Bottom, PRAP Archive. J. Bennet.*

DAVID STONE *and* AXEL KAMPKE

FIGURE 89
Roman mosaic at Dialiskari. PRAP Archive. R. J. Robertson.

Dialiskari are quite clearly marked by a distinct drop-off in artifact densities; the site appears to cover some 900 by 400 meters, or some 36 hectares.

Apart from this intensive surface collection, other types of investigation were carried out at the site, including the use of one powerful weapon of the twentieth-century archaeologist. A team undertook the architectural mapping of the site with the use of an electronic TotalStation (Fig. 92). A TotalStation is an instrument that measures both distance and elevation by shooting an infrared beam to a reflecting prism; these measurements are then recorded on a hand-held computer attached to the machine. This equipment allowed us to make plans of the entire site, and of individual architectural features, which are accurate to within a single centimeter. Given

DIALISKARI: *A* LATE ROMAN VILLA *on the* MESSENIAN COAST

FIGURE 90
Hypocaust from Roman bath at Dialiskari. PRAP Archive. J. Bennet.

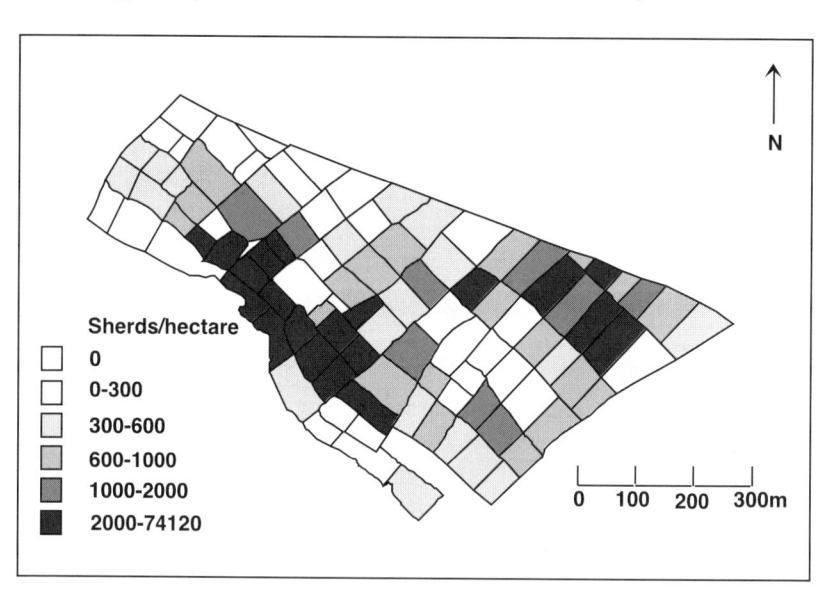

FIGURE 91
Sherd density at Dialiskari. PRAP Archive. D. Stone and S. Heath.

FIGURE 92
TotalStation in use. PRAP Archive. J. Bennet.

the ongoing threat to the site, with vacation homes being built within its very confines, such detailed mapping seemed a wise idea.

With its rich architectural remains, Dialiskari was an excellent candidate for TotalStation work, but running the Station (a temperamental instrument) in the hot summer sun and the soft sandy soils of southwestern Greece proved not an easy task. Three people were normally involved in this work: one taking readings with the machine, one holding a pole with the reflecting prism at the point to be measured, and a third sketching and noting down all data. Sometimes a fourth person would be needed to hold back olive branches or other foliage out of the beam's path: trees and reed beds that blocked views from one feature to another were among the major obstacles to overcome at Dialiskari. To acquire a plan of the site as a coherent whole, we made maps of all individual features, then linked them together through readings on a series of intermediate bench marks. All in all, it took us two weeks, and approximately 1,200 readings, to map the remains at Dialiskari.

Besides plotting all the surface features, the PRAP team from the University of Braunschweig, Germany, attempted to "see beneath the soil" with the aid of instruments for geophysical prospection (similar in principle but more powerful than recreational metal detectors). Two techniques of prospection were used at Dialiskari during the 1994 and 1995 seasons:

magnetometry and geoelectrical testing. By taking readings at one-meter intervals, we recorded variations in the earth's magnetic field with the magnetometer, and fluctuations in the earth's electrical currents with the electrical resistivity meter. Differences between buried archaeological structures and areas with no subsurface building are usually significant, enabling researchers to plot the layout of things they can't actually see. At Dialiskari, the results indicated the presence of high resistivity "caverns" and other anomalous features adjacent to where PRAP surveyors had discovered the hypocaust heating system of the Roman bath. It seems certain that the bath continued to the north and east of where it was exposed in the field boundary.

What do these forms of evidence—the artifact collection, the Total Station mapping, the geophysical results—suggest? With apologies to Valmin, we no longer believe Dialiskari to be Erana, nor even a town or village settlement at all. We now argue that the site at Dialiskari is a Roman villa, the residence of a wealthy inhabitant of the region, complete with bath, mosaics, and fine marble decorations. Defining a "villa" is a difficult task: no standard meaning for the word existed even in antiquity, and modern scholars have not arrived at any consensus. It is principally the high-status elements that figure most prominently at the site that have led us to this conclusion. There is a large proportion of imported materials—marble columns, millstones, fine pottery—and a restricted scatter of artifacts across the site. Yet the villa was more than a luxury beachfront home: its owner would have controlled substantial lands in the region, for which this site may have been an agricultural processing center; the fish pond or salt pan and quarry also indicate economic activity in the vicinity. Sites such as Dialiskari, with their size and ostentation, are a new feature in the landscape of Messenia, and are indicative of many major social and economic changes in Greece during the Roman period.

DAVID STONE *and* AXEL KAMPKE

FOCUS

POWER *from the* DEAD: TOMB CULT *in* POSTLIBERATION MESSENIA

A prominent feature of the Messenian landscape is the presence of tombs—tholos tombs, chamber tombs, or tumuli—dated by modern archaeologists to the period of the Bronze Age. These tombs have attracted much modern-day interest and much archaeological attention. Yet many basic and compelling questions are only now beginning to be asked about these prehistoric graves: How would inhabitants of Messenia at other periods in the past have viewed these tombs? What would they have made of them? How might they have used them?

In some cases, the answer is undeniably prosaic. Chamber or tholos tombs were occasionally turned into temporary houses or sheep pens; the pit created by a collapsed tholos tomb clearly made a very attractive and convenient garbage dump. Sometimes, it seems, prehistoric graves either were not recognized for what they were, or were disregarded nonetheless. In other periods of the past, however, these ancient tombs could become the focus for ritual and celebration; many were offered veneration and respect. The remains of animal sacrifices, of votives, and of pottery can testify to ritual activity, or "tomb cult," at these graves, first built and used hundreds of years earlier.

Tracing and understanding this post-prehistoric activity at these Bronze Age tombs is not an easy matter. Many of the tombs were dug during the early years of archaeology in Messenia, at a time when most attention was focused on the heroic Bronze Age epoch. Pottery or other finds dating to later periods were often just viewed as intrusive "garbage" and barely mentioned in publication. Despite this, tomb cult at Messenian Bronze Age graves can be argued for historic times. Intriguingly, some of this ritual activity may have been carried out during the centuries of Spartan control (at places such as Volimidia, Vathirema, or Nichoria); tomb cult, then, may have been one means by which the Messenians maintained a sense of their own local identity and traditions. The real florescence of tomb cult in Mes-

SUSAN E. ALCOCK

senia, however, seems to take place in later Classical and Hellenistic times, that is, *after* the liberation of Messenia (Fig. 93). Two illustrations can be given of tomb cult in Messenia at this time.

At Voidokoilia, on a promontory directly opposite and in full view of the city site of ancient Coryphasion, stands the remains of a tholos tomb dating to the Late Helladic I period, itself placed within a Middle Helladic tumulus (Fig. 94). Both tholos and tumulus are believed to have been visible in historic times; indeed, it is usually assumed that Pausanias means Voidokoilia when he remarks that "the tomb a little distance from Pylos is said to belong to Thrasymedes"—a son of the mythic king Nestor. When the upper levels of the tholos were excavated, the remains of an entire bull were found, although the date of this impressive sacrifice could not be determined. More clear-cut was the discovery of several deposits in the vicinity of the tholos, deposits containing Hellenistic vessels, figurines, and hundreds of small terracotta plaques, dated to the end of the fourth or beginning of the third century B.C. The plaques depict a variety of images, including scenes of worship, horse-and-rider motifs, and funerary banquets: all scenes familiar from heroic and funerary cults elsewhere in the Greek world. Some of these finds were made in association with a small construction of Hellenistic date, interpreted as a "chapel" for hero-funerary worship by the tomb's most recent excavator, George Korres.

Our second example lies in the heart of modern Hora, the "home base" for PRAP activities. The famous chamber-tomb cemetery of Volimidia, excavated in the 1950s and 1960s by Spyridon Marinatos, presents a case of tomb reuse that is without doubt the longest and among the most complicated in Greece (Fig. 95). In just one tomb (Angelopoulos Tomb 2), the entranceway, or *dromos*, contained two pyres for burning. One, in the middle of the passage, held charcoal and a Hellenistic vessel. The other, right by the door of the tomb, contained fragments of cups and cooking wares (dated to approximately 300 B.C.). At the upper level of the *dromos*, other objects of Hellenistic date were discovered, including loomweights, a coin, a lamp fragment, and part of an unguentarium—a vessel associated with funerary activity. The tomb chamber proper contained yet another pyre, with a pig sacrifice dated to the Hellenistic era, as well as much other later pottery, lamps, glass, and metal finds—including a coin from the city of Argos, dating to the third century B.C. Even if some of this abundant material was not specifically intended as votive offerings, enough evidence remains to make a strong case for late Classical and Hellenistic cult at Angelopoulos Tomb 2.

Another tomb (Angelopoulos Tomb 6) is the largest of all those at

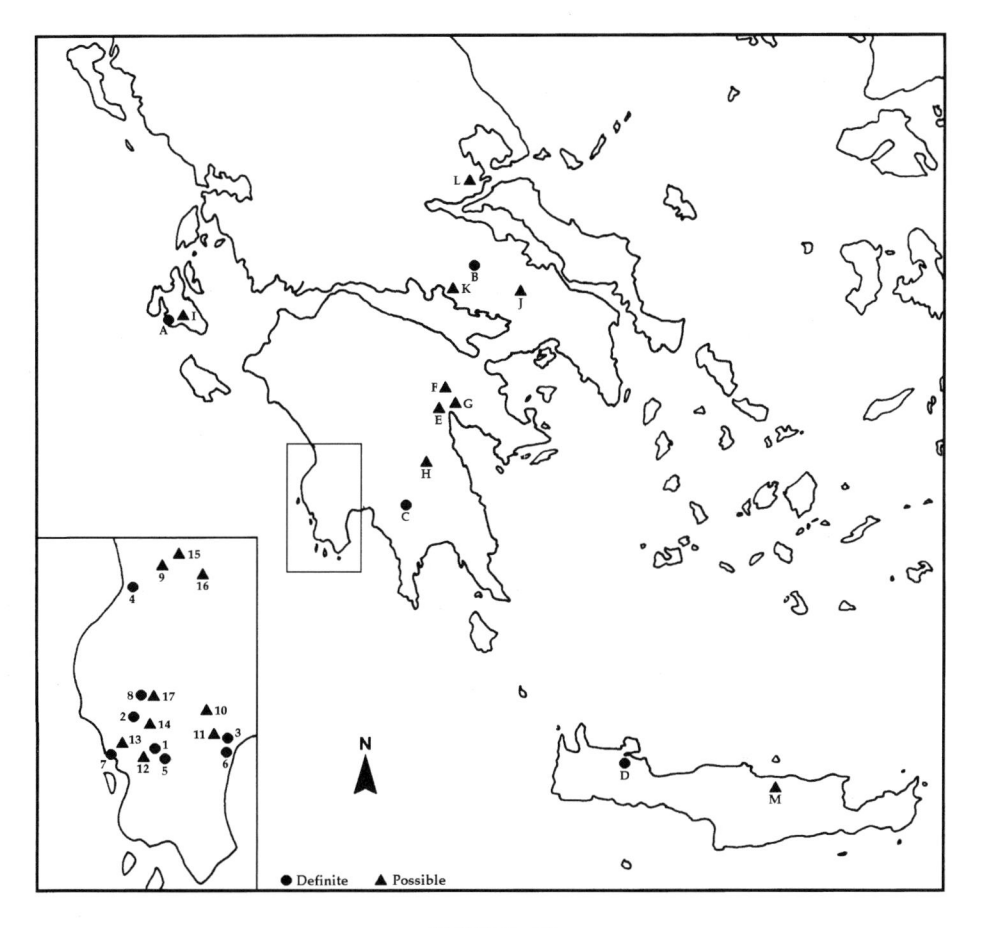

FIGURE 93
Location of definite and possible sites of Late Classical and Hellenistic tomb cult in southern Greece. After S. E. Alcock, "Tomb Cult and the Post-Classical Polis,"
American Journal of Archaeology *95 (1991): 450, fig. 1.*
A = Cephallenia; B = Orchomenus; C = Sparta; D = Stilos; E = Argos; F = Mycenae; G = Prosymna; H = Analipsis; I = Cephallenia; J = Thebes; K = Medeon; L = Pteleon; M = Episkopi; Messenia: 1 = Kremydia: Kaminia; 2 = Myrsinohori: Routsi; 3 = Nichoria; 4 = Peristeria; 5 = Soulinari: Tourliditsa; 6 = Vathirema; 7 = Voidokoilia; 8 = Volimidia; 9 = Ano Kopanaki: Akourthi; 10 = Dafni/Daras; 11 = Karpofora: Akones; 12 = Koukounara: Tomb 4, Gouvalari I; 13 = Osmanaga: Koryfasion; 14 = Papoulia: Ayios Ioannis; 15 = Psari; 16 = Vasiliko: Xerovrisi; 17 = Volimidia: Angelopoulos 10.

FIGURE 94
*View north from the promontory of Coryphasion. The "Tomb of Thrasymedes"
lies in the bare patch on the further headland. S. E. Alcock.*

FIGURE 95
J. Bennet inspecting Volimidia graves. PRAP Archive. R. Dupuis-Devlin and E. Dallagher.

Volimidia. Marinatos located a human burial before the door of the tomb, which he dated (if largely on the basis of the corpse's stature!) to the Hellenistic period. The chamber of the tomb itself was filled with a wide variety of pottery, including Hellenistic and Roman material; numerous animal remains (of ox, deer, pig, and stag) were also found. In the floor of the chamber were two pit burials, in both of which were found Mycenaean and Hellenistic pottery in association with skeletal remains.

Angelopoulos Tomb 6 is an excellent example of how difficult it can be to interpret the archaeology of tomb cult. Marinatos believed, for example, that these pit burials were of the Mycenaean dead, given additional Hellenistic offerings in a later cult ceremony. The animal offerings, notably the deer bones and stag horns found, he took to reflect a cult of "hunting heroes." It is also possible, however, that the pit burials are of *Hellenistic* date, with Mycenaean pots added as "extras" to their grave offerings. Several other late Classical and Hellenistic burials were found either within or in the vicinity of the Volimidia tomb group at large, suggesting that at least some local families had a strong desire to associate themselves in death with these ancient tombs. Yet a third interpretation, that of George Korres, dismisses most of these finds as simply the product of refuse dumping and disposal, apart from the pit burials in the tomb-chamber floor. Whichever interpretation one follows, a profound later interest in the prehistoric Volimidia tombs seems undeniable.

Precisely whom the Messenians of the postliberation period thought they were venerating at these tombs remains unclear, and it is unlikely we will ever know. In some cases, they may have attached names of specific heroes to these rituals, as is suggested by Pausanias's reference to the "Tomb of Thrasymedes" at Voidokoilia. They may have seen these graves as the resting places of family ancestors, a powerful force in ancient Greek society. Or they may simply have seen the tombs as anonymous but numinous places where authority and power, drawn from the distant and revered past, could be tapped for the benefit of the present.

Tomb cult is not a phenomenon confined to Messenia; other regions in Greece (the Ionian islands, the Argolid, Attica) boast similar cases of tomb veneration. Yet we should not try to seek identical explanations for this behavior in all areas. In postliberation Messenia, there would have been particular and particularly strong reasons to appeal to the past, to ancestors, to heroes. Such practices affirmed the long and noble history of the Messenian people, a history "truncated" by the Spartan conquest. Tomb cult can be associated with the Messenian fascination with "local heroes," manifested at Messene's foundation when various heroes were summoned to "return and dwell with them," as well as in the cult of Aristomenes, still popular and functioning well into the Roman empire.

Heroes and legends were, of course, good propaganda weapons, working both to bolster the confidence of the Messenians themselves and to demand respect from other Greek states. An even simpler explanation is less political and more spontaneous. Tomb cult and hero worship celebrated the longed-for, long-denied freedom of Messenia, a celebration that transcended temporal boundaries to embrace all Messenians, of both past and present.

FOCUS

BOUKA

Survey archaeology has long been used to identify sites for subsequent excavation, or to analyze large-scale regional issues, but small sites can also be usefully studied through intensive survey. The site of Bouka, identified by PRAP in 1993, provides a perfect demonstration of this. PRAP's work at Bouka also shows the benefit of combining different methods of approaching the past, drawing on the expertise of several specialized disciplines in order to understand the ancient world.

In the 1993 season, a field team walking tracts in an area adjacent to the coast about 5 kilometers north of the large Late Classical and Hellenistic urban center of Coryphasion identified the small site of Bouka (Fig. 96). The site was marked by large quantities of ceramic material, both pottery and roof tiles. It was clear to the team in the field that the material at Bouka was unlike any yet found by PRAP. This pottery scatter was exceptional on several counts. First, the large size of the pottery fragments and their very good state of preservation were unusual for this survey. Survey pottery is often very small and worn, but due to its chemical composition, the soil of Messenia is particularly damaging, often stripping off all the surface of the pottery. Also, a large proportion of the pottery the team found that day was what is called fine ware. As the name implies, fine ware is the ancient equivalent of "the good china," which, given its fragile nature, is often not found in survey, whereas thicker, heavier types of pottery are more likely to be preserved. Finally, the ceramic material was very concentrated.

The exceptional nature of the finds led to the decision to study the site in a more systematic way and to collect more pottery. A grid of 10-meter squares was laid down over the site, in order to be able to precisely document the location of artifacts, and the site was "vacuumed," meaning all pottery, tile, and other artifacts were collected. The site today constitutes three separate fields. The two areas on either side of the field where finds

ANN B. HARRISON

FIGURE 96
S. E. Alcock at the site of Bouka. PRAP Archive. J. Bennet.

were initially discovered yielded little material, although in one case this may be due in part to poor visibility.

During our collection at the site, it appeared that the distribution of pottery and tile fell into patterns. Site center was placed at the apparent point of highest concentration of the ceramic material; therefore grid squares nearest site center were the richest. Areas of high concentration of material spread out in a diagonal swath to the northeast and southwest from this central point, following the line of the original tract, a fallow field. On either side of this original tract, there was a clear and sharp drop-off in densities, which may be due in part to differing treatment of the fields.

To give some idea of what is meant, an examination of the density of ceramic material from three adjacent squares is helpful: the square nearest center had 285 sherds and 395 tile fragments, the next square had 127 sherds and 362 tile fragments, whereas the third had 14 sherds and 1 tile fragment. This pattern of sharp density drop-off is repeated throughout the site. Also, the drop-off in sherd count could be traced on an even smaller scale within different portions of the 10-meter grid squares. For example, in three squares that had moderate amounts of ceramic material, there was a clear difference in the quantity of material found in the different parts of the grid square, with almost all the material being collected from the northern half of these squares.

Many archaeological projects learn more about a site located through survey by then excavating it, but this is not the only way. There is also the option of essentially being able to "see" through the covering soil any structures or large man-made objects lying below the surface. The distinctive pattern of pottery scatter on the surface at Bouka made the site a perfect candidate for subsurface investigation through geophysical remote-sensing techniques. Therefore, in 1994, the grid was reestablished, and electromagnetic investigation of the site took place.

The geophysical work was carried out by the PRAP team from the Institute for Geophysics and Meteorology of the Polytechnical University in Braunschweig, Germany. A portion of the site was analyzed using instruments called gradiometers, which measure variations in the earth's magnetic field. Various man-made elements such as fired clay, iron objects, or trenches cause distortions in the magnetic field, which can be measured and analyzed. And indeed, at Bouka, "anomalies" in the earth's magnetic field were noted. When the results are plotted graphically on a computer, the anomalies at Bouka take the form of a linear variation over 45 meters long, with at least two perpendicular offshoots (Fig. 97). Looking at the mapping of the anomaly with an archaeological eye, it appears to show the corner of a building and interior cross walls. And in fact, these magnetic

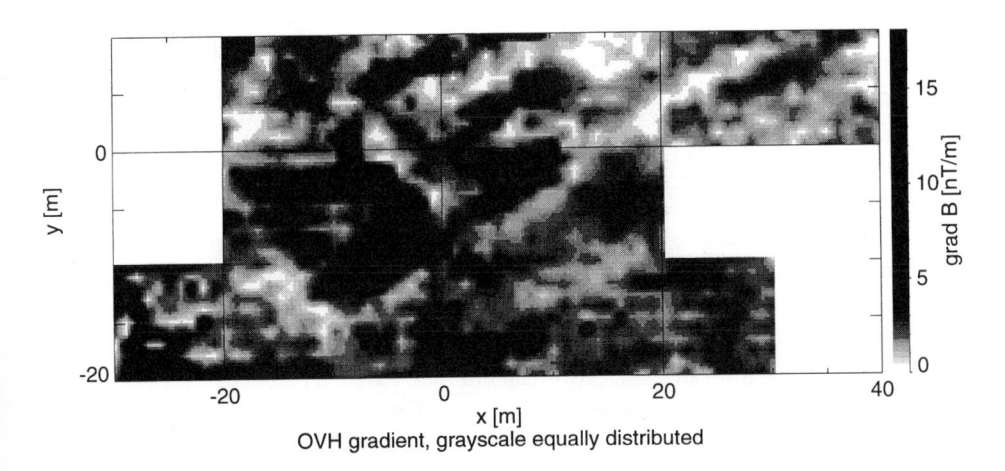

FIGURE 97
Magnetometric map showing the plan of an unexcavated building at Bouka. PRAP Archive. F. K. Kuhnke and F. C. Fieberg.

FIGURE 98
*Weights for weaving threads on a loom, from Bouka. PRAP Archive.
R. Dupuis-Devlin.*

anomalies follow the precise distribution pattern of the pottery and roof tiles from the survey collection.

Since the magnetic anomalies were relatively weak, it seemed likely that what the gradiometer was detecting were not actual walls, but the foundation trench from which the walls had been robbed. Sample coring along the line of the anomalies supported this interpretation, finding no evidence of the walls themselves. The building stone of the base of the walls appears to have been removed in the course of farming and plowing, but the foundation trench was still marked by a disruption in the earth's magnetic field.

The site at Bouka appears to represent a very large structure, for the 45-meter measurement does not reach the other corner of the wall, but merely indicates the limit of the electromagnetic study area. The pottery evidence dates the structure to the period from the mid-third to the mid-second centuries B.C., and tells us of its function. The types of pottery found, including fine wares, cooking wares, storage vessels, loomweights (Fig. 98), lamps, and gaming pieces, indicate a domestic structure.

The people living in this house (perhaps the term "villa" is not too extravagant) may have had some connection with those buried in the nearby cemetery at Tsopani Rahi, with graves dating from the late third to early second centuries B.C. These graves contain numerous clay vessels, gold jewelry, a silver vase, and elaborate glass bowls. The evidence from Tsopani Rahi and Bouka indicates that the Messenians in the Pylos area in this period had access to imported and luxury goods. Local potters and artisans were also imitating these imported wares. At least some Messenians had a very affluent standard of living.

FIGURE 99
Fortifications of Methoni, as seen from the Venetian marketplace. PRAP Archive.
R. J. Robertson.

CHAPTER 8

MEDIEVAL MESSENIA

*The small peninsula of Pedasos, present-day Methoni,
is near the site that long ago was called Pylos, now called Avarino,
the homeland of Nestor, praised by Homer.*

LATE BYZANTINE COMMENTARY ON CONSTANTINE VII
PORPHYROGENITUS *De thematibus*

The names of Nestor and Pylos never lost their poetic resonance in the medieval East, even when the site of the palace later brought to light by Blegen lay buried beneath centuries of soil. But the very transformation of the name Pylos to Avarino, a toponym associated with Slavic settlement, signals the enormous changes that this region would undergo from the Bronze Age to the late medieval period.

Throughout the Byzantine period, Messenia was part of the Peloponnesian "lands down under," far from centralized imperial rule in distant Constantinople. Located on the margins of the Byzantine empire, washed by the waters of the Ionian and Aegean seas, Messenia's ports formed a stopping point on the maritime routes between the autonomous cities of medieval Italy, Byzantium, and the Holy Land. A fifth-century geographical list of cities in the Eastern empire, known as the *Synekdemos*, cites five cities in present-day Messenia: Messene, Koroni, Asine, Methoni, and Cyparissia, four of them on the coast. In the tenth century, the Byzantine saint Nikon would visit the same cities listed by the Roman geographer. "In turn," according to the biography of the holy man, "he quickly visited Koroni, Methoni, and Messene, which the locals call Bourkanos, and came to Arcadia (Cyparissia)." For both the fifth- and the tenth-century traveler, Messenia was characterized by its thriving port towns. But a long coastline and rich agricultural resources made Messenia attractive to less-desirable visitors, such as imperial tax-collectors and foreign invaders. Visigoths,

SHARON E.J. GERSTEL

Vandals, Slavs, Franks, Venetians, and Turks all played a role in forming and transforming medieval Messenia. As in many complex societies, the history of the region is characterized by reaction to these outsiders as much as by interaction with and absorption of them.

Medieval Messenia's political and societal vicissitudes are recounted in written texts and can be inferred from archaeological data. For the Byzantine period, ecclesiastical texts, including saints' lives and lists of bishops, provide sporadic information about the region. However, with the invasion of the Peloponnese in the early thirteenth century by the soldiers of the Fourth Crusade, and with the later control of valuable coastal areas by the Venetians, Messenia became one of the best-documented regions of the medieval East. In addition, numerous texts referring to the area, its population, and its economic status are found in Italian archives. These documents provide a detailed picture of medieval life in this region.

Archaeological data for the Middle Ages are less known, perhaps ignored, in the rush to explore Bronze Age remains in the region. However, the absence of excavated medieval remains is counterbalanced by the plethora of ruins dating to the Middle Ages. These structures, originally built to protect the region during the later medieval period, now stand desolate, silent reminders of a period of crusades and conquest.

EARLY BYZANTINE MESSENIA (FIFTH–SIXTH CENTURY)

Life in the Late Roman and Early Byzantine Peloponnese was punctuated by destruction and natural disaster. The Herulian invasions of the third century, Visigothic pillaging of the fourth century, Vandalic incursions of the fifth century, earthquakes (A.D. 522 and 551), and bubonic plague (A.D. 541–544) resulted in depopulation of the region. Despite these trials, remains of Late Roman villas or bath structures from the fourth to seventh centuries at Dialiskari, Hora, and Ayia Kyriaki demonstrate the survival of Roman ways in a turbulent time.

The construction of Christian monuments contemporaneous with these Roman structures signals the gradual conversion of the region. Textual, epigraphical, and archaeological evidence demonstrate that, by the fifth century, the church must have played an increasingly important role, not only in the daily lives of the people, but also in their eternal afterlife. A local bishop, John of Messenia, participated in the ecumenical church Council of Chalcedon in 451, and the name of a priest, Eudochios, is recorded in an inscription discovered in Cyparissia. A fragmentary inscription found in the excavations of the Ayia Kyriaki basilica refers to episcopal patronage of that church. The inhabitants of the ancient city of Messene, decimated by

Gothic raids in the second and third centuries, relocated further north on the safer slopes of Mt. Ithome. Numerous artifacts and the remains of ecclesiastical structures and furnishings, as well as grave markers with Christian invocations, confirm that ancient Messene, though Christianized and diminished in size and splendor, continued to exist.

The excavated remains of a large basilica at Ayia Kyriaki on the coastline near Filiatra indicate the existence of a thriving Christian community in the Early Christian period (Fig. 100). Two later churches were built on these same foundations. The first church, a five-aisled basilica, was erected in the first half of the sixth century. Built in a provincial manner—carved stone of high quality was imported from Attica, and the mosaic pavement discovered in the sanctuary was retrogressive in its style—the basilica was probably destroyed in the A.D. 551 earthquake. A smaller, three-aisled basil-

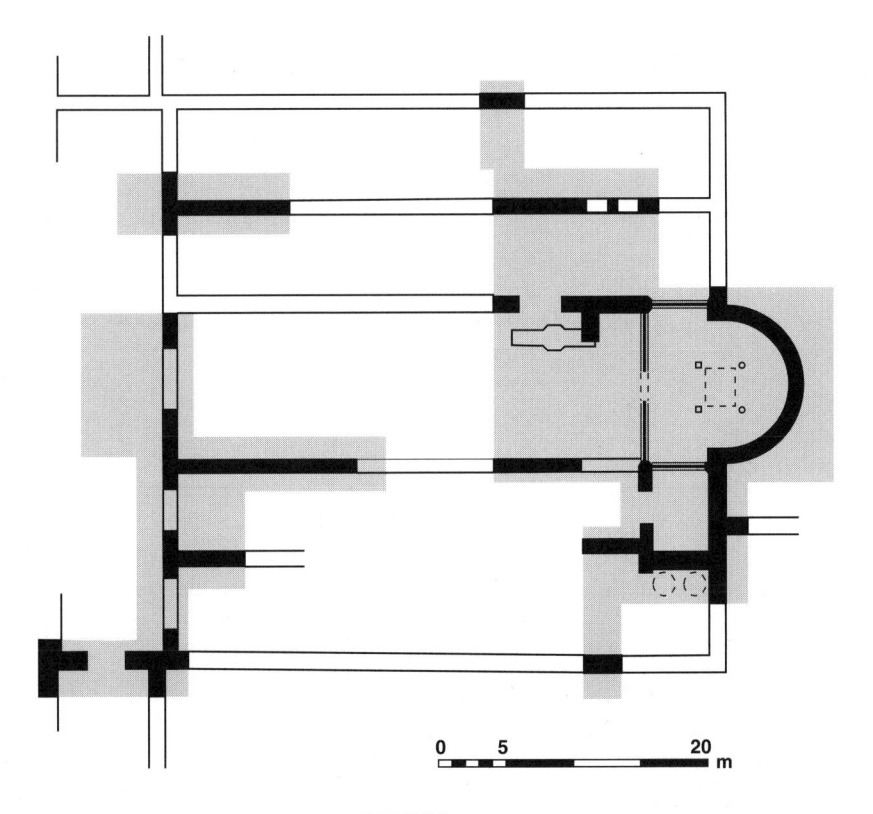

FIGURE 100

Plan of the basilica of Ayia Kyriaki near Filiatra. Area of excavation shaded. After D. I. Pallas, "'Ανασκαφὴ εἰς Φιλιατρὰ τῆς Τριφυλίας," Πρακτικὰ τῆς ἐν Ἀθῆναις Ἀρχαιολογικῆς Ἑταιρείας (1960): fig. 1. R. J. Robertson.

ican church was built on the ruins of the larger church at the end of the sixth century. Finally, a small, single-aisled structure was constructed on the site of the first two churches in the fourteenth century. The architectural contraction of this building sadly parallels the waning fortunes of the region. Coastal settlements protected in the Roman and Early Christian periods fell prey to marauding pirates and invaders in the later Middle Ages, and the Ayia Kyriaki basilica probably lay in ruins for some time, until a period of relative stability in the fourteenth century, when the coastline would again be safe, this time also protected by a strong power from the Italian peninsula.

In the Early Byzantine period, several pagan structures were reused for Christian burials. At Routsi, Myrsinochori, burial spaces were carved to the right of the *dromos* of a Mycenaean tholos tomb. Identifiable pottery buried with the skeletons provides a date early within the Christian era for the departed. The same is true of a Mycenaean tomb at Kefalovryso. Christians also made use of Roman structures for the purposes of burial. A small underground heating chamber (hypocaust) of a Roman bath in modern-day Hora was used for Christian burials from the fourth century A.D. onward. In the Turkish period, the appearance of walls and human bones in the area gave rise to the mistaken notion that an earlier church had been constructed on the site, and the Roman bath complex was once again used for a second and much later phase of Christian burial. Near Methoni, in the southwest corner of Messenia, Early Christian remains have been discovered inside a cave. The burials take the form of both arcosolia (burial niches) and shaft graves.

Aside from the small amount of information provided by excavation in the region, we know little about the daily lives of the people in the Early Christian era. The site of Dialiskari, on the western coast, provides a tantalizing view of a seaside villa that thrived in the turbulent fourth through seventh centuries (see Chapter 7 and Fig. 87). What was once a luxurious villa built by the sea is currently imperiled by the construction of modern coastal vacation homes. Its mosaic pavements are now built into a modern house, and the storage vessels and cookpots used by the residents are now found worn away by the sea or broken into hundreds of pieces and scattered across the cultivated fields. The household bath, heated against the cool breezes of the winter sea, was revealed by a modern bulldozer in the soil built up after centuries (see Fig. 90). Yet, walking through the rows of tomatoes that now cover the site, one wonders whether the inhabitants knew of impending Slavic penetration into the region or felt the aftershocks of the great earthquake of 551, or whether they, like many travelers on a hot summer day, simply enjoyed the sea vista.

THE DARK AGES (SIXTH TO NINTH CENTURIES)

The Slavic occupation of the Peloponnese from the late sixth to early ninth centuries is well known to all historians of the period, though not easily identified in archaeological remains. According to many scholars, the Slavs took Corinth between 582 and 586. Their residency in the Peloponnese and their migration to the south and west effectively prevented communication between Constantinople and its subjects in this region. The tenth-century emperor Constantine VII Porphyrogenitus noted that "the whole country [the Peloponnese] was Slavonized and became barbarous when the deadly plague [744–747] ravaged the universe, when Constantine, the one named after dung [Constantine V Kopronymos], held the scepter of the Romans." A letter of the patriarch Nicholas the Grammarian (A.D. 1084–1111) to the Byzantine emperor Alexios I Comnenos comments on the repulsion of the Avars and Slavs from the Peloponnesian city of Patras in 807 and notes that they "had held possession of the Peloponnese for 218 years and had so completely separated it from the Byzantine empire that no Byzantine official dared to set his foot in it."

The period of the Slavic occupation of the Peloponnese has often been viewed as an early medieval "Dark Age." Indeed, archaeologically, few Slavic remains can be identified with absolute certainty, and so the period is notable for its lack of evidence rather than its material remains. Although fragments of "Slavic" pottery have been identified at Olympia, Argos, and other sites in the Peloponnese, no remains that can be characterized as Slavic have yet been identified from Messenia.

What does remain from this period, however, are changes in the names of sites. "Avarino," mentioned in *De thematibus* as the new name for Messenian Pylos, is the Slavic name for "place of maples." In addition, nearby Sklavohori (Village of Slavs) indicates the settlement of a non-indigenous, non-Greek population. Even as these new place names were being established, however, Greek toponyms continued to be used. It is therefore unlikely that the Slavs ever ruled over the region. Rather, they were cohabitants of an area that would continually absorb and assimilate other new peoples.

THE MIDDLE BYZANTINE PERIOD (A.D. 900–1204)

The Middle Byzantine period, based on textual and archaeological evidence, appears to have been a time of relative stability and prosperity. According to firsthand accounts such as that of the English pilgrim Benedict of Peterborough, the region was agriculturally fertile and was known for its olives, much as it is today. In religious terms, this was the time in which St. Nikon was able to travel through parts of Messenia, stopping at the port towns of Kalamata, Koroni, Methoni, and Cyparissia (Arcadia). Saint Athanasios was a bishop of Methoni in the ninth century. His biography, written in the tenth century by Peter of Argos, unfortunately provides no information concerning contemporary events in Messenia.

Perhaps the greatest sign of economic stability was the construction of numerous churches in the region. In the eleventh and twelfth centuries, several small churches were built in Kalamata. These were reconstructed or enlarged in later centuries but were greatly damaged in an earthquake in 1986. The presence of the churches of the Holy Apostles, St. Haralambos, St. Dimitrios, St. Athanasios, and St. Nikolas, however, indicates an upsurge in piety, or in the finances to support pious foundations at this period. The biographer of St. Nikon notes the religious fervor of the residents of Kalamata, even in the tenth century: "Grace has always been measured out in relation to faith, even for all others, but more so for the inhabitants of Kalamata." In the town of Filiatra, the churches of the Hrysospiliotissa and the Ascension, dated to the eleventh and twelfth centuries respectively, await further publication. The Middle Byzantine church of Zoodohos Piyi in Samarina, standing in the middle of a lush valley, preserves important wall paintings from a slightly later date (Fig. 101). Stone remains of older structures were built into the walls of this church, providing a glimpse of the many phases that comprise the history of the region and the Byzantine tendency to architecturally sanctify previously pagan sites.

One of the most important ecclesiastical constructions of the Middle Byzantine period is the church of the Transfiguration of the Savior in Hristianou (Fig. 102). Situated at the foot of Mt. Aigaleon, Hristianou is the site of medieval Hristianoupolis, mentioned in Byzantine ecclesiastical documents from 1086 as an archbishopric. The large size of the building, its innovative construction, and the presence of an adjoining structure identified as the episcopal palace all confirm the importance of Hristianou in this period. The church's position is further demonstrated by an expression still heard in the village and throughout Messenia: "Holy Savior in the Morea, Holy Wisdom in Constantinople," a telling parallelism between the seat of Hristianou's episcopate and the distant patriarchal church of the Byzantine capital, Ayia Sophia.

As is the case with the medieval history of Messenia, the very fabric of the church bridges the chronological gap between the Classical and Modern periods. The lower courses of masonry are constructed of large limestone blocks presumably taken from Classical monuments in the region

FIGURE 101
The church of Zoodohos Piyi, Samarina, Messenia. S.E.J. Gerstel.

(Fig. 103). Furthermore, marble cornices and architraves of Roman date are used to ornament the building's interior. Archaeologists have not yet established the provenance of these ancient blocks and carvings. Despite these elements, the church has a somewhat modern appearance. The building was reconstructed after its dome collapsed in the earthquake of 1886. Architecturally, the Church of the Savior at Hristianou belongs to the Greek-cross octagon type, an unusual plan found in only a few other important eleventh-century religious structures and in several Byzantine copies of a later date. On the basis of the selection of this architectural type, one may postulate that the builders of this church had some knowledge of architectural trends of their period.

While the surviving churches of Messenia furnish information about the religious life of the period, recent archaeological work offers some insight into the everyday life of its medieval inhabitants. Excavation at the site of Nichoria, in eastern Messenia, from 1969 to 1975 provided important information about domestic architecture in a small village of the Middle Byzantine period. Abandoned in the middle of the eighth century B.C., this ridge, 2 kilometers inland from the northwest corner of the Messenian Gulf, shows traces of rehabitation in the Late Roman/Early Byzantine periods and then again in the Middle Byzantine period. Excavation of several medieval domestic structures led archaeologists to hypothesize that the houses may have been two-storied, with the lower level used as shelter for animals or for storage. The discovery of a small, two-apsed chapel of rubble construction, together with evidence provided by the domestic architecture, led the excavators to posit the existence of a small village at Nichoria. According to the archaeologists, evidence provided by the excavation demonstrates that the Nichoria villagers enjoyed a standard of living "not conspicuously inferior" to city dwellers of this period. The villagers used imported pottery and lit glass lamps similar to those manufactured in the relatively large medieval city of Corinth. Analysis of animal bones suggests that both beef and pork were part of the diet.

Although Late Roman and Early Byzantine settlements of Messenia were commonly by the coast, Hristianou, Nichoria, and many later sites are removed from the sea. One explanation for this uphill migration was the vulnerability of the maritime settlements in this region. In the Middle Ages, pirates sailed along the Messenian coast. Methoni, in the southwest corner of the peninsula, had become such a center of piracy that in 1125, the

FIGURE 102
The church of the Transfiguration of the Savior in Hristianou as seen from the southwest. PRAP Archive. S.E.J. Gerstel.

SHARON E.J. GERSTEL

FIGURE 103
Church of the Transfiguration of the Savior in Hristianou, showing Classical blocks used in the construction of its walls. PRAP Archive. S.E.J. Gerstel.

Venetian ruler Domenico Michiel ordered the city to be burned to the ground in order to protect the Serenissima's commercial interests.

By the end of the twelfth century, Messenia boasted several coastal towns—rebuilt Methoni, Koroni, and Kalamata—with relatively large populations. The remaining inhabitants resided in smaller villages, probably dependent on an agricultural economy. Nominally, the area was under Byzantine rule, though it is unlikely that the tentacles of that bureaucracy ever had a firm grasp on this far corner of the empire. Heavy taxation on hearths (households) and land animals must have fostered an enormous resentment toward a central administration that provided few services for the steep taxes that it collected. In 1198, the Byzantine emperor signed an imperial writ allowing Venice open trading privileges at Methoni. Venice's control of this port, evident even at the end of the twelfth century, would establish a pattern for the following centuries.

FRANKISH MOREA (A.D. 1205–1430)

The history of Frankish Messenia begins with the untimely arrival of Geoffrey de Villehardouin of Champagne, whose ship was blown off course during his attempt to join the Fourth Crusade. Together with a local Greek ruler, he conquered a large segment of the western Peloponnese, now to be called the Morea. The name Morea is derived from the similarity between the shape of the Peloponnese and the leaf of the mulberry tree (*morea*). These trees flourished in the medieval Peloponnese, for which silk production was a major industry.

Following the conquest of Constantinople in 1204, Villehardouin sought further assistance for his territorial aspirations from his compatriot, Guillaume de Champlitte. According to a contemporary chronicle, Villehardouin told his friend:

> I've just come, sir, from a very prosperous land which is called Morea. Get together as many men as you can and leave this army, and with God's help we'll go and conquer it. When we've won it, I'll hold from you whatever part of it you're pleased to give me, and serve as your vassal.

By 1212, the entire Peloponnese was Frankish, with the exception of Monemvasia in the southeast corner, the last stronghold of Byzantium, and Methoni and Koroni in the southwest corner, held by the Venetians. Villehardouin, for his enterprising spirit, was awarded Arcadia and Kalamata. Soon after, by means of an ingenious sleight-of-hand, he became ruler over the entire region.

The wealth of the land delighted the Franks. The contemporary *Chronicle of the Morea* states that "after the Franks had won Kalamata, they saw the land was fertile, spacious and delightful with its fields and waters and multitudes of pastures." For these crusaders, the Morea would become a small kingdom to which many of the Western medieval customs would be imported. Jousting, for example, was known to have taken place in the plains of Laconia. More lasting marks of the Frankish period are left in the Gothic architecture of several Morean churches, such as the ruined cathedral at Andravida or the small single-aisled chapel at Androusa, now serving as the cemetery church of the Messenian village (Figs. 104, 105).

In the Frankish period, western Messenia was divided into two sections. The northern half, in the area of Arcadia, was controlled by the Franks of Champagne, Geoffrey de Villehardouin and his descendants. The southern half, Methoni and Koroni and its dependent towns, remained firmly in the hands of the Venetians. This arrangement had been confirmed in negotiations, according to a contemporary source, whereby the Frankish ruler "should give to the Commune the castle of Koroni with its villages and the land around it and, likewise, Methoni for the Commune of Venice to hold as an inheritance."

FIGURE 104
Cemetery church at Androusa, from the southeast. PRAP Archive. S.E.J. Gerstel.

The Frankish system of governance of the Morea was based on a feudal constitution known as the "Book of the Customs of the Empire of Romania." These laws governed the complex hierarchy of obligations between lord and liege, vassal and serf, as well as relationships between family members. One of the more intriguing passages of the law code refers to what one must do when a treasure is found. Clearly this statute had interesting implications for a feudal territory built on an ancient land. According to the code:

> When a treasure is found in some place by a freeman and on his own land, he who finds it gets half of it and the Prince the other half. And if he finds it in the land of another, the lord gets the third part of it—that is, he who is lord of the fief or of the bourgeois land—the finder receives a third, and the Prince the remaining third. And if the finder is a serf, the right of the serf passes to his lord.

For much of the time that the Franks were overlords of the region, there was relative stability. A strong, centralized authority, facilitated by a feudal

MEDIEVAL MESSENIA

FIGURE 105
*"Gothicizing" pointed arch in the north wall of the cemetery church at Androusa.
PRAP Archive. S.E.J. Gerstel.*

system, had replaced the distant Byzantine bureaucracy that was so ineffective prior to the Frankish occupation. The land was subdivided into fiefs and placed in the charge of various knights who had participated in the conquest of the region. These knights, according to the feudal system, owed military service to their liege lords. The perception of feudal efficiency is measured in laudatory comments about Geoffrey de Villehardouin's successor, his son Geoffrey II, who, according to a contemporary chronicle, "possessed a broad domain and great riches; he was wont to send his most confidential advisers from time to time to the courts of his vassals, to see how they lived and how they treated their subjects." In order to protect the land, fortresslike castles were constructed at vantage points over the seas and plains, and a number of these are to be found in Messenia. The castles at Kalamata, Androusa, Arcadia, Aëtos, Old Navarino, and Arhangelos are but a few examples of fortifications erected at this time that still show traces of the Frankish construction phase.

The Morea, however, was not built of castles alone. This chain of fortifications girded a preexisting peasantry that resided in smaller villages and farmed the land that fueled the medieval economy. A letter from Pope Innocent III in 1212 to the bishop of Methoni provides important evidence for the existence of certain towns in the Frankish period. Early Modern Ligoudista and Skarminga, for example, are recorded as "Levoudist and Escaminges" (the towns renamed Hora and Metamorfosis in the twentieth century). Ceramic finds in these two locations confirm the existence of what, until now, had been recorded only on paper. Surface collection of pottery in the region of Skarminga in 1993–94 included lamp fragments and pieces of fine glazed bowls, signs of an established community (see Fig. 106 and Focus in this chapter).

Fiscal censuses of serfs and properties also provide demographic and economic information for this region. Important feudal lords, such as the Florentine banker Niccolò Acciaiuoli, left inventories of the villages in their possession (see Focus in this chapter). The villages held by Niccolò were inhabited primarily by extended families whose surnames clearly indicate that they were indigenous Orthodox Greeks. The inventories paint a picture of the rural economy of the region. The chief crops were grains, such as wheat, barley, oats, millet, and a vetch for cattle. Olive groves, as now, flourished in the region. Wine, sold extensively at Venetian Methoni and praised by travelers to that trading port, must have come from local vines. Silk, honey, wax, figs, raisins, nuts, oranges, acorns, cotton, and flax contributed to the economic prosperity of medieval Messenia. Salt was also produced in the region, as evidenced by the presence of salt pans on the coast at the Bay of Navarino.

The Frankish knights did not maintain control of the entire Morea for long. Portions of the peninsula were reluctantly ceded to the Byzantines in a 1262 treaty, and the imperial power established a local capital at Mystra in Laconia. The Frankish dominance over the Morea, so brilliant in the thirteenth century, was much diminished by the fifteenth. In the absence of

FIGURE 106
Pierced handle of a Byzantine double-saucered lamp with traces of burning at the lower edge. PRAP Archive. R. Dupuis-Devlin.

stable rule in the region, the Morea fell prey to petty squabbling between local lords and was vulnerable to another wave of invaders. The local population was decimated by the Black Death in 1347–48, and incursions by Catalans and Turks in the fourteenth century destabilized a region that had seen a century of social and economic stability under the Franks. Further changes in the region were effected by the influx of Albanians in the late fourteenth and fifteenth centuries.

As noted, many of these invasions were the result of the weakening of the Frankish hold on the region. Despite their glorious dreams of conquest, most of the Frankish nobility had been wiped out in a distant battle with Catalan mercenaries in 1311. The absence of strong knights such as

Villehardouin, who had brought about the Latin conquest of the region, left the land in the hands of absentee bankers and princes from Flanders, Naples, Florence, and Genoa, who sought to make a profit at the expense of the villagers. By 1430, the remnants of the glorious crusader state were ceded to the Byzantines after the Franks were defeated by Constantine XI Palaiologos, Despot of Mystra.

THE VENETIANS IN THE 14TH AND 15TH CENTURIES

Numerous deliberations in the Venetian Senate of the fourteenth and fifteenth centuries concern the twin ports of Methoni and Koroni. The records of these deliberations indicate two predominant areas of Venetian interest: the legal protection of trade rights and tariffs, and the physical defense of these cities. In order to protect its coastal ports, Venice broadened the region under its control by the addition of the castles of Zonchio (called Navarino), Grisi, and Manticori, recorded in a resolution of January 27, 1411. Further land acquisition on the eastern coast of Messenia meant that the Most Serene Republic was in firm possession of much of the southern portion of the Messenian Peninsula. The focus of Venetian concerns, however, was the twin trading posts of Koroni and Methoni (see Focus in this chapter).

Venice's concern for the protection of its territories is evidenced by the sources. The commercial success of its ports, and their virtual monopoly over such industries as the transportation of pilgrims to the Holy Land, was sure to have inspired the envy of a number of competitors. Senatorial deliberations in March and May 1334 concerned the continual pillaging by the followers of a certain Zassi, assumed to be a pirate. Following investigation by a Senate committee, Venice authorized Corfu, Koroni, and Methoni to defend their Venetian subjects from piratical devastation. Assaults against the Venetian holdings in the Morea, however, also came from more organized sources. In 1391, the Senate acknowledged the severity of Turkish attacks on Nauplion, Koroni, and Methoni. The region was equally plagued by Albanians and by threats from neighboring areas of the Morea under Byzantine control. Fourteenth- and fifteenth-century deliberations concerned increased Genoese interests and hostilities in the area. A response sent by the Senate in May 1431 refers to supplemental measures taken to protect Methoni and Koroni from pillaging by the Catalans and the Genoese.

The large number of deliberations concerning the weakened fortifications of Methoni and Koroni suggests that the Senate feared for the physical security of Venice's Morean holdings. One revealing document of December 23, 1410, states that many of the inhabitants had left the city of Methoni because it seemed insufficiently fortified. This perception of vulnerability was caused not only by the decaying walls, but also by the decimation of troops assigned to these forts. Senatorial deliberations of 1348, 1358, 1360, 1398, and 1410, for example, name the plague as a reason for the reduction in the number of soldiers stationed at the fortresses. The Senate in these two centuries continually authorized new troops to be sent to Methoni and Koroni, crossbowmen and infantrymen. Not even these reinforcements, however, could assist the residents of the city against the plague, or even famine, referred to in several documents.

Although Methoni and Koroni suffered from the Black Death, depleted supplies, and weakened fortifications, the cities thrived as important centers of Venetian trade and as strategic ports for the Venetian navy. Numerous documents witness Venice's concern with the upkeep of the port and storehouses. Taxes on products were thoroughly regulated. These official documents, combined with travelers' reports, provide a vivid image of centers specializing in the traffic of wheat, olive oil, wine, meat, and humans.

Several standing ruins attest to this phase of Messenia's history. One fortress, Old Navarino, is situated on a cliff towering above Osmanaga Lagoon. Originally built for the Frankish prince Nicholas II of the St. Omer family, the castle changed hands as Frankish power weakened in the region. At various times, it was under the control of the Genoese and the Navarrese. In 1423, however, the castle was purchased by the Venetians as the northernmost post in the defense of the republic's Messenian holdings. The maritime placement of the fortress is significant and reflects a strategic transition from the Frankish period. Whereas the Franks looked to the land and protected it with feudal castles ruled over by the crusaders and their descendants, the Venetians' fortresses protected the coast and assured that the city's thriving commercial ventures would not be impeded.

TURKISH MESSENIA (1460–1684)

The conquest of the Morea by the Turks once again created a unified peninsula, now under the control of a centralized and distant authority in Ottoman Istanbul. The fear engendered by this conquest is foreshadowed even in Venetian senatorial deliberations of 1401 that stressed the dangers of falling into the hands of the infidels. Certainly the downfall of Constantinople in 1453 must have terrified both Latins and Greeks in the Morea, who could only wait their turn; and indeed, following the conquest of the Byzantine capital, the Ottomans turned to the capture of the Morea. The holdings of the last Byzantine rulers of the Morea were easily taken due to infighting among the Greeks. One by one, the castles of the Peloponnese, built by the Franks, taken by the Byzantines, then bought by the Venetians, fell to these new invaders. In 1470, the Venetians burned the castle of Kalamata, the original fief of the Villehardouin family, rather than allow the Turks to take it. A subsequent peace between the Venetians and the Turks in 1479 assured that the republic would retain Koroni, Methoni, and Navarino as well as several other important possessions in the Peloponnese. This peace, however, was not to last. By 1500, Venice had lost all three sites.

The period of the First Turkish Occupation is well documented, though little explored. Archival materials exist in Istanbul, Venice, and Athens. On the basis of preliminary analysis, one scholar, Peter Topping, observed several patterns in population figures for this period. A low point in the population is noted around 1480, following wars between the Turks and Venetians. In 1502–3, according to Topping, Sultan Bayezit II ordered the transfer of heretic Turkomans from Anatolia to Methoni and Koroni, severely altering the demographic picture of these areas. The population drain also resulted from the forced tribute of Christian boys for the janissary corps of the Ottoman court in addition to the recruitment of foot soldiers from this region. The decline of the Morea in general, and Messenia in particular, thus resulted from a large-scale exodus of Christians from the region, who sought to avoid the "Ottoman draft" and who searched for lands still under Christian control.

Changes in population during this period are nearly impossible to trace in the archaeological record through ceramic analysis. No firm chronology has been established by archaeologists for Turkish pottery in the distant provinces. Moreover, despite changes in the region's political structure, small villages such as Skarminga would have continued to employ the same clays, kilns, and ceramic techniques, making the establishment of a ceramic typology based on historical periodization anachronistic.

One of the best-preserved fortresses in Greece, New Navarino, or Neokastro, was built by the Turks in this period of occupation. Now serving as the headquarters of the branch of the Greek Archaeological Service concerned with underwater archaeology, the fortress was constructed in 1573 in order to guard the western coast of the Peloponnese.

VENETIAN RULE, 1686–1715

A second period of Venetian power in the Morea began with the Serenissima's conquest of the region in 1685–88. The reconquered land, severely depopulated and undercultivated, was not in the condition in which they had last seen it, however. The Venetians set about surveying the region that they would now rule. The Morea was divided into four provinces, one of which was Messenia, and new populations were invited into the region, thus reactivating industries that had lain dormant under the First Turkish Occupation of the area.

Three Venetians, Girolamo Renier, Marin Michiel, and Domenico Gritti, arrived in the Morea in the summer of 1688 with the express purpose of recording the resources of the region. Both Michiel and Gritti wrote long reports that were read to the Venetian Senate. The underpopulation of the region, resulting in a lack of agricultural enterprises, was notable. The Venetians lured residents from other areas of Greece to settle in the Peloponnese, now called the Kingdom of the Morea, offering them reduced tithes on their land and long-term leases. Michiel's report describes the topography of the region and the character of the people. Gritti is more concerned with economic issues. In order to increase agricultural productivity, Gritti suggested that large shelters be erected to protect flocks from the cold winters, and that more storage buildings be constructed to match more closely produce with the supply and demand of the marketplace.

The Venetian registers and reports provide critical information for Messenia, giving not only actual population statistics, but observations on the residents of the area. Francesco Grimani, who served as *provveditor* of the Morea from 1698 to 1701 noted of the Morean inhabitants that

> lying comes naturally to them; they think of ways to deceive one another and are always afraid of being deceived. They place their own interest above everything: this is the first lesson a son learns from the father. They live mostly in huts in order to spend less on their own houses, thus making a show of poverty even when well-off. They love idleness and cultivate only enough land for their precise needs, being inclined to maintain large flocks in order to get a return without sweat.

These, however, were the comments of an outsider and a Westerner observing people who had lived under an unstable political regime.

Venetian suggestions for improvements in the region included the consolidation and repair of the fortresses. But these plans were to no avail. Venice was not as strong in the seventeenth and eighteenth centuries as it was in the days when its trading ports in Messenia were the envy of the Mediterranean. No amount of repair could change the course of history. In 1715, the Turks reconquered the Morea, and there they would remain until the Battle of Navarino in 1827.

FOCUS

The ESTATES *of* NICCOLÒ ACCIAIUOLI

Evidence for medieval Messenia is provided by numerous documents held in Italian archives. Several texts assess the landholdings of Niccolò Acciaiuoli, a Florentine banker who had close ties to the rulers of the Morea in the mid-fourteenth century. Through his own cleverness, Niccolò gradually amassed a number of properties in the Morea, including many in the region of Messenia.

On May 27, 1354, when Niccolò took possession of the castle of the Holy Archangel, an inventory was compiled listing all of the holdings belonging to that property. The inventory, written on forty-six pages, is located in the State Archives of Florence. One of the properties assessed by the document is the village of "Cremidi," presently divided into the two towns of Upper and Lower Kremydia (Fig. 107). What follows is the inventory of the landholdings of the peasants of a single town of the fourteenth century. The names have been preserved in the Italianate form found in the document. In the text, the name of the head of the family is followed by the amount of taxes that he owes for his *stasia*, or landholding. According to the text, these *acrostica*, or taxes, were to be paid in the currency of the period; hyperpera, sterlings, and denier tournois. Each hyperperon equalled twenty sterlings, and each sterling was equal to four tournois.

HOLDINGS OF NICCOLÒ IN THE VILLAGE OF CREMIDI

The said count has possessions in the village of Cremidi of all persons, vassals, and goods, hereunder recorded and described in detail.

Georgi Philippopoli has a wife and two sons, Johanne and Nicola, one ox, and for the land that he holds and for his tax, he is obligated to pay 3 hyperpera, 3 sterlings.

The Orthodox priest Theofilato Carazopolo has a wife, two sons,

---

SHARON E.J. GERSTEL

FIGURE 107
Aerial photograph of the modern town of Kremydia. Courtesy of H. I. Koutsoumbos.

Nicola and Andreas, and has a brother Johanne, and is obligated to pay for his tax 4 hyperpera.

Legorius Sisuvalanus has a wife, two cows, eight pack animals, and for the land that he holds he must pay the tax of 2 hyperpera, 17 sterlings, 1 tournois.

Johannes Sisuvalano has a wife, a daughter, and a brother Theodero and two cows, and must pay for his tax 5 hyperpera, 17 sterlings, 1 tournois.

Gregorius Balanus has a wife, one cow, five vineyards, and must pay for his tax 2 hyperpera, 13 sterlings.

Costa de Cuniati, must pay for his tax 5 hyperpera, 3 ½ sterlings.

Trifona Roccana has a son Ligori, one ox, and for his tax owes 2 hyperpera, 4 sterlings.

Anna Marinu has a son Nicola, pays for the tax 1 hyperperon, 15 sterlings.

Nicola Macri has a wife, two sons, Lione and Andrea, and three daughters, two oxen, two cows, ten sheep, and must pay for his tax, 4 hyperpera, 4 sterlings.

Argirius Macri has a wife and son Paulu, and a brother Basili, two oxen, one cow, six sheep, for his tax owes, 4 hyperpera, 17 sterlings, 1(?) tournois.

Vasili Carzopolu has a wife and is obligated to pay 3 ½ hyperpera.

SHARON E.J. GERSTEL

Vasili Zangaropolu has a brother Tefilato and is obligated to pay for his tax 2 hyperpera, 17 ½ sterlings.

Leu Blasi has a wife, two daughters, one ox, eight sheep, and owes for his tax, 1 hyperperon, 13 sterlings, 3 tournois.

Leu Guacava has two nephews, Johanne and . . . , two oxen, six sheep, and for his tax he must pay 4 hyperpera, 8 sterlings, 1 tournois.

Andreas Poteras has a wife, two daughters, a nephew Christopheru, one ox, and must pay for his tax 18 sterlings, 1 tournois.

Sire Revechena is obligated to pay 3 hyperpera, 10 sterlings.

Leu Pavlucazi has a wife and must pay 1 hyperperon, 10 sterlings.

Nicola Pavlucazi has a wife and must pay 1 hyperperon, 12 sterlings, 1 tournois.

Johannes Nicolia has a wife, two daughters and is obligated to pay 2 hyperpera, 17 sterlings, 1 tournois.

Johannes Laroseu has a wife, and son Lione, one ox, one ass, five sheep and is obligated to pay 1 hyperperon, 14 sterlings.

Lariseu has two nephews, Nicolau, Christoforu, one ox, five sheep and is obligated to pay 17 sterlings.

Demetrius Lariseu has three sons, Johanne, Georgium, Sevadetu, and Johannes has a wife, two oxen, six sheep and is obligated to pay 1 hyperperon, 6 sterlings, 1 tournois.

Johannes Curea has a daughter and must pay 1 hyperperon, 15 sterlings, 1 tournois.

Chiriachius Laroseu has a wife and daughter, a nephew Nichiforu, one ox, and is obligated to pay 1 hyperperon, 5 sterlings, 2 tournois.

Nichiforius Laroseu has . . . , and is obligated to pay 1 hyperperon, 15 sterlings.

Basilius Sarburi has a wife, and brother Nichita, two oxen, two cows, fifteen sheep, and must pay 5 hyperpera, 1 sterling, 3 tournois.

Johannes Sarburi has a wife and son Georgiu, a daughter, one cow, one ox, one ass, and must pay 2 hyperpera.

Manolius, the magistrate from Basilopoli, has a wife, one ox, three sheep, and must pay 2 hyperpera, 17 sterlings, 1 tournois.

Porcopis, the magistrate from Vasilopli, has a wife and daughter, and a brother Stasinu, and is obligated to pay 3 hyperpera, 10 ½ sterlings.

Basilius Fundari has a wife, a son Theofilatu, two daughters, one ox, three sheep, and must pay 3 hyperpera, 10 ½ sterlings.

Theophilatus Capiseus has a wife, a brother Cossta, two oxen, one cow, four sheep, and must pay 1 hyperperon, 6 sterlings, 1 tournois.

Sirianu Pumpo has a wife and daughter and pays 2 hyperpera, 17 sterlings, 1 tournois.

Costa Mercevele has a wife, a son Nicola, and two oxen, one cow and must pay 2 hyperpera, 16 sterlings, 1 tournois.

Nicolaus Siliberti has a wife and son Paulu, and two daughters and is obligated to pay 1 hyperperon, $17\frac{1}{2}$ sterlings, and for the land of his brother, he must pay 1 hyperperon, $17\frac{1}{2}$ sterlings.

Stefanu Condo has a wife, a son Georgiu, a daughter, and a brother Basili who has a wife and a son Stamati, and two oxen, one cow, ten sheep, [and] is obligated to pay 2 hyperpera, 5 sterlings.

Costa Fundari has a wife, and four sons, Nicolau, Johanne, Georgius, Athanasiu, and one ox, ten sheep, and must pay 2 hyperpera, 14 sterlings, 1 tournois.

Athanasius Fundari has a wife and son Denemetri [sic], a daughter, and two nephews Niclina and Johanne, two oxen, one cow, fifteen sheep, and must pay 2 hyperpera, $2\frac{1}{2}$ sterlings.

Migaeli Fundari has a wife and brother Johanne, and must pay 1 hyperperon, 19 sterlings.

Johannes Fundari has a wife and a daughter, one cow, and must pay 1 hyperperon, 3 sterlings.

Stamatis Fundari has a wife and son Johanne and a daughter and is obligated to pay 1 hyperperon, 3 sterlings.

Nicolaus Fundari has a wife and is obligated to pay $1\frac{1}{2}$ hyperpera.

Johannes Fundari, son of Calogree, has a wife and pays $1\frac{1}{2}$ hyperpera.

Georgi Agrocantu has a wife and a brother Johanne and pays 3 hyperpera, $9\frac{1}{2}$ sterlings.

Heleni Agrocanta has a son Theoderu and a daughter and is obligated to pay 1 hyperperon, 8 sterlings, 1 tournois.

Argirius Agrocantu is obligated to pay 1 hyperperon, 2 tournois.

Georgi Nicita has a wife and a son Johanne and pays 1 hyperperon, 18 sterlings.

Manueli Agrocanti has a wife and a son Nicolau and a daughter, and one cow and is obligated to pay for this landholding 1 hyperperon, $11\frac{1}{2}$ sterlings.

Gollelmo Agrocantu is obligated to pay for the landholding of Demetri Agrocantu, his father, 1 hyperperon, 2 tournois.

Georgius Agrocanto has one ox, and is obligated to pay for the landholding of Manuli Agocato 1 hyperperon, $11\frac{1}{2}$ sterlings.

Stamatis Agrocato has a wife and four daughters and two oxen, one cow, and pays 1 hyperperon, 2 tournois.

Johannes Rapana has a wife and a brother Nicolau, one ox, and is obligated to pay 5 hyperpera, 3 sterlings, 3 tournois.

Basilius Calados has a wife and two sons, Theoderu and Johanne, two oxen, one cow, five sheep, and must pay 3 hyperpera, 3 sterlings.

Johannes Martarus has a wife and a daughter, one cow, and is obligated to pay 1 hyperperon, 9½ sterlings.

Tharapos Calandos has a wife and a son Exeducusu, one ox, five sheep, and is obligated to pay 1 hyperperon, 17 sterlings, 1 tournois.

Georgius Calados has a brother Theodore, one ox, three sheep, and must pay 18 sterlings, 1 tournois.

Theoderu Calados is obligated to pay for his share of the land tax 18 sterlings, 1 tournois.

The Orthodox priest Nicola Cundo is in the hands of his nephews Stefanu, Basilius, and Johanne Cundor, who are responsible to pay for the tax of the aforementioned priest Nicolay 1 hyperperon, 5 sterlings.

Basilius Cundo is responsible for the tax of 1 hyperperon, 5 sterlings.

The Orthodox priest Christodolu Laruseu [no amount recorded].

Simeon Revezena [no amount recorded].

The Orthodox priest Leu Sarburi has a son, the priest Christodulu [no amount recorded].

Lucas Ninivea has to pay the tax for the aforementioned Basil of Tray in the amount of 3 hyperpera, 2 sterlings, 1 tournois.

This section of the inventory provides interesting information about a typical fourteenth-century town. Though the area was under Latin overlordship, the names of the villagers demonstrate that they were predominantly Orthodox. Most are named after such popular saints of the Eastern calendar as George, Basil, Andrew, and Constantine (Costa). Typically, only the names of the male members of each household are provided. However, in three cases, that of Anna Marinu, Sire Revechena, and Heleni Agrocantu, the inventory cites a female as head of the family. In these cases, one must assume that the male head of the household was deceased.

Several families dominated the village, among them the Fundari, Agrocanti, and Caladoi. In several cases, brothers or nephews joined the nuclear family, thus extending the number of men available for agricultural work. In the case of Stefanu Condu, who lived with his brother Basili and his family, the inventory provides evidence for an extended family sharing the same residence. The agricultural basis for the village economy is further evidenced by the number of oxen, often paired, that would have been required to farm the land.

FOCUS

VENETIAN METHONI (MODON)

Walls and wind are what one remembers of Methoni. The massive walls, built by the Venetians to protect the medieval trading center, now enclose a vast wasteland of desolate buildings and acres of grass-covered history (Fig. 108). The wind comes from the sea, blowing the high grass to and fro, impeding the modern visitor from walking the overgrown streets of the once-flourishing town. It was the blustering ancestor of this wind that brought Geoffrey of Villehardouin, returning from a crusade to the Holy Land in 1204, to the welcome shelter of Methoni, a visit that would change the history of the city. A chronicle of the event tells us that once there, "He and his companions were approached by a local Greek archon who wanted to use this unexpected troop to expand his territories. The prospect of adventure and profit led Geoffrey to join the Greek, and together they conquered all the western Peloponnese as far north as Patras."

But Villehardouin could not hold on to Methoni, and in 1206 ceded it and neighboring Koroni to the Venetians, who would maintain control of this peninsula for the ensuing three centuries. These twin cities, forming the "right eye of Venice," strategically placed at the tip of the Peloponnese, would serve as the base for the Venetian reconquest of Crete in 1363–64. Methoni became the main port of the Most Serene Republic of Venice (Fig. 109), trafficking wares to traders who stopped to rest their weary sea legs on the way to eastern Mediterranean ports, and to pilgrims who rested and purchased supplies for their journey to the Holy Land. Travelers of the fourteenth and fifteenth centuries have left a vivid account of this now-abandoned city at its most flourishing moment. The image sketched by their accounts is of a fortified city built of wooden houses. The population was mixed: Latins, Greeks, Jews, Turks, and Gypsies. Trade proliferated, but what these travelers most remember is the high quality of the wine.

SHARON E.J. GERSTEL

FIGURE 108
Relief of the lion of St. Mark in the fort of Methoni. PRAP Archive. S.E.J. Gerstel.

FIGURE 109
Town and harbor of Methoni. Detail from F. de Wit engraving of the Peloponnese. Courtesy of Dumbarton Oaks, Trustees of Harvard University, Washington, D.C. © 1997.

THE CITY AND ITS POPULATION

Opposite to the port of Modona is a very large mount which is called the Hill of Wisdom, to which mount in ancient times used to go the philosophers and poets to exercise their arts; and in this very big mount, on the summit is a certain tower fortified with planks, and on it are certain guards; and as sails come to appear on the sea, they make signs with certain white cloths on sticks, according to the direction from which they come, because they have details and signs are required for defence and offence, so that the port, which is between two mounts, that is, between that of Modona and that of Wisdom, is very secure both from the corsairs and the winds.

LEONARDO DI NICCOLÒ FRESCOBALDI (1384)

I found there a German master-gunner called Peter Bombadere, who gave me good company and friendship. He showed me the strength of the town and the artillery, and it is in truth a small town but strong. On the land side it has three suburbs with three walls and three ditches hewn out of the natural rock, on which they are building daily. He took me around the innermost wall, which was very thick and built of rough stones: in addition there is a rampart against the wall on which stood many fine cannon, great carthouns and slings. We went further beyond the gate into the first suburb in which is a very long street inhabited solely by Jews, whose women-folk do beautiful work in silk, making girdles, hoods, veils, and face coverings, some of which I bought. We proceeded through the suburb, which is inhabited by many poor black naked people who live in little houses roofed with reeds, some three hundred families. They are called gipsies: we call them heathen people from Egypt who travel about in our countries. These people follow all kinds of trade, such as shoemakers, cobblers and smiths.

SIR ARNOLD VON HARFF (1497)

COMMERCE

There are two thousand inhabitants, and the sea encloses it on both sides. It is well walled and sufficiently strong, but flat. I saw there numerous gardens supplied with all kinds of fruit, and the soil is very productive, like that of Andalucia. Lodging is good, the language is Greek, but the place is governed from Venice. . . . The Venetians have these possessions in the Morea because they are vital for their trade. The people are very wealthy, for these places are the ports of discharge for Greece and the Black Sea for all classes of merchandise.

PERO TAFUR (1436)

We went over to the market, and saw many Turks bargaining with the Christians. For there are Turks, neighbors of the people of Modon, and these Turks raise hogs, and fatten them, and bring them to Modon to sell to the Christians, because, like the Jews, they themselves do not eat pork; and especially when they see a fleet or a convoy arrive, they come with their herds of swine, and do such a good business that for less than one mark one may buy a fat porker. The men from the galleys buy and kill them, burn off the hair—saving only the bacon fat, and all the bacon and lard of two or three pigs they cram into the hide of one, sew it up with a needle and so carry it to Venice. . . . I believe that in those days while we remained at Modon over 6,000 such hides were brought on board the galleys . . . and every pig thus equivalent to three or four; for the city of Venice gets its bacon and lard from this place; and sausages are also made there in great quantities.

FELIX FABER OF ULM (December 15, 1480)

THE WINE

And we arrived here at vintage-time and found no old wine, and for the new Romania [wine] they make, they fill all the barrel inside with resin like plaster; and if they do not do so, through the fatness of the wine, all would become verminous; and of these two things I know not which was worse, the one to the eye and the other to the taste.

LEONARDO DI NICCOLÒ FRESCOBALDi (1384)

But of the wine which grows there, what shall I say, since the very thought of it alone delights me! For there, there grows a muscat wine whose bouquet and noble name a certain wine has taken to itself which grows in Calabria . . . which in comparison to the wine of Modon is hardly as water. It is plentiful and cheap, and finer than the Cretan wine, wherefore at Ulm, Modon wine is sold at a higher price than Cretan—and both are called Malmsey. But the market is good for other things also and is exceedingly prosperous; and it is extraordinary that the Turks

---

VENETIAN METHONI (MODON)

have not long ago destroyed the place; but perhaps they spare it on account of the trade that they have with the Christians, which would cease if they sacked the city.

FELIX FABER OF ULM (December 15, 1480)

This city is governed by a Captain and a Governor of the castle, who are sent by the Signoria, and they are changed every two years. Good malmsey, muscatel wines and Roumanian wines are also found there.

CANON PIETRO CASOLA (June 26, 1494)

FOCUS

BYZANTINE SGRAFFITO WARE

Broken pots are scattered over the Greek landscape. These pieces of pottery all tell a story, whether they are chance remains of civilizations long gone or careless refuse discarded by recent inhabitants. Each ceramic fragment is a physical link to the artisan who fashioned a vessel and to the civilization that supported his craft. Moreover, the analysis of these broken pots may provide detailed information about their owners: their economic status, their religious practices, their aesthetic preferences. Archaeologists examine sherds to address a wide range of issues. For civilizations that preserve no written records, ceramic remains often provide critical evidence for the everyday life of people and for their interaction with other cultures. Even for societies that have left ample documentation, the analysis of pottery may help to supplement the written record.

A dirt-encrusted sherd is not always the most picturesque artifact when collected in the field or excavated in a trench. When brought into the pottery shed, each fragment must be washed, examined by a specialist, sorted into a meaningful category, measured, drawn and photographed. Only through such systematic examination do these artifacts reveal more synthetic information about the cultures that produced them. Specialists strive to create accurate chronologies by which to date pottery. For archaeology, pottery with a secure chronology provides one of the most accurate means of dating an excavated or surveyed site.

The study of pottery of the eastern medieval world is still in its infancy. But this pottery promises to reveal information about the interaction of three great cultures of the Middle Ages: the medieval West, Byzantium, and Islam. Pottery of this period demonstrates the transmission of shape and decoration from one culture to another. The establishment of local workshops and patterns of importation and exportation are all areas of concern to pottery specialists of the medieval period.

SHARON E.J. GERSTEL

In order to study Byzantine ceramics, the material evidence is divided by some specialists into specific categories that facilitate analysis: coarse, cooking, and fine wares. Coarse-ware containers such as amphoras were used to ship and store products such as oil and grains. Cooking pots, made from a gritty, micaceous clay, are associated with household use. Fine wares are the tableware of the family. Intricately decorated and coated with a lead glaze, fine wares have received the most attention from scholars, due to the beauty of the vessels. Some scholars have linked these vessels to the Byzantine aristocracy, but examples of this class of pottery are found throughout the empire, even in excavations of the poorest sites.

Sgraffito ware is the best known of Byzantine fine-ware types (Figs. 110, 111). The sgraffito technique, which was influenced by Islamic models, involved incising a design through a thin white or cream-colored slip that coated the surface of the vessel. The darker color of the clay was revealed by the incised design and formed a contrast to the lighter-colored surface. The incised lines vary in width, from thick to thin, depending on the instrument used to incise the design through the slip and the predilections of the artisan. The play of dark and light colors, incised and excised spaces, which provided a sense of depth and relief, were intentional contrasts used by the potter to create a lively vessel guaranteed to delight its owner. Beginning in the twelfth century, paint was often applied to the surface, either

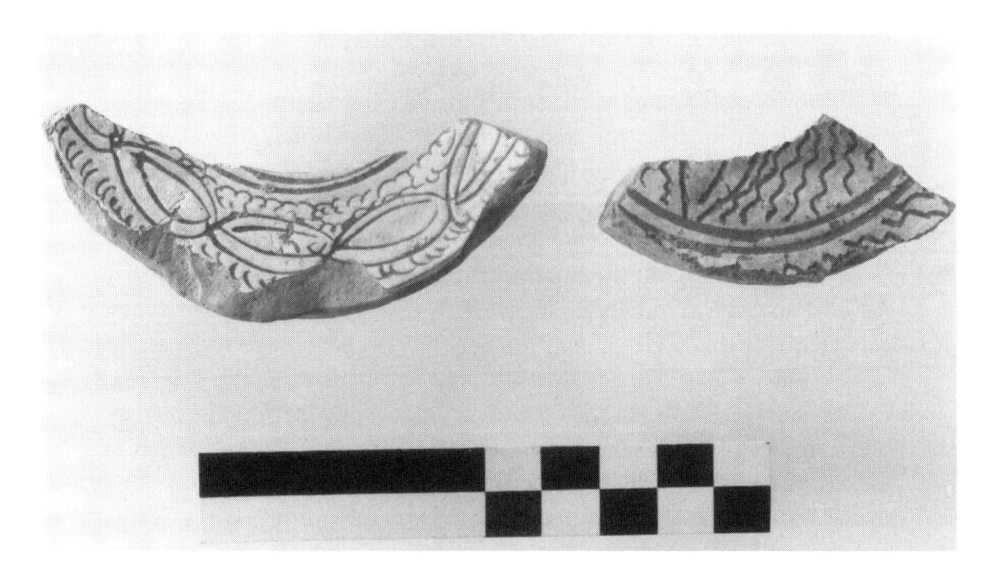

FIGURE 110
Two bases of bowls with sgraffito decoration from Skarminga. PRAP Archive. R. Dupuis-Devlin.

FIGURE III
Fourteenth-century chalice, interior with sgraffito decoration. Courtesy of the Pierides Foundation Museum, Larnaka, Cyprus.

a yellow-brown or green tint, that complemented and enlivened the sgraffito design.

Sgraffito decoration is found mainly on the interiors of bowls and plates and on the exteriors of goblets and jars (Fig. III). Vessels are often decorated with geometric, vegetal, interlace, or curvilinear motifs. However, the design repertory also included animals, humans, scenes of marriage, and illustrations of popular romances and legends. As in decorated pottery of the ancient world, motifs incised on pottery might be related to the function of a specific vessel. The prevalence of hares as a decorative motif in the central medallion of bowls, for example, alludes to the inclusion of the meat of this animal in the medieval diet.

A number of sherds of sgraffito ware, created in the manner described above, were collected by PRAP (Fig. 110). Their decoration, however, did not consist of the sophisticated patterns normally associated with this ware. Rather, the Messenian sherds, created far from known pottery-manufacturing centers such as Corinth, Thessaloniki, or Serres, were plainer, characterized by concentric incised circles or sloppy loops following the shape of the bowl. Dated to the twelfth and thirteenth centuries, the collected sherds provide evidence for the flourishing community of Skarminga, mentioned in an early-thirteenth-century document as "Escaminges." The existence of sgraffito ware at Skarminga is proof that popular pottery styles could be imported even into the provincial "lands down under."

FIGURE 112
Central square of the modern town of Pylos with a monument to the Battle of Navarino. PRAP Archive. R. J. Robertson.

CHAPTER 9

The SECOND OTTOMAN PERIOD *and the* GREEK REVOLUTION

When the Greek Revolution erupted in 1821, the Turkish, or Ottoman, empire controlled the Morea. The seat of power for the Ottoman sultan, modern Istanbul, the former Byzantium/Constantinople and capital of the Eastern Roman empire, had fallen centuries earlier to the onslaughts of Mehmet the Conqueror, in the year 1453. Nonetheless, we have already seen in Chapter 8 that the conquest of southern Greece by the Ottomans was a gradual process—there were even parts of the Morea, such as the Mani (the middle finger of the Peloponnese), that were only nominally under Turkish authority and preserved intact many of their traditional social and political institutions.

Messenia, however, was not one of these favored regions. It was occupied by the Ottomans already in the fifteenth century, and was to remain Turkish for the better part of three centuries—except for a few decades on either side of 1700, when Venice succeeded in replacing the Turks as overlords of the Morea and secured its prize with a series of strategic coastal forts (see Chapter 8).

Already by the eighteenth century, the central Ottoman government had weakened, and its economy was in a state of decline. In contrast, northern European markets were expanding rapidly. In such a climate, a new kind of commercial relationship formed between the eastern Mediterranean and western Europe: at the center of this economic system were countries like England, France, and Holland; at the periphery were Greece and other marginal provinces of the Turkish empire.

The Ottoman state could no longer hope to monopolize trade. Now there arose a new dynamic, by which Western merchants might exploit Greece as a source either for raw materials and produce or for cheap manufactured goods. Opportunities for private initiative rose. Enterprising Turkish landholders intensified cultivation on estates, often with dire consequences for peasant Christian populations who worked the land. Greek

---

JACK L. DAVIS

notables promoted the expansion of Hellenic maritime trade by investing in the construction of ships, often sailing under Russian flags to avoid taxes levied on Ottoman subjects, or in industries like those on Mt. Pelion in Thessaly, which supplied yarn to the West.

Some Greek families grew rich, as the condition of most deteriorated in areas of southern Greece like Messenia. Prosperous expatriate Greek communities thrived in Venice, Trieste, Leghorn, Bucharest, and Marseilles—only a few of the many centers where Greek mercantile interests were established. The powerful "Phanariot" elite of Istanbul (so-called from the district of the city where most lived) held influential and lucrative offices in the Turkish court—buying and selling and exploiting ecclesiastical posts. Even the office of the patriarch itself, the head of the Orthodox church, did not escape such venality.

It is in such a context that we must view the political and economic history of the Second Ottoman period in Messenia. It is a complicated history, confused by frequent threats to the authority of the Turks, from both within and without their empire. It is a time of increasing interference by western European powers not only in the economy but also the politics of the southern Balkans. By the end of the eighteenth century, the ability of the Ottomans adequately to protect their own borders and resources almost invited local insurrections, rampant piracy, and military interventions.

The most famous among the latter were the incursions of Catherine the Great of Russia and of Muhammad Ali of Egypt. As supposed champion of the Orthodox faith, Catherine dared to sponsor an invasion of the Peloponnese by Russian troops under the command of Alexei and Fedor Orlov, an expedition that succeeded in occupying the fort at Navarino for a brief time (Fig. 113). A few decades later, in an even more daring move, Muhammad Ali occupied virtually the entire Morea, nominally by authority of the sultan, but with the intent of joining it to his own domain.

But, despite the intrinsic interest of such episodes for both Western and Eastern historians, many details of the history of the Peloponnese in the eighteenth century are still poorly understood, until recently owing to difficulties in access to the Ottoman archives in Istanbul. For this reason, many historians have relied on Western sources, principally reports written by consular agents of the Western merchant states, or by Western travelers and explorers. These can provide in many instances a rich and varied description of Ottoman Greece, but one that is almost always unnuanced and generally lacks detail—even with regard to basic matters like the census of the Greek population or the location of Greek villages.

Messenia figures prominently in the story of the Second Ottoman period in the Morea; in a sense, the period both starts and ends there, since

FIGURE 113
Line of fortifications at Neokastro and the southern end of the island of Sphacteria. PRAP Archive. J. L. Davis.

the siege of Methoni completed the Turkish conquest of the Peloponnese, and the Battle of Navarino brought Ottoman rule to an end more than a century later. The first chapter in this story begins in 1715, the year in which Venetian rule was brought to a sudden and violent conclusion.

THE SECOND OTTOMAN PERIOD

The Second Ottoman period was established in the Morea through a bloody campaign of vengeance launched against Venice by Sultan Ahmet III. On May 22, 1715, the powerful Grand Vizier of the Ottoman empire, Çorlulu Ali Paşa, set forth from Thessaloniki to accomplish the conquest. By June 25 he had marshaled his forces before Corinth—the key to Venetian defenses against a land attack (Fig. 114). After a council among his advisers, Ali delivered an ultimatum to the Venetian commandant (the *proveditor*) of the fort:

> I am the first minister and *generalissimo* of the most powerful emperor in the World ... if you ... through bad advice, want to oppose yourself against the invincible forces of our powerful emperor, with the help of God we will invade your fortress, we will put all men within to the sword,

FIGURE 114
Two views of the Venetian citadel of Corinth. Reproduced from R. Carpenter and A. Bon, Corinth, *vol. 3, pt. 2:* The Defenses of Acrocorinth and the Lower Town *(Cambridge, Mass.: Harvard University Press for the American School of Classical Studies at Athens, 1936), 155, fig. 98. With permission of the American School of Classical Studies.*

and all the women will be enslaved . . . and it will be you who are responsible to Heaven for the blood spilt and for the enslavement of the women.

Giacomo Minetto, the *provveditor*, rejected this command, trusting in his own God and firm in his commitment to preserve the stronghold for Venice. Consequently, the following day, the responsibility for besieging Corinth was passed to Sari Ahmet Paşa, chief of the elite Ottoman palace guard, the Janissaries, and the battle commenced. A week later, Corinth lay in ashes; Minetto had disappeared. A Turkish promise to transport safely his second-in-command and other citizens of Venice to Corfu was honored, but the Greeks—men, women, and children—found inside the fortress were sold into slavery. In the aftermath, Greeks from all parts of the Peloponnese flooded to Corinth to submit themselves to the rule of the sultan.

The result of the siege, if not quite so dramatic as Byron's explosion in the powder magazines—

> Many a tall and goodly man,
> Scorch'd and shrivel'd to a span,
> Like a cinder strew'd the plain
>
> . . . .
>
> Some fell on the shore, but far away,
> Scatter'd o'er the Isthmus lay;
> Christian or Moslem, which be they?
> Let their mothers see and say!

—nonetheless led within a few decades to a more substantial intermingling of Eastern and Western populations in the Morea and the formation of a quite cosmopolitan culture, particularly in the important coastal merchant centers.

Messenia shared in the tumult of 1715 and was in turn radically altered by its consequences, in part by events played out on its own stage. After Corinth, other Venetian castles soon fell, notably Nauplion. The Turkish forces next marched unopposed across the Taygetus range, through the valley of the Pamisos, to the outskirts of Pylos, and camped at Handrinou. The important Messenian stronghold of Koroni was forsaken by its commander, after he had wrecked the walls and demolished its houses himself. Not a shot was fired. Venice also destroyed Navarino, and the decision was taken that forces be massed at Methoni for a last-ditch effort.

But within days, the garrison there was slaughtered, and the Peloponnese was entirely in Turkish hands. The four Venetian provinces were eliminated; ultimately, a new seat of government was established at Tripolitsa (modern Tripolis) in the center of the Morea, far from the Most Serene Republic's former seats of administrative power at Patras, Nauplion, Monemvasia, and Methoni.

The Morea under the Ottomans was appointed into thirty-six administrative districts, a structure maintained, *mutatis mutandis*, after 1821 by the modern Greek state. The area of Messenia in which PRAP has conducted research is divided among three of these. Arcadia, with its capital at modern Cyparissia, included towns in the northwestern part of our study area—for example, Gargaliani, Ligoudista, Floka, and Valta. Skarminga, Maniaki, Styliano, Romanou, and Hasanaga were under the jurisdiction of Navarino. And in the far northeast, the village of Maryeli was administered from Androusa.

One can, with some perseverance, gain a graphic picture of the character of life in the coastal centers of Messenia during this Ottoman occupation—but glimpses of the daily existence of Greek and Turkish peasants in the rural hinterlands are few and far between. Though foreigners often visited the town of Kalamata, the village of Navarino, or the ruins of Messene, they seldom ventured elsewhere, and, if they did so, they tell us little about their experiences. This is especially true of the areas of western Messenia that we have studied most closely through archaeological survey—the lands that lie between Pylos and Gargaliani. Indeed, it is hardly less true for the Ottoman period than for antiquity, as Leake noted, that "there is no portion of the Peloponnese less noticed by ancient authors, than the part of Messenia lying between Coryfasion and Cyparissia, though its length is not less than twenty miles."

Sometimes, however, precious information can be culled even from quite laconic notes, like those included in William Gell's valuable *Itinerary of the Morea* (1817) and his *Narrative of a Journey in the Morea* (1823). The former work is little more than a list of places, appended with charts providing the times needed to travel between them and occasional memoranda on sources of water and provisioning. But Gell, unlike so many other Westerners in Messenia, traveled the coastal route north from Pylos to Gargaliani. His observations along the way provide us with uniquely important information about sites that we would otherwise know only from their material culture, such as Hasanaga and Ordines.

After passing the north end of the Bay of Navarino and Voidokoilia, Gell noted that "an eminence approaches the road r. The plain extends on r. See the villages, or tchitliks of Osman Aga and Haslan Aga." The position of Osmanaga, modern Koryfasion, is not in doubt. Haslan Aga must be the site of Hasanaga. Fortunately for us, Gell is comparatively garrulous in his *Narrative of a Journey in the Morea*, describing the same trip from Navarino to Gargaliani in much greater detail: "The track runs along the eastern shore of the port for some time, after which it descends into an alluvial plain, leaving the little villages of Petrachorio and Leuka on the left, and Gephyrae and Lisaki on little knolls on the right." A description of Hasanaga follows that invites comparison with the material remains of the place (see Focus in this chapter).

North of Gargaliani, Gell notes another significant archaeological site—just before crossing the Langouvardos River. Here are the "ruins of Ordina, or Ortina," clearly our site of Ordines; this is the first written reference to the existence of antiquities in this important location (see Chapter 5).

A second, much more graphic account of a journey over these same horsepaths through the Messenian outback is that of A. L. Castellan—a trip that occurred a decade or so earlier than Gell's and was filled with considerably more excitement. After departing Navarino on an "ancient road" well-built with large slabs of irregular shape and bordered at intervals with fountains, a vast plain planted with large olives, apparently untended, loomed ahead. The plain itself was marshy near the base of the hills skirted by the road, and the bridges were half-ruined, making the going difficult for the horses. After traveling all day within this olive forest (called "100 villages," although not even a single house was in sight), Castellan and his party emerged from it at sunset.

The travelers found themselves opposite the island of Proti, in the midst of a barren terrain covered with heather. Ahead lay yet another forest, which their guide claimed was inhabited by pirates, who swept forth from the island to prey on the unwary. Suitable precautions had to be taken. The party pitched camp for the night, but soon a whistle was heard from inside the forest, followed by more, approaching closer and closer until several men emerged. These supposed night guards for fields in the vicinity invited the travelers to join them in their own camp; but after their offer was declined, the whistlers retreated into the forest, later to reemerge and attack. Finally they were driven away only by a gunshot, and a sentinel was posted for the remainder of the night.

Piracy and brigandage of this sort, particularly in areas within striking distance of the Mani, had proliferated since the wars of the late eighteenth century. Turks fortified their rural estates. Greeks chose to leave land uncultivated rather than risk living in the countryside. Offshore islands such as Proti often served as a base for scoundrels. As Castellan and his party observed, the entire coast opposite the island was entirely deserted.

The interior of western Messenia was, however, hardly desolate, although we have few accounts of journeys by Western travelers inland. Reports of the French Expédition scientifique de Morée, organized by the French government in conjunction with its military occupation of the Peloponnese (about which see more below), are exceptional in this regard and are especially helpful; beginning in 1829, scientists and historians attached to this mission ranged the Peloponnese, engaged in studies so diverse as geology, botany, archaeology, and geography.

From statistics reported by the Expédition, even though they were gathered after Greece had been severed from the Ottoman empire, it is possible to deduce a great deal about the way life had been in western Messenia under Turkish domination. For example, we learn much about patterns of settlement and the distribution of population. In 1830, there were several towns of substantial size in the area studied by our project: 200 families lived at Gargaliani; modern Hora (Ligoudista, Tchifphliki [sic], and Kavelaria [sic]), with 153 families, was nearly as big. But of as much interest to us are the smaller settlements recorded by the French. Indeed, several of those, abandoned today, were the object of investigations by our project: for example, Panitsa, with eleven families, and Hasanaga, with five.

It was life in the centers that was generally of most interest to travelers, however, and in western Messenia, that meant Navarino. This was the most cosmopolitan settlement, and that in which a foreign traveler was most likely to find himself after disembarkation. Influences of both East and West were imprinted on the very fabric of a port-village like Navarino. Here, as elsewhere in the Levant, Western fashions played a role in shaping local culture—to such an extent that they sometimes provoked acrimonious debate between the French and the English. For though Gallic conceit might view "French flounces and caps" as a test of progress for a developing nation, the use of "*modiste* showing rooms of the Rue Vivienne" as a touchstone of culture was a foible roundly condemned by English travelers.

Ottoman Messenia was a rich embroidery of Italian, Turkish, Greek, Albanian, and Western traditions. Some resulted from intermingling populations, others were introduced and continuously reinforced through the constant interaction of merchants. The Turks were nominally in control, but the subject population had often more to fear from prosperous Greeks of their own communities. Religion and power were hardly coextensive, and embracing the Islamic faith brought with it no guarantee of earthly prosperity.

This kaleidoscopic human landscape is well documented by the accounts of our travelers. Castellan, for example, after his encounter with the pirates of Proti, next found himself confronted by Albanians, distinctly un-Hellenic in costume, character, and language. Some villages were entirely non-Greek, populated by immigrants transported by the Turks from the far reaches of their empire. The largest communities, however, were ethnically Greek. Gargaliani was one such.

Gell describes life there in some detail. Led by his dragoman (interpreter), a Greek doctor from Filiatra, and a guide from the island of Zante (Zakynthos), who spoke "very bad Greek and worse Italian, and, of course, knew nothing of his profession," Gell discovered that the wealthiest resident was a man named Andrianopoulos, a priest and *protosygkellos* (or chief overseer) of the Orthodox church. Adrianopoulos spoke the "Italian of the Ionian islands." He, like other ambitious Greeks in Messenia and elsewhere in the Ottoman territories, sought to obtain the protection of a foreign government through the conference of "consular status."

Such a position endowed a Greek with honorary citizenship in a powerful foreign nation with diplomatic standing in Istanbul, and placed him outside the legal control of the Ottoman government. Economically, there was much to gain. A wealthy Greek, like the priest of Gargaliani, could accumulate cash through graft as a subcontractor for the collection of Turkish taxes, then hide his ill-gotten gain under the cloak of a foreign flag. A common saying in the Peloponnese at that time was that "the country labors under three curses, the priests, the *coghia bashis* [Greek tax subcontractors], and the Turks"—in that order!

Major mercantile powers maintained consuls, in Greek ports—Britain, France, Austria, Russia, Holland, and even states long-since vanished from the stage of European power-politics, such as Venice and Ragusa (modern Dubrovnik). These agents often were authority figures who dominated the lives of their communities. At Navarino, for example, Gell was welcomed by Anastasios Pashalopoulos, resplendent in garb and bearing. Pashalopoulos met Gell on board his ship, accompanied by his Turkish guard and servant Mustafa, and "dressed in a long tunic of cotton and silk, studded with flowers, and varied in stripes," worn under "a long robe of brown cloth,

FIGURE 115
Two sailors at Pylos in the service of the admiral of the Turkish fleet. Reproduced from W. Gell, Narrative of a Journey in the Morea *(London: Longman, Hurst, Rees, Orme, and Brown, 1823), 25.*

The SECOND OTTOMAN PERIOD *and the* GREEK REVOLUTION

with a deep fur cape and front," with red boots, a hat, and a long cane to express his dignity.

Other aspects of local society in Navarino also reflected this mix of East and West. Dinner at the house of a wealthy Greek merchant named Ikonomopoulos was decidedly European in character: a table and chairs betrayed the non-Eastern habits of the household. Guests dressed in Western suits were in attendance, including both a merchant from Ragusa and his Greek consul at Methoni.

The town itself was a mix of Mediterraneans—predominantly Greeks and Turks. But a Turkish commander controlled the small garrison assigned to the seedy, dilapidated fort of Neokastro at Navarino, and forces of the Ottoman navy anchored in the harbor under command of the Turkish vice-admiral, Shiramet Paşa (Fig. 115).

THE GREEK REVOLUTION

The Peloponnese rose against the Ottoman government in 1821 (while it was distracted by a revolt by the renowned Ali Paşa, the "lion" of Ioannina [Fig. 116]) and soon after was joined by islands of the Aegean and towns north of the Isthmus of Corinth. Athens and Corinth were quickly recovered by the Turks, but in the Peloponnese there evolved a standoff that lasted for the next three years. National assemblies were held, independence proclaimed, and a president elected for the new Hellenic republic—although by 1823, a civil war had erupted among the Greeks themselves.

The maintenance of a strong and frequent military presence in the Bay of Navarino had been as important to the Ottomans as to their predecessors who sought to control politics in the Balkan Peninsula (Fig. 117). Indeed, as the capture of the Messenian fortresses of Methoni, Koroni, and Navarino marked the end of the beginning of Islamic domination of southern Greece, just so martial conflict at Pylos in 1827 introduced the beginning of its end. This battle at Navarino, its consequences for Ottoman naval might, the international attention that it focused on the Greek War of Independence and its concomitant horrors—these led almost ineluctably to the evacuation of southern Greece by the Turks and their agents, and the consolidation and stability of the borders of the modern Greek state.

There are, however, a number of modern misconceptions about the nature of the engagement that we call the Battle of Navarino. It may, therefore, be useful to outline certain basic facts. First, the battle was not fought principally against Turks, but against the forces of Ibrahim Paşa, the son of Muhammad Ali, a Turkish vassal born in the Balkans who had designs on establishing for himself an independent Egyptian kingdom to be governed

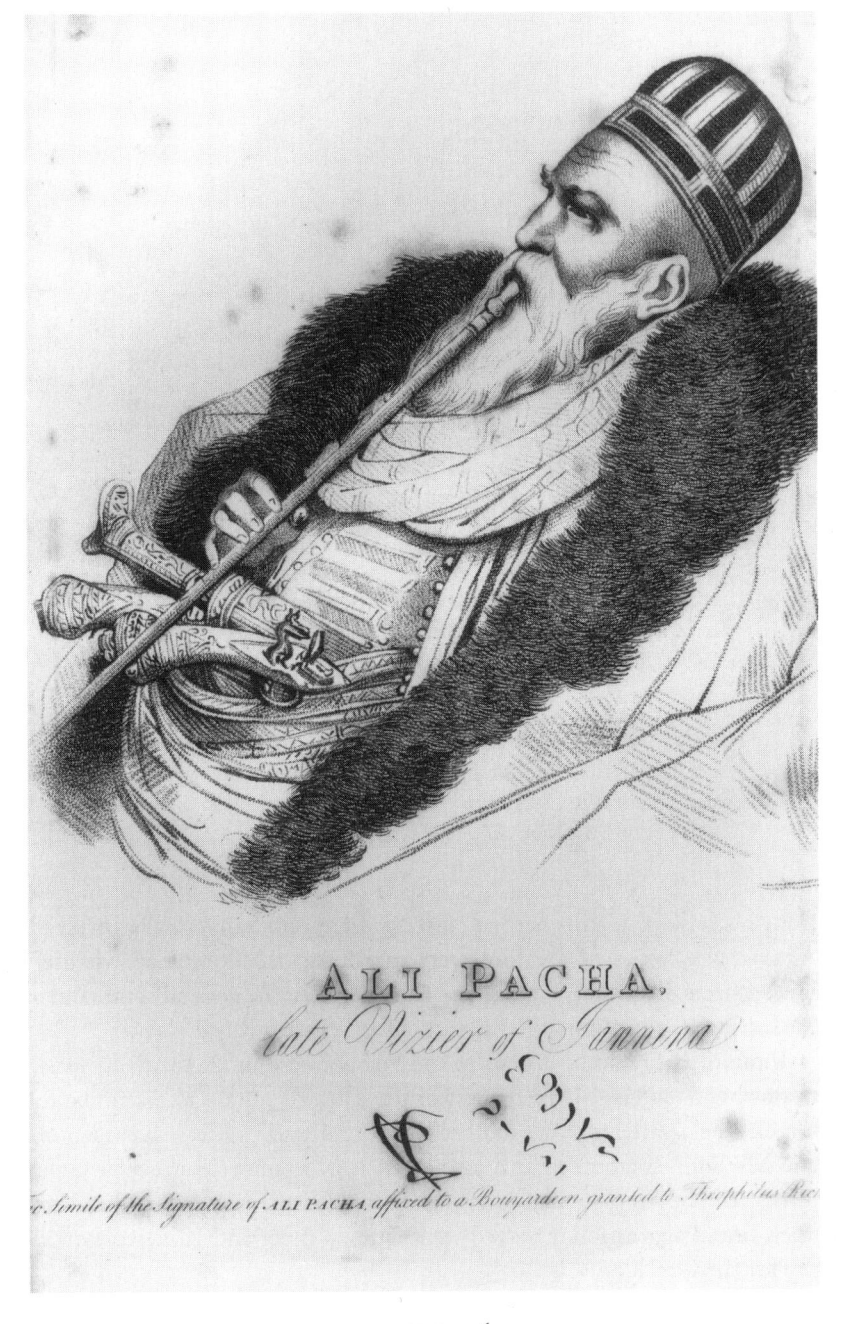

FIGURE 116
Ali Paşa, vizier of Ioannina, a prominent Albanian potentate of the early nineteenth century. Reproduced from A. de Beauchamp, The Life of Ali Pacha of Jannina: Late Vizier of Epirus, Surnamed Aslan, or the Lion. Including a Compendious History of Modern Greece, *2d ed. (London: L. Relfe, 1823), frontispiece.*

FIGURE 117
*The gate of the fort at Neokastro in the early nineteenth century. Reproduced from
A. Blouet,* Expédition scientifique de Morée, ordonée par le gouvernement
français: Architecture, sculptures, inscriptions et vues du Péloponèse, des
Cyclades et de l'Attique, *vol. 1 (Paris: Didot frères, 1831–38), pl. 2, fig. 3.*

from his base in Cairo. Second, Greeks were only tangentially involved. Against the forces of Ibrahim were marshaled the combined Mediterranean fleets of Britain, France, and Russia, under the general command of Sir Edward Codrington, vice-admiral of the British Royal Navy.

Ibrahim Paşa had been sent to the Peloponnese in 1824 with Egyptian troops by his father, at the request of the Turkish sultan, to discipline the Greek rebels. After gaining footholds in Crete, and in Messenia at Koroni and Methoni, Ibrahim campaigned extensively against the irregular Greek forces, and began systematically to devastate Greek villages and farmland. Such brutal aggression attracted international press and garnered sympathy for the Greek cause.

In an attempt to end this destruction, the Greek revolutionary government at Nauplion sent Grigorios Dikaios "Papaflessas" into the field against the Egyptians. His Christian forces met the Moslems at Maniaki. Sentinels placed by Dikaios atop Mt. Maglavas announced that Ibrahim had arrived at Hilia Horia on May 19, 1825. The following day, the Greeks saw the Egyptians on the march two hours after dawn. When the armies clashed, the defeat of the Greeks was decisive: nearly all of the 2,000 troops were killed. Ibrahim's cavalry impeded retreat or flight. Dikaios perished, so the story goes, admired by Ibrahim for his courage as he lay dead on the battlefield.

But the chief concern of the powers of Europe was the maintenance of a balance of power in the Mediterranean: the destruction of the Ottoman empire was, in this regard, not desirable. In 1827, consequently, a treaty was concluded in London between England, France, and Russia, its aim to make Greece an autonomous but tributary state of the Ottoman empire. The agreement contained a secret clause authorizing the use of force should it be necessary to compel the Turks to cease hostilities. Stratford Canning, the British ambassador at Constantinople, minister and architect of the plan, described the intent in his own words rather enigmatically as "a peaceful interference, recommended by a friendly demonstration of force."

The sultan refused to accept this mediation, however, and reinforcements for Ibrahim Paşa arrived in Pylos in early fall. Meanwhile, Codrington's armada had received orders to prevent the Egyptian fleet, now joined by the Ottoman fleet, from leaving the port of Navarino to pursue any further hostilities against Greeks. Of particular concern was the real possibility that Ibrahim might attempt an attack on critical Greek naval resources on the island of Hydra, of a sort that had resulted a few years earlier in the annihilation of the population of the island of Psara.

One essay by Ibrahim's forces to break loose from Pylos failed, and his ships were driven back by the British. But Codrington and his allies feared that, with the advent of winter storms, they would be unable to hold their posts outside the bay. From this concern, the decision was taken on October 20, 1827, to deploy the allied fleet inside the bay, thus commencing the Battle of Navarino (see Focus in this chapter). The Islamic ships were already arrayed in a horseshoe-shaped maneuver and faced the entrance to the port, at the southern end of the island of Sphacteria; their flanks were protected by batteries of guns both on the island and in the fort of Navarino (Fig. 118).

The allies were outnumbered, nearly three to one. The Islamic commanders, trusting in their numbers, fired first, but waited too late. The British and French had already entered the harbor without harm. The battle lasted until evening. When morning dawned, only a third of the Egyptian and Turkish ships remained afloat: these warships had been burned or sunk in only three hours.

On November 5, 1827, news of the disaster reached Alexandria, Egypt,

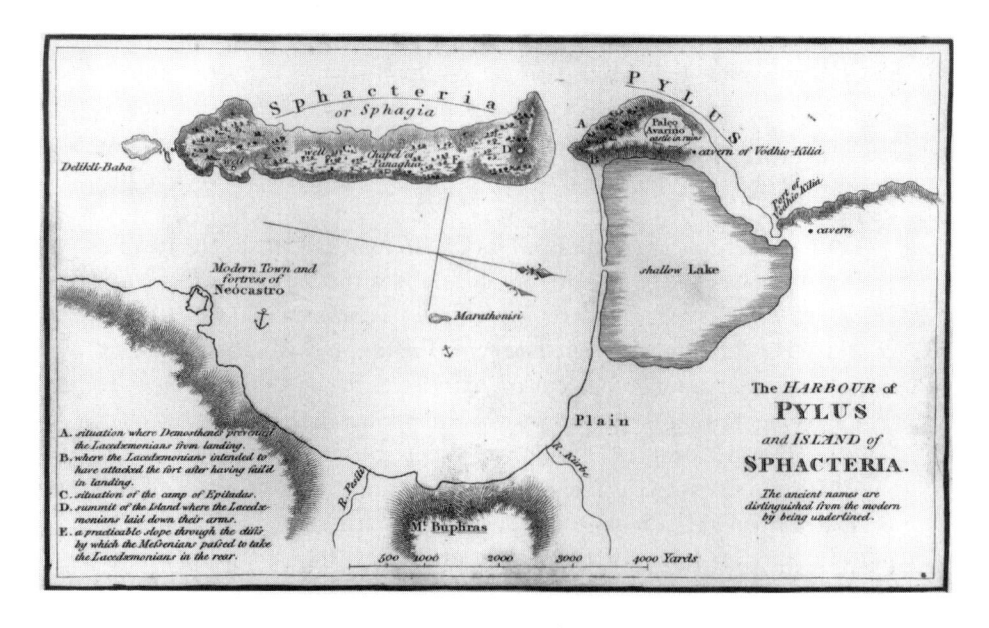

FIGURE 118
The harbor of Pylos and the island of Sphacteria. Reproduced from W. M. Leake,
Travels in the Morea, *vol. 1 (London: J. Murray, 1830), pl. 4.*

carried by an Egyptian corvette, announcing a battle so fierce that it had resulted in nearly total destruction of Muhammad Ali's fleet. But despite this information, neither the Turks nor the Egyptians were brought to terms; it was finally only through a succession of events set in motion by the incidents at Navarino that Ibrahim was to concede his territory in the Peloponnese.

In the first instance, the allies returned to bases in the western Mediterranean for refitting, leaving Ibrahim to continue campaigning. Then, almost immediately, many Greeks (the exact number is in dispute) were deported as slaves to Egypt, and it was widely believed in the capitals of northern Europe that Ibrahim contemplated the removal of the entire Greek population of the Morea. The devastation of villages and fields in Messenia continued.

Bory de Saint Vincent of the Expédition scientifique in 1830 was told about this deliberate destruction and could see the results all around him in the plains north of the Bay of Navarino: it was reported to him that the Egyptian soldiers had regularly been assigned, under the supervision of their officers, the duty of systematically destroying the fruit trees of the country—an act that he found not only incredibly barbaric but totally incomprehensible. But the facts about the extent of the havoc and rapine are not always so conclusive. De Rigny, the French general at the Battle of Navarino, later wrote to Codrington that, in 1828, when Ibrahim finally exited the Peloponnese, a large number of Greek women, supposedly slaves, insisted on accompanying his troops and, indeed, had to be forced by the French to remain in Greece.

This final withdrawal was accomplished when England, France, and Russia ordained that France should occupy the Peloponnese and *compel* Ibrahim to retire. But before this plan could be effected, Codrington sailed to Egypt and negotiated a treaty with Muhammad Ali on his own—one that provided both for an exchange of prisoners and for evacuation. Thus, on August 30, the French general Nicolas Joseph Maison arrived in the Peloponnese with 14,000 troops, to inherit a "done deal." In September, the Egyptian army was removed on transports without bloodshed. Although Codrington had agreed that Egyptian garrisons could be left in Messenia at Navarino, Koroni, and Methoni, General Maison summoned their immediate surrender.

FIGURE 119
The church at Navarino after liberation. Reproduced from A. Blouet,
Expédition scientifique de Morée, ordonée par le gouvernement français: Architecture, sculptures, inscriptions et vues du Péloponèse, des Cyclades et de l'Attique, *vol. 1 (Paris: Didot frères, 1831–38), pl. 4.*

The SECOND OTTOMAN PERIOD and the GREEK REVOLUTION

FIGURE 120
The modern town of Pylos with the Bay of Navarino and Mt. Aigaleon in the background. PRAP Archive. J. L. Davis.

For the next two months of the occupation, the French army was employed in rebuilding and restoring the villages, forts, and fields. The devastation left by war was almost total. At Pylos, the Expédition scientifique de Morée found only a church (long since converted into a mosque) and a palm tree intact amidst piles of rubble (Fig. 119). The church had been used by the French army as a grain magazine. French soldiers labored to restore the best-preserved secular structures to serve as government offices and as quarters for their officers.

Some local families had survived and returned to settle on the coast. Greeks from the islands, merchants from Trieste, and even a vagabond French couple from Marseilles had set up shop. Coffeehouses were established, complete with billiards. And in the countryside, young girls were to be found in European dress, in pretty bonnets and fine frocks of percale with painted patterns, courtesy of relief efforts by philhellenes in the United States of America.

But impromptu repairs could not mask the horrors of the Egyptian occupation and of the Battle of Navarino. Whitened human bones lay scattered on the shores of the bay, rolled by the waves into the form of "lately living pebbles." The countryside, too, was filled not only with the survivors

JACK L. DAVIS

but also with the dead. A young girl of seventeen, enslaved by the Egyptians, had escaped their clutches only at the moment of embarkation. "Returning to the place of my birth," she reported painfully to the Expédition members, "I found only the bones of my parents, scattered among the collapsed walls of their house."

In November, the army of occupation withdrew from the Peloponnese, leaving garrisons to guarantee the peace only at Koroni and Navarino; Maison was recalled to France in May of 1829. His passing clearly and decisively brought the Second Ottoman period to a close.

FOCUS

HASANAGA: *A GLIMPSE into the* OTTOMAN COUNTRYSIDE

Recording his journey from Navarino to Gargaliani, William Gell gives us one of our rare glimpses into the rural settlement of Messenia during the late Ottoman era. One place he mentions in both his *Itinerary of the Morea* (1817) and his *Narrative of a Journey in the Morea* (1823) is Hasanaga. Gell says little enough, describing the place in the latter book as a "village" or "tchiflik" (a Turkish term meaning a country estate) near Osmanaga, also reporting:

> The country house and cypress of a certain Osman Aga are soon after seen on the right, between which and the village of Hasanaga is a pretty wooded valley watered by the river Romanus, which is crossed by a bridge. These residences generally consist in a tower, overlooking the humble dwellings of the peasants, who cultivate the soil, which form a quadrangle inclosing the house.

That a settlement at Hasanaga had existed for some time before Gell's travels is documented by the Venetian census of 1700 (during Venice's brief repossession of the Morea), when Cassan Agà (Chasan-Agà, Chasánaga) is mentioned as a village in the territory of Navarino. Hasanaga also appears as a "tchiflik" in an unpublished early-eighteenth-century Ottoman census, the principal feature of which was a two-story estate house and compound. At that time, the estate was farmed by nine Greek families who were tithed in wheat, barley, sheep, rice, lemons, other fruit, and cotton; olive presses were also specifically taxed. That life at this settlement continued after the tumultuous period of the Battle of Navarino is attested by its reappearance in the report of the Expédition scientifique de Morée, where it is listed as being home to five families.

Apart from brief and tantalizing glimpses such as these, we know little of small villages such as Hasanaga, and even less about their inhabitants.

SUSAN E. ALCOCK

What could *archaeological* evidence tell us about this small and "insignificant" place?

In 1992, as a PRAP field team examined the area of the Englianos Ridge, they encountered traces of settlement—including walls and a small but dense concentration of artifacts—on a knolltop to the west of that ridge, off the main road running from Hora to modern Koryfasion (the former Osmanaga). At the foot of the knoll was a two-story edifice with a surrounding walled courtyard (Fig. 121). We were informed that the local toponym for this area was Hasanaga.

Further work at this site, undertaken in 1994, took two forms: intensive surface collection and mapping by our TotalStation team. The additional collection gave us some sense of the extent of the site, which today appears largely confined to the top of the knoll itself. The hilltop possesses a retaining wall around parts of its perimeter (visible at points, though terribly overgrown), which has served to keep artifacts from eroding downslope. Below this wall, however, slope erosion is very likely, given the hill's soft limestone composition; fields at the knoll's base may well have been buried by eroded marl, explaining the very low densities of artifacts we discovered there. All in all, the preserved extent of the site appears to be at most some 200 by 200 meters (4 hectares). The material collected from Hasanaga has been dated primarily to the Early Modern era (nineteenth and early twentieth centuries A.D.). Some of the sherds discovered, however, can be specifically assigned to the late seventeenth/early eighteenth centuries, and the later eighteenth/early nineteenth centuries—the time of the Venetian occupation and of the second period of Turkish occupation in the Peloponnese.

Reconnaissance at Hasanaga revealed a number of features worth recording with our electronic TotalStation. On the hilltop itself, overgrown to a great extent by intimidating scrub and weed cover, several walls were identified. Some of these were clearly mortared, and thus were intended to be more permanent constructions; others were simple rubble field walls. Bedrock cuttings observed on the hilltop may be remnants either of a water channel or of bedding trenches for other walls.

Lying at the eastern foot of the knoll today is a two-story dwelling, said to have been constructed in the early twentieth century. This structure, interestingly, has an elevated, second-floor entranceway: a very characteristic feature of the residences of the provincial elite under Ottoman rule. In front of this building lie the foundations of another rectangular structure, a forerunner of the present-day house. An enclosure wall, with a beveled molding on top and with narrow slits (gun slits?) in one side, was originally attached to this ruined structure. The enclosure was subsequently remodeled

FIGURE 121
S. E. Alcock leaning against enclosure wall with molded top surrounding the yard of a house at Hasanaga. PRAP Archive.

FIGURE 122
The "Hasan Paşa tower" at Troy in Turkey, as it appeared in 1776. Reproduced from M.-G.-A.-F. Choiseul-Gouffier, Voyage pittoresque de la Grèce, *vol. 2, pt. 1 (Paris: J. J. Blaise, 1809–22), pl. 32.*

to surround the later house; at least two phases in the construction of this wall are clearly visible. For both houses, the enclosure offers a pleasant—and protected—courtyard space, which is today marked by the growth of large trees. Both houses, past and present, and their enclosure face out toward modern Koryfasion (Osmanaga) to the southeast.

The best-published (indeed, practically the only published) Ottoman farmstead, the "Hasan Paşa tower" on the plain at Troy in Turkey, is known to have boasted a tower (*kule*) with an attached walled enclosure, as well as having an associated village settlement (Fig. 122). The tower, which belonged to Grand Admiral Cezayirli Hasan Paşa and which dates to the late eighteenth century, is infinitely more impressive than anything we have, or ever have had, at Hasanaga. Nonetheless, one wonders if the present-day house emulated its predecessor in terms of its design (with two stories and an elevated entrance), and if that predecessor might not have been the home of the local "lord." If so, the foundations seen today at Hasanaga could be correlated with Gell's "tower" and the two-story building mentioned in the Ottoman census. Traces of the "humble dwellings of the peasants, who cultivate the soil" remain more elusive, but may quite possibly lie on the hilltop above.

At the other side of the knoll, to the northwest, lies the chapel of Ayia Paraskevi (Holy Friday), a small rural chapel whose courtyard bell bears a date of 1897, although the church itself may be older than that. Less typical is the enclosure wall about this structure, much of which is almost identical to the enclosure to the east—including its beveled molding. All of these features and structures—the hilltop walls, the bedrock cuttings, the two-story house, the house foundations, the enclosure walls, the chapel—were mapped by the TotalStation crew to give a general picture of the site and its features.

Though walls are notoriously hard to date, it seems reasonable to link our two enclosures with the traces of Venetian, Ottoman, and Early Modern settlement lying on the hill above, and to associate this site with the place our documentary sources called Hasanaga. The activities of this village's inhabitants would have been almost entirely agricultural, as they worked to feed themselves and to pay dues to their overlords. As testimony to these labors, we discovered two limestone agricultural presses at the site, one of which still lies embedded in the slope below the knolltop, directly above the two-story house and its fine enclosure wall.

FOCUS

The BATTLE of NAVARINO

Under the plane trees, in the central square of modern Pylos, stands a monument to three foreign admirals who played a decisive part in winning Greek independence from the Ottoman empire. It was their decimation of a Turkish fleet in the Bay of Navarino on October 20, 1827, that forced the Western Great Powers finally to commit themselves to the Greek cause (Fig. 123). But for the diplomats, the battle was an "untoward event," an accidental bloodbath in which thousands died. And for Sir Edward Codrington, the admiral-in-chief, it was a Pyrrhic victory that caused the ruin of his distinguished career.

The background to the battle lies in the Treaty of London, signed between Britain, France, and Russia in July 1827, to protest the renewed violence of Ottoman repression in the Peloponnese. The treaty demanded an armistice from both Greeks and Turks and threatened peaceful but forceful intervention should either side not accept it. In Britain especially, this solution grew out of a political compromise between powerful philhellenes and those ministers who saw more stability for trade in continued Ottoman unity.

When Sir Edward Codrington had become commander of the Mediterranean Station in February 1827, he had anticipated that his main task would be the same as his predecessor's: the suppression of pirates. Now, however, he also had to play the diplomat. On the one hand, he was expected to limit the Ottoman army's excesses on land by a blockade of its supply lines. On the other, he needed to restrain young British noblemen who, following Lord Byron's example, were harassing the Turkish forces on land and sea. The treaty's signatories, four weeks' journey away, provided little practical advice on how this was to be done. Their later accusation that he had failed to obey orders was to make Codrington understandably bitter.

CHARLES WATKINSON

FIGURE 123
Painting of the Battle of Navarino with ships of the combined fleet still entering the harbor at the start of the battle. The artist, G. P. Reinagle, was in the British vanguard. National Maritime Museum, London. BNC0623.
Courtesy of National Maritime Museum.

Navarino was a perfect natural harbor, protected by Turkish gun batteries. In late 1827, the Ottoman fleet had anchored there to await reinforcements for a proposed attack on the Greek naval stronghold of Hydra and to keep in contact with the Turkish army, which was ravaging the rich plain of Kalamata. It consisted of sixty-five fighting ships mounting over 2,000 guns and with a crew of almost 22,000 men.

The hostile intent evident in this massing of Ottoman naval power, and the fortuitous arrival of the Russian and French fleets, suggested to Codrington that this was the ideal opportunity for a peaceful show of force. He hoped that this alone could persuade the Turkish captains to return to Alexandria. His blood was also stirred by the return of Captain Hamilton of the *Cambrian*, whom he had sent into the Bay of Kalamata to spy on Turkish movements. Hamilton gave a vivid picture of Greek suffering there at the hands of the Ottoman commander, Ibrahim Paşa:

> The distress of the inhabitants driven from the plain is shocking! Women and children dying every moment of absolute starvation and hardly any having better food than boiled grass! I have promised to send a small quantity of bread to the caves in the mountains, where the unfortunate wretches have taken refuge. . . . It is supposed that if Ibrahim re-

mains in Greece, more than a third of its inhabitants will die of absolute starvation.

On the evening of October 19, Codrington, Henri-Daniel Gaultier, Count de Rigny (the French admiral), Longuine Petrovitch Heiden (the Russian), and their senior captains gathered on the flagship *Asia* to agree on plans for the showdown. Their combined force was inferior numerically, with about 17,500 men on twenty-seven ships, but the quality of their vessels was superior. Their sailors' resolve was also better, since most of the Ottoman crews were composed of press-ganged prisoners of war, many of whom were manacled and treated as slaves. But the Ottoman superiority in number was magnified by the days during which the Turkish captains (with the advice of French mercenaries) had perfected a complex nooselike formation in the bay.

It is important to stress, as all this warlike preparation took place, that the three admirals, while prepared for battle if necessary, were not expecting any armed struggle. The degeneration of a peaceful show of force into bloody battle was an accident that only a careful study of the day itself can explain.

After weeks of rain, the morning of October 20 was fine, with a light breeze. It took all morning to prepare the combined fleet, and it was not until 2 P.M. that the first English ships passed under the guns of the Neokastro, which still guards the harbor mouth. As the lead ships cruised by, the Turkish soldiers in the fort cleaned their guns and watched silently. As the *Asia* turned into the bay, Codrington ordered a marine band to play on deck to break the tense silence. The fleet began to anchor, each ship with its broadside guns covering an enemy. As Codrington had ordered, "In the case of a regular battle ensuing and creating any of that confusion which must naturally arise from it, it is to be observed, that, in the words of Lord Nelson, 'No captain can do very wrong who places his ship alongside that of an enemy.'"

There was little room for the allied fleet, and near the harbor entrance, English ships were forced to anchor uncomfortably close to Ottoman fireships, empty hulks packed with gunpowder (Fig. 124). An attempt by one of the English captains to move these fearful weapons was met by musket fire in which a lieutenant was killed. An Egyptian corvette, confused by the gunfire, fired its cannon at the French admiral's ship, and after that misunderstanding, as de Rigny later wrote, "L'engagement devint bientôt général."

A stone's throw apart, with cannons blazing, the last great ships of the

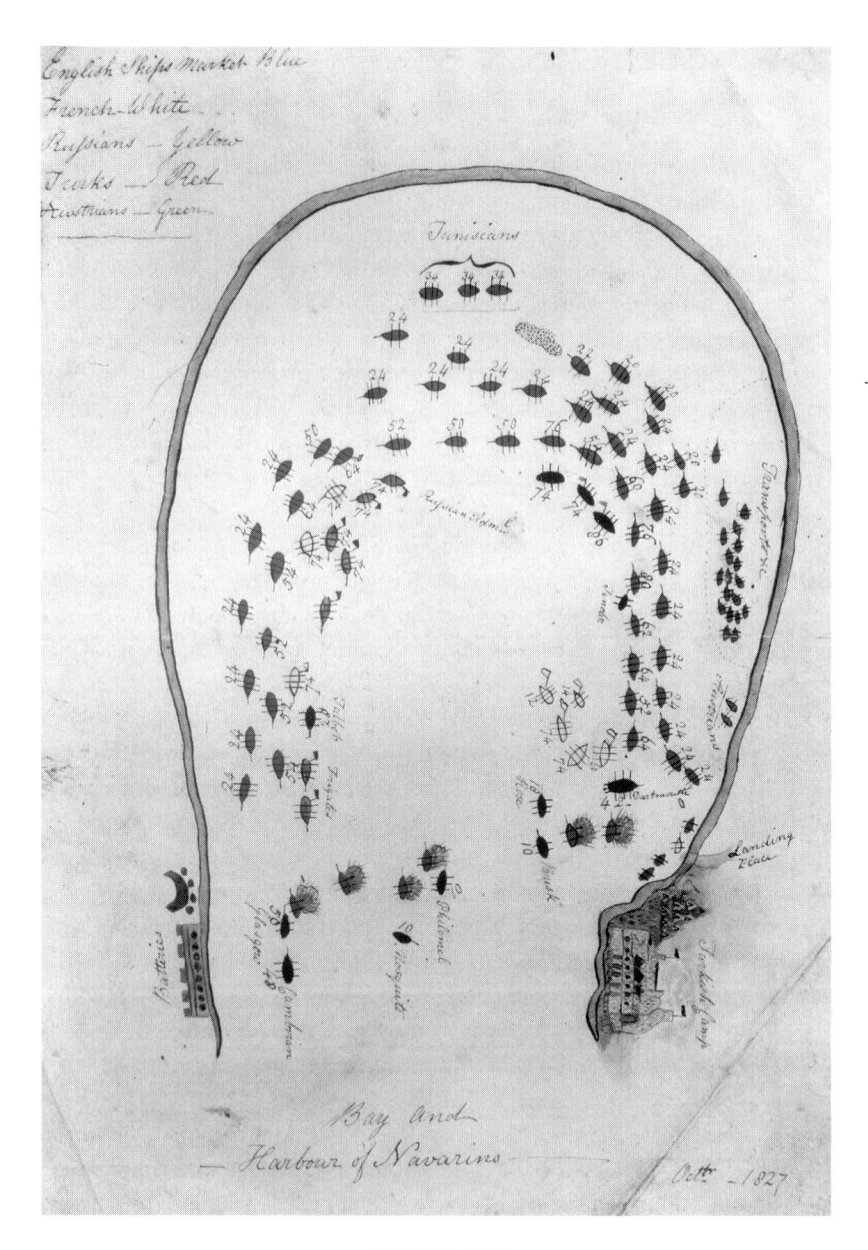

FIGURE 124
Map of Ottoman formation at Navarino, produced by Codrington on the basis of reports from spies, and circulated to the captains of the combined fleet to show them where to anchor. National Maritime Museum, London. A5898. Courtesy of National Maritime Museum.

age of sail and wood tore each other to fragments. The men on the lower decks suffered as much from huge splinters as from the shot itself. In the galleys, on makeshift tables, the surgeons performed rough amputations. Fireships, drawn toward their victims by the gentle breeze, torched the sails and then the hulls and gunpowder kegs of some ships. Charred rice and olives from the stores were thrown into the air. At one stage, the smoke was so thick that the Russian ships were firing at their English allies. There was no plan of battle, the only rule being blind destruction.

By 6 P.M., as darkness fell, the firing abated. The comparative silence of night was occasionally broken by the sound of fireships exploding, and the smaller boats were kept busy protecting the battleships from the flames. The battle had been decisively won by the French, Russians, and English. Codrington estimated that from the combined fleet there were 174 dead and 474 wounded, and that all their ships had survived. His suggestion that the Turks had lost 6,000 men and had 4,000 wounded with sixty ships lost is clearly overblown, but the number of manacled sailors of the Ottoman navy who found a watery grave that day may have run into the thousands. Nobody kept count.

The British, French, and Russian ships had left the bay within a week, and by Christmas the Turkish fleet also had limped away. The sea closed over the shattered hulls of the remaining ships, and the sheltered Bay of Navarino returned to its accustomed calm. Little seemed to have changed, and for another year Ottoman armies pursued the Greek rebels on land, and diplomats in Constantinople and London tried to salvage amicable relations by making Codrington a scapegoat. But, after the destruction of an entire Turkish fleet, the balance could never be quite the same. For Russia especially, Navarino signaled the start of open hostility against the Ottoman empire. In France and England, the philhellenes reveled in the euphoria that any national victory provoked. And within the next few months, an independent Greek state took form.

CHAPTER 10

From PAUSANIAS *to the* PRESENT

AN INTERLUDE

PRAP came to Messenia in 1991, a century and a half after the Greek Revolution. Messenia has long been a province in a modern nation-state, its capital at Athens; it has a governor, democratically elects representatives to a national parliament, and chooses mayors and city councils in like manner for its towns and villages. Greek is the sole official language; Turkish and Albanian have entirely vanished from the PRAP study area as spoken languages, although toponyms still lurk in the landscape. As in other parts of the country, former Albanian speakers consider themselves ethnically Greek.

The opportunity to earn cash has drawn thousands of Messenians to large cities outside Messenia—Kalamata, the provincial capital; Chicago; Melbourne; and, above all, to Athens. The drain in human resources is evident in the landscape. Many terraced slopes now lie abandoned; agriculture has been mechanized. Better roads have promoted (particularly Greek) tourism in recent years; fields near the coasts are increasingly subdivided into building lots for summer houses. Larger towns of the Ottoman period, like Gargaliani or Filiatra, bustle, their economies integrated into provincial, national, and international structures.

The sheer quantity of evidence at our disposal for studying the recent Messenian past is staggering. The establishment of an independent Greek nation marks an enormous watershed for historians, archaeologists, and anthropologists. One recent collection of accounts of foreign visitors to Greece during the years of the Greek Revolution (1821–29) alone runs into five volumes, while the same author devotes only four volumes to the accounts of travelers during the entirety of the Byzantine, Venetian, and Ottoman periods.

But no longer are we dependent only on the evidence of material culture

---

JACK L. DAVIS

or the accounts of visits to Messenia by outsiders for our information. Greek sources for the social and economic history of Messenia are for the first time plentiful, thanks both to the bureaucratic machinery of the state and to the efforts of the many Messenian historians and antiquarians who have labored to record and preserve its past (see Focus in this chapter). And many fine histories and anthropologies both of Messenia and of modern Greece already exist.

For all of these reasons, rather than attempting in the final chapter of this book to provide the reader with any comprehensive review of the history of modern Messenia (which would in any case tax our resources, and probably also the patience of readers), we have instead chosen to shift gears from writing prehistory and history, as in previous chapters.

In place of constructing stories about the pasts of others, we shall attempt to provide information that others will require if they are to contextualize *our* research within the history of Messenia and the history of archaeological research in Greece. In this chapter, therefore, we discuss the nature of our fieldwork more extensively, the possible significance of its results, and the relationships that have developed since 1991 between us and the contemporary Messenians, whose past we have pursued. Such a strategy requires that readers be provided with some understanding of the conditions in which members of PRAP have lived and worked in the community where the project has been based—Hora.

Modern Hora, currently a town of about 3,000 people, is a creation of the nineteenth and twentieth centuries, formed by the unification of three old villages—Ligoudista, Kavalaria, and Tsifliki (see Chapter 8). Following the Greek Revolution and the institution of a national government, these villages found themselves conjoined in a single administrative unit, with Ligoudista as capital. In 1927, Ligoudista was one of many communities to be purified by the state of a non-Greek toponym, taking the name Hora, today its official name, but one that means no more than "place" or "town."

There is a sense locally that its present name inadequately reflects the significant role that the town has played in Messenian history. Indeed, it could be argued that Hora has a strong moral claim on the name Pylos (given its geographical proximity to the Palace of Nestor), but that name was snatched long ago by the port town of Navarino: old Pylos (Palaipylos) has been recently proposed instead. But with or without an ancient name, Hora has flourished in recent years as a regional supplier of agricultural equipment, as a market for the buying and selling of produce, and as a center for light industry. Since the discoveries of Marinatos and Blegen, it has also developed as an important way-station on the touristic map of the Peloponnese: its museum, built in 1967, holds the finds from Trifylia (northwestern Messenia), including such significant sites as the Palace of Nestor, Volimidia, and Peristeria.

Other than the antiquities treasured in its museum, there is little within the present limits of the town that reflects its prominence while under Byzantine, Ottoman, or Venetian control, or that is even as ancient as the nineteenth century; an important exception is the recently restored mansion of the Kokkevis family (1857), which attests to the power and influence of this prominent local clan in both Messenian and national politics. A few grave markers in the several cemeteries of the town retain the name Ligoudista. The toponym Kato Rouga ("The Lower Road") hints that the Albanian language was once familiar, although the name itself is hybrid—combining a Greek adverb, *kato*, with an Albanian noun, *rouga*. But few structures built before 1900 are standing. Of those that are, most are in a bad state of repair, in part the result of ruin inflicted in 1957 by a severe storm, after which damage was repaired in contemporary styles with materials, such as reinforced concrete, that are now staples of the Greek contractor.

This is the community in which PRAP has operated since 1991: renting a house; borrowing public schoolrooms for use as dormitories, laboratories, and offices; arranging meals for forty or more project members each evening at a local restaurant. It was in this modern town of Hora that we began to construct our version of the Messenian past.

A PRAP CASE STUDY

In July and August of 1994, a small team of archaeologists from the Pylos Regional Archaeological Project was assigned a particularly difficult mission—the survey of rugged uplands north of the Palace of Nestor, between the modern town of Gargaliani and the village of Lefki (Fig. 125). This is a remarkably isolated and desolate area, a broad basin ringed by ridges, with a floor of jagged limestone outcrops, covered by a virtual sea of scrubbrush. Arable land is scarce, particularly in the north, and there is little cultivation anywhere.

Prior to exploration by PRAP, the area of the basin, several square kilometers in extent, had been archaeological terra incognita. No ancient remains had ever been reported there, despite the investigations of western Messenia sponsored by earlier teams—notably the University of Minnesota Messenia Expedition and the Swedish Messenia Expedition. Indeed, it seems unlikely that, before us, any archaeologist had explored this basin

FIGURE 125
The Gargaliani-Lefki uplands. PRAP Archive. R. Dupuis-Devlin and E. Dallagher.

in detail. Perhaps its very barrenness had persuaded most that these uplands would have been of little economic importance in antiquity and thus were not worthy of examination.

Earlier in the summer, PRAP archaeologists had convincingly demonstrated that such assumptions were without foundation. Indeed, although we had confirmed that archaeological remains *were* scarce, at the same time, our survey team had succeeded in locating a fascinating array of discoveries of considerable archaeological interest: for example, pottery and stone tools from both prehistoric and historical times; an extensive complex of early modern quarries, from which stone had been extracted to construct the town of Gargaliani; and two unusual geological features that between them seem to have served to focus human activities in this wasteland for thousands of years.

We did not find, however, any evidence that the uplands have ever been a location of permanent settlements. We found no residue of towns or villages, nor did we find traces of burials, the remains of which are otherwise rather common in western Messenia. Cemeteries are to be expected in places that served as the primary abode for ancient Messenians. Instead, our finds in the Gargaliani uplands suggest that people throughout the ages have visited this area to exploit particular resources, but have never stayed to settle.

Archaeological remains are concentrated around the two geological features, each of which may once have provided a source of water—otherwise in short supply. The first feature, a shallow depression in the floor of the basin, is now covered with low grasses and is ringed on all sides by the low but dense complex of wild Mediterranean shrubs and weeds that botanists call macchia or maquis. On the edges of the basin, signs of a very early human presence are evident.

Extremely old soils are exposed where bushes have been bitten down by pasturing livestock, and a meandering network of goat trails has promoted erosion. The stone tools that lie on the surface of these soils are of great antiquity—most seem to date to the Palaeolithic (before 10,000 B.C.), before the introduction of agriculture to Greece. Of much later times, but still quite ancient, were shattered fragments of ceramic vessels in a coarse fabric previously found by our teams only at coastal sites several kilometers to the west. These appear to be products of people living in the area during the Early Bronze Age in the third millennium B.C., long before the emergence of Mycenaean civilization.

Why would humans have been attracted to such a desolate place? Geological reconnaissance suggested that in prehistoric times, the depression may have been a marsh. There is no evidence that people lived year-round on the margins of the marsh, but it certainly seems possible that in earliest prehistory, wild game was attracted here by the availability of water and perhaps hunted by those humans whose stone tools we found. Later, in the third millennium, it is not difficult to imagine that domestic stock was watered in the marsh by shepherds, who, from their homes on the coast, brought flocks here to browse and graze.

If this reconstruction is correct, the scanty remains discovered by our team on the edges of the depression would mark the location of what archaeologists often call a "special activity area"—that is, a place where a limited range of affairs is conducted by a group of people who live elsewhere. Indeed, it is only by examining the sum of all such locations *and* the places where people lived in the past that archaeologists can understand the full array of actions conducted by the human societies that are the objects of their study.

In the next two millennia following the Early Bronze Age, all evidence suggests that the uplands continued to be used only for special purposes. But the focus of this activity shifted several hundred meters to the south, to what appears to be a natural sinkhole in the limestone floor of the basin.

Today the sinkhole is filled with trees and brambles so dense that it would require a flamethrower or napalm to clear it! We were consequently unable to explore its bottom, although we could determine that it was at least 3 meters deep.

Natural features of this sort occur sporadically in the Peloponnese, and it is likely that this sinkhole, as others, served at least seasonally as a source of water. But whatever its precise importance to the ancients, we were startled to find that human beings continued to be attracted here over an astonishingly long period of time — off and on for more than 1,500 years.

There was fine pottery of the Early Mycenaean period around its rim, from times when the Palace of Nestor was just beginning to establish its domination over Messenia; we also found fine pottery of the Archaic and Classical periods, the time of Spartan domination. The site does not, however, seem to have been used in the Late Mycenaean period, at the time of the floruit of the Mycenaean bureaucracy at Pylos, or, in historical times, after the reestablishment of Messenian independence.

The presence of fine pottery in historical times around such an odd natural phenomenon, where there is no reason to believe there existed a village or farmhouse, raised in our minds the possibility that some local rustic cult was focused on the sinkhole. But how, then, were we to explain the lapse in observation of the ritual following Messenian liberation? One might speculate that, with the emergence of new coastal settlements in the last centuries before the birth of Christ, individuals responsible for the maintenance of such religious observances were attracted elsewhere and their obligations forgotten. Or was the focus of the worship transferred to another location? Excavation could no doubt assist us in distinguishing among such possibilities. But survey itself was soon to complement the picture by offering us additional facts.

By the first week of August, our survey team was nearing completion of its assignment. After a month and a half in sweltering heat, picking their way through maquis (and picking its prickles from their clothes and flesh each evening), these determined young archaeologists were about to finish their exploration of the Gargaliani-Lefki uplands. On the very last day of survey, they at last reached the top of a hill bordering the northwest side of the basin, where, as so often happens on archaeological projects worldwide, they made a discovery of considerable significance. (Any archaeologist will confirm that significant discoveries are invariably made on the last day of the season!)

On top of the hill was a modern chapel (Fig. 126). After a break for lunch in the shade of its walls, the team proceeded to examine the church and found, from the icons inside, that it was dedicated to two Orthodox saints,

FIGURE 126
The church of Saints Constantine and Helen. PRAP Archive. J. Bennet.

Constantine the Great, the first emperor of the Christian Roman empire, and his mother Helen. They together had ruled the Roman empire in the early fourth century A.D. from Constantine's imperial throne in his new capital at Constantinople on the Bosporus, the straits leading from the Mediterranean to the Black Sea.

The walls of the chapel, our archaeologists found, were almost completely covered by recent plaster and whitewash, obscuring most older parts of the structure of the building. But here and there in the walls outside, they could see large, rectangular, carefully cut blocks of stone, very different from the smaller stones from which most of the church had been built. These blocks appeared to our surveyors to have been reused from some older structure, earlier in date than the Roman conquest of Greece in the second century B.C. The remains were dutifully recorded in their notebook, but in 1994 there was no time for us to examine them in greater detail.

The following summer we did, however, have the occasion to return to this church, as part of regular revisits to all areas that had been investigated by survey teams in the 1992–94 field seasons. In 1995 our goal was to reexamine all sites and other locations of interest identified in previous years so that full and accurate descriptions of our results could be composed and then incorporated into subsequent professional publications. We therefore sent no teams into the field to explore new territory. Our revisitation team consisted of just three archaeologists: myself; the project's codirector for historical archaeology, Sue Alcock of the University of Michigan; and the field director of PRAP, John Bennet of the University of Wisconsin, who in previous seasons had organized the operations of our survey teams.

Much to our surprise, the three of us discovered that the church of Constantine and Helen had been razed, and a thoroughly modern replacement erected in its stead. The blocks previously set into the walls of the old church were now strewn about in the vicinity, some pushed into piles of rubble and construction debris in the churchyard, others shoved unceremoniously down the hillside. In the clearing ripped by a bulldozer into the maquis around the new church, we found fragments of fine pottery of the later fourth or early third centuries B.C., the time of Messenia's liberation from the Spartans.

The instincts of the members of our original survey team had indeed been correct. It seems likely that a building of monumental form, perhaps a pagan temple, stood here in Late Classical and Hellenistic times. It is also interesting that the earliest pottery we found around the church of Constantine and Helen is only slightly later than the latest pottery found around the sinkhole, in the floor of the basin to the east. In other words, it is arguably the case that activity at the sinkhole ceased when activity at the church of Constantine and Helen began.

Was the function of one site usurped by the other? The choice of location for the new shrine would have offered commanding views not only of the uplands but of the coastal areas that were increasingly becoming a focus of settlement. But our discoveries did not end with Classical antiquity. Finds from the Byzantine and Ottoman periods suggest that the church demolished in 1994–95 had predecessors on this same spot. Indeed, it is possible that ritual was practiced on this hilltop continuously for over two millennia.

PRESERVING THE PASTS

The exploits of our survey teams in the Lefki-Gargaliani uplands have been discussed at such length in this final chapter because in many ways they are illustrative of our experiences elsewhere in the Pylos area. They also explain, to a large extent, why we believe that PRAP has been of considerable archaeological and historical importance.

In the first place, our encounters in the field generally justify our concern that the archaeological resources of Greece are endangered; those of Messenia are perhaps even more seriously threatened than those of other, more isolated parts of the country and require immediate scientific attention. The destruction of the old church of Constantine and Helen is only one of dozens of similar incidents that occur annually—in western Messenia alone. Each individual act of despoliation marks an irreversible step in the destruction of the archaeological heritage of the ancient Mediterranean.

During the five years that we have received permission and funding to conduct fieldwork in western Messenia, we have witnessed the total or near-total demolition of several archaeological sites of real significance. This depredation is hardly the result of any organized campaign of vandalism, but is incidental to the lives of those who are both fortunate and unfortunate, unlike us, to reside permanently in an archaeological landscape that is, in its entirety, of interest to all students of the history of world civilization.

The progress of the carnage is largely random. When archaeological remains stand in the path of economic development, sites are chosen for destruction without prejudice to their date or function. The oldest Palaeolithic site yet discovered in Messenia was severely damaged when an agricultural track cut through its center (Fig. 127). A small Mycenaean site has been entirely bulldozed into a single pile of rubbish. A beehive tomb from the period of the Dark Ages between the demise of Mycenaean civilization and the emergence of Classical Greek city-states has been swept away by the broadening of a highway. Historical burial mounds have been leveled to form floors for drying currant grapes for raisins or to enlarge fields (Fig. 128). The agents of the destruction are remarkably diverse, sometimes private individuals struggling to bring unproductive land under cultivation, sometimes public corporations or governmental agencies striving to improve facilities for their citizens, sometimes the pious dissatisfied with less-than-perfect houses of worship.

The environment itself can also be cruel to archaeological remains. The introduction of new agricultural techniques opens up steep slopes to cultivation, but without stone terrace walls to retain the soil, storms can in a few years wash away archaeological sites that required millennia to form. Even without human agency, earthquakes can lead to the subsidence of entire hillsides and, with them, any artifacts they supported.

There will always be the temptation to place the blame for human destruction of archaeological remains on the shoulders of archaeologists whose job it is to protect them. But such a perspective is naive. The scale of the problem of preservation is far too great ever to be controlled by policing alone. Surface archaeological studies of the sort sponsored by PRAP have, since they first became popular in the 1970s, demonstrated conclusively that archaeological sites are thickly scattered across the landscape of

FIGURE 127
Severe erosion of Palaeolithic remains near the mouth of the Veryina River. PRAP Archive. J. Bennet.

FIGURE 128
Bulldozed knoll with graves at Tsouka, near Pyrgos. PRAP Archive. J. Bennet.

Greece. In some parts of the country, there may indeed be a dozen or more sites of substantial size within a single square kilometer.

At the same time, it is not just large sites or very ancient sites that are important for the reconstruction of the past, or rather of the multiple pasts whose recreation relies on the interpretation of the basic physical remains that are threatened. Scanty remains may also have real significance. Archaeologists who specialize in regional studies, such as the authors of this book, stress the importance of determining the locations even of very small places, sites that usually lack the prestige goods that attracted our predecessors to ancient towns, villas of the wealthy, major ritual centers, or palaces. Relatively recent sites and artifacts may also acquire importance, when little written documentation is available to historians. Indeed, the past decade has even witnessed the beginnings of an industrial archaeology in Greece, focused on exploration of the factories and residue of the manufacturing revolution and its aftermath. Their study can enable the writing of otherwise unobtainable chapters in the history of the development of the economy of modern Europe.

Such a broad range of sites and other remains of archaeological interest cannot be adequately protected by methods designed to safeguard the Greek heritage at a time when most archaeologists viewed the landscape of Greece as occupied by a finite number of "official" sites that could be fenced and guarded. We now know that the official sites are merely the tip of a very large, and largely still submerged, iceberg. To control access to even a portion of the archaeological patrimony of Greece would require turning the country into one gigantic archaeological park—hardly a viable option! (A solution to this conundrum is proposed in the final section of this chapter.)

PRAP IN ITS OWN HISTORICAL CONTEXT

In addition to recording information about the past that may soon disappear, we think that PRAP has been able to improve greatly the quality of the data about the past that are available to historians and prehistorians. Indeed, we came to Messenia in part because we were uncertain about the accuracy and completeness of much data gathered by previous expeditions and wanted to do something about the situation. Grave doubts had been cast by some scholars on the reliability of archaeological reconstructions of settlement patterns in ancient Messenia. The only systematic attempt to locate sites in the entire province had been that of UMME. But the directors of that project frankly admitted that its goal had been to study the locations of Late Bronze Age towns and villages named in the Linear B tablets from the Palace of Nestor.

Historical periods were of secondary importance. Although several hundred were recorded in UMME's published catalogue of Messenian sites, the experiences of more recent, more intensive surveys elsewhere in Greece suggested that this number was unbelievably low. Even for prehistoric periods, we were anxious about the completeness of UMME's gazetteer. UMME had made certain assumptions about where prehistoric sites were likely to be found, but were those assumptions valid?

For example, William McDonald and Richard Hope Simpson tell us how in the winter in North America, they inspected maps and aerial photographs—seeking to identify those places that were the most likely candidates for Mycenaean settlements. The following summer they located these places in the field, and experienced a remarkably high success rate in finding sites. But there was no way to be certain that archaeological remains did not also exist in other locations, overlooked because they did not conform to prior expectations.

There are large parts of western Messenia where no prehistoric sites were found by UMME. Was their absence in these areas "real"? Had people actually not lived or worked in these places? Or was the explanation even simpler: Had no archaeologist ever looked for the evidence? In frustration, we decided that fresh fieldwork would be required to answer these questions.

The results of that fieldwork have now allowed us to begin to evaluate in this volume the completeness of more than a century of previous research in Messenia. In some areas, we did find that there really are no sites of certain periods. This "negative evidence" about where there are not sites is sometimes as important as knowledge about where sites do exist, and several authors of this book have made reference to it as they have attempted to make sense of the archaeological history of Messenia. But at the same time, we found many new sites, and a large percentage of these are not situated on naturally fortified hilltops or in other locations where UMME is likely to have searched. The Palaeolithic and Early Bronze sites we found on the upland plateau between Gargaliani and Lefki are, in fact, good examples: few archaeologists would have expected to find artifacts there. There are no wells or springs. The ground is largely flat; no nearby ridge offers protection. And the land in the vicinity is hardly productive.

THE SIGNIFICANCE OF INTENSIVE SURFACE SURVEY

Why was our project successful in finding archaeological remains where they had been previously unknown? The short answer is that the survey conducted by PRAP was considerably more "intense" than those organized in the Pylos area by our predecessors. By "intense" we mean that our teams inspected a far larger percentage of the landscape than is customary for more "extensive" surveys like UMME, which have tended to search for sites only in particular parts of the countryside. The trade-off is in the cost, in human and other resources, of mounting an archaeological expedition. An intense survey like that of PRAP required providing for the support of nearly forty men and women each summer in the field, while UMME never comprised more than a handful of archaeologists.

With large amounts of labor, an intensive survey is capable of looking very closely for archaeological remains in all parts of a landscape in a relatively short time. In under five months in the field (spread over three summers), we were able to invest nearly seven-and-a-half "person-years" of work into the exploration of an area only 35 square kilometers in size. In contrast, extensive survey by a two-person team would have required nearly four years of continuous year-round effort to accomplish the same end—and the ground we covered is only a tiny fraction of the total area investigated by UMME.

The strategies adopted by PRAP are the only tactics currently available to the archaeologist who chooses to study the history of a region, rather than a single site or two. Excavation is inappropriate, since the digging of only a single 20-by-20-meter trench can easily cost thousands of dollars. Intensive surface survey is, therefore, the regional archaeologist's principal tool, and has in the past two decades become a fundamental component of research in Greece. Survey (as aficionados know it) is now as common as excavation. Some thirty or more projects are in progress or have recently been completed.

Readers who are hearing about survey for the first time usually express amazement that artifacts can be found without digging. Much of Greece is, however, so rich with antiquities that it is nearly impossible to walk 100 meters anywhere without finding something ancient. The problem confronting surveyors is not in finding artifacts but in investigating, in a systematic manner, an entire landscape full of them.

How does survey work? Intensive surface surveyors, instead of digging vertically into the ground, work horizontally, collecting artifacts from the surface of the earth, wherever they are to be found (Fig. 129). The archaeologists walk in rows across the landscape, separated one from the other by about 15 meters. As they walk, they observe artifacts on the surface, they count them, and they collect them. Frequently, following initial reconnaissance, they return to gather more artifacts, from those locations where they are most dense: we often call these places "sites." The work is hot, dirty,

FIGURE 129
PRAP archaeologists surveying in the field. PRAP Archive. R. Dupuis-Devlin and E. Dallagher.

dusty, and sometimes even dangerous, but also generally fun and rewarding (see Focus in this chapter).

The findspots of artifacts are duly recorded in the field. They must next be brought to the museum to be cleaned, labeled, sorted, described, and dated. But even after these initial stages of analysis, the job is just beginning. Data from both field and museum must be entered into computers, and maps must be produced, both by hand and by machine. Our task is not only to find artifacts. We must also look for patterns in the masses of data that we gather, patterns that allow us to describe changes that have occurred in the locations of settlement and in the way in which land has been used and differences between one part of western Messenia and another.

Once we believe that we have identified meaningful patterns, it is the work of our geological team to examine them from the perspective of a geomorphologist. Have we failed to find artifacts in a valley bottom because they are covered with soil eroded from hillsides above? Are the surface indications of a site more extensive than the buried deposits beneath? Has the soil, and with it the archaeological deposits, been stripped by erosion from some slopes, but not from others?

JACK L. DAVIS

Natural scientists were, however, an essential component of PRAP, not only because of their role in evaluating the reliability of archaeological data. Some of the most exciting results of our project have emerged from their efforts—including the discovery of the Mycenaean port near Romanou (Focus, Chapter 3) and the reconstruction of the agricultural history of western Messenia through the study of pollen cores. Increasingly, too, remote sensing is proving to be an effective and reliable means of following up the discoveries of surveyors by mapping subsurface remains of walls, hearths, and other structures (Focus, Chapter 7).

We are confident that the sum of all the aspects of our research now enables us to offer our colleagues and the public a far more accurate picture of physical remains of the Messenian past than was available seven years ago, when PRAP began. Clearly, there remain sites of archaeological interest that we have not found because there are no surface indications of their existence, but we remain cautiously optimistic that the sample we have investigated is sufficiently meaningful to support the archaeological and historical generalizations drawn in this book.

THE INTEGRATION OF INFORMATION

The improvement of field techniques described in the preceding section of this chapter can increase our confidence that the data we have are reliable. The real challenge for a research team like ours comes, however, when we are called upon to interpret that data. How has PRAP responded to this challenge?

At the most basic level, we have stressed the integration of diverse categories of information gathered by the many different specialists associated with PRAP, and we believe we have been successful in doing this. The advantage of such an integrated approach to the study of the past should be obvious. Multidisciplinary categories of evidence brought to bear on a particular problem always add up to more than the simple sum of the individual components. Truly interdisciplinary investigations of the sort we espouse do not simply consist of many academic endeavors traveling on parallel tracks. Rather, the goal is for researchers to cooperate, regardless of their specialization, to build a better locomotive to pull the entire project.

For example, we have found that by combining information from the analysis of texts with physical evidence from excavated and surveyed Mycenaean sites, it has been possible to reconstruct the geography and even something of the history of the kingdom of Nestor, as it developed in the thirteenth century B.C. From analysis of the Linear B documents, we have expectations about the nature of the hierarchy of Mycenaean settlements. Archaeological discoveries, on the other hand, allow us to hypothesize how relations of power between the Palace of Nestor and outlying centers (attested in Linear B at only a single moment in time) came to be. The natural sciences also contribute significantly. The existence of a Mycenaean port suggests that substantial human resources were at the disposal of the Palace of Nestor. Moreover, pollen analysis testifies to the expansion of olive cultivation when both pots and texts suggest the manufacture and export of perfumed oil was at its height.

For the period of Spartan domination of Messenia (eighth to fourth centuries B.C.), we believe that we have also been successful in integrating diverse categories of information. Ancient Greek texts led us to expect that through surface survey we would find plentiful numbers of small rural installations: here helots would have lived and worked in the service of their Spartan masters. But this was not the case. We instead discovered that the pattern of rural settlement in western Messenia when it was part of Sparta was radically different than elsewhere in Greece. This revelation in turn encouraged us to think about other ways in which Sparta might have organized its enslaved population. Could it have controlled helots not by scattering them, but by aggregating them in a small number of large residential centers? The natural sciences have again played an important role in our attempts to reconstruct the past. Agricultural production expanded considerably under Spartan control. The Messenia that Sparta converted into its breadbasket had been substantially underutilized.

In our way of thinking, archaeological, textual, and natural scientific data are reflexively related. Any category of information may contradict another, forcing us to reconsider received wisdom and long-cherished interpretations of the past. Over the next few years, we will redouble our efforts to interpret the data gathered in years of laborious fieldwork. Many specialist reports will be published in scholarly journals, but we hope that we will not lose sight of a resolve to produce fully integrated interdisciplinary reconstructions of the past. For this reason, we plan after several years to publish a second summary of our results—this time written principally for our archaeological colleagues. But it will hardly be the final word.

Our ultimate goal is to establish a base of information that will remain useful for future generations of archaeologists to explore, when many of the antiquities we have been fortunate to study will no longer be preserved. No doubt their vision of the Messenian past will be as different from ours as ours is from that of Pausanias. But it is important for us to provide the future with a rich body of observations that *can* be reinterpreted, as we can now reinterpret the texts of the ancient Greek and Roman authors in bringing their words to bear on our modern concerns and constructs.

Readers will, however, probably be more interested in our success in meeting the specific tasks we set for ourselves in the preface to this volume. The need to protect the physical remains of the past has already been addressed in this chapter; other concerns have not yet been—at least, not explicitly. What about Messenian identity? What is Messenia? What is a Messenian? How have the geography and natural resources of the region we now call Messenia determined the form of the successive cultural systems that have evolved in this landscape over the past millennia? Has the long-term perspective adopted in this book contributed to our ability to address such questions?

Messenia, as we saw in Chapter 1, is naturally segregated from the remainder of the Peloponnese. Its geography effectively defines it as a region. Nonetheless, a Messenia has often not existed in the past. Seldom have political borders been coextensive with the natural definition of the modern Greek province. For the Ottomans, there was, strictly speaking, no Messenia; the southwestern Peloponnese was divided into several distinct administrative districts. Earlier, before the Turkish conquest of the Peloponnese in the fifteenth century, authority was split between Franks and the Most Serene Republic. In contrast, the Venetian province that incorporated Messenia was larger than the modern province, also including Elea and parts of what is today Arcadia.

In Classical antiquity, Messenia was more often divided than not. Not even after the foundation of the city of Messene was the entirety of modern Messenia brought immediately under a single political authority. Only in the thirteenth century B.C. (probably an unstable temporary phenomenon resulting from the expansionist policies of the Palace of Nestor), and much later under the Roman and Byzantine empires, is it clear that all major parts of Messenia (the western coast, the Soulima Valley, the Akritas Peninsula, and the Pamisos Valley) were one.

The geographical resources of the region we now call Messenia, notably the extraordinary fertility of its land, have remained more or less constant. More than those resources, the particular political or economic systems into which Messenia has been incorporated have defined the role it has played in the larger Mediterranean world. Although often a backwater remote from contemporary centers of power, it is important to consider the circumstances that have from time to time brought the southwestern Peloponnese to center stage in Greek history—for example, the establishment of independent local states in later Mycenaean times and in the Hellenistic period, or its domination by empires based in the western Mediterranean, like Venice and Rome. These events provide a stark contrast with the marginal situation of Messenia when subservient to more Eastern-oriented centers of power, such as Istanbul or Byzantium. Today, Greece's membership in the European Community and increased tourist traffic between western Greece and Italy are gradually reshaping the character of the region. Geographical position is relative, and natural resources are only valuable when the mechanisms exist for their exploitation.

If the concept of Messenia has been so dependent on the form of the political systems that have dominated this region, who, then, are the Messenians? Have those who have lived in the geographical unit now known as Messenia always had a sense that they belong to the same group? Is there a Messenian identity? How long has it existed? Although geography offers the potential for the creation of Messenians, it certainly does not guarantee that this will happen. The earliest Mycenaean texts, as we have seen in Chapter 5, hint, in fact, that the original Messenians may have been a minority group of peoples, distinct in some uncertain way from those Greeks who controlled the Mycenaean state established by the Palace of Nestor.

Indeed, the individual contributions to this volume suggest that a Messenian identity is hardly a natural concept. It is one that has resulted when a political and intellectual elite has actively and consciously employed the physical remains and intellectual legacy of the past to construct a sense of togetherness among peoples of diverse origins, often by distinguishing themselves from an external otherness—Sparta, Rome, or the anonymity of the central government of modern Greece. Nor need Messenians live in Messenia! Now, as in the fifth century B.C., the creation of a Messenian identity can be of great concern to members of a diaspora, whether they live in ancient Naupactus or in contemporary Athens.

The preceding observations may seem obvious in light of the archaeological history sketched in the chapters of the present volume, and the events we have described may well seem familiar to many readers, particularly to those with multicultural backgrounds, in light of their own experiences. We hope this is the case. Many of the processes that have promoted the creation of a group identity in Messenia are universal to humankind, and similar stories about the interplay between peoples and their landscape could be written for most other regions of the world. We have chosen to focus *our* investigations on Messenia because this small part of our planet has proven to be an excellent place to document the diversity of the past, thanks to the long and detailed record we have of its past. It has been our experience, too, that many modern visitors to Messenia are hardly aware of the millennia of struggle on which rests the extraordinary homogeneity of this region today—or of Greece *in toto*. Such diversity should, in our view, always be recognized and celebrated.

SHARING THE PAST

Our work in Messenia has also, we hope, been less intrusive than that of traditional archaeologists. We have expropriated no fields, destroyed no trees, forced the rerouting of no roads. Indeed, our teams have not even disturbed the earth with a shovel or trowel. This is intentional. Archaeology can strike terror into the hearts of Mediterranean landowners—and with good reason! Valuable property that contains antiquities may be requisitioned, and just compensation received only years later. No wonder many Messenians were anxious about where and when we planned to dig, despite our disclaimers!

Only after years of informal conversations and formal lectures (see Focus in this chapter) have we begun, I think, to make our message understood. We are a different kind of archaeologist. We view our research as a partnership with the residents of Messenia. We do not consider our view of the past superior to their own. We do not intend to dig. We are not interested in precious objects. We do not intend to disrupt lives. It is, in fact, of great importance to us that daily practices continue, for they help us, consciously and not, in our attempts to document the distribution of archaeological remains in the Messenian countryside. The routine labor of cultivation restores the past to the present. Only then can it be documented.

The contribution of other Messenians to our work has been, of course, more purposeful. The educated and the curious in the many towns and villages through whose fields we have tramped have shared with us their personal knowledge of their own archaeology, often by guiding us to items of archaeological importance. But regardless of their station in life, all these men and women of Messenia have welcomed us as visitors in their land. The land itself remains for the most part unfettered by barbed wire or chain link; its very openness gives a sense of community to the landscape—a sense of ownership that transcends the individual. We shall forever be grateful to all those who have included us in that community, and we hope that this book in some small way might repay their hospitality.

FOCUS

MESSENIA'S MULTIPLE PASTS

Messenian brothers! Hear the voice of the afflicted soul of our justly lamenting motherland Messenia. Let us then fittingly honor her sacrificed dead, those worthy of both our gratitude and honor, our ancient and recent ancestors, the great as well as the small heroes of our own Messenia, the eternal memory of whom will be always sacred in our minds, the names of whom, as well as their ethnic spirit and their actions worthy of commemoration, remain unknown to Panhellenic history, and are thus unfortunately condemned to darkness, thanks to the guilty indifference of their young descendants.

Thus concludes the preface to the first of three projected volumes of *A History of Messenia*, published in 1935, with subventions from dozens of Messenians living in and out of Messenia, by Ioannis Kefalas, a lawyer in Athens. The quote also introduces a theme common to modern historical and archaeological writing about Messenia: Messenia's past is relevant to its future. The past is also an active part of its present, capable of being employed (as did Pausanias; see Chapter 6) to shape images of personal and group identity, potentially with profound positive consequences for the economic, social, and cultural development of the region.

We should not have been surprised (although it did surprise us at the time) at the intensity of interest shown by the present residents of Messenia in our investigations of their past. Already in the first year of our archaeological fieldwork, we were invited to address the youth of Hora, the community in which we were living, on the subject of our personal research—with risible outcomes at times when our Greek did not prove equal to the task of describing complex topics normally discussed in English, even with Greek academic colleagues. On a subsequent occasion, we related the results of our own fieldwork in Messenia to members of the

JACK L. DAVIS

town cultural association, then in 1994 lectured to the entire population of Hora in its newly refurbished public square at the intersection of Blegen and Marinatos streets, as a major event in the Nestoreia, an annual festival in celebration of King Nestor, sponsored by the town and the "Association of Residents of Hora Living in Athens."

Each of these activities clarified for us the magnitude of the esteem in which Messenians hold their past. The past is powerful. But the past created by contemporary Messenians is very different from that typically constructed by professional archaeologists like us, who choose to emphasize scientific objectivity, often trivializing the particular in favor of broader themes that may be of greater interest to academic colleagues.

The images of Messenia past that appear in Pausanias have themselves played a significant role in the creation of modern Messenian ethnicity. Indeed, one early modern history of Messenia, written by Ilias Zervos Iakovatos (1857), chose as its central theme the ancient hero Aristomenes, whose life the author represents as instructive for both the present and the future—it is an obvious mythological antecedent for an all-too-recent resistance against the oppression of the Ottomans. His goal:

> To write a history of the antiquities, the alterations, the wars of one small Peloponnesian land, Messenia, and of its great hero Aristomenes, who by fighting bravely against his overlords, gained great glory and shared her fate. Noble souls comprehend neither a homeland that lacks freedom and independence, nor a life without honor and glory. Wherefore, the knowledge of such great souls and of the fortunate places where they are born offers an instructive lesson, and a very effective example worthy of imitation, both for contemporary Messenians and for their progeny.

And the success of this work and others similar to it is reflected in the contemporary toponymy of Messenia, where non-Greek names were systematically shed in favor of more noble appellations of Greek derivation; even the name of Aristomenes himself is now applied to the town formerly known as Mustafa Paşa.

Local historians of Messenia, like professional archaeologists, have sometimes pursued their vision of the Messenian past by initiating fieldwork and by compiling catalogues of ancient sites and descriptions of artifacts found at them. More often than not, however, their efforts have escaped the notice of professional archaeologists. It is difficult entirely to understand why. In part, it almost seems that we academics have arrogantly judged the worth of information more by examining its source than by weighing its quality. We are the losers. No matter who compiled them, catalogues of archaeological materials are of great potential value, all the more so when the objects themselves have long been destroyed.

PRAP, too, is guilty of such a lapse. Although, prior to the start of our fieldwork, a year was devoted to the compilation of references to previous archaeological research, the extensive bibliography we carried to Messenia in 1992 did not contain a single reference to the work of a local Messenian antiquarian.

The subsequent process of our "discovery" of the modern Messenian historical voice has been gradual. At the site of Dialiskari (see Foci in Chapter 7 and in this chapter), for example, we had already conducted extensive fieldwork of our own before discovering the long history of modern exploration of the site. Dialiskari did not come to the attention of the professional archaeological community until it was "rediscovered" by the Swedish scholar Natan Valmin in a report published in Sweden in 1934. But a basic description of its monuments (including references to a Roman city, ruins of a temple, monolithic and Doric columns, and many mosaics in the ruins of houses) had been published already in 1900 in the pages of the Greek philological journal *Parnassos*.

One might plead in defense that academic libraries rarely hold such publications in their collections. Such an excuse would, however, explain little. Why is this so? Why are these publications not more widely available? Part of the explanation must be that Messenian authors understandably have not regularly composed their scholarship with the professional archaeological establishment in mind, and, consequently, professional scholars have generally not found the writings of Messenian authors particularly relevant to their own academic concerns. Messenians, like many or even most Greeks, partly define who they are on the basis of their place of birth or family origin (*patrida*) within Greece, and their histories reflect the greater practical value that the Messenian past holds for them than for others.

Antiquities may from a local Messenian perspective be viewed as resources—one of a range of resources, natural and cultural, valuable to contemporary inhabitants, *not* simply for the profit they can bring by promoting tourism. Indeed, in 1936, long before foreign visitors to Messenia became a significant factor in the economy of the province, a resource-management questionnaire addressed to those living in the Messenian sub-district of Trifylia (investigated in part by PRAP) by the Association of Trifylians living in Athens and Piraeus explicitly solicited information about archaeological resources, boundaries of communities, communication routes, water resources, and the extent of both waste and cultivated land. Furthermore, a White Paper published two years later incorporating responses to this survey devoted half of its 200 pages to history and the description of archaeological monuments of times before Greek independence.

But the publication of our own book also marks one explicitly stated and significant step in a continuing process of exploitation of the past of Messenia by individuals who do not live there. For whom did the White Paper imagine the Messenian past would be useful—for those actually resident in Messenia, or for educated Messenians now living, for example, in Athens? The source of the questionnaire is instructive, emphasizing that the definition of the word "Messenian" had changed substantially in the nineteenth and early twentieth centuries. The growth and industrialization of Athens created chances for employment that attracted tens of thousands of families from the Peloponnese; opportunities for emigration to America, Canada, Australia, South Africa, and northern Europe drew as many or more abroad. As a consequence, the voice of Messenians in Athens became increasingly a force in the politics of the countryside of Messenia itself—even to the extent that nonresident Messenians could make the claim that they knew best what was right for Messenia. Such a privileged position is claimed in the ornately composed prologue to the 1938 White Paper:

> The present Administrative Council of the Trifylian Association in Athens feels the necessity to communicate to all Trifylians in general, but especially to the ecclesiastical, public, and social authorities and the various Associations, Organizations, and Cooperatives of Trifylia the following: first, it makes manifest its thinking, as it pertains to its attempt at the social and economic elevation of Trifylia within a governmental and social framework, and, second, it invites all Trifylians to a spiritual and ideological exchange of ideas, for the better and quicker success of this objective.
>
> The Association undertakes this effort, because, finding itself in the Capital, far from Trifylia, it is in a position to examine and to judge more objectively the needs and potentialities of Trifylia, as well as its obligations and rights. For this reason, it is initiating and executing a movement which has as its goal the spiritual, productive, cultural, and social development of Trifylia. It does this because the members who constitute the Association feel deeply the necessity to offer their services without the slightest recompense, but rather as a down payment of one part

of the interest on the capital of obligations which they owe the environs of Trifylia, and which they are only in a position to execute inasmuch as today they live outside Trifylia.

This proclamation was published only one year before the district of Trifylia was rocketed to international fame through the discovery of the Palace of Nestor (a site, like Dialiskari, previously known to local historians before its "discovery" by archaeologists [see Focus in Chapter 2]). The cultural heritage of Messenia now had another serious claimant—professional academicians like us, more concerned with Blegen's finds for their value in reconstructing the economy of earliest *Greek* (not Messenian) kingdoms (the oldest in *Europe*) than for any significance that such treasures might have for the residents of Messenia. An international community of scholars is *our* audience. We share first with them our discoveries and ideas (and sometimes we ignobly hope for a promotion, a new post, or a pay raise). Why should we exchange ideas with those who live where we work? Where is the benefit for us?

Such a self-centered attitude can be deduced from the fact that, despite the hundreds of articles and books directly concerned with the archaeology of Messenia that now repose in university libraries, more than fifty years elapsed between the first season of excavation at the Palace of Nestor and the publication in Greek of the first guidebook to it in 1994.

The authors of *Sandy Pylos* believe that the attitudes that have resulted in such a disgrace are fundamentally elitist in that they presuppose that concerns of professional archaeologists should take precedence over those of the Messenians themselves. But it is not only tolerance for the requirements of others that we should learn; we need also to appreciate the real advantages that can accrue from discarding outmoded chauvinistic perspectives.

Attention to Messenian scholarship has more than repaid us for the efforts we have invested to learn about it, even if judged in terms of objectives set by our own research design. We have recovered details of the past that would otherwise have been lost to us. We have also learned that there are other ways of looking at the Messenian past than our own, and we are now in a better position to appreciate the advantages and disadvantages of our own approaches to the acquisition of knowledge. And even in those instances where our perspective and local viewpoints may diverge most widely (e.g., in our attitudes toward the use of the past to shape group identity), there remains much common ground of mutual interest to explore. Pride in the past and scientific interest in the past may represent very different perspectives, but both rely on the preservation of the past as their object of inquiry.

Our experiences since 1991 have, in fact, encouraged us to continue to grope our way through uncharted waters, searching for ways in which useful partnerships may be constituted between archaeologists, those who live in the area of our archaeological enquiry, and Messenians elsewhere. We simply cannot continue to appropriate local pasts exclusively for our own national and international ends. It would indeed be as arrogant for us to privilege our views of Messenian history over those of Messenians, as it was for Athenian Trifylians in 1938 to claim a vantage point superior to that of Messenians remaining in the Peloponnese.

Old habits die hard. The struggle to create a polyvocal archaeology in Messenia may well be as protracted as the wars with Sparta, but perhaps some progress has been made. We are especially proud of our participation in a ceremony of dedication that occurred in Hora in early August 1995, when a bust of Carl Blegen (see the drawing at the head of Chapter 2) was erected in the garden of the town museum, opposite that of Spyridon Marinatos—both men symbolic of the best that professional archaeology has contributed to Messenia.

The proceedings were cosponsored with the Society for Friends of Antiquities of Hora. Presiding was the president of the society, a man who, as mayor, had in 1991 welcomed us with open arms, had attended to our needs, and with whom we had frequently cooperated in planning cultural events for the community. In attendance were Greek and foreign professional archaeologists and historians—including those civil servants given custodial care of antiquities; academic scholars; a delegate from the American School of Classical Studies in Athens, the research institution under the auspices of which PRAP conducted its fieldwork; officers of the state, both federal and local; mayors; the American ambassador; and representatives of the clergy, including His Holiness, the Archbishop of Cyparissia. Hundreds of residents of Hora also came in no official capacity to welcome Carl Blegen to the garden of their museum, and engage their past by harkening to a harmony of non-Messenian and Messenian voices.

FOCUS

COMPUTERS *and* MAPS *at* PRAP

As digital computers have become more commonplace, they have also become increasingly powerful tools for archaeological research. From its inception, PRAP has been employing these machines in the field, for data analysis and mapping, and for publication. This focus discusses only some of the many ways that information stored "online" in computers can further the objectives of an archaeological project.

The most straightforward archaeological use of computers is to maintain databases of the pottery, small finds, and sites that have been identified and recorded by the project. The single greatest advantage of an electronic filing system over paper-based alternatives is its searchability.

For example, during the 1993 and 1994 field seasons, PRAP defined an archaeological site (Site G01) on the western coast of Messenia at a place known locally as Dialiskari (see Focus in Chapter 7). From this site, 220 closely datable pottery sherds were collected. An easily performed search of the online PRAP pottery database shows that forty-six of these sherds, that is, 21 percent of the total, were dated to the Late Roman period (fifth to seventh centuries A.D.) by the project's ceramic specialists, far more than were assigned to any other single period. The abundance of well-dated Late Roman sherds at Site G01, in conjunction with its substantial Roman-period architectural remains, including a bath, support our hypothesis that it was the location of a villa complex that was still in use as late as the sixth century A.D.

Two further observations about Site G01 are possible, on the basis of information easily culled from the searchable pottery catalog. On the surface at the site were recovered sherds of African Red-Slip (a very popular type of pottery produced in or near modern Tunisia), fine ceramic wares from the western coast of Turkey, and amphoras that carried wine from the Aegean and Palestine. The diversity of this imported pottery strongly suggests that Site G01 was an important settlement whose inhabitants had ac-

SEBASTIAN HEATH

cess to the same interregional exchange systems that were also supplying high-quality pottery to large urban centers such as Rome, Athens, and Alexandria during the Late Roman period. The exceptional nature of the site is further emphasized by the fact that, of 108 firmly dated Late Roman sherds collected from the entire PRAP study area, 44 percent come from Site G01. Moreover, no more than four sherds were found at any of the other fourteen sites where Late Roman pottery was gathered.

Because information about pottery collected by PRAP is stored in a computerized database, the number of finds of various types of pottery can easily be calculated for all sites and periods, as for Dialiskari and the Late Roman period. Calculation of the number of sherds of a given date found at a particular site is, however, only one way of viewing the data that is greatly facilitated by the use of computers.

Our efforts have also focused on the generation of maps that can illustrate how patterns of settlement have changed through time. Computer-based mapping has become an indispensable tool that has transformed a previously labor-intensive activity into an interactive analytical technique. For example, in Figures 130 and 131 are mapped the locations of Archaic and Classical Greek sites and Roman sites—images that now take minutes rather than hours to prepare and can be immediately modified and updated and reproduced without substantial cost in time and effort. Patterns in the distribution of the sites are clear: not only is there a marked increase in the number of Roman sites, but the Roman sites are closer to the coast.

There are, of course, other possible explanations for such a shift in the locations of settlements between Greek and Roman times, but it is perhaps most likely that the change is indicative of an increased interest in having access to the sea and to seaborne commerce. The rise of the Roman empire and the political stability and elevated economic activity that it brought also seem to have resulted more or less directly in an increase in population in this corner of southwest Greece.

The analyses discussed above make use of computerized database and mapping tools. These have steadily improved over the past decade. In contrast, the recent rapid development of the Internet and the World Wide Web offers opportunities to facilitate collaboration between members of PRAP and to share our findings with the general public—opportunities that we are actively pursuing and encouraging. Members of PRAP are based in many different institutions, in several countries. Problems of communication are complex: for example, the academic affiliations of the authors of this book alone, only part of the PRAP team, include the University of Athens (Greece), the University of Braunschweig (Germany), the University of Cincinnati, the University of Ioannina (Greece), the Univer-

FIGURE 130
Archaic and Classical Greek finds identified by PRAP: on-site (circles) and off-site (crosses). PRAP Archive. S. Heath.

sity of Maryland, the University of Michigan, Oxford University, the University of Texas, and the University of Wisconsin.

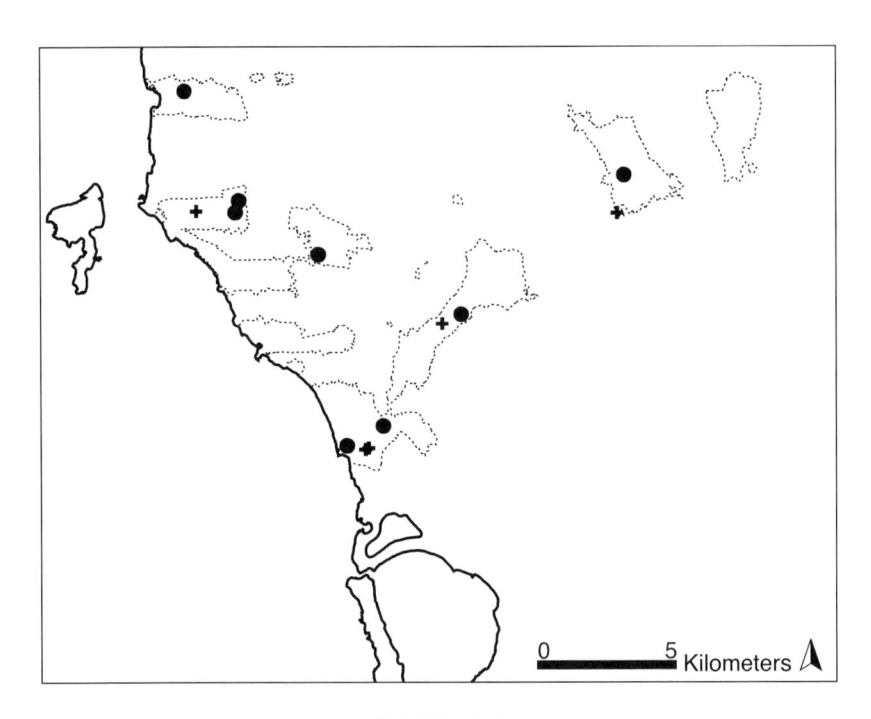

All members of PRAP need to have at their disposal the latest data in the archives of the project, but how to get it to them? How to ensure that everyone is studying the same data? We believe that we have found an excellent solution to the problem by using a computerized database program that can be run on either Apple Macintosh or Windows-compatible computers. This database program allows files of information to be accessed via the Internet from a single computer where the "master copy" resides.

For the general public and for scholars who are not members of our team, PRAP has made available on the World Wide Web (the part of the Internet where "point-and-click" interfaces to publicly available information can be created) scientific reports describing the progress of our fieldwork year by year, descriptions of all archaeological sites investigated by our teams, descriptions and illustrations of many ancient artifacts, as well as discussions of other matters of more particular interest. This Web site is also a convenient place for students to follow the work of the archaeolo-

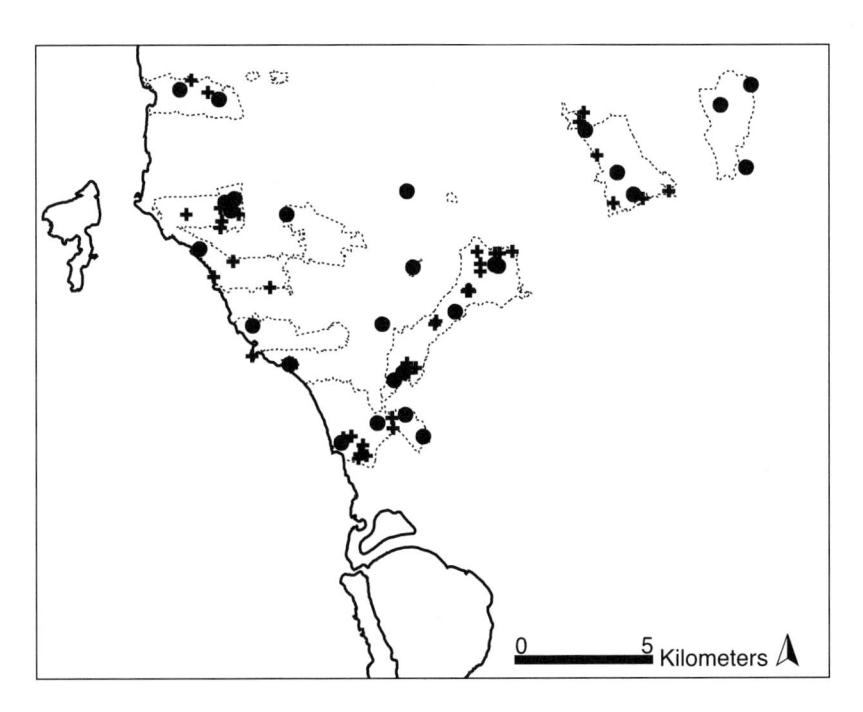

FIGURE 131
*Roman finds identified by PRAP: on-site (circles) and off-site (crosses).
PRAP Archive. S. Heath.*

gists, historians, and scientists on the PRAP team who are continuing to analyze the PRAP data.

The World Wide Web has also dramatically reduced the time that it takes us to publish archaeological information. In fact, our site was made public only six months after the completion of our last full season in the field—a savings of years in the normal scheme of academic publishing.

FOCUS

A FIELDWALKER'S PERSPECTIVE *on* PRAP

The adventures of a PRAP fieldwalker could fill a whole book, as each day yielded a variety of events. Our survey day began at the crack of dawn, when we almost jumped into our work clothes. It was amazing to notice the silent agreement among fieldwalkers who had never met before to dress in exactly the same style: boots, long trousers, long-sleeved shirts, gloves, and hats. Next we had to find our way to breakfast by walking quite a distance, through the still-sleeping village. It was there, during breakfast, while eating all colors of jams, nutella, and peanut butter, that we got the first hint of our daily field schedule.

The conditions in the field were difficult because of the climate and geomorphology of Messenia. Like most of southern Greece, Messenia is usually hot, dry, and dusty in summer. Its landscape consists largely of olive groves dissected by deep gorges and ravines, most of which are completely choked with thorny bushes. Only close cooperation among ourselves, our team leader, and our field director made study of such terrain practicable (Fig. 132).

Naturally, a sense of humor was always a powerful weapon against pain and tedium. Indeed, we needed it as we made our way through the thick Mediterranean underbrush known as "macchia" and through mazes of vines, often finding our path blocked by scorpions, snakes, or spider webs.

As we walked, we often followed a line of flags that we had previously implanted to mark our course, or we took bearings on our compass. At other times, we traced the lines of agricultural terraces along steep hillslopes. Whenever it was impossible to see each other, we yelled our positions, feeling sorry at the same time for disturbing the silence of nature. Situations like this made us realize the importance of the individual, not only as a member of the team, but also as a separate personality.

Well, things were not always that bad! We are still recalling the moments of finding artifacts. Our enthusiasm did not even diminish when we

---

MARIA ANTONIOU *and* KALLIOPE KALOYERAKOU

FIGURE 132
Leader of a survey team (Charles Watkinson) consulting with the field director of PRAP, John Bennet. PRAP Archive. R. Dupuis-Devlin and E. Dallagher.

were faced with the task of transporting them. The pottery, lithics, metals, and bones, after being properly labeled, next had to be carried in backpacks to our van, sometimes parked some distance away. In our backpacks, they, of course, shared space with our daily food rations, such as sardines in chili sauce or hot red peppers and, for vitamins, seasonal fruits.

Occasionally, the routine was interrupted by short rest breaks, when we would chat about the progress of the day and our most significant finds. Of course, it was such a nice and welcome surprise when after a break, the route on the topographic map led us away from the inland areas, toward the more pleasant and picturesque coastal sites.

Wherever possible, we tried to collect ethno-archaeological information—that is, descriptions of material culture of the present and most recent past. As we were making our way through cultivated fields and passing nearby fenced gardens, we took the opportunity to chat with the local homeowners and farmers. These Messenian natives were almost always a valuable source of information about local history and recent landscape changes, and sometimes they even told us about archaeological remains we had not yet found.

We could hardly blame our potential "informants" for sometimes being surprised, suspicious, or curious when they first saw a row of foreigners

FIGURE 133
The makeshift dormitory in the Hora schoolhouse used by PRAP. PRAP Archive.

walking through their fields. Almost always, after explaining who we were and what we were doing, we found ourselves deluged with stories, told in good faith and with great gusto, such as sagas about golden treasures buried by pirates. The hospitality we received, especially from older people, was extraordinary, and we gratefully accepted many an invitation to sip coffee and nibble sweets or fruits in their yards. We, as Greeks, had a special role to play in the field. Since there were relatively few cultural and linguistic differences between ourselves and the locals, it often fell on our shoulders to explain our goals in an appropriate manner and to try to eliminate any possible misunderstandings; although in some cases such misunderstandings offered us much amusement. Once, we came across an odd old woman who said she had dreamt of a man telling her that she would find a magnificent treasure if she "pulled down her houses," something that, for one second and under the heat of the sun, was heard as "pulled down his trousers"!

As soon as the heat of midday became unbearable, we found shelter in our dormitories, set up in one of the two elementary schools in Hora (Fig. 133). As they say, "life is a struggle," and for us this often proved true, especially when the whole field crew had to line up outside to use our only cold shower. After this luxury, a short nap was what we were looking for, but this effort was usually interrupted by special events, organized for us by the field directors and team leaders: usually lectures and discussions, but occasionally "worst-dressed" competitions or weekly awards to honor both our most noble and our most ignominious achievements in the field. Sometimes we visited archaeological sites, or even relaxed on a beach when one could be found nearby. A traditional family-style dinner, meant to be the appropriate antidote to homesickness, was followed by a game of volleyball in the schoolyard, for those with any energy remaining.

Another aspect of our involvement, not directly connected with fieldwalking but necessary for the operation of our work, was the survey's museum. This was not a real museum but rather a temporary affair, as it was housed in the same school as our living quarters. Every day we would provide help with all sorts of museum tasks, such as the counting, sorting, cataloging, drawing, photographing, and studying of artifacts. A special challenge for us was trying to explain all these activities as well as the survey methods and the principle of teamwork to groups of local youngsters. Our new friends brightened our days and gave us a bit of excitement when babbling some village gossip during the dull work of washing potsherds (Fig. 134).

FIGURE 134
PRAP surveyors washing pottery after the completion of work in the field. PRAP Archive. J. L. Davis.

FIGURE 135
The PRAP team in 1993. Maria Antoniou and Kalliope Kaloyerakou are second and third from the left in row 2. PRAP Archive. R. Dupuis-Devlin and E. Dallagher.

Now that the fieldwalking has come to an end, we can stand back and reflect in a more relaxed (and comfortable) environment on the good moments created by a multinational team (Fig. 135). We can now also appreciate the methods with which we, as young archaeologists, became more familiar while taking part in PRAP. The opportunity to examine artifacts from different periods of the past was a valuable educational source, as it gave us a special insight into the history and topography of Messenia. Moreover, from the natural scientists on the team, we personally learned much about the importance of close collaboration between archaeologists, botanists, and geologists in reconstructing ancient landscapes.

MARIA ANTONIOU *and* KALLIOPE KALOYERAKOU

TIMELINE

Dates in early prehistory are by convention reported in years B.P. ("Before Present;" "present" being set at 1950 A.D.). Dates in prehistory are based on those suggested in "Reviews of Aegean Prehistory," published in *American Journal of Archaeology* since 1992, especially those by Curtis Runnels (1995), Jeremy Rutter (1993), and Cynthia Shelmerdine (1997).

ARCHAEOLOGICAL PERIODS	HISTORICAL EVENTS
Upper Palaeolithic (ca. 35,000–11,000 B.P.)	
Mesolithic (ca. 9500–8000 B.P.)	
Neolithic (ca. 6000–3100 B.C.)	Introduction of farming to Greece
Early Bronze Age	First use of the plow?
Early Helladic I (ca. 3100–2650 B.C.)	
Early Helladic II (ca. 2650–2200 B.C.)	
Early Helladic III (ca. 2200–2050 B.C.)	
Middle Bronze Age	
Middle Helladic (c. 2050–1680 B.C.)	
Late Bronze Age (Mycenaean Period)	
Late Helladic I (c. 1680–1600 B.C.)	
Late Helladic II (c. 1600–1400 B.C.)	
Late Helladic IIIA (c. 1400–1300 B.C.)	
Late Helladic IIIB (c. 1300–1180 B.C.)	Ca. 1200 B.C.: Palace of Nestor destroyed
Late Helladic IIIC (c. 1180–1060 B.C.)	

ARCHAEOLOGICAL PERIODS	HISTORICAL EVENTS
Submycenaean and Early Iron Age or Dark Age (ca. 1060–900 B.C.)	
Geometric Period (ca. 900–700 B.C.)	Late eighth century: First Messenian War (with Sparta)
Archaic Period (ca. 700–480 B.C.)	Seventh century?: Second Messenian War
Classical Period (480–323 B.C.)	ca. 460 B.C.: Third Messenian War—Messenians exiled to Naupactus 431–404 B.C.: Peloponnesian War 425 B.C.: Battle of Sphacteria 408 B.C.: Spartans take Pylos 402 B.C.: Messenians expelled from Naupactus 371 B.C.: Battle of Leuctra 369 B.C.: Foundation of Messene 365 B.C.: Pylos (Coryphasion) captured by Argos, given over to Messenians 338 B.C.: Battle of Chaeronea
Hellenistic Period (323–31 B.C.)	191 B.C.: Messenia joins Achaean League 146 B.C.: Achaean War with Rome First century B.C.: *floruit* Strabo 31 B.C.: Battle of Actium
Roman Period (31 B.C.–ca. 400 A.D.)	67 A.D.: Nero declares freedom for the Greeks Mid-second century A.D.: Trajan declares Methoni a free city Mid-second century A.D.: *floruit* Pausanias Third century A.D.: Herulian invasions of Greece
Late Roman Period (400–700 A.D.) or Early Byzantine Period (400–600 A.D.)	451 A.D.: Bishop John of Messenia participates in Council of Chalcedon 582 or 586 A.D.: Slavs take Corinth
Dark Age (600–900 A.D.)	

ARCHAEOLOGICAL PERIODS	HISTORICAL EVENTS
	1086 A.D.: Hristianoupolis becomes an archbishopric
Middle Byzantine Period (900–1204 A.D.)	1125 A.D.: Methoni burned by Venetians for piracy
	1128 A.D.: Venetians receive Byzantine imperial writ to trade at Methoni
Frankish Period (1204–1430 A.D.) or Late Byzantine Period (1261–1453 A.D.)	1204 A.D.: Venetians take Methoni, Koroni
	1204 A.D.: Following the Fourth Crusade, Franks establish a feudal kingdom in the Peloponnese
	1347–48 A.D.: Black Death
	Fourteenth century A.D.: Catalan and Turkish incursions
	Fifteenth century A.D.: Influx of Albanians
	1430 A.D.: Constantine IX Palaiologos, Despot of Mistra, recovers Peloponnese for the Byzantines
	1453 A.D.: Constantinople falls to the Turks
First Ottoman Period (1460–1684 A.D.)	By 1500 A.D.: Venice loses Methoni, Koroni, Navarino
	1573 A.D.: Neokastro built
Venetian Rule (1686–1715 A.D.)	
Second Ottoman Period (1715–1827 A.D.)	
Early Modern Era (1800–1950 A.D.)	Early nineteenth century A.D.: William Gell's travels
	1821 A.D.: Greek War of Independence begins
	1827 A.D.: Battle of Navarino
Modern Greek State (1834 A.D.–present)	1834 A.D.: Establishment of the Modern Greek State

TIMELINE

SOURCES *of* QUOTATIONS

Passages from Pausanias, Strabo, and Tyrtaios are original translations by J. Bennet, based on F. Spiro's Teubner text of Pausanias, *Pausaniae Graeciae descriptio* (Leipzig: B. G. Teubner, 1903), H. L. Jones's text of *Strabo: The Geography of Strabo* (Cambridge, Mass.: Harvard University Press, 1917), and E. Hiller and O. Crusius, *Anthologia lyrica sive Lyricorum graecorum veterum praeter Pindarum reliquiae potiores post Theodorum Bergkium quartum* (Leipzig: B. G. Teubner, 1913), frags. 3–5.

Other quotations are drawn from the following sources.

INTRODUCTION

Monomitos inscription, from *Inscriptiones Graecae*, vol. 5, pt. 1, 1431 (Berlin: George Reimer, 1913), trans. J. L. Davis; on the character of Ottoman Greece, W. M. Leake, *Travels in the Morea*, vol. 1 (London: J. Murray, 1830), v.

CHAPTER 2

Pouqueville at Pylos, from F.C.H.L. Pouqueville, *Travels in Greece and Turkey, Comprehending a Particular Account of the Morea, Albania, &c.*, 2d ed. (London: Henry Colburn, 1820) 10; Grundy's discovery of the tholos at Voidokoilia, from G. B. Grundy, "An Investigation of the Topography of the Region of Sphakteria and Pylos," *Journal of Hellenic Studies* 15–16 (1895–96): 49; address by Oikonomos from "῎Εκθεσις περὶ τῶν κατὰ τὸ ἔτος 1925 ὑπὸ τῆς Ἀρχαιολογικῆς Ἑταιρείας πεπραγμένων" (Πρακτικὰ τῆς ἐν Ἀθῆναις Ἀρχαιολογικῆς Ἑταιρείας, 1925): 17, trans. N. Spencer; Blegen's address at the University of Pennsylvania, from C. W. Blegen, "Preclassical Greece," in C. W. Blegen et al., *Studies in the Arts and Architecture, University of Pennsylvania Bicentennial Conference* (Philadelphia: University of Pennsylvania Press, 1941); McDonald on the purpose of his regional studies: W. A. McDonald and R. Hope Simpson, "Prehistoric Habitation in Southwestern Peloponnese," *American Journal of Archaeology* 65 (1961): 222 n. 2.

In Focus: Unpublished notebook entry of C. W. Blegen for April 4, 1939, with permission of the Department of Classics, University of Cincinnati; published announcement of the discovery of the Palace of Nestor, from K. Kourouniotis and C. W. Blegen, "Excavations at Pylos, 1939," *American Journal of Archaeology* 43 (1939): 557.

CHAPTER 3

Unpublished notebook entry of C. W. Blegen for March 31, 1939, with permission of the Department of Classics, University of Cincinnati.

CHAPTER 4

Unpublished telegram of April 21, 1939, from C. W. Blegen, with permission from the American School of Classical Studies at Athens; original translations of Linear B documents by C. W. Shelmerdine after texts published in E. L. Bennett Jr. and J.-P. Oliver, *The Pylos Tablets Transcribed*, vol. 1: *Texts and Notes* (Rome: Edizioni dell'Ateneo, 1973), with unpublished revisions by E. L. Bennett Jr., included with his permission.

CHAPTER 5

Original translations of Linear B documents by J. Bennet after texts published in E. L. Bennett Jr. and J.-P. Olivier, *The Pylos Tablets Transcribed*, vol. 1: *Texts and Notes* (Rome: Edizioni dell'Ateneo, 1973), with unpublished revisions by E. L. Bennett Jr., included with his permission.

CHAPTER 6

Thucydides 4.3.2, on Messenia, from the text of *Thucydidis Historiae*, ed. H. S. Jones and J. E. Powell (Oxford: Clarendon Press, 1942), trans. J. L. Davis; Euripides on the climate and natural resources of Messenia, from Strabo 8.5.6; the status of helots, from Aristophanes of Byzantium 3.83, in E. Bethe, ed., *Pollicis Onomasticon*, vol. 1 (Leipzig: B. G. Teubner, 1900); helot settlement and the Five Rivers survey, from F. E. Luckerman and J. Moody, "Nichoria and Vicinity: Settlements and Circulation," in G. R. Rapp, Jr. and S. Aschenbrenner, eds., *Excavations at Nichoria in Southwest Greece*, vol. 1: *Site, Environs, and Techniques* (Minneapolis: University of Minnesota Press, 1978), 95.

CHAPTER 7

Sentiments of King Archidamus on the loss of Messenia, from Isocrates, *Archidamus* 28, text from G. Norlin, *Isocrates: Works* (Cambridge, Mass.: Harvard University Press, 1928–45), trans. J. L. Davis; "holding the ox," from Strabo 8.4.8; clouds in the west, from Polybius 5.104.10, ed. L. Dindorf and rev. T. Buettner-Wobst, *Polybii historiae* (Stuttgart: Teubner, 1882–1904); the fertility of Messenia, from Strabo 8.5.6; the dispute over the Ager Dentheliates, from Tacitus 4.43, in C. D. Fisher, ed., *Cornelii Taciti Annalium ab Excessu Divi Augusti Libri* (Oxford: Clarendon, 1939).

CHAPTER 8

Byzantine reference to Pylos, trans. S.E.J. Gerstel, from Constantine Porphyrogenitus *De thematibus* (Bonn: E. Weber, 1840), 280–83; places visited by St. Nikon, from Anonymous, *The Life of Saint Nikon*, trans. D. Sullivan (Brookline, Mass.: Hellenic College Press, 1987), 109; the repulsion of the Avars and Slavs from Patras, after W. Miller, *Essays on the Latin Orient* (Cambridge: Cambridge University Press, 1921), 34–35; Villehardouin's call to action from G. Villehardouin, "The Conquest of Constantinople," in M.R.B. Shaw, *Chronicles of the Crusades* (New York: Dorset, 1963), 113; the Frankish assessment of Kalamata and relations with Venice, from *Crusaders as Conquerors: The Chronicle of the Morea*, trans. H. Lurier (New York: Columbia University Press, 1963), 113, 121, 152; on Frankish legal practice, P. Topping, *Feudal Institutions as Revealed in the Assizes of Romania: The Law Code of Frankish Greece* (Philadelphia: University of Pennsylvania Press, 1949), 77; remarks regarding feudal efficiency are those of Marino Sanudo Torsello in "Istoria de regno di Romania," in C. Hopf, *Chroniques gréco-romanes inédites ou peu connues* (Berlin: Weidmann, 1873), 100–101 (translated in W. Miller, *The Latins in the Levant* [London: J. Murray, 1908], 87); and Grimani's caricature of Peloponnesians, and discussion of the reports by Renier, Michiel, and Gritti, are found in P. Topping, "Premodern Peloponnesus: The Land and the People Under Venetian Rule (1685–1715)," *Annals of the New York Academy of Sciences* 268 (1976): 95.

In Focuses: Documents concerning the estates of Acciaiuoli, trans. S.E.J. Gerstel, from texts published in J. Longnon and P. Topping, *Documents sur le régime des terres dans la principauté de Morée au quatorzième siécle* (Paris: Mouton, 1969), 73–76; Villehardouin at Methoni, from Anonymous, *Crusaders as Conquerors: The Chronicle of the Morea*, trans. H. Lurier (New York: Columbia University Press, 1964), 5–8; texts of Frescobaldi, from L. di N. Frescobaldi, *Visit to the Holy Places of Egypt, Sinai, Palestine, and Syria in 1384*, trans. T. Bellorini and E. Hoade (Jerusalem: Franciscan Press, 1948), 36, 37; von Harff, from *The Pilgrimage of Arnold von Harff*, trans. M. Letts (London: Hakluyt Society, 1946), 81; Tafur, from P. Tafur, *Travels and Adventures*, trans. M. Letts (New York: Harper and Brothers, 1926), 49–50; Faber, from S. B. Luce, "Modon: A Venetian Station in Mediaeval Greece," in L. W. Jones, ed., *Classical and Mediaeval Studies in Honor of Edward Kennard Rand* (New York: published by the editor, 1938), 201–2; Casola, from *Canon Pietro Casola's Pilgrimage to Jerusalem in the Year 1494*, trans. M. M. Newett (Manchester: Manchester University Press, 1907), 194.

CHAPTER 9

Ultimatum of Çorlulu Ali Paşa, trans. J. L. Davis, from text in B. Brue, *Journal de la campagne que le grand vesir Ali Pacha a faite en 1715 pour la conquête de la Morée* (Paris: Ernest Thorin, 1870), 15–16; explosion in the powder magazine, from George Gordon, Lord Byron, *The Siege of Corinth: A Poem; Parisina: A Poem* (London: John Murray, 1816), 52–53; W. Gell, from *Narrative of a Journey in the Morea* (London: Longman, Hurst, Rees, Orme, and Brown, 1823): in Gargaliani, pp. 63–72; comments on Greek tax-collectors, pp. 65–66; with Pashalopoulos in Navarino, pp. 6–7; and the site of Hasanaga, pp. 61–62 (also discussed in the Focus). Leake on the lands between Coryphasion and Cyparissia: W. M. Leake, *Travels in the Morea*, vol. 1 (London: J. Murray, 1830), 425; Castellan's adventures: A. L. Castellan, *Lettres sur la Morée et les iles de Cérigo, Hydra et Zante*, vol. 2 (Paris: H. Agasse, 1808), Letter 22, pp. 90–100.

In Focuses: Hamilton's report to Codrington, from the papers of Captain G. W. Hamilton, now in the collection of the National Maritime Museum, London (courtesy of the National Maritime Museum); Codrington's orders in case of battle, from C. M. Woodhouse, *The Battle of Navarino* (London: Hoddler and Stoughton, 1965), 107.

CHAPTER 10

I. D. Kefalas's plea from Ἱστορία τῆς Μεσσηνίας (Athens: A. Dialismas, 1935), 14–15; I. Zervos Iakovatos's emulation of Aristomenes, from Ἡ ἀρχαία Μεσσηνία καὶ ὁ Ἀριστομένης (Cephallenia: Cephallenia, 1857), 1; passages from the Trifylian White Paper, from Anonymous, Λεύκωμα Ἐπαρχίας Τριφυλίας (Athens: Association of Trifylians in Athens and Piraeus, 1938), 3–4. All translations by J. L. Davis.

FURTHER READING

The following brief list of references (for the most part to books) should be consulted by those who are interested in learning more about some aspect of Messenia. The bibliographies of these references in turn will direct readers to more specialized papers and books that have been consulted by the authors of this volume. Most are in English, and intentionally so; but it should not be forgotten that Greek archaeology, history, and prehistory are fully international disciplines. Important research is published not only in English, but also in French, German, Italian, and, of course, Greek.

INTRODUCTION

Angelomatis-Tsoungarakis, H., *The Eve of the Greek Revival: British Travellers' Perceptions of Early Nineteenth-Century Greece* (London: Routledge, 1990). Discussion and analysis of the published accounts of British travelers to Greece at the end of the Second Ottoman period.

Barber, R., *Blue Guide: Greece* (London: A. and C. Black, 1987). The best tourist guide to mainland Greece, including Messenia. Unlike other guides, the Blue Guide speaks with authority about archaeological sites.

Cherry, J. F., J. L. Davis, and E. Mantzourani, *Landscape Archaeology as Long-Term History: Northern Keos in the Cycladic Islands* (Los Angeles: Institute of Archaeology, UCLA, 1991). Part 1 describes methods used by most recent intensive archaeological surveys in Greece—as applied to the study of one small Greek island—and argues the virtue of taking a chronologically broad view of the past and of the relationship between humans and the environment in which they live.

Eisner, R., *Travelers to an Antique Land: The History and Literature of Travel to Greece* (Ann Arbor: University of Michigan Press, 1991). General synthesis of travel literature written about Greece, from the Middle Ages until the twentieth century.

Pausanias, *Guide to Greece*, vol. 2: *Southern Greece*, trans. Peter Levi (London: Penguin Classics, 1971), book 4. The most accessible English translation of the most comprehensive ancient description of Messenia.

Simopoulos, K., Ξένοι ταξιδιώτες στην Ελλάδα (Athens: n.p., 1970–75). Even Greekless readers will find the bibliographies of this four-volume series a gold mine of information about works in English, French, and German written about journeys to Greece prior to the Greek Revolution of 1821–29.

CHAPTER 1

Jameson, M. H., C. N. Runnels, and T. H. van Andel, *A Greek Countryside: The Southern Argolid from Prehistory to the Present Day* (Stanford, Calif.: Stanford University Press, 1994). A regional archaeological project, similar to PRAP; discoveries made through surface survey and geomorphological research are well integrated.

Kraft, J. C., G. R. Rapp, Jr., and S. E. Aschenbrenner, "Paleogeomorphic Reconstructions in the Area of the Bay of Navarino: Sandy Pylos," *Journal of Archaeological Science* 7 (1980): 187–210. How the area north of the Bay of Navarino appeared in prehistoric times; changes in the course of the Selas River.

Wright, Jr., H. E., "Vegetation History," in W. A. McDonald and G. R. Rapp, Jr., *The Minnesota Messenia Expedition: Reconstructing a Bronze Age Regional Environment* (Minneapolis: University of Minnesota Press, 1972), 188–99. The first study of fossilized pollen in Greece.

CHAPTER 2

McDonald, W. A., and G. R. Rapp, Jr., *The Minnesota Messenia Expedition: Reconstructing a Bronze Age Regional Environment* (Minneapolis: University of Minnesota Press, 1972). The grandfather of modern regional-studies projects in Greece, and one of the most important studies of the archaeology of Messenia ever published.

McDonald, W. A., and C. G. Thomas, *Progress into the Past: The Rediscovery of Mycenaean Civilization*, 2d ed. (Bloomington: Indiana University Press, 1990). Still the only systematic history of the study of prehistoric Greece, from the time of Schliemann through the 1980s.

Valmin, M. N., *The Swedish Messenia Expedition* (Lund: C.W.K. Gleerup, 1938). Its author was a pioneer of Messenian archaeology—both prehistoric and historic; the volume includes a detailed report on excavations at Malthi and references to other papers by Valmin.

CHAPTER 3

Blegen, C. W., M. Rawson, W. Taylour, and W. P. Donovan, *The Palace of Nestor at Pylos in Western Messenia*, vol. 3: *Acropolis and Lower Town, Tholoi, Grave Circles and Chamber Tombs, Discoveries Outside the Citadel* (Princeton: Princeton University Press, 1973). The final part of Blegen's monumental publication of his explorations at the Palace of Nestor. Volume 3 describes archaeological finds near the Palace of Nestor and on the Englianos Ridge, except the remains of the palace itself.

Dickinson, O.T.P.K., *The Aegean Bronze Age* (Cambridge and New York: Cambridge University Press, 1994). The only comprehensive book in English about the archaeology of the prehistoric Aegean; by a leading authority.

CHAPTER 4

Blegen, C. W., and M. Rawson, *The Palace of Nestor at Pylos in Western Messenia*, vol. 1: *The Buildings and Their Contents* (Princeton: Princeton University Press, 1966). The first volume of Blegen's publication; a description of the Palace of Nestor and the artifacts found in it.

Chadwick, J., *Linear B and Related Scripts* (London: British Museum Publications, 1987). For beginners, a general guide to Linear B. How was the script used to write Greek? What sorts of document exist?

Chadwick, J., *The Mycenaean World* (Cambridge: Cambridge University Press, 1976). Mycenaean society and economy, based on documentary evidence as viewed by one of the decipherers of the Linear B script.

Killen, J. T., "Thebes Sealings, Knossos Tablets and Mycenaean State Banquets," *Bulletin of the Institute of Classical Studies—London* (1994): 67–84. Presents evidence, based on new readings of Linear B texts and comparison with other societies, for feasting among the Mycenaean elite on Crete and mainland Greece.

Shelmerdine, C. W., *The Perfume Industry of Mycenaean Pylos* (Göteborg: Paul Åströms Förlag, 1985). A groundbreaking attempt to integrate archaeological and textual evidence; the production of scented oils was an important aspect of the Mycenaean economy at Pylos.

CHAPTER 5

Bennet, J., "Space Through Time: Diachronic Perspectives on the Spatial Organization of the Pylian State," in W.-D. Niemeier and R. Laffineur, eds., *POLITEIA: Society and State in the Aegean Bronze Age* (Liège [Aegaeum 12], 1995), 587–602. A review of the evidence for the geography of the Pylian kingdom and a consideration of the means by which Pylos expanded its control from western Messenia to the Pamisos Valley.

Chadwick, J., "The Geography of the Further Province of Pylos," *American Journal of Archaeology* 77 (1973): 276–78. Names of towns recorded in Linear B are associated with specific archaeological sites in Messenia.

McDonald, W. A., and N. C. Wilkie, eds., *Excavations at Nichoria in Southwest Greece*, vol. 2: *The Bronze Age Occupation* (Minneapolis: University of Minnesota Press, 1992). Full publication of the prehistoric buildings and artifacts from the site.

Rapp, Jr., G. R., and S. Aschenbrenner, eds., *Excavations at Nichoria in Southwest Greece*, vol. 1: *Site, Environs, and Techniques* (Minneapolis: University of Minnesota Press, 1978). Excavations of an important Messenian settlement by the organizers of the University of Minnesota Messenia Expedition; as in earlier regional studies, the integration of archaeology and natural and physical sciences is emphasized.

Shelmerdine, C. W., "Nichoria in Context: A Major Town in the Pylos Kingdom," *American Journal of Archaeology* 85 (1981): 319–25. Artifacts and analysis of documents in Linear B both support identification of the site of Nichoria with the town of *ti-mi-to-a-ke-e*.

CHAPTER 6

Cartledge, P., *Sparta and Lakonia: A Regional History, 1300–362 B.C.* (London and Boston: Routledge and Kegan Paul, 1979), chapters 7–8. The early history of Sparta and of its military involvement with and subsequent occupation of Messenia.

McDonald, W. A., W.D.E. Coulson, and J. Rosser, *Excavations at Nichoria in Southwest Greece*, vol. 3: *Dark Age and Byzantine Occupation* (Minneapolis: University of Minnesota Press, 1983). The archaeology of Nichoria after the destruction of the Palace of Nestor.

Popham, M. R., "Pylos: Reflections on the Date of Its Destruction and on Its Iron Age Reoccupation," *Oxford Journal of Archaeology* 10 (1991): 315–24. Did people live amidst the ruins of the Palace of Nestor after its destruction? When exactly was the palace destroyed?

Pritchett, W. K., *Studies in Ancient Greek Topography*, vol. 1 (Berkeley and Los Angeles: University of California Press, 1965). A distinguished historian and topographer of Greece analyzes the Battle of Sphacteria.

Thucydides, *History of the Peloponnesian War*, trans. R. Warner (London and New York: Penguin, 1972), book 4, chapters 3–23, 26–41. Translations of the fifth-century B.C. historian Thucydides' descriptions of the Athenian blockade of the island of Sphacteria and Athens's victory over the Spartans.

CHAPTER 7

Alcock, S. E., *Graecia Capta: The Landscapes of Roman Greece* (Cambridge: Cambridge University Press, 1993). The archaeology of Roman Greece reviewed, with special emphasis on new evidence from surface surveys.

Antonaccio, C. M., *An Archaeology of Ancestors: Tomb Cult and Hero Cult in Early Greece* (Lanham, Md.: Rowman & Littlefield, 1995). Veneration of tombs of the Mycenaean Age by historical Greeks—why and how?

Cartledge, P., and A. Spawforth, *Hellenistic and Roman Sparta* (London and New York: Routledge, 1989). Sparta after the liberation of Messenia, and as part of the Roman empire.

Cavanagh, W., J. Crouwel, R.W.V. Catling, and G. Shipley, *The Laconia Survey: Continuity and Change in a Greek Rural Landscape* (London: British School at

Athens, 1996). Regional studies in the territory of ancient Sparta, under the auspices of the British School of Archaeology.

Habicht, C., *Pausanias' Guide to Ancient Greece* (Berkeley: University of California Press, 1985). A series of provocative lectures by the foremost scholar of Pausanias, including a detailed discussion of Pausanias's description of the city of Messene.

Roebuck, C., *A History of Messenia from 369 to 146 B.C.* (Chicago: Private edition distributed by the University of Chicago Libraries, 1941). Old but useful review of sources for Messenian history after liberation from Sparta and before Roman conquest.

CHAPTER 8

Andrews, K., *Castles of the Morea* (Princeton: American School of Classical Studies at Athens, 1953). Full description and history of medieval and early modern forts in the Peloponnese—Frankish, Ottoman, and Venetian.

Anonymous, *Crusaders as Conquerors: The Chronicle of the Morea*, trans. H. Lurier (New York: Columbia University Press, 1964). The only English translation of our principal medieval description of the conquest of the Peloponnese by Western European knights in the wake of the Fourth Crusade.

Anonymous, *The Life of Saint Nikon*, trans. D. Sullivan (Brookline, Mass.: Hellenic College Press, 1987). Biography of an Eastern Orthodox saint, but an important source for medieval Messenian history.

Longnon, J., and P. Topping, *Documents sur le régime des terres dans la principauté de Morée au XIVe siècle* (Paris: Mouton, 1969). Translations of important documents, and commentaries on them, that tell us who owned land in the Peloponnese in the final century before the Ottoman conquest and who profited from it. Messenian villages are included.

Miller, W., *The Latins in the Levant: A History of Frankish Greece (1204–1566)* (London: J. Murray, 1908). The standard English history of the states established in Greece by Western Europeans in the late Middle Ages.

Soulis, G., "Notes on Venetian Modon," *Peloponnisiaka* 3–4 (1958–59): 267–75. Clips from travelogues by Western European visitors to Methoni in the late Middle Ages.

Topping, P., "Premodern Peloponnesus: The Land and the People Under Venetian Rule (1685–1715)," *Annals of the New York Academy of Sciences* 268 (1976): 92–108. Short history of Venice's occupation of the Peloponnese between the First and Second Ottoman periods.

Topping, P., "The Post Classical Documents," in W. A. McDonald and G. R. Rapp, Jr., *The Minnesota Messenia Expedition: Reconstructing a Bronze Age Regional Environment* (Minneapolis: University of Minnesota Press, 1972), 64–80. Written testimonies for the history of Messenia between the foundation of Constantinople (A.D. 323) and the Greek Revolution in the early nineteenth century.

CHAPTER 9

Arel, A., "About the 'Hasan Paşa Tower' at Yerkesiği, on the Plain of Troia," *Studia Troica* 3 (1993): 173–89. An architectural and archaeological study of an estate in northwestern Turkey, once belonging to a member of the Turkish elite. PRAP's site of Hasanaga may preserve remains of a similar, if less grand, foundation.

Dakin, D., *The Unification of Greece, 1770–1923* (New York: St. Martin's Press, 1972). Perhaps the best one-volume political history of the modern Greek state during its formation and first century of existence.

Finlay, G., *History of Greece from Its Conquest by the Romans to the Present Time, B.C. 146–A.D. 1864*, vols. 6–7: *History of the Greek Revolution and the Reign of King Otho* (London: Zeno, 1971). The Greek Revolution and independence seen through the eyes of a nineteenth-century English philhellene.

Woodhouse, C. M., *The Battle of Navarino* (London: Hoddler and Stoughton, 1965). The most authoritative history of the battle, incorporating British documentary sources.

Woodhouse, C. M., *Modern Greece: A Short History*, 3d ed., rev. (London and Boston: Faber and Faber, 1984). Less dense than Dakin's history.

CHAPTER 10

Keller, D. R., and D. W. Rupp, *Archaeological Survey in the Mediterranean Area* (Oxford: British Archaeological Reports, 1983). Papers from a conference in Athens in the early years of surface survey.

Lolos, Y. G., Πύλος ημαθόεις· η πρωτεύουσα του Νέστορος και η γύρω περιοχή · ιστορία, μνημεία, μουσείο Χώρας (Athens: Ekdoseis Oionos, 1994). Authoritative guide to the Palace of Nestor, archaeological monuments of interest in its vicinity, and the museum of Hora.

Mouzelis, N. P., *Modern Greece: Facets of Underdevelopment* (New York: Holmes and Meier, 1978). Marxist analysis of the economic development of Greece since independence.

"The Pylos Regional Archaeological Project: Internet Edition," http://classics.lsa.umich.edu/PRAP.html. Resources of PRAP, available to scholars and the general public.

van Andel, T. H., and C. N. Runnels, *Beyond the Acropolis: A Rural Greek Past* (Stanford, Calif.: Stanford University Press, 1987). An introduction to regional studies in Greece.

INDEX

Page numbers in italic indicate illustrations.

Abia, 188
Absolute chronologies, 165
Accelerated Mass Spectrometer (AMS) radiocarbon dating, 18
Acciaiuoli, Niccolò, 223, 229–233
Achaea, xxix, 168, 185, 186
Achaean League, 184
Achaean War, 184
Acrocorinth, 183
Actium, 184–185
Administrative records. *See* Palace of Nestor administration
Aegean Sea, 5
Aetolia, 149
Aëtos, 223
African plates, 1–2
African Red Slip ware, 194, 298
Ageladas, 187
Ager Dentheliates, 186. *See also* Artemis Limnatis temple
Agriculture: and botanists, xli; and enceinte walling systems, 180; and environmental changes, 5–7; and foreign invaders, 211; in Greece, 5; and Hasanaga, 266; and helots' role, 155–156, 158–159; and Hora, 274; in Late Byzantine Period, 233; and marginal sites, 136; mechanization of, xlii; of Messenia, xxxi, xxxix; in Middle Byzantine Period, 216, 219; in Modern Period, 273; of Mycenaean Period, 6; and Palace of Nestor, 136; in Pamisos River valley, xxxix; and postliberation Messenia, 183; of Roman Period, 185; and Sparta, 288; and Venice, 228. *See also* Pollen studies

Ahmet III (Sultan of Ottoman Empire), 247
Ahmet Paşa, Sari, 111, 122, 124
Aigaleon Mountains: as border, xxxiii, 114; formation of, 2; and Mycenaean centers, 64; photographs of, *115*, *116*; and Pylos, 113; ridges of, 44
Akovitika, 40
Akritas Peninsula, 289
Akrotiri, 47, 49
Albania: and Frankish Morea, 224, 225; and Hora, 275; and Modern Period, 273; and Ottoman rule of Greece, xxxviii; and Second Ottoman Period, 252
Alcock, S. E., *264*, 280
Alexander the Great, 182
Alexios I Comnenos (Byzantine emperor), 215
Ali Paşa (of Ioannina), 254, *255*
Ali Paşa, Çorlulu, 247–248
Amber, 65–66, 77
American Journal of Archaeology, 43

American School of Classical Studies in Athens, 297
Amphoras, 240, 298
AMS (Accelerated Mass Spectrometer) radiocarbon dating, 18
Anatolia, 227
Andravida, 220
Andrianopoulos, 252–253
Androusa, 220, *221*, *222*, 223
Angelopoulos Tomb 2, 200. *See also* Volimidia
Angelopoulos Tomb 6, 200, 203. *See also* Volimidia
Animal husbandry: in Early Iron Age Period, 149–150; and Linear B tablets, 130, 136; in Mycenaean Period, 6; in Nichoria, 167; of seventh millennium B.C., 5; and water supply, 277
Ano Englianos. *See* Englianos Ridge
Antigonid kingdom, 182
Antony, Mark, 184
Apollo Korythos shrine, 28, *29*
Arabs, 172
Araxos, 56
Arcadia: Damophon of Messene's sculpture in, 183, *184*; and First Messenian War, 153; and founding of Megalopolis, 180; in Frankish Morea, 223; Mycenaean hydraulic systems of, 73; and Second Ottoman Period, 249; settlement patterns of, 159; and Sparta, 155; and Venice, 289; and Villehardouin, 220. *See also* Cyparissa
Arcadian Gate, *181*
Archaeological fieldwork: approaches to, 23, 285, 291; description of, xix–xx, 302–306, *303*, *304*, *305*, *306*; and erosion, 8; improvement of, 287; interdisciplinary nature of, 23, 25–26, 35, 39
Archaeological investigations: of Bronze Age, 24, 26, 27, 30, 35, 39; of early twentieth century, 27–28; of eighteenth and nineteenth centuries, 24–27; and fieldwork approaches, 23, 285; of historical periods, 24, 26–27, 28, 30, 33, 35, 284; and Linear B script, 23–24; and Roman Period, 24; between World Wars, 28–35
Archaeological sites: and computers, 298, 299; of Dark Age, 149; of Early Iron Age, 149; Linear B place names compared to, 134; and place names, 112; PRAP's contribution to, 134–135; preservation of, 280–283; size of, 135; and tourism, 55; underrepresentation of, 134–135, 284; and University of Minnesota Messenia Expedition, 134, 159–160, 283. *See also* specific sites
Archaic Period: in Messenia, 148; and Poseidon temple, 40; settlement patterns in, 159–160, 162, 299, *300*; and Spartan society, 155
Architectural monuments, 163
Arcosolia, 214
Argive Plain, 5
Argives, 154, 183
Argolid: and agriculture, 5; Cyclopean marvels of, 56; Mycenaean sites of, 45, 66; settlement patterns of, 159; and Spartan domination of Messenia, 154; and tomb cult, 204
Argos, 56, 153, 155, 215
Arhangelos, 223. *See also* Holy Archangel, castle of the
Aristomenes, 180, 187, 204, 293
Aristotle, 155
Artemis Limnatis temple, 33, 186
Artifact typology, xl–xli
Ascension church, 216
Aschenbrenner, Stanley, 69
Asclepieia, 26, 39, 41, 187, 188, *189*
Asia, 269
Asine, 154, 188, 211

Assyria, 101
Athanasios, Saint, 216
Athens: archaeological investigations in, 25; and Classical Period, 129; defenses of, 56, 87; and First Ottoman Period, 227; and Greek War of Independence, 254; and Messene, 182; Messenians living in, 295, 297; Modern Greek State, 273; naval battle with Sparta, 26; and Peloponnesian War, 157, 171–174, *175*, 176; rule of Messenia, xxxv
Attica, 159, 171, 173, 176, 204, 213
Attic red-figure work, 166
Augustan Age, 186
Augustus (emperor of Rome), xxix, 184–185
Aulon, 156
Austria, 253
Avarino, 211, 215
Avars, 215
Ayia Kyriaki, 32, 124, 212, 213–214, *213*
Ayia Paraskeva, 265–266
Ayia Sophia, 216
Ayios Floros, 31–32
Ayios Hristoforos, 68
Ayios Nikolaos, 192

Balkans, 246, 254
Bassiakos, Yiannis, 13
Bayezit II (sultan), 227
Benedict of Peterborough, 216
Bennet, John, 280, *303*
Bennett, Emmett L., 38–39
Beylerbey, 63, *64*, 76, 135
Black Death, 224, 226
Blegen, Carl W.: and Beylerbey, 63; bust of, *22*, 49, 297; on fortification wall, 56, 58, 68; and Grave Circle, 76; and Hora, 274; and interdisciplinary focus, 39; Palace of Nestor dating, 126; Palace of Nestor discovery by, xxxvi, 33, 35, 42–46, 81; and Palace of Nestor excavation, 23, 40; and Palace of Nestor ruins, 97–99; photograph of, *45*; and Tholos Tomb IV, 76; and tombs, 75; value of findings of, 296
Blegen, Elizabeth, 44
Blouet, Abel, 25
Boeotia, 158, 159, 179, 185
Bombadere, Peter, 236
"Book of the Customs of the Empire of Romania," 221
Botany: and agriculture, xli; and environmental evolution, 4–5; and pollen studies, 14–16, *17*, *19*, 71, 287, 288; and PRAP study, 3, 14–20; and vegetation history, 11, 14–20
Bouka: electromagnetic investigation of, 207–208; and geophysicists, 12, 207; loomweights from, *208*; magnetometric map of, *207*; photograph of, *206*; villa site of, 191, 205–209
Bouleuterion, 27
Bourkanos, 211
Brigands, 251
Bronze Age: Aigaleon Mountains as political border during, xxxiii; archaeological investigations emphasizing, 23–24, 26, 27, 30, 35, 39, 41; and interdisciplinary study, 35; Linear B archive at Knossos, 113; and Nichoria, 140; and Palace of Nestor discovery, xxxvi, 23; and perfumed oil, 109; political boundaries during, 111; in Pylos area, xxii; Pylos as toponym in, xx, 125; tholos tombs of, 27–28, 37–38, 199. *See also* Early Bronze Age; Late Bronze Age; Middle Bronze Age; Mycenaean Period
Bronze figurine, from Apollo Korythos shrine, *29*
Bronze industry: curved strip of bronze, *95*; and Linear B tablets, 89, 92–94; in Nichoria, 143; and Palace

INDEX

323

of Nestor administration, 114, 130;
widespread nature of, 130–131
Bronze statues, 163
Bronze votive statuette of bull, *152*
Bubonic plague, 212
Bucharest, 246
Byron, Lord, 248–249, 267
Byzantine Period: Byzantine lamp, *224*; and Church of Saints Constantine and Helen, 280; and First Ottoman Period, 227; historical sources of, 212, 273; in Messenia, 211–212. *See also* Early Byzantine Period; Late Byzantine Period; Middle Byzantine Period
Byzantium, 211, 290

Cambrian, 268
Cambridge-Bradford project, 159
Canning, Stratford, 257
Casola, Canon Pietro, 238
Cassan Agà, 262
Castellan, A. L., 250–252
Catalans, 224, 225
Catherine the Great (empress of Russia), 246
Cave of Nestor, 1, 26, 60–61, *61*
Ceos, 159
Ceramics. *See* Pottery
Chadwick, John, 40
Chaeronea, Battle of, 182
Chamber tombs: of Bronze Age, 199; and erosion, 8, *9*; and Marinatos, 48; and Palace of Nestor destruction, 78; of Volimidia, 35, 60, 77, 78, 200, 203, *203*
Chariot industry, 87, 89, 94, 95–96
Chasan-Agà, 262
Chasánaga, 262
Chochieva, Dodo, 16
Christianity: and First Ottoman Period, 227; influence of, 212–214; in Methoni, 237; and Second Ottoman Period, 245

Chronicle of the Morea, 220
City-states, 154
Civic authority, 93
Classical Period: archaeological investigations of, 41; and Athens, 129; and Coryphasion, 61; environmental changes during, 6–7; gods of, 89; in Messenia, 148; and Messenian identity, 289; and Middle Byzantine church construction, 216–217, *219*; and modern Greek nationality, xxxix; and neoclassical style, 183; perfumed-oil industry in, 106; pottery of, 278; and PRAP, 159–160; and Pylos as toponym, xx, 113; settlement patterns in, 159–160, 162, 299, *300*; and Spartan society, 155. *See also* Late Classical Period
Cleopatra VII, Queen of Egypt, 184
Clepsydra spring, 187, 188
Climatic shifts, 14
Coarse wares, 165, 240
Codrington, Sir Edward, 256, 257, 259, 267–269, *270*, 271
Computers, 298–301
Constantine V Kopronymos, 215
Constantine VII Porphyrogenitus, 211, 215
Constantine XI Palaiologos, 225
Constantinople, xxxiv, 211, 220, 226
Cooking ware, 240
Corcyra, 171, 173. *See also* Corfu
Corfu, 171, 225, 248
Corinth: and Achaean War, 184; and Greek War of Independence, 254; Middle Byzantine Nichoria compared to, 218; pottery of, 242; refounding of, 185; and Second Ottoman Period, 247–248, *248*; Slavic occupation of, 215
Corinthia, 45, 153
Coryphasion: and Late Classical Period, 205; and Mycenaean Period, 62; Pausanias on, 190; and Pelopon-

nesian War, 172–173, *175*; photograph of, *146*; and Pylos as toponym, xx, 113; and Schliemann, 26, 61; and Sparta, 183; tourists' interest in, 25. *See also* Cave of Nestor; Palaionavarino
Council of Chalcedon, 212
Cremidi, 229–233
Crete, 33, 47, 88, 234
Cultural homogeneity, xxxix–xl
Cycladic Islands, 25
Cyparissia (formerly Arcadia): Eudochios' inscription in, 212; Pausanias on, 190; as perioikic town, 156, 160; and Second Ottoman Period, 249; and Sparta, 183; and St. Nikon, 216; in *Synekdemos*, 211; as town of Messenia, 1; travelers' descriptions of, 25
Cyparissia Valley, 129

Damophon of Messene, 183, *184*, 186–187
Damos, 92–93, 132
Dark Age (1060–700 B.C.): archaeological sites of, 149; and burial practices, 78; and Englianos Ridge, 97; and fortification wall, 56; literacy during, 148; in Messenia, 147–151; in Nichoria, 100, 150; and Palace of Nestor ruins, 97–100, *98*, *99*; tholos tombs in, 149, *150*, *151*
Dark Ages (600–900 A.D.), 215
Deforestation, 5–6, 14
Demosthenes, 171–173, 174, 182
De Rigny, Count (Henri-Daniel Gaultier), 259, 269
Despoina, 183
De thematibus (Constantine VII Porphyrogenitus), 215
Dialiskari: chronological range of site, 193–194; Column House at, *194*; and computer databases, 298; and Early Christian Period, 214; geophysicists' study of, 12, 197–198; and local Messenian historians, 294, 296; photograph of, *178*; plan of, *193*; pottery of, 298, 299; and Roman influence, 212; Roman mosaic at, *195*; sherd density at, *196*; and Valmin, 32–33, 294; villa site of, 191, 192–198
Dikaios, Grigorios, 256–257
Dodwell, Edward, 25
Dubrovnik, 253
Dye materials, 94, 106, 131

Early Bronze Age: archaeological sites of, 284; and Palace of Nestor administration, 67; and Tragana, 65; and Voidokoilia, 62–63
Early Byzantine Period: and coastal settlements, 218; in Messenia, 212–214; in Nichoria, 217. *See also* Late Roman Period
Early Christian Period, 213–214
Early Hellenistic Period, 159, 160
Early Iron Age, 149–150, 167–170. *See also* Dark Age
Early Modern Period, 223, 263, 266
Earthquakes: churches damaged by, 216, 217; and Dialiskari, 214; in Early Byzantine Period, 212, 213; and preservation, 281; in Sparta, 157
Eastern Roman empire, 245
Egypt, 101, 106, 254, 257–259, 269
Elea, xx, 190, 289
Electromagnetic investigation, 207–208
Elis, 149. *See also* Elea
Elite class: and flax, 130; and Hasanaga, 263; in Nichoria, 127, 169; Phanariot elite of Istanbul, 246; and pottery, 163, 165–166, 239; and Roman taxation, 191; and tholos tombs, 60, 68, 77, 78, 125–127, 132, 140; and tumuli, 125; and valuable goods, 131

Elliniko, 128–129. *See also* Mouriatada

Englianos Ridge: chamber tombs located on, 8, *9*; and erosion, 6; fortification wall around, 67–68, 126; and Hasanaga, 263; and Mycenean centers, 33, 35, 63, 67, 68; and Palace of Nestor, xxxv, xxxvi, 42, 44, 53, 55, 122, 123, 126; after Palace of Nestor destruction, 97–100, 149; photographs of, *xxxv*, *3*; settlement patterns on, 58–59; tholos tombs of, 78, 126, 149, *150*; tomb sites of, 75

Environment: and agriculture, 5–7; and erosion, xli, 8, 9, *9*; evolution of, 1–5, 9, 10, 11; geographical features of, 1; and human land use, xxi–xxii, xli, 3, 14; and landslide near Palace of Nestor, *xlvi*; and Mycenaean civilization, 5–6; natural resources, 2–3, 9, 289; of Nichoria, 140, 144; and preservation, 281; and rivers, 4–5; and vegetation history, 11, 14–20

Epaminondas: and archaeological investigations, 23; and Asclepiea, 188; and Battle of Leuctra, 158, 179; and founding of Megalopolis, 180; and Messene, xxix, 179, 186–187; sculpture of, 187

Erana, 32–33, 192, 198

Erosion: and environmental changes, xli, 8, *9*; and Hasanaga, 263; of Palaeolithic site, *282*; and soil scientists, 12–13; and surface survey, 286; and vegetation history, 14

Études topographiques sur la Messenie ancienne (Valmin), 31, 33

Eudochios, 212

Euripides, 155, 185

Europe: and Battle of Navarino, 258, 267; and economic system, 245; Greek nostalgia of, 24–25; and Mediterranean balance of power, 257; and Second Ottoman Period, 246, 253

European Community, xliii, 290

European plates, 1–2

Eurotas Plain, 154

Evans, Arthur, 33

Excavations at Nichora in Southwest Greece (McDonald and Rapp), 40–41

Expédition scientifique de Morée: archaeological investigations of, 25–26, 259, 261; and Battle of Navarino, 258–259; and Hasanaga, 262; interdisciplinary methods of, 39; and Second Ottoman Period, 251–252

Faber, Felix, 237–238

Filiatra, 216, 273

Fine wares, 165, 198, 205, 240, 298

First Messenian War, 153–154

First Ottoman Period, 214, 226, 273, 280

Five Rivers Survey, 160–161, 191

Flanders, 225

Flax production, 130, 143–144

Floka, 249

Floodplains, 10

Florence, 225, 229

Fourth Crusade, 212, 220

France: and Battle of Navarino, 256, 259, 268, 269, 271; and economic system, 245; and Greek War of Independence, 257; and Second Ottoman Period, 253; and Treaty of London, 267

Frankish Morea: feudal system in, 221–223; and Messenian identity, 289; and Villehardouin, 219–220; weakening of, 223–225

Franks, 212, 220

Further Province: boundary of, 114; bronze industry in, 93; coastline of, 117; flax production in, 143; four sectors of, 124; Hither Province compared to, 119–120, 122, 128; Hither Province links of, 129, 138; incorporation of, in Palace of Nestor administration, 128; Leuktron as capital of, 122, 123; and Linear B tablets, 113–114; map of, *121*; Nichoria as subcapital of, 40, 128, 142, 167; place-name list of, 117, 119–120, *120*, 122, 125, 128

Gargaliani: in Modern Period, 273; and PRAP study, 275, 276–277; and Second Ottoman Period, 249, 250, 251, 252–253; size of, 135; as town of Messenia, 1. See also Ordines
Gargaliani-Lefki uplands, 275–280, *276*, 284
Gaultier, Henri-Daniel (Count de Rigny), 259, 269
Gell, Sir William, 25, 250, 252–254, *253*, 262
Genoa, 225, 226
Geoarchaeology, 11
Geochemistry, 11
Geochronology, 11
Geoelectrical testing, 198
Geoffrey II (son of Villehardouin), 223
Geology, xli, 3
Geometric Period, 40, 97, 99
Geomorphology, 3, 11, 134–135, 286, 302
Geophysics: and Bouka, 12, 207; and buried walls near Palace of Nestor, 58; and Dialiskari, 12, 197–198; and Nichoria, 140; and PRAP study, 3, 11–12, *12*
German Archaeological Institute, 61
Gla, 73
Gothic architecture, 220, *221*, 222
Gothic raids, 212–213
Governmental administration. *See* Palace of Nestor administration
Gradiometers, 207, 208
Grave Circle, 60, 76, 126

Great Britain: and Athens/Sparta naval battle, 26; and Battle of Navarino, 256, 259, 268, 269, 271; and economic system, 245; and Greek war for independence, xxxvii, 257; and Second Ottoman Period, 253; and Treaty of London, 267
Greece: agriculture in, 5; archaeological resources of, 280–283; economic system of, 245; and European Community, xliii; European nostalgia for, 24–25; expatriate Greek communities, 246; and fortification walls, 56; map of, *xxi*; and Messenian identity, 290; modern Greek state, xxxix–xl, 254, 273; perfumed oil used in, 101; regional studies of, xli–xliii; and Second Ottoman Period, 245–246; slavery in, 155–156; town/countryside interdependence, 54–55; trade of, 246; travelers to, 25; war for independence from Ottoman empire, xxxvii, 254–261
Greek Archaeological Service, 40, 44, 48, 227
Greek Archaeological Society, 26, 28
Greek language, and Linear B tablets, 38, 45–46, 88
Greek War of Independence (1821–1829): and Pylos, 172; in Second Ottoman Period, 245, 254–261. *See also* Navarino, Battle of
Grimani, Francesco, 228
Grisi, 225
Gritti, Domenico, 228
Grundy, G. Beardoe, 26–27, 28, 37
Guide to Greece (Pausanias), xxxvii
Gypsies, 234, 236

Habicht, Christian, 186
Hamilton, Captain, 268
Handrinou, 249
Harakopeio, 47
Haratsari, 63, 64, 68, 76

Harrison, A. B., *164*
Hasanaga (also Cassan Aga; Chasan-Aga; Chasánaga), 249, 250, 252, 262–266, *264*
Hasan Paşa, Cezayirli, 265
Hasan Paşa tower, 265, *265*
Heiden, Longuine Petrovitch, 269
Hellenistic Period: and Achaean War, 184; and Actium, 184–185; alliances/betrayals of, 182; and Coryphasion, 205; and Dialiskari, 193; pottery of, 280; settlement patterns of, 162; and tomb cult, 200, *201*, 203. See also Early Hellenistic Period
Helots: agricultural role of, 155–156, 158–159; and Athens, 157; and founding of Messene, 180; harsh treatment of, 156; and Peloponnesian War, 176; revolts of, 157–158, 179; slaves distinguished from, 156; Spartan control methods for, 160–162, 288; and Sparta's rule, xxxi, 148, 155, 157
Heraklidai, 149
Herodotos, 157
Herulian invasions, 212
Hill, Bert Hodge, 44
Hill, Ida, 44
Hill of Wisdom, 236
Historical sources: biases of, xxxv–xxxvii; of Byzantine Period, 212, 273; and cultural homogeneity, xl; from Italy, 212, 229; lack of, 148; Leake as, xxxvii–xxxviii; and Modern Period, 273–274; native Messenian sources, xxxv, xl, 293–297, 303; PRAP's use of, xl–xli; for Spartan conquest, 152–153, 191; of Venice, 273
History of Messenia, A (Kefalas), 292
Hither Province: boundary of, 114; bronze industry in, 93; coastline of, 117; Further Province compared to, 119–120, 122, 128; Further Province links of, 129, 138; and Linear B tablets, 113–114, *119*; map of, *121*; and Nichoria, 138; place-name list of, 117, 119–120, *119*, *120*, 122, 125; and power relations with Palace of Nestor, 128; Pylos's location in, 117
Holland, 245, 253
Holy Apostles Church, 216
Holy Archangel, castle of the, 229. See also Arhangelos
Holy Land, 211, 225, 234
Homer: and Greeks' cultural homogeneity, xxxix–xl; and King Nestor, 25; and Marinatos, 48; Messenian visit in *Odyssey*, xxxv–xxxvi, 43; and oil with textiles, 109; Pausanias on, 190; and perfumed oil, 109; and Pharae, 26; and Sandy Pylos as term, xx; and Schliemann, 25–26; seafaring trade descriptions of, 74; and Trojan War, 26; and *wanax*, 90
Hope Simpson, Richard, 39, 40, 284
Hora: in Frankish Morea, 223; and Palace of Nestor, xxxvi, 274, 275; and PRAP study, xli, 274–275, 292, 304; and prehistoric communities, 59; Roman influence in, 212; and Second Ottoman Period, 251; as town of Messenia, 1. See also Katavothra cave; Kato Rouga; Kefalovryso; Kokkevis family mansion; Ligoudista; Museum of Hora; Society of the Friends of Antiquities of Hora; Tsifliki; Volimidia
Hristianou, 216, 218
Hristianoupolis, 216
Hristofilopoulos, Haralambos, 44, 63
Hrysospiliotissa church, 216
Human land use: and deforestation, 5–6, 14; and human cultures, xxi–xxii, xli, 3, 14; and pollen studies, 16; and Selas River diversion, 69. See also Agriculture
Hydra island, 257, 268

Hydroengineering, 11, 13, 73–74
Hypocaust, 193, 194, *196*, 198, 214

Iakovatos, Ilias Zervos, 293
Ibrahim Paşa, 254, 256–259, 268–269
Ice Age, 4–5
Iklaina, 48
Iliad (Homer), 90, 109, 190
Industrialization, xlii, 283
Infrared aerial photography, 40
Innocent III, 223
Institute for Geophysics and Meteorology of the Polytechnical University in Braunschweig, Germany, 207
Internet, 299–300
Ionian islands, 204
Ionian Sea, 69, 71
Islam, 239, 240, 252
Ismail-Zade, Gulia, *17*
Istanbul, xxxiv, 227, 245, 246, 290. *See also* First Ottoman Period; Second Ottoman Period
Italy: historical sources from, 212, 229; and Messenia, 211; and *Rhomaioi*, 185–186; and Second Ottoman Period, 252; tourism of, 290
Ithaca, 149, 168
Itinerary of the Morea (Gell), 250, 262

Janissaries, 227, 248
Jews, 234, 236, 237
John of Messenia, 212

Kakovatos, 77
Kalamata: as capital of Messenia, 1; churches constructed in, 216; fertility of, 185; in Frankish Morea, 223; Greek population of, xxxviii–xxxix; and Nichoria, 139; in Second Ottoman Period, 250, 268; and St. Nikon, 216; and tourism, xlii; and Venice, 227; and Villehardouin, 220. *See also* Pherae
Kalopsana, 126, *127*, 135, 138

Kaloyeropoulos tumulus, 66–67
Karpofora, 139
Katarrahaki, 48
Katavothra cave, 59
Kato Rouga, 275
Kavalaria, 251, 274
Kefalas, Ioannis, 292
Kefalovryso, 59, 214
Keftiu, 59
Kinadon, 158
King: functions of, 84, 92; initiation of, 112; perfume offerings to, 106; and *wanax*, 90, 92, 112
Kleon, 173–174, 176
Kleroi, 156
Knauss, Jost, 13, 73–74
Knolls, 8
Knossos: craftsmen belonging to gods/goddesses in, 92; Linear B archive of, 88, 113; Palace of Nestor administration compared with, 131; and Palace of Nestor discovery, 33; and perfumed-oil industry, 101, *105*, 106; woolen industry at, 93, 130
Kokkevis family mansion, 275
Kopanaki, 161–162, *161*
Koroni: and Battle of Navarino, 259, 261; and First Ottoman Period, 227; fortifications of, 225–226; and Ibrahim Paşa, 256; and Roman Period, 188; and Second Ottoman Period, 249; and St. Nikon, 216; in *Synekdemos*, 211; Turkish attacks on, 225; and University of Minnesota Messenia Expedition, 159; and Venice, 24, 220, 225, 234. *See also* Petalidi
Korres, George: archaeological excavation of, 41, 48; and Myrsinohori, 66–67; and Routsi, 77; and tomb cult, 203; and tombs, 75; and Viglitsa, 65; and Voidokoilia, 62; and Voidokoilia tholos tomb, 200; and Volimidia, 60

INDEX

Koryfasion (formerly Osmanaga): and Beylerbey, 63; and Hasanaga, 265; size of, 135; and tholos tombs, 43–44, 60; tomb sites of, 75
Koukounara, 38, 39
Kourouniotis, Konstantinos: and Blegen, 35, 42; and Haratsari, 63, 64, 76; and Mycenaean settlements, 33; and tholos tombs, 43–44; and tombs, 75
Koutsouveri, 135, *136*
Kraft, John, 69
Kremydia, 229, *230*
Krypteia, 157
Kuhnke, Falko, 11

Laconia: boundary of, xxxiv, 111, 148; in Dark Age, 149; in Frankish Morea, 220; kleroi not in, 156; and Nichoria, 168–169; settlement patterns of, 159; and Spartan society, 155, 156. *See also* Sparta
Land shortages, 154–155
Land tenure, 90, 92–93, 229–233
Langsam, Julia, *45*
Langsam, Walter, *45*
Late Bronze Age: and Marinatos, 47, 48; and Myrsinohori, 37–38; and Nichoria, 149, 167; and perfumed oil, 109; and Pylos's fortification wall, 56, 68; scholars' interest in, 38; and Selas River diversion, 69–74; and University of Minnesota Messenia Expedition, 283. *See also* Late Helladic I; Late Helladic IIIA; Late Helladic IIIB; Late Helladic IIIC; Mycenaean Period
Late Byzantine Period, 223, 225, 233
Late Classical Period, 200, *201*, 203, 205, 280
Late Helladic I: and Routsi, 66; and tholos tombs, 125–126, 127, 200; and Tragana, 65; and Voidokoilia, 62; and Volimidia, 59–60

Late Helladic IIIA: monumental structures of, 126; and Nichoria, 66, 127, 128; and tholos tombs, 126, 127
Late Helladic IIIB: archaeological sites of, 134; and Mouriatada, 129; and Nichoria, 127; and Palace of Nestor construction, 86, 126, 128; and Palace of Nestor destruction, 82, 97, 126; and Palace of Nestor's administrational reach, 125, 126; settlement sites' size, 123; and tholos tombs, 131–132
Late Helladic IIIC, 149
Late Neolithic Period, 59
Late Roman Period: and coastal settlements, 218; and Dialiskari, 191, 193, 298, 299; and Nichoria, 217. *See also* Early Byzantine Period
Leake, William, xxxvii–xxxviii, 32, 250
Leather-working, 94, 169
Lefkas, 173
Lefki, 275
Leghorn, 246
Leonidas (king of Sparta), 44
Leuctra, Battle of, 158, 179
Leuktron, 122–125, *124*, 130
Ligoudista, 223, 249, 251, 274, 275
Linear A script, 88
Linear B tablets: administrative purpose of writing, 89–90; and Aigaleon Ridge boundary, 111; and animal husbandry, 136; and archaeological investigations, 23–24; and Bennett, 38–39; and Greek language, 38, 45–46, 88; and industries, 93–96; interdisciplinary approach to, 287–288; and Koukounara, 38; and land tenure, 90, 92–93; and Late Helladic IIIA, 126; and Mycenaean industry, 89; and Nichoria, 40, 143, 167; nodule Wr 1480, *91*; number of place names listed in, 134; and perfumed-oil industry, 89, 90, 93, 101, 103, 104, *104*, 106, *108*;

photographs of, *34*, *43*, *91*; and PRAP study, xli; as prehistoric archives, xxii, xxxvi; and Pylos as toponym, 113; and ritual feasting, 87; structure of, *118*; toponyms of, 39; and University of Minnesota Messenia Expedition, 283; writing system of, 88. *See also* Palace of Nestor administration
Literacy, 89, 148
Literary evidence: and Christian conversion, 212; and Dark Age, 147; and Erana, 192; interpretation of, 289; and Marinatos, 47–48; of settlement patterns, 160; and Sparta's dominance of Messenia, 158
Lolos, Yannos, 64
London, Treaty of, 267
Loomweights, from Bouka, *208*
Lycosura, 183, *184*

Macchia, 7
Macedon, 182
Magnetometry, 63, 198, *207*
Maison, Nicolos Joseph, 259, 261
Malthi, 30, *31*, 32, *32*, 44, 56, 68
Mani, 245, 251
Maniaki, 249, 256
Manticori, 225
Mantinea, 161
Mapping, 299–301
Marathon, 157
Marathoupolis, 192
Marble statues, 163
Marinatos, Spyridon: archeological investigations of, 23; bust of, 49, *49*, 297; death of, 41; and Hora, 274; Katavothra cave, 59; and Koukounara, 38; in Pylos, 47–50; and Routsi, 77; and tombs, 75; and Tragana excavation, 65; and Voidokoilia, 62–63; and Voidokoilia tholos tomb, 27; and Volimidia, 59–60; and Volimidia chamber tombs, 35, 77, 200

Marseilles, 246
Maryeli, 135, *136*, 138, 249
Mavromati, 188
McDonald, William A.: and archaeological sites, 284; and Beylerbey, 63; and Nichoria, 40–41, 139–140; and Palace of Nestor location, 44; surface studies of, 39, 40; and University of Minnesota Messenia Expedition, 139
Mediterranean region: empires dominant in, 290; map of, *ii*; Messenia's place in, *ii*, 289; prehistory and history of, xxiii
Megalopolis, 180
Mehmet the Conqueror, 245
Messene: archaeological excavation of, 26, 28, 30, 39, 41, 187–188; and Athens, 182; Christian influence in, 213; enceinte walling system of, 180, *181*; and Epaminondas, xxix, 179, 186–187; as federal capital, xxx; foundation of, 153, 179–180, 182, 186, 289; Gothic raids in, 212–213; Mt. Ithome associated with, 132; Oikonomos' investigations of, 27; Pausanias on, 186–187; in Roman Period, 186; in Second Ottoman Period, 250; in *Synekdemos*, 211; travelers' descriptions of, 25
Messenia: allies of, 153; coast of, *xxxiv*; in Early Byzantine Period, 212–214; fertility of, 155, 185, 289; geographical boundaries of, xxx–xxxi, 1, 111, 289; identity of, xxix, xxxvii, 289–291, 292–295; isolation of, 9; landscape of, xxix–xxxiv; local historians of, 293–297, 303; maps of, *xxxii*, *xxxiii*, *121*; within Mediterranean region, *ii*, 289; and Messenia/Sparta border, xxxi; and Peloponnesian War, 171; and Philip II of Macedon, 182; postliberation relations with Sparta, 182, 186; Spartan conquest

INDEX

of, 151–155, 204; Spartan domination of, 111, 148, 152, 162, 170, 191, 288; travelers' view of, xxxiv–xxxix; wars of, 152–153. *See also* specific archaeological periods
Messenian Gulf, 154
Metal shield boss, *169*
Metallurgy, 169, *169*
Metamorfosis, 65, 223. *See also* Skarminga
Metaxada, 135
Metaxada Valley, 126, *127*, 138
Methoni: archeological investigations of, 24; and Battle of Navarino, 259; Christian burial in, 214; engraving of, *235*; and First Ottoman Period, 227; fortifications of, *210*, 225–226, 234, *235*; and Ibrahim Paşa, 256; in Middle Byzantine Period, 218–219; and Peloponnesian War, 171; as perioikic town, 156, 160; in Roman Period, 188; and Second Ottoman Period, 247, 249; and Sparta, 154; and St. Nikon, 216; in *Synekdemos*, 211; and trade, 219, 234, 236–237; travelers' descriptions of, 234, 236–238; Turkish attacks on, 225; and Venice, 24, 219, 220, 223, 225, 234–238
Mezana/Messana, 132–133
Michiel, Domenico, 219
Michiel, Marin, 228
Micropaleontology, 11
Middle Ages. *See* Dark Ages (600–900 A.D.); Early Byzantine Period; First Ottoman Period; Frankish Morea; Middle Byzantine Period; Venice
Middle Bronze Age: and Englianos Ridge fortification wall, 68; and Malthi, *32*; and Palace of Nestor construction, 75, 99; settlement at Palace of Nestor site, 81. *See also* Middle Helladic Period

Middle Byzantine Period: agriculture in, 216, 219; church construction in, 216–217; domestic architecture in, 217–218; environmental changes during, 7; in Messenia, 215–219; and Nichoria, 140; piracy in, 218–219; stability of, 216–217
Middle Helladic Period: and Osmanaga Tholos, 64; settlements of, 58, 135–136; and Tragana, 65; and tumuli construction, 125, 126, 200
Midea, 56
Minetto, Giacomo, 248
Minoan culture, 88, 89
Modern Period: agriculture in, 273; and Messenian historical sources, 273–274; and Middle Byzantine church construction, 216–217. *See also* Early Modern Period
Monemvasia, 220, 249
Monomitos: inscription of, *xxviii*, xxix; and Messenian landscape, xxxiii; and Messenia/Sparta border, xxxi, 111; and Messenia/Sparta rivalry, 133
Morea: and First Ottoman Period, 226–227; and Muhammad Ali, 246; and Niccolò Acciaiuoli, 229; and Second Ottoman Period, 245, 249; and Venice, 225–228. *See also* Frankish Morea; Messenia
Mosaic tesserae, 194
Most Serene Republic of Venice. *See* Venice
Mothone, 188. *See also* Methoni
Mouriatada, 44, 48, 128–129
Mt. Aigaleon, xxxiii, *xxxv*, *110*, *260*
Mt. Eira, 154, 180
Mt. Ithome: and First Messenian War, 153–154; and Gothic raids, 213; Messene associated with, 132, 180; and Philip V of Macedon, 184; photograph of, *158, 181*; prominence of, xxxiii; strategic importance of, 182–183; and Third Messenian War, 157

Mt. Lykodimos, 114, *115*
Mt. Maglavas, 114, *115*
Mt. Taygetus, border of, xxxi
Muhammad Ali, 246, 254, 256, 258, 259
Museum of Hora, 22, *49*, 50
Mustafa Paşa, 293
Mycenae: destruction of, 88; fortification wall of, 56, 87; houses burned at, 87; hydraulic systems of, 73; Palace of Nestor compared to, 135; Royal Tombs of, 27; and Schliemann, 25, 42, 75; settlement plan of, 56; Shaft Graves of, 65–66; stirrup jars from, 106
Mycenaean Period: and Blegen, 33, 35, 42; chamber tombs of, 8, 35; and environmental changes, 5–6; and erosion, 8; gods of, 89, 92; and Koukounara, 38; literacy during, 89; and Messenian identity, 290; and Mycenaean sites, 40, 44–45, 55, 58–67; and Palace of Nestor administration, 67; and perfumed oil, 109; and Schliemann, 26; tholos tombs of, 30, 75–78; near Tragana tholoi, 37. *See also* Late Bronze Age
Mycenaean port basin. *See* Nestor, port of
Myron, 129. *See also* Peristeria
Myrsinohori, 37–38, 65, 66, 68, 75, 214. *See also* Routsi
Mystra, 223

Naples, 225
Narrative of a Journey in the Morea (Gell), 250, 262
National Museum (Athens), 33, 44
Natural sciences, 288, 306
Naupactus, 157, 171, 176
Nauplion (formerly Nauplia), 154, 225, 249, 256
Navarino: and Castellan, 250; and Catherine the Great, 246; church at, 260; in First Ottoman Period, 227; and Pylos, 274; in Second Ottoman Period, 250, 251, 253–254. *See also* Neokastro; Neokastro, Fort of
Navarino, Battle of: effects of, 259, 261; and Europe, 258, 267; and Ibrahim Paşa, 254, 256–259; map of, *270*; misconceptions concerning, 254, 256; monument to, *244*; painting of, *268*; and Second Ottoman Period, 228, 247
Navarino Bay: evolution of, 4, 6; and Greek War of Independence, 254; and Palace of Nestor location, 44, 52; photograph of, *2*, *260*; and Pylos as toponym, xx; salt pans of, 223; and Selas River, 69; unspoiled nature of, 1
Navarino Ridge, 1
Navarino (Zonchio), 225
Navarrese, 226
Neda River valley, xxxi
Negotiatores, 185
Neleus (Nestor's father), xxxvi, 25, 188, 190, 191
Nemea Valley Archaeological Project, 159
Neoclassical sculpture, 183
Neokastro, xx, 227, *247*. *See also* Navarino
Neokastro, Fort of, *172*, 254, 256. *See also* Navarino
Neolithic Period, 5, 59, 62
Nero (emperor of Rome), xxxiv, 185
Nestor, port of, *4*, 64, 69–74, *70*, *72*
Nestor (king of Pylos): and archaeological investigations, 23; and Homer, 25; and interdisciplinary approach, 287; and Nestoreia, 293; and *Odyssey*, xxxv; Pausanias on, 190, 191; poetic resonance of, 211. *See also* Palace of Nestor
New Navarino, 227
Niccolò Frescobaldi, Leonardo di, 236, 237

INDEX

333

Nicholas the Grammarian, 215
Nicholas II (Frankish prince), 226
Nichoria: archaeological excavation of, 39–41, 160, 217–218; in Dark Age, 100, 150; in Early Iron Age, 149, 167–170; Early Iron Age house of, *168*; in Further Province, 124, 142, 167; and Hither Province, 138; megaron of, 127; metal shield boss from, *169*; Mycenaean House of, *142*; Mycenaean street in, *141*; and Palace of Nestor, 141–142; and Palace of Nestor administration, 127–128, 142; road of, 128, *137*, 138, 144; in Roman Period, 191; site of, 139; size of, 127–128; tholos tombs of, 66, 127, 140, 141, *143*, 168; and tomb cult, 199; University of Minnesota Messenia Expedition excavation of, 139–144, 147, 149; view from, *140*
Nicopolis, 185
Nikias, 174
Nikon, Saint, 211, 216

Odyssey (Homer), xxxv–xxxvi, 43, 90
Oikonomos, Yioryios, 27, 28, 30, 33, 39
Old Navarino, 223, 226
Olive oil, 87, 99, 101, 104, 109
Olive trees: and archaeological fieldwork, 302; erosion measured with, 8; in Middle Byzantine Period, 216; in Mycenaean Period, 6; and pollen studies, 288; during Spartan control, 7
Olympia, 149, 150, 176, 183, 185, 215
Ordines, 12, 135, 250. *See also* Gargaliani
Orlandos, Anastasios, 39, 41, 187
Orlov, Alexei, 246
Orlov, Fedor, 246
Orthodox church, 246, 252
Osmanaga. *See* Koryfasion
Osmanaga Lagoon: evolution of, 4, 5, 6; as geographical feature, 1; photograph of, *2*; pollen cores from, *17*, *19*, 71; sediments from, 5, 6, 7; and Selas River diversion, 69, 74
Osmanaga Tholos, 64. *See also* Haratsari
Ottoman Periods. *See* First Ottoman Period; Second Ottoman Period
Oxford University, 300

Pagan sites, 216
Pagan structures, 214
Palace of Minos, 33. *See also* Knossos
Palace of Nestor: and agriculture, 136; and Aigaleon Mountains as political border, xxxiii; archives room of, 53, 85; bathtub in Room 43, *86*; Blegen's discovery of, xxxvi, 33, 35, 42–46, 81, 296; Blegen's excavation of, 23, 40; and burial customs development, 75; citadel of, 55–58; Court 3 of, 82, *83*; Court 88 of, *99*; dating of, 126; dependencies of, 67–68; destruction of, 67, 78, 88, 97, 126, 133, 144, 148; and environmental evolution, 9; and erosion, 8; and feasting, 84, 87–88; fortification wall of, 81; geophysicists' study of, 12, *12*; and Greek-American collaboration, 35, 47; and Hora, 274, 275; Knossos administration compared with, 131; landslide near, *xlvi*; Main Building of, 81–88; megaron of, 53, *80*, 82–85, 106, 112; and Nichoria, 141–142; Northeast Workshop of, 87, 90, 94–96, 97, 99; Pantry 19, 84, *85*; and pantry access, 87–88; photograph of site, *xxxv*, *52*, *54*; plan of, *36*, *82*; political territory of, 111–112, 288; prehistoric communities near, 58–67; and Pylos as toponym, xx, 113; remodeling of, 86–88; Room 5 of, 83, 84, *84*; ruins of, in Dark Age, 97–100, *98*, *99*; and Schliemann, 26; settlement surrounding, 135; South-

western Building, 81, 84, 97; state apartments of, 53; storerooms of, 53, *80*, 86, 87, 88, *107*; and tourism, 53–55; and University of Minnesota Messenia Expedition, 283; Wine Magazine, 99. *See also* Linear B tablets; Nestor (king of Pylos)

Palace of Nestor administration: archaeological evidence of, 67; and boundaries, 114; and bronze industry, 114, 130; and *damos*, 92–93, 132; domination of sites within territory, 134; and fiscal grouping of place names, 119–120, *120*, 122, 123, 128; and fixed order of place names, 114, 116–117, *118*, 126, 135; and geographical structure, 114, 116–117, 122, 125; and industries, 93–96, 130; and king's function, 84, 92; and megaron, 85; and Messenian identity, 290; and Nichoria, 127–128, 142–143; and political territory integration, 112; and PRAP, 134–138; and ritual feasting, 131; settlement hierarchy of, 123–126, 135–138; and writing's administrative purpose, 89–90. *See also* Further Province; Hither Province; Linear B tablets; Taxation

Palace of Nestor at Pylos in Western Messenia, The (Blegen), 40

Palaeolithic Period, 277, 281, *282*, 284

Palaiohoria, 48

Palaionavarino, *2*, 60, *146*, *172*. *See also* Cave of Nestor, Coryphasion

Palaipylos, 77, 274

Palynology, 11, 14–18, *17*, *19*, 71, 287, 288

Pamisos River valley: agriculture in, xxxix; as Dark Age site, 149; ethnicity of population in, xxxviii; fertility of, xxxi; and Messenian identity, 289; and Nichoria, 139; photograph of, *140*; Spartan control of, 154, 156; and University of Minnesota Messenia Expedition, 159

Panitsa, 252

Papaflessas. *See* Dikaios, Grigorios

Papoulia, 35, *37*

Parnassos, 294

Pashalopoulos, Anastasios, 253

Patras, 185, 215, 249

Pausanias: and Apollo Korythos shrine, 28; and archaeological investigations, 24; and Artemis Limnatis, 186; bias of, xxxvii; and Cave of Nestor, 60; and Coryphasion, 25; on helots, 156; on Messene, 179–180, 186–187; and Messene excavation, 26; and Messenian history, 147, 292, 293; on Messenian wars, 153–154; PRAP study compared to, 288; on Roman Period cities, 188, 190–191; and Spartan/Messenian hostilities, 150; and Tomb of Thrasymedes, 27, 62, 190, 200, 204

Peloponnese: and fortification walls, 56; Fourth Crusade invasion of, 212; map of, *xxx*; and Messenian identity, 289; Nemea Valley Archaeological Project of, 159; Ottoman rule of, xxxviii; and Philip V of Macedon, 182–183; Pylos as toponym in, 113; Roman colonists in, xxix; Slavic occupation of, 215

Peloponnesian War, 157, 171–176, *175*

Perfumed-oil industry: description of, 101, 103–104; and Knossos tablets, *105*, 106; and Linear B tablets, 89, 90, 93, 101, 103, 104, *104*, 106–107, *108*; and olive cultivation, 288; stirrup jars for, 87, 101, *102*, *103*, *105*, 106, 109; storerooms for, 86, 106, *107*; and trade, 131

Perikles, 44

Perioikoi, xxxi, 155, 160, 162

Peristeria: beehive tombs of, 48; fortifications of, 68; and Hora, 275; and Mouriatada's foundation, 129;

INDEX

335

Mycenaean sites of, 44, 47; tholos tombs of, 77, 129
Pernice, Erich, 26, 31
Petalidi, 139
Peter of Argos, 216
Petrohori, 44, 125–126. *See also* Voidokoilia
Phanariot elite, 246
Pharae, xxxvi, 26, 153. *See also* Kalamata
Philip II (king of Macedon), 182
Philip V (king of Macedon), 182–184
Phrygana, 7
Physical science, 3–4, 10–13
Pine forests, 5–6, 18, 20
Pirates: and coastal settlements, 214, 218–219; and Codrington, 267; in Second Ottoman Period, 246, 251, 252; and Venice, 225
Plague: in Athens, 171; Black Death, 224, 226; in Dark Ages, 215; in Early Byzantine Period, 212; and Methoni's fortifications, 226
Plate movements, 1–2, 9
Plato, 157
Pleistocene Era, 2
Politics (Aristotle), 155
Pollen studies, 11, 14–18, *17*, *19*, 71, 287, 288
Polychares, 150
Port of Palace of Nestor. *See* Nestor, port of
Portes, 63, 64, 76
Poseidon temple, 40
Post, Lennart von, 16
Potnia (goddess), 94, 106
Pottery: and archaeological fieldwork, 305, *305*; of Archaic Period, 278; and Bouka, 205–209, *208*; Byzantine sgraffito ware, 239–242, *240*, *241*; chronology of, 45, 163, 165, 227, 239; of Classical Period, 278; and computer databases, 298–299; and Dialiskari, 192, *196*, 198; of Early Bronze Period, 277; and First Ottoman Period, 227; of Hasanaga, 263; of Late Classical Period, 280; of Mycenaean Period, 44, 278; in Nichoria, 167, 168–170; photographs of, *164*; and PRAP study, 276; and Slavic occupation, 215; and tomb cult, 199; and trade, 163, 165, 166, 209, 218, 239, 242, 298–299; and transport vessels, 165; typology of, 163–166. *See also* African Red Slip ware; Amphoras; Coarse wares; Cooking ware; Fine wares; Stirrup jars
Pouqueville, François, 23
PRAP (Pylos Regional Archaeological Project): and agricultural resources, xxxi; Archaic and Classical site identification, 159–160; and Bouka, 191, 205, 207; and Byzantine sgraffito ware, 241–242; composition of, xxii; computer use by, 298–301; and Dialiskari, 191, 192, 197–198; fieldwork of, 23, 274; and Greece as modern nation-state, 273; and Hasanaga, 263; and Hora, xli, 274–275, 292, 304; and integration of information, 287–291; interdisciplinary focus of, 39, 287; and mapping, 299–301, *300*, *301*; and Mycenaean Period, 48; and natural sciences, 287, 288; and Palace of Nestor administration, 134–138; physical scientists of, 3–4, 10–13, 16; purpose of, xx; and Pylos (ancient town), 58; region examined by, *xxxiii*, 41, 127, 275–280, *276*; relationships with Messenians, 274, 291, 292–294, 296–297, 303–304; and reliability of data, 283–284; role of, 280–283; and Romanou, 64; and scientific aids, 40; and Second Ottoman Period, 249, 250; and Selas River, 69–74; and surface survey technique, xl
Priene, 162

Procession fresco with bull, *84*
Profitis Ilias, 62
Propylon, 27
Proti, island of, 251, 252
Protogeometric Period, 40, 88
Psara, island of, 257
Pylos (ancient town): Avarino as Slavic name of, 211, 215; as center of polity, 113, 122, 123, 124; in Dark Age, 149; flax production in, 130; and Peloponnesian War, 173, 176; settlement patterns of, 160; size of, 58; and Sparta, 157, 183; and University of Minnesota Messenia Expedition, 159; work force of, 122. *See also* Coryphasion; Palace of Nestor; Palaionavarino
Pylos (modern town): and Battle of Sphacteria, 26; and Greek War of Independence, 172, 257; and Ibrahim Paşa, 257; map of, *258*; photograph of, *244, 260*; as population center, 1; and Second Ottoman Period, 250; and Sphacteria Island, 60. *See also* Navarino; Neokastro; Neokastro, Fort of
Pylos, as toponym, xx–xxii, 25, 60, 113, 125
Pylos Regional Archaeological Project (PRAP). *See* PRAP

Quarries, 276

Ragusa, 253
Rapp, George R., Jr., 40, 69, 139
Rawson, Marian, *45*
Regional archaeology: and ancient political territory, 112; and Blegen, 35; and Greek countryside, 159; physical scientist's role in, 10–13; and preservation, 283; and University of Minnesota Messenia Expedition, 139, 159. *See also* PRAP; Surface survey
Relative chronologies, 165

Religious authority: and Linear B tablets, 92–93, 94; in Second Ottoman Period, 252
Religious offerings/practices: and Christian monuments, 212–214; and founding of Messene, 179–180; in Frankish Morea, 220; and Linear B tablets, 90, 92; in Messene, 186–188; in Middle Byzantine Period, 216–217; perfumed oil as, 101, 106; and pottery, 239; and sinkhole, 278, 280; and tomb cult, 199–204. *See also* specific churches
Remote sensing, 207, 287. *See also* Geoelectrical testing; Geophysics; Gradiometers; Infrared aerial photography; Magnetometry; Resistivity meter
Renier, Girolamo, 228
Resistivity meter, 40
Rhomaioi, 185–186
Rizomylos, 124, 127, 167. *See also* Nichoria
Roman baths, 193, *196*, 198, 212, 214
Roman mosaic, *195*
Roman Period: and archaeological investigations, 24; and Aristomenes cult, 204; and Church of Saints Constantine and Helen, 279; and coastal settlement, 191, 214; and Dialiskari, 192–198; environmental changes during, 6–7; and Messene, 186–188; Messenia as part of Roman empire, 185, 290; and Messenian identity, 290; and Middle Byzantine church construction, 217; and Pausanias, 188, 190–191; prosperity of, 185–186; settlement patterns of, 299, *301*; villa sites of, 191. *See also* Late Roman Period
Romanou: environment of, 4; hydrological studies of, 13; as Mycenaean center, 63, 64, 287; and Palace of Nestor location, 44; and PRAP

INDEX

337

study of Dialiskari, 192; in Second Ottoman Period, 249; and Selas River, 69–70, 74
Rome: civil wars of, 184; and Greek identity, xxxvii; "hands-off" rule of, 186; Messenia as province of, xxix–xxx, 183–185; and Messenian taxation, xxxiv, 185; Monomitos as representative of, xxxiii; and Spartan domination of Messenia, 111
Routsi, 48, 60, 65–66, 77, 214. *See also* Myrsinohori
Royal authority, 93
Russia: and Battle of Navarino, 256, 259, 268, 269, 271; and Greek War of Independence, 257; and Second Ottoman Period, 253; and Treaty of London, 267

Saints Constantine and Helen, Church of, 278–280, *279*, 281
Saint Vincent, Bory de, 258–259
Samarina, 216
Schliemann, Heinrich: and Cave of Nestor, 60–61; and Homeric sites, 25–26; and interdisciplinary investigations, 26, 35; and Mycenae, 25, 42, 75
Scribes, 89, 106–109
Sebasteion, 188
Second Messenian War, 153, 154, 157
Second Ottoman Period: character of life in, 249–250; and Church of Saints Constantine and Helen, 280; and Çorlulu Ali Paşa, 247; diplomats of, 252–253; and Expédition scientifique de Morée, 251–252; and Greek War of Independence, 245, 254–261; and Hasanaga, 262, 263, 266; settlement patterns in, 251; and trade, 245–246; and travelers' descriptions, 250–253, 262, 273; and Venice, 228, 247–249, 253. *See also* Navarino, Battle of

Sediments: and archaeological sites, 10; and plant pollen studies, 14–16; and Selas River diversion, 70–71, 73–74; and thermoluminescence dating, 13
Selas River: core sample drilling, *72, 73*; diversion of, 69–74; evolution of, 4; hydrological study of, 13; photograph of, *4*
Serenissima, 219, 227, 289. *See also* Venice
Serres, 242
Shaft Graves, 38, 65–66, 214
Shiramet Paşa, 254
Sicyon, 153
Silk production, xxxix, 220
Sinkhole, 277–278, 280
Skarminga, 223, 227, *240*, 242, 249. *See also* Metamorfosis
Skias, Andreas, 27–28, 31
Sklavohori, 215
Slavery: and Battle of Navarino, 258–259; in Greece, 155–156; in Second Ottoman Period, 248
Slavic settlement, 211
Slavonic invasions, 7, 214, 215
Slavs, 212
Society for Friends of Antiquities of Hora, 297
Sofoulis, Themistoklis, 26, 27, 39
Soil science, 3, 11, 12–13, 144
Soulima Valley, 161, 289
Sparta: and Augustus, 184–185; and Battle of Leuctra, 179; conquest of Messenia, 151–155, 204; and Corinthia, 153; domination of Messenia, 111, 148, 152, 162, 170, 191, 288; environmental changes during control of, 7; and Epaminondas, xxix, 23; and founding of Messene, 180; and helot revolts, 157–158; land needs of, 154–155; and Messenian identity, 290; and Messenian towns remaining loyal to, 183; Messenia/Sparta border, xxxi; naval battle with

Athens, 26; and Peloponnesian War, 157, 171, 173–174, *175*, 176; and Philip II of Macedon, 182; postliberation Messenian relations, 182, 186; pottery of, 168; Spartan society, 155–157; subject population control methods, 159, 160–162. *See also* Laconia

Spartiates, 155, 156

Special activity area, 277

Sphacteria, Battle of, 157, 171–176, *175*

Sphacteria, island of: and Battle of Sphacteria, 26, 172, 173–174, *175*, 176; and Greek War of Independence, 258; map of, *258*; Pausanias on, 190; photographs of, *146*, *172*, *247*; and Pylos, 60; and tectonic faults, 2

Sphagianes, 112

Spyropoulos, Leonidas, 44

St. Athanasios church, 216

St. Dimitrios church, 216

St. Haralambos church, 216

St. Nikolas church, 216

Status. *See* Elite class

Stenyclarus Plain, 149, 154, 156, 159

Stirrup jars, 87, 101, *102*, *103*, *105*, 106, 109

Stone, David, *xlii*

Strabo: and archaeological investigations, 24; and Erana, 32; and Palaipylos, 77; and political boundaries, 114; on productivity of Messenia, 185; and Pylos as toponym, 113, 125; and Spartan encroachment into Messenia, 153

Stratigraphy, 165

Styliano, 249

Submycenaean Period, 149. *See also* Dark Age; Early Iron Age

Surface survey: of Beylerbey, 63; and Blegens, 35; of Bouka, 205; of Dialiskari, 192, 195; of Hasanaga, 263; and Marinatos, 47; and McDonald, 39; of Nichoria, 141; and pottery, 163, 165; and preservation, 281, 283;

significance of, 284–287; of Skarminga, 223; technique of, xl, 285–286, *286*

Swedish Messenia Expedition, 275

Swedish Messenia Expedition, The (Valmin), 33

Synchronisms, 165

Synedrion, 27

Synekdemos, 211

Tacitus, 186

Tafur, Pero, 236–237

Taxation: and agricultural resources, 211; and bronze industry, 130; fiscal units in provinces for, 120, 122, 128; and Linear B tablets, 90, 114, 116; of Messenia, xxxiv; in Middle Byzantine Period, 219; and Niccolò Acciaiuoli estates, 229–233; and political territory, 112; purpose of, 129–130; and *Rhomaioi*, 186; Roman taxation, 185, 186, 191; in Second Ottoman Period, 253; and Venice, 226

Taygetus Mountains: disputes with Sparta over, 186; fertility of, 185; as Messenian border, xxx–xxxi, 1, 111; and Nichoria, 139; and Second Ottoman Period, 249

Teleklos (king of Sparta), 153

Telemachus, xxxv–xxxvi, 26, 43

Textile industry, 86, 89, 90, 109, 169

Thebes, 92

Themelis, Petros, 41, 187

Thermoluminescence dating, 13

Thessaloniki, 242, 247

Thessaly, 5

Third Messenian War, 157

Tholos Tomb I, 47

Tholos Tomb III, 78, 126

Tholos Tomb IV: and Middle Helladic Period, 126; and Mycenaean Period, 60, 76–77; and Palace of Nestor, 82; photograph of, *57*; plundering of, 77; road to, 56; and tourism, 53

INDEX

339

Tholos tombs: of Bronze Age, 27–28, 37–38, 199; Christian burials in, 214; in Dark Age, 149, *150*, *151*; and elite class, 60, 68, 77, 78, 125–127, 132; emergence of, 75; of Englianos Ridge, 78, 126, 149, *150*; and Harakopeio, 47; of Haratsari, 63, 64, 68, 76; and Hristofilopoulos, 44; and Koukounara, 38; and Late Helladic I, 125–126, 127, 200; and Late Helladic IIIA, 126, 127; and Late Helladic IIIB, 131–132; and Marinatos, 48; and Mouriatada, 129; and Myrsinohori, 37–38, 66, 68; of Nichoria, 66, 127, 140, 141, *143*, 168; Osmanaga Tholos, 64; and Palace of Nestor's location, 43–44; of Peristeria, 77, 129; of Routsi, 65–66; and Skias, 27–28; and tomb cult, 199; and Tragana, 27, 37, 60, *66*, 68; and Valmin, 30, *31*; of Viglitsa, *66*, 77–78; of Voidokoilia, 60, 62, 68, 125–126, 200. See also specific tombs
Thouria, xxxiii, 124, *124*, 157
Thrasymedes (Nestor's son), xxxvi. See also Voidokoilia tholos tomb
Thucydides, 148, 157, 160, 173
Timpson, Michael, 12–13
Tin, 169
Tiryns, 56, 69, 73, 87, 88
Tombs: archaeological investigation of, 75; beehive (tholos) tombs, 56, 64, 65, 75; and Christian burial, 214; of Dialiskari, 193; of Nichoria, 40; shaft graves, 214; tomb cult, 199–204, *201*; at Tsouka, 281, *282*. See also Chamber tombs; Tholos tombs; Tumuli; and specific tombs
Tomb of Thrasymedes. See Voidokoilia tholos tomb
Topography, xxxi, xxxiii–xxxiv, 26–27
Topping, Peter, 227
TotalStation: and Dialiskari, *193*, 195, 197, *197*, 198; and Hasanaga, 263, 266

Tourism: and Coryphasion, 25; effect of, on archaeology, *xlii*, xliii; and Hora, 275; and local Messenian historians, 294–295; and Messenian identity, 290; in Modern Period, 273; and Palace of Nestor, 53–55; and regional studies, xli–xliii
Trade: and amber, 66, 77; and Bouka, 209; and Methoni, 219, 234, 236–237; and perfumed oil, 131; and perioikoi, 155; and pottery, 163, 165, 166, 209, 218, 239, 242, 298–299; and Second Ottoman Period, 245–246; and Selas River diversion, 74; and Tholos Tomb III, 78; and valuable goods, 131; and Venice, 219, 225, 226, 234; and villa sites, 198; and Voidokoilia, 62
Tragana: dominance of, 67; and Late Helladic I, 65; and Navarino Bay, 4; photograph of, *4*; tholos tombs near, 27, 37, 60, *66*, 68; tomb sites of, 75
Trajan (emperor of Rome), 188
Transfiguration of the Savior in Hristianou, Church of, 216–217, *218*, 219
Trieste, 246, 259
Trifylia, 275, 294–296
Trifylian Association, 294, 295, 297
Trigonometric markers, 8
Tripolitsa, 249
Trojan War, 26, 149
Troy, 265
Tsakonas, Periklis, 44
Tsifliki, 251, 274
Tsopani Rahi, 209
Tsouka, 281, *282*
Tumuli: of Bronze Age, 199; as form of burial, 75; and Marinatos, 48; in Middle Helladic Period, 125, 126, 200; and Myrsinohori, 66–67; and Papoulia, 35, *37*; replacement of, 68; and Valmin, 30; of Voidokoilia, 62
Turkey, *xxi*

Turkomans, 227
Turks: and Battle of Navarino, 257–258, 267–269, *270*, 271; conditions of Greece under, xxxviii–xxxix, 212, 293; depictions of, *253*; in Frankish Morea, 224; Greek War for Independence from, xxxvii, 172; in Methoni, 234, 237; and modern Greek state, 273; and Venice, 225. *See also* First Ottoman Period; Istanbul; Second Ottoman Period
Tyrtaios, 151, 153, 154, 155, 156

Uluburun wreck, 131
UMME. *See* University of Minnesota Messenia Expedition (UMME)
United States, 259
University of Athens, 60, 61, 65, 66–67, 299
University of Braunschweig, Germany, 197, 299
University of Cincinnati, 44, 299
University of Ioannina, 299
University of Maryland, 299–300
University of Michigan, 300
University of Minnesota Messenia Expedition (UMME): archaeological evidence found by, 275; and archaeological sites, 134, 159–160, 283–284; interdisciplinary focus of, 39; and Marinatos's map of Messenia, 48; and Nichoria excavation, 139–144, 147, 149; PRAP compared to, 285; publications of, 40; and regional archaeology, 139, 159; and settlement sites' size, 123, 124, 134
University of Texas, 300
University of Wisconsin, 300

Valmin, Mattias Natan: archeological investigations of, 23, 30–33; and Ayios Floros, 31–32; and Dialiskari, 32–33, 192, 193, 198, 294; and tholos tombs, 30, *31*

Valta, 249
Valvi, Elisavet, 22, *49*
Vandals, 212
Vari, 162
Vathirema, 199
Venice: and Arcadia, 289; expatriate Greek communities in, 246; and First Ottoman Period, 226, 227; in fourteenth and fifteenth century, 225; and Hasanaga, 262, 263, 266; historical sources of, 273; and Koroni, 24, 220, 225, 234; and Methoni, 24, 219, 220, 223, 225, 234–238; rule of Messenia, xxxiv, 24, 212, 227–228, 245, 289, 290; and Second Ottoman Period, 228, 247–249, 253
Ventris, Michael, 38, 40, 88
Vespasian (emperor of Rome), xxxiv, 185
Viglitsa, 65, *66*, 77–78
Villa sites, 191, 192–198, 212, 298
Villehardouin family, 227. *See also* Geoffrey II
Villehardouin, Geoffrey de, 219–220, 225, 234
Vischer, Daniel, 74
Visigoth, 211–212
Voidokoilia: and Athens/Sparta naval battle, 27; dominance of, 67; landscape of, 1, 4; Marinatos's excavation of, 62–63
Voidokoilia Bay, *146*
Voidokoilia tholos tomb, 60, 62, 68, 125–126, 200; excavation of, 37–38; Grundy's discovery of, 27, 28; Marinatos's exploration of, 27; photograph of, *38*, *202*; as Thrasymedes' burial place, xxxvi, 27, 62, 190, 200, 204; and tomb cult, 200
Volimidia: chamber tombs of, 35, 60, 77, 78, 200, 203–204, *203*; and Hora, 275; and Late Helladic I, 59–60; and Middle Helladic Period, 126; and Mycenaean Period, 48, 59–

INDEX

341

60; photograph of, *110*; prehistoric communities of, 59–60; and tomb cult, 199, 200, 203–204; tomb sites of, 75
Volimnos, 169
Von Harff, Sir Arnold, 236
Voroulia, 48

Wace, Alan, 45
Wagner, Günther, 13
Wall of the Dymaians, 56
Wanax, 89, 90, 92, 112
Water supply, 14, 277–278
Watkinson, Charles, *303*
White Paper, 295–296
Wine, 234, 237–238, 298
Wine-storage building, 88

Women: and Battle of Navarino, 259; in Late Byzantine Period, 233
Woolen industry, 93, 130
World War II, 33, 48
World Wide Web, 299–301

Yazvenko, Sergei, 11, *17*
Yialova, 44
Yiannitsa, 26

Zangger, Eberhard, *72*, *73*
Zante island, 252
Zassi, 225
Zeus Ithomatas, 180, 188
Zeus statue, 183, 187
Zonchio (Navarino), 225
Zoodohos Pigi, Church of, 216, *217*